RED ODYSSEY

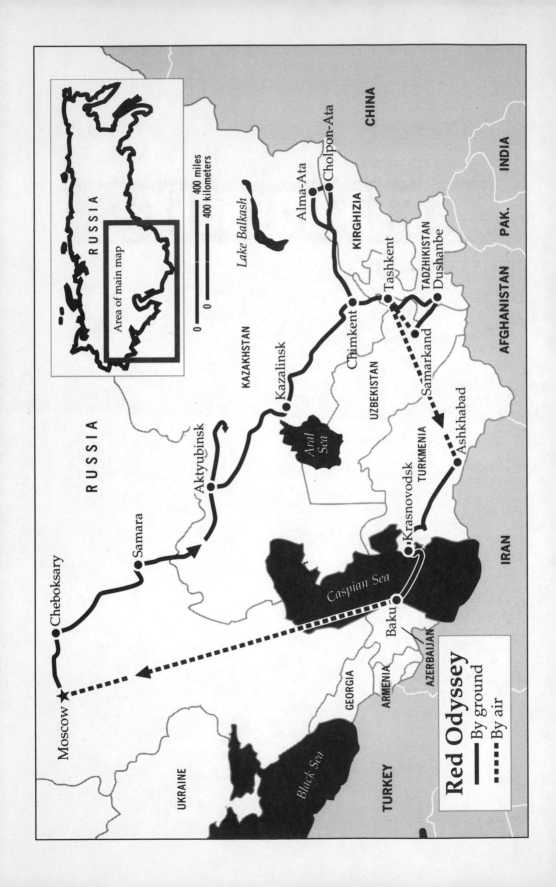

Red Odyssey

— By ground
----- By air

RED ODYSSEY

A JOURNEY THROUGH THE
SOVIET REPUBLICS

MARAT AKCHURIN

HarperCollins*Publishers*

RED ODYSSEY. Copyright © 1992 by Marat Akchurin. All rights reserved. Printed in the United States of America. No part of this book may be used or reproduced in any manner whatsoever without written permission except in the case of brief quotations embodied in critical articles and reviews. For information address HarperCollins Publishers, Inc., 10 East 53rd Street, New York, NY 10022.

HarperCollins books may be purchased for educational, business, or sales promotional use. For information, please call or write: Special Markets Department, HarperCollins Publishers, Inc., 10 East 53rd Street, New York, NY 10022. Telephone: (212) 207-7528; Fax: (212) 207-7222.

Designed by George J. McKeon
Map by Paul Pugliese

Library of Congress Cataloging-in-Publication Data
Akchurin, Marat.
      Red odyssey : a journey through the Soviet republics / by Marat Akchurin.—1st ed.
         p. cm.
      Includes index.
      ISBN 0-06-018335-7
      1. Soviet Central Asia—Description and travel.   2. Transcaucasia—Description and travel.
3. Volga River Region (R.S.F.S.R.)—Description and travel.   4. Akchurin, Marat—Journeys—
Soviet Union.   5. Soviet Union—Civilization—1917–   6. Soviet Union—Description and
travel—1970–   7. Soviet Union—Ethnic relations.   8. Minorities—Soviet Union.   I. Title.
DK854.A63   1992
947.085'4—dc20   91-58363

92 93 94 95 96 ❖/HC 10 9 8 7 6 5 4 3 2

Beautiful is when we least expect it. And where.

—William Minor

Contents

Illustrations follow page 246.

Acknowledgments

First of all, I am grateful to Esther Dyson, who introduced me to Frank Clines and to John Brockman, who gave me the idea for this book. Once these three people had entered my life, each of them influenced my astrological destiny in a very special way.

I am most thankful to my old friends in the former Soviet Union, who helped me both in word and deed during my wanderings across our long-suffering country. Many thanks are due to my wife, Alexandra, and my daughter, Mary, for their help in creating this book and their endless stoic patience while I was writing it.

I am especially appreciative of my friend Arkady Morgulis, who did so much to make the writing and translating of this book possible.

Sincere gratitude to Jamie James for his fine remarks concerning the style of the book.

All places and events in this book are real.
No names have been changed.

Prologue

In 1222 the mother of Genghis Khan, who called himself the Sovereign of the Universe, died. He had known it was coming, for he himself was old and nearing the completion of his journey through this life. He had spent the last twenty years completing his conquest of half the world without having seen his mother, whom he honored and loved.

He knew that he would encounter his death far away from his homeland, thousands of miles away on the shores of the river Kerulen, where his mother was finishing her days. Therefore, Genghis Khan decided that if his mother died before him, her remains should be embalmed by Chinese medicine men and brought to his headquarters, no matter how far away it might be or how long it might take. Bury us next to each other side by side, he ordered his sons and his grandson Bhatu-Khan, who he thought would be his successor.

But a terrible thing happened. On the ninety-third day of its journey, the mournful caravan with the body of Genghis Khan's mother was looted by a detachment of Turks. One young lieutenant was destined to survive. He managed to defend with his sword the camel carrying its precious cargo. Pierced with arrows, he galloped away at full speed. He carried the royal remains wrapped up in a Persian rug woven by the twelve-year-old virgins of Khorossan.

According to the legend, the young lieutenant lost his mind while he was searching for Genghis Khan's headquarters, visiting all the places where the monarch had once passed with his men. The youth never allowed anyone to come near him as he carried his strange baggage through Russian lands and the Golden Horde's holdings down the banks of the Volga, across the steppes of Turan and deserts of Iran, which are today called Central Asia, Kazakhstan, and the Transcaucasus. Then he vanished forever, leaving not a trace. Apparently, he violated the ancient custom: trying to render homage, he buried the mother of his emperor still wrapped in that precious rug.

Because of the insane warrior's mistake, for seven centuries the Tartar czarina has appeared time and again to her posterity in their dreams. She comes to them in the shape of the young, wandering woman, demanding that they find her lost grave and remove the cursed rug, which prevents her bones from being joined with Mother Earth.

When she appears to one of her descendants in his early-morning dreams, whether he is in blossoming youth, mature adulthood, or wise old age, he must leave behind him all the duties of his life and depart on a long journey.

No one has yet managed to fulfill her adjuration.

1

Preparations and Departure

All the great books have been about journeys. Even *The Odyssey* and *The Divine Comedy* were stories about wanderings.

This, at least, was the argument I made one spring night in 1990, as my wife and I were sitting having supper in our modest apartment in the north part of Moscow. Naturally, it had no effect on Alexandra, who from the very beginning had declared her opposition to the trip I was planning. At first, it seemed to me that these conversations about my possible journey would never lead to anything at all. What kind of strange force could possibly compel me to drop everything I was doing in Moscow and temporarily abandon my family, just for the sake of a weird and dangerous journey? The Soviet system was in death throes, everything was bursting at the seams and crumbling: at times like this, it's better to sit quietly at home. The next day, though, I started up the previous night's discussion again, with a new vigor. My wife's arguments, however emotional, had been to the point, and it was hard to make any good comebacks. She claimed that nowadays people learn the news not from books by adventurers, but from newspapers and television. Gulliver and Robinson Crusoe turned into children's stories long ago.

But that's not quite true. You could find out the news from Moscow or the Baltics from the newspapers or television, but the southern republics of the pre-breakup Soviet Union were still cut off from the rest of the world by an iron curtain. None of us in the U.S.S.R., nor especially people abroad, know exactly what is happening there. Even the failed coup in August 1991, which led to the collapse of the Communist regime in Russia, changed almost nothing in many Central Asian republics. Naturally, after the Moscow hard-liners' failure, the republican-level Communist parties changed their names and began to call themselves socialist or national democratic parties, but they had no intention of letting go of the power. As the influence of the central authorities continued to weaken, both before the coup and especially afterwards, local and republican-level party authorities got stronger. Censorship in these areas became even stricter, and in some cases leaders of pro-democracy movements were actually arrested.

At the beginning of perestroika, the liberal Moscow newspapers were just starting to write about party mafias in the Moslem republics, but the faucet was quickly shut off. Why? Then, no one knew. Any opposition voice who spoke out against the power of the local party-dominated bureaucracy was immediately accused of reviving Islamic fundamentalism. But the whole Islamic fundamentalism issue wasn't that simple. We could believe the Soviet propaganda and suppose that it was sprouting up in Tadzhikistan. After all, Tadzhikistan is culturally very close to Iran and shares a common border with Afghanistan. But where would Islamic fundamentalism come from, for instance, in Kazakhstan, where the people, as a result of their nomadic heritage, are considerably less inclined to be religious?

Something was wrong. Each time I thought about the ethnic conflicts that have been tearing our country apart for the past few years, I got a strange feeling, as if there were some intangible similarity between all of them. In the first phase, new pro-democracy movements in these republics began to threaten the old political order. Then suddenly, as if on some mysterious signal, ethnic conflicts erupted, which the Western mass media knew nothing about—or pretended to know nothing about. And of course the blame for the deaths of hundreds of people, which resulted from these clashes, was invariably placed on the democratic opposition, and then the local authorities would ask Moscow to send in troops. After the arrival of the troops, martial law would be introduced, and the people, fearful of pogroms, would welcome it. Martial law would be accompanied by an information blackout and a reinstitution of local censorship. As a result, one-third of the populated territory of the then U.S.S.R., so rich in human and natural resources, continues to be a blank spot on the map for the rest of the world. This is not tiny, courageous Lithuania with a population of only one million, and with little mineral wealth and few energy sources. More than fifty million people live in the Moslem republics in the southern backbone of the Soviet Disunion, well-known for its vast number of natural treasures, which include everything from huge undeveloped oilfields and major gas pipelines to gold and uranium mines. If the growth rates in this terra incognita stay the same as they are today, in ten years the majority of the population of the Commonwealth of Independent States will be Moslem.

"There's absolutely no way that could happen!" Alexandra exclaimed. Like all Muscovites, she is excessively politicized and therefore reacts to talk about the future of the Soviet Union very emotionally. "Won't all the Moslem republics leave the U.S.S.R., now that all the other republics are trying to break away?"

"It doesn't look that way," I said. "Just about everyone says they're leaving the Union. And yes, all the republican bosses are trying to get much more political and economic independence than they were even a year ago. But in Central Asia they have a better chance of staying in power if they hold on to the power structures they have now."

"Why do you care?" My wife's tone changed, as she realized that I really was planning to leave. "What do you think you're going to do, write a political treatise?"

"No," I said. "This is going to be a book about the people who live there. I want to see what perestroika has done for people in different republics. In Moscow, no one believes Gorbachev anymore. Maybe it's different in the other republics. Something must have changed there over the past few years."

"Then I will go with you," my wife said angrily.

"And who will stay here with Mary?" I laughed nervously.

We had an eight-year-old daughter who needed to be taken care of. "Besides, I want to go incognito; I am not taking a business trip for a newspaper or magazine, so that means the authorities won't know about my journey."

"But that means that you won't have the protection of the authorities," my wife said, worried. In places of ethnic conflicts, journalists with official assignments are usually protected by local authorities or even the military. "Now I am even more against this trip."

I tenderly drew the protesting Alexandra to me and stroked her hair, but she angrily tore herself out of my embrace. She understood, of course, that as a private citizen I could go places where neither Soviet nor foreign journalists have free access. She knew as well as I did that the KGB still controls the movements and contacts of foreign journalists. Of course, now it's much easier than it was before to get permission to travel. But many visitors from abroad don't even think about the fact that except in a few large cities, it is the Soviet authorities who decide what to show the guests and which KGB informers and undercover officers will play the role of "independent" sources.

"Oh, I almost forgot to mention this," I said as nonchalantly as I could, and held my breath, as if I were about to dive into cold water. "I'm not flying there. I'm going to take our car."

"In a car? No way!" was my mother Farida's alarmed reaction when Alexandra called her in Tashkent to tell her about my trip; and Farida immediately switched from Russian to her native Tartar. My mother has long been convinced that telephone conversations in our country are always tapped, and therefore, when talking with me, she always discussed anything important only in Tartar. As if there couldn't be anyone among the eavesdroppers who understood the Tartar language.

"You don't know what it's like in Central Asia now. People are being robbed and killed on the roads. The director of a city cab company was just shot and killed along with his wife. Their neighbor tried to save them and he was killed, too."

"But that happened inside their house," I answered in Russian, trying to calm her down, though I knew that this argument would not give her much consolation.

I was grateful that my emotional mother, who lives in remote Uzbekistan, cannot watch the Leningrad television show "600 Seconds," which daily portrays Soviet life as a bloody slaughterhouse. I pictured one of yesterday's news items about an independent businessman who was impaled and grilled over a fire by racketeers, but incredibly survived this torture and was found crawling from the forest barely alive. Or take another sickening story, broadcast yesterday by "Moscow Nightly News," reported by a journalist acquaintance of mine. The story concerned a psychopath who cut his mother up and then baked her head in an oven. Our news reports are a charnel house: half-burned rotten dismembered crushed human bodies, rapists, prostitutes, and hoodlums visit our homes on a nightly basis. Confronted with such nightmares, people begin to fear leaving their homes.

Alexandra shouldn't have told my mother about my plans to drive from Moscow to Tashkent, which is only about two thousand miles out of the ten-thousand-mile journey I have planned. I had decided to drive through the Volga region and North Kazakhstan to Central Asia, and then, after ferrying across the Caspian Sea, come back to Moscow via Azerbaijan, Daghestan, and southern Russia.

Yet from the very beginning the idea of this fantastic journey— rather like a video travelogue straight out of the Brezhnev era—was inexplicably attractive to me. Ever since ancient times, the chroniclers have tried to convey the details of just such events. Of course, it is much more pleasant to live and raise children in an era of peace and prosperity, but those times are rarely rewarded with more than a few lines in the chronicles.

Like many of my countrymen and millions of people abroad, I joyfully greeted Gorbachev and perestroika in 1985. Just as the words "market economy" and "free enterprise" were first being spoken in the Soviet Union, I left a prestigious job in the national publishing house and, with my wife, founded a small private company that specialized in literary publishing. More precisely, it was not a private company but a cooperative, since the word "private" remained an ideological taboo. However, in a few short months, even "cooperative" would become a Soviet curse word, for the Communist system, with good reason, considered private business to be its grave-digger and did everything in its power to compromise free enterprise in the eyes of a confused citizenry.

I soon realized that the Communist system had no intention of surrendering. The first book published by my company was seized by the authorities, for its very existence was perceived by the Communist bureaucracy as a challenge to the state monopoly on book publishing. Now hundreds, perhaps thousands of books are being published in the former Soviet Union by private publishers. The book I published was among the very first, and therefore it was attacked savagely.

Some time later, I ventured into the world of the theater, producing a performance of *The Cherry Orchard* with some of the most famous actors in Moscow. Theater production had also been a state monopoly in our country, and my production of the play was the first time in more than sixty years that the play had been presented by a private individual rather than by the state.

I enjoyed my new job; it quickly became very clear, however, that the system was driving private enterprise into a corner. Every day new restrictive decrees and regulations appeared, for the laws concerning the market economy still had not been adopted and were not forthcoming. For example, the 1988 law on cooperation stipulated moderate taxes for new companies during the first five years. However, not even a year had passed before the government decided to increase the tax on profit to 50 percent. Gorbachev vacillated desperately, from left to right, while the party-dominated bureaucracy shamelessly blackmailed private businessmen on behalf of the state. In this specially created tangle of laws and resolutions, any action by a private enterprise could easily be interpreted as a violation of the new laws, which in our country were often retroactive. Corruption became epidemic. Everyone who wanted to survive had to pay bureaucrats of all levels for every little step they took. I decided to go out of business and return to writing.

I knew that what was going on in our country—the last huge empire on this planet—was historic. Even if they read the mass media reports, my Western readers, members of a different civilization, cannot understand the surreal nightmare of the struggle being waged by the common people in the U.S.S.R. daily, simply in order to survive. Conversely, a lot of my countrymen, especially those of the older generation, still do not believe that there exists a different way of life—an existence that is reasonably peaceful, polite, and satisfying.

However, I must admit that even then I had serious doubts about using the automobile to travel between cities in our country. I had very few options for my journey: a choice between a Lada and a Zhiguli, basically two names for the same car, which was itself a knockoff of the Fiat of the mid-sixties. However, another problem arises from the fact that there are no reliable automobile repair services except for the privileged few, with political connections or influence—*blat*, as the Russians call it—well-greased with bribe money. That is the case not only in the remote steppes and deserts of Kazakhstan or Turkmenia, where such service stations have never really existed, but even in Moscow.

To attempt to cover even part of such a vast area in an old car without so much as a tune-up is a prescription for disaster. That much was clear even to me, a person with no technical background or experience. When I asked my auto mechanic and friend Vladimir Liberman (known to his friends as Vova) to prepare my car for a long trip, he became curious about where I intended to drive his precious car. He had bought it, wrecked in an accident committed by a criminal who was being chased by the police. Then he completely rebuilt it and sold it to me, on the condition that no other mechanic would ever touch his creation as long as he lived. When he found out my route, he thought seriously, cleaned his hands with greasy rags, and said resolutely:

"I would pick a different car for this trip."

"Which one?" I asked casually, as I didn't want to scare off this vague sense of luck I felt when I saw the face of this Mozart of the automotive art light up. Even though I could guess what his answer would be, I still could not believe it would happen.

"We must go in my car, the red one," he finally said, watching me out of the corner of his eye to see what effect his words would have on me.

In the former Soviet Union, service-related state employees—sales people, waiters, airline and railroad cashiers, furniture loaders, doormen and hotel clerks, cab drivers, nurses, electronics and refrigeration repairmen (have I mentioned them all?)...oh, yes, and auto mechanics, especially auto mechanics, as well as their immediate supervisors—make up a specially privileged caste in our Wonderland, with its constant shortages of all goods and services. Swollen with their petty power, they choose only clients useful to them, and treat the rest like dirt, since they know well that their customers are helpless without them. One of the worst facts of Soviet life today is the absolute defenselessness of the people before all government institutions, and the resulting decline in normal human values.

Foreigners who ride the Moscow subway notice that people here never smile. During rush hour, slow or clumsy people are silently beaten and pushed so that they move faster.

Two American friends of mine, psychologists Wendy Kohli from the State University of New York and Philip Bennett from Cornell University, made a startling observation during one of their trips to the Soviet Union. When they were riding in a subway car, they noticed that an old woman right across from them was looking with hostility at Philip's shorts. When Wendy met the old woman's eyes, she did something very natural—she smiled in a friendly way. The old woman, however, interpreted her smile as an insult, and she spat on her and cursed her. As psychologists, Wendy and Philip were excited by this informal contact, but as human beings they were deeply shocked by the hopeless despair of this miserable and desperate woman. They recounted this story to us in a small restaurant of the Malyi Theater in Moscow, where Alexandra and I invited them for a traditional lunch, made possible by the *blat* we have there. We did everything we could to console them, trying to find a justification for the crazy woman, who had gone over the edge from frustrating years of standing in lines, but we felt agonizingly ashamed of our country.

In comparison with his thieving, insolent colleagues, Liberman is a phenomenal exception. When we were introduced to each other, I was simply amazed when I suddenly realized that he was a rare, decent man and not just another jerk from the notorious service industry. He seems to be puzzled by his own honesty. By the age of twenty-five he had obtained both an auto engineering degree and gastritis in his native Moscow. He did his apprenticeship at an automobile plant in the Tartar city of Naberezhnye Chelni, which he stubbornly continues to call Brezhnev, although the old name has been returned to the city. There he married an art teacher from Chuvashia, Sveta, who gave birth to two children, Ksyusha and Motya. Liberman and his family returned to Moscow to live with his parents. In a small two-room apartment, equivalent to a one-bedroom apartment in the United States, three generations of Libermans share their lives together; Vova and his family could not buy or rent an apartment of their own in Moscow for any amount of money.

"I could go with you as far as Cheboksary, and maybe even farther," Liberman said, smiling radiantly. "I've never been to Central Asia, I've never seen mountains or seas. It would be so nice to drive around and see the world and people," he said, closing his eyes dreamily. He opened them and asked casually, "Your Uzbek buddies ain't going to kill us?"

"I hope not," I replied. "You can't imagine how many friends and acquaintances I have in every republic, and in almost every city on our route."

I happily accepted all his conditions: I took full responsibility for all travel expenses, and paid him as well. This seemed to me quite fair. Besides that I had to permit his father to use my car while we were gone.

The next problem was shopping. Stores in Moscow have nothing but empty shelves and angry crowds. Is there any other country in the world besides the former U.S.S.R. where people must stand in line even for bread, and anesthetics and heart medication may be purchased only under the counter, in exchange for considerable bribes?

Russian fairy tales have a recurring motif about a young blue-eyed woman with light brown hair who falls under the power of an ugly, crooked old man. Unable to possess her, he tortures and torments the unfortunate girl, and she keeps waiting for her foolish lover, who misses his opportunity to save her. That prophetic plot strikingly resembles reality before the failure of the 1991 August coup. The faded beauty is Russia, and the malicious little old man is the party apparatus, which will not let our country free from its bloody metal claws.

The morning before we started our trip, I ran into transistor radios on sale at a store called Dosug (Leisure), which is attached to the first floor of our apartment building. These radios worked only in long- and medium-wave frequency ranges, which meant that I would only be able to tune in three or four stations with it. I would have preferred a short-wave radio, so that I could listen to the foreign stations formerly called "enemies' voices." But half a loaf is better than no bread at all. Only two years ago these ugly things were sitting idly on the shelves, next to the antique television antennas, domestically produced tape-cassette recorders, and cameras that somehow resembled the face of the late Brezhnev; nowadays even this trash is in short supply.

Liberman had a cassette player but no radio in his car, so the purchase would be worthwhile. The line moved quickly, for the department had nothing else for sale. Then an old woman trying to return a radio in front of me became a problem. I have noticed that there are more old women than old men in Moscow: men, I theorize, go faster because they smoke more and are never sober.

"Only one per person," the crowd behind me grumbled, becoming agitated.

"I'm listening to you," the saleswoman said sternly, through clenched teeth. In our stores they do not ask a customer, "May I help you?" The professional code of Soviet sales employees directs them to address the customer as though he is an inferior breed: "I'm listening to you." Or, better yet: "Next." Any cashier in a department store can scream at the crowd of obedient customers: "You're many, I'm one!" And no one will argue with her; after all, it is true. All the other cash registers will be closed no matter how long the line is. And everybody understands that it is not a matter of disorganization or lack of skill; rather, it is how our system works. Our system was designed that way, and it cannot be changed: it can only be destroyed.

"I bought it here right before lunch break, and it doesn't work," the old woman mumbled nervously. She looked and smelled like a typical retired representative of the "supreme class of the revolutionary movement," as the working class was referred to in our political jargon.

"So what?"

"Will you exchange it, dear? Please?"

"We don't exchange merchandise. Next!" The saleswoman indifferently turned her swinish eyes to me.

"Wait a minute, sweetheart, why not?" wailed the miserable customer loudly. "Or give me my money back. I paid twenty-seven rubles for the damn thing. I bought it just before lunch break. Just one hour ago! Look, I have the receipt, too."

"Go to a warranty shop. Next!" The impassive saleswoman turned to me again, a slight grin flashing in her stony eyes.

The crowd behind us was pushing forward more and more insistently. "Hey, come on, move it, let's go!" A few impatient ones began to shove. It is strange, but Soviet people in lines always side with the sales people, because they represent the authorities. But at the same time, in full accord with Marxist dialectics, sales people are commonly despised; only intellectuals, co-op businessmen, and Raisa Gorbachev are hated more.

"Replace the radio for her!" I shouted authoritatively. She almost obeyed, but then regained her composure with a visible effort. My eyes betrayed me again, damn it! My wife often tells me that to wear such a cynical and bitter face in Moscow is quite dangerous; either thugs will thrash you or the police will make note of you.

"I'm trying to tell her that she should go to a repair shop," the saleswoman explained. "We are not responsible for manufacturer's defects."

"Well, she just bought this rubbish from you, took it home, and it doesn't work," I said, starting a useless argument. I felt like jumping over the counter and boxing her ears. "So, why not replace it? That's what you're here for. Surely you have an agreement with the manufacturer or distributor. Doesn't it provide for such things?"

I should not have been polite with her; that gave her an advantage. "It's not me who made the agreement; it's not me who signed it."

"And the store manager is not available because today is Saturday, right?" I tried not to fall into the standard state of mind of a Soviet customer, a blind and helpless rage.

The crowd became aroused with indignation: "What kind of idiots are you?" "If you're so smart, you should have checked it in the first place."

The saleswoman looked me in the eyes, sizing me up, and said, "Okay, let her write a letter of complaint."

"What kind of a complaint? And where?" The old woman tried to find a pencil and a piece of paper in her bag, all in vain. But the saleswoman knew that the old woman had no such things in her purse. A short moment of celebration, and then the old woman was pushed mercilessly from her position in line by the crowd. The saleswoman shrugged her shoulders and barked at the crowd: "Next!"

The old woman dragged herself to the exit in her worn-out felt overshoes, looking with disgust at her unfortunate purchase. To my surprise I found myself running after her. Even more surprising, I offered to buy it from her.

Hesitantly, afraid of a dirty trick, the old woman handed over the box to me. She counted her money several times and then, all of a sudden, shared her innermost thoughts with me: "See what they did to Russia, those goddamn aliens? They are all over Moscow now. They are not Russians, they are Satan's children!"

And she went back to the far end of the same line.

2

Never Stop at Rest Areas

We drove in a drizzle, at our nighttime cruising speed of fifty-five miles per hour, on a road called the Gorkovsky Highway. According to its name, it was to bring us to the city of Gorky, which used to be and was soon to become Nizhny Novgorod again. In reality the Gorkovsky Highway is only a 250-mile stretch of road my map called a "Nationally Important Highway." The atlas designated it M-8, but according to the road signs it was M-7. A discrepancy of just one is not bad for the U.S.S.R.

If the road atlas could be trusted, Highway M-8 or M-7 is 575 miles long and connects Moscow with the cities of Cheboksary and Kazan. I hoped that information was accurate. Both these cities are capitals of autonomous republics, Chuvash and Tartar respectively; now, both are part of the present-day Russian federal republic.

The great Bulgar kingdom once flourished on these lands along the Volga. But after the hordes of Genghis Khan poured into this area in the thirteenth century, his slant-eyed army mixed with the blue-eyed, red-bearded Bulgars and formed a formidable new state, known to the world as the Golden Horde. It dominated the region for several centuries, until Timur the Great founded a new empire a thousand miles to the south, with the ancient city of Samarkand as its capital. These two rival states both had their origins in kingdoms formerly held by sons of Genghis Khan, who divided his empire into five portions among his five sons.

Few people in modern Russia know that it was the prolonged conflict between these two bordering superpowers that determined the historical destiny of the embryonic Russian nation. The official patriotism of Russian historians even today does not allow them to include in the history curriculum the obvious fact that it was Timur the Great who broke the back of the Golden Horde at the turn of the fifteenth century. Genghis Khan's empire fell to pieces with a roar, leaving behind scattered Russian princedoms without any sort of federal government to unite them. After almost three hundred years of Tartar rule, the princedoms had become accustomed to the Russian-Tartar symbiosis.

For decades, many Soviet historians took it for granted that secretaries of the regional committees of the party, the powerful rulers of their huge provinces, had to be appointed by Moscow's Politburo. But try reminding them that the Russian princes of the past, including Alexander Nevsky himself, canonized by the Russian Orthodox Church, were required to appear before the "politburo" of the Golden Horde to receive permission to reign and collect taxes. Five centuries later, history repeats itself almost identically, only the actors have swapped roles. Today Moscovia is losing its strong central role, while its vassal republics, populated by the direct descendants of the former conquerors of Russia, are now in their turn reaching for some kind of independence.

Liberman had many interesting things to say about Chuvash people. His testimony is that of an expert; he was married to a Chuvash woman. By Soviet standards, this was quite an exotic marriage for a Jew. When we were planning the first part of our trip, Liberman suggested that we should spend our first night with his wife's parents. I gladly accepted this offer to meet some new people, even though I have some friends in Cheboksary.

"You'll like my father-in-law," Liberman said enthusiastically. Even behind the wheel, he managed to gesture like an Arab while speaking. He has always expressed his feelings, both positive and negative, with great force. "He is just a working man, but he is an outstanding person. He subscribes to a lot of magazines, he understands politics. He even paints pictures. I like to visit my wife's family. They're sincere, hospitable, and down-to-earth folks. So what if they're Chuvashes? All our nationalities are equal, aren't they?"

"Of course they're not," I answered, laughing at Liberman's fervor.

"I mean, I know they're not, but I like Chuvashes," he rejoined sternly. He was ready to rebuff any manifestations of Russian chauvinism with an argument, but then he remembered that I was not Russian either. "You should see how they sing and dance when they get together at family celebrations. A very peaceful nation, too. They wouldn't kill or disturb anyone, not like your Central Asians or Caucasians."

"Well, first of all," I argued, "it is Central Asia and the Caucasus where they came from. The ancestors of the modern Chuvashes, the ancient Bulgars, originally lived in the northern Caucasus, until the Khazars forced them out in the seventh century. By the way, the Khazars' religion was Jewish. So your marriage, Vova, is not the first contact between these two great nations."

Liberman smiled at my joke approvingly. "What happened then?"

"Then the ancient Bulgars moved up to the banks of the Volga, where Finno-Ugric tribes had been living for nearly five thousand years. They are still living there. Who do you think the Mari and the Udmurts are?" I asked him, referring to the native inhabitants of the neighboring ethnic republics, who have almost lost their national identity. "They are the cousins of the Hungarians and Finns, who decided a thousand years ago that this area wasn't worth staying in. Have you ever noticed that the names of so many lakes and rivers in Central Russia are of Finno-Ugric origin? Even the Moscow River, which gave its name to our capital, means 'the bear's creek' in the language of the pre-Slavic population of the region."

Liberman looked at me in amazement: "You've got to be kidding! Are you saying that *Moskva* is not a Russian word?"

"Well, after eight hundred years it became Russian," I conceded, continuing my argument. I recalled my slavophile acquaintances from the Central Club of Writers, who, upon hearing this, would immediately accuse me of being a member of the Jewish-Masonic conspiracy against Russian national identity. "Ethnic groups disappear or are assimilated into new nations, but the names of the lakes and rivers are inherited by the new inhabitants. In the United States and Canada many of the lakes and rivers have retained their original Indian names."

"What has Central Asia got to do with it?" Liberman would not give up. Like a majority of Muscovites, he hated Central-Asian and Caucasian market profiteers for the monstrously high prices of vegetables, fruits, and flowers they sell at the markets. And he simply could not accept the fact that he was related to these people, even indirectly.

"What Central Asia has to do with it is that it provides the northern Iranian element for the formation of the Chuvash ethnos," I said.

"What element?" said the stubborn Liberman, taken aback. He was horrified by the mention of Iran. "You mean..."

"I mean, your son Motya and Ayatollah Khomeini are distant relatives." I was getting annoyed with his Eurocentrism. I turned on the bright orange compact radio I had bought the day before and tried to tune in the news. The old woman could not make it work because she had not put the batteries in it. It was as simple as that. But the car body and engine created such horrible static that I turned it off.

Five minutes later, Liberman started a game on his own field. "Here, we are on one of the 'Nationally Important Highways,' as they call them. Do you know why they call them that?"

"I would guess that they are designated for troop movements, or some strategically important freight traffic in case of war."

Liberman flashed his snow-white teeth in an instant smile and shook his head with feigned distress, as if to say, You stupid intellectuals, you know nothing worthwhile. Then he explained that the "Nationally Important Highways" are those paved with asphalt rather than dirt.

"You were in America and saw their highways, right? These national roads are our 'khaivays.'" He laughed, delighted that he remembered the word in English at the right time, which meant that he had not completely wasted so many years in high school and college studying English.

Whenever I hear the word "highway" now, I picture the multilane expressway between Washington, D.C., and New York City. I traveled with my wife on this road in a Greyhound bus last spring, during our first visit to the United States. Our friends were meeting us in New York, but we had only managed to buy tickets from Moscow to Washington, and at that we had paid a double fare. The Soviet state-owned airline, Aeroflot, has no competition, which permits its employees to establish their own, unofficial "tax" on tickets—in reality a bribe equal to the price of a full fare. "If you don't want to pay, then stand in line and wait," they say cheerfully, nodding at lines they have organized themselves. To fly abroad you need to sign up for one of these lines half a year in advance, and then wait days and nights outside the cashier's office, displaying at the entrance a number written on your palm in ink, certifying your place in line.

"If you want to compare our roads with American highways," I said, re-creating in my mind the multilane Interstate 95, "then imagine the difference between an East German two-cylinder Trabant, with a body made of compressed sawdust, and the latest Mercedes."

Liberman sighed. Like the majority of Soviet people, he had never traveled outside the U.S.S.R. "As for our roads, so far so good, I would say. But after Kuybyshev—forget it!"

He was right; our road had been just fine so far. Oncoming traffic was separated from our side most of the time by a concrete border, poor flower beds, or sometimes by a narrow strip of land, which is especially important on intercity roads at nighttime, because drivers of state-owned vehicles, such as trucks, buses, and cabs, do not even think about switching to low beams when they come toward you. You can flash your brights as many times as you like, but nine times out of ten your request to be polite will be simply ignored.

Americans would have a hard time understanding the typically Soviet antagonism between professional state drivers and the owners of private passenger cars, officially classified by the traffic police as amateurs. There are about 588 passenger cars per thousand people in the United States while in the U.S.S.R. there are only fifty-three cars per thousand people. Accordingly, the percentage of people who drive cars is different too. In the United States it is a majority of the population, while in the U.S.S.R. it is a small minority. And, as we know now, the truth in a Communist country always lies with the majority.

A professional driver sincerely believes that he owns the road and, with true proletarian class hatred, disdains any private owner who may get in his way. That attitude is especially intense after a night of heavy drinking. A woman behind the wheel is no exception. Quite the contrary, profies discriminate against women even more ferociously, especially when they are young and attractive. Even now, there's a widespread belief in the U.S.S.R. among ordinary people that you cannot become an owner of a private car by honest means. The professional drivers have a contemptuous slang name for the owner of a private car: in Russian, the word for teapot, *tchainik,* closely resembles the word for a private owner, *tchastnik.* So we are known as teapots, *tchainiks.*

Some *tchainiks* decorate the back windows of their cars with humorous pictures of a teapot in the form of a road sign. They display this self-demeaning image in the hopes of pacifying the masters of the Soviet roads. "Here you go!"—the pros spit out their windows with satisfaction, cutting corners on hated amateurs, getting a wink from the traffic cops, who nearly explode from the proud feeling of belonging to the elite.

The car bounced over a particularly deep bump, and Liberman cried, "Why, oh, why are our roads so beat up and neglected, even in the capital?"

"The roads in Russia crawled away like lobsters in the night," I said aloud, quoting *Dead Souls.*

Liberman did not seem to like the quotation: "Did you just make that up?"

"Vova, it's Gogol," I informed him.

"Gogol-shmogol." Liberman disrespectfully rolled his eyes in his head. "Is it true that he was crazy?"

Gogol is near the top of the list of my favorite writers, and twenty years ago I would have quarreled with Liberman over this. If it had happened ten years ago, I would have started an educational campaign on the road in order to persuade Liberman that Gogol was not an anti-Semite. Today I decided to do neither. There are certain prejudices that Soviet people absorb with the ideological milk from their motherland's tit, and even perestroika cannot change them.

Liberman's generation went to school when universal hypocrisy reached its highest level. For instance, your literature instructor told you that General Secretary Brezhnev of the Communist Party of the Soviet Union (CPSU) was not only four or five times the Hero of the Soviet Union but also one of the world's greatest writers. The Soviet people unanimously demanded that he be awarded the highest Soviet literary award, the Lenin Prize. You had to read his books as your homework assignments, and you were not alone; the entire adult population of the U.S.S.R. was expected to study him diligently, too. Or pretend to, for those who openly refused to read the masterpieces of

Lenin's faithful follower usually wound up in the lunatic asylum. These masterpieces were put together by a team of hack writers, who had everything but integrity and literary talent. The literary Frankensteins they created are ugly, pretentious, and painfully boring.

Thanks to television, it was obvious to everyone that the Boss was not playing with a full deck even in his younger days, but by the end of his life he completely spaced out. Then, we asked ourselves, how can the teachers not understand that? Of course they understood, but nobody wanted to be sent to a madhouse, and so they lied. Teenagers can tell when their teachers are lying, but they do not really care why. The next hour the same teacher told you that Gogol was more or less a great writer, but he never fought against the czar for the working-class cause, and what's worse, he believed in God. That was why he was out of it, you know...So if you wanted to be accepted into a college, you knew it was better to pick as the topic of your Russian composition the immortal works of the General Secretary. If you did not, chances are you would not make it through the competition, and the odds of your being accepted into a college were slim. But you would still be able to get a job on an assembly line at a factory. No need to write compositions there!

Naturally, confronted with such a dilemma, the more ambitious students would enthusiastically lie their way to the top, while the rest, the majority, decided that they would never trust anyone or anything. That was how the country's young entered their adult lives. And that is why for most of my contemporaries, educated during the era of "stagnation," Gogol is no more than a patient of a madhouse.

We have covered the first hundred miles of our trip. I look at the map: M-8. The signs of the road still say M-7.

"What difference does it make as long as we get to the right place?" says Liberman good-naturedly. "The map could be outdated as easily as the road could be renamed."

He is right. One of the principal problems in getting around the U.S.S.R. is trying to keep up with the constant rewriting of the map to suit ideological needs. Hundreds of ancient cities, thousands of old towns all over the country have been renamed. After the coup in 1917, the old place names were replaced by the names of the new rulers, who did not suffer from excessive modesty and would lend their names to big cities and entire regions while still alive. Thanks to the reviving nationalism of the intelligentsia, the list of today's populist demands includes the reestablishment of the old place names, such as St. Petersburg (to replace Leningrad), and more often now the old names are finding their way back. But it is a huge country, and its maps are still stained with the names of leaders of the departing bloody epoch, like the face of a person who once had smallpox.

It gets dark very late in mid-Russia in May. It was after ten, but the night was still young, the darkness not complete. If it were not for the scattered rains, we could see almost as if it were day. On both sides of the deserted road there were such dark, dense forests that it seemed as if Russian partisans had been hiding there since World War II.

After the ancient Russian city of Vladimir (named not for Vladimir Lenin but rather for the medieval prince), we passed small villages already sleeping.

At midnight, I took the wheel. Liberman is an early bird while I am a night owl, so we decided in the beginning of our trip that he would drive until nightfall, and I would be the nighttime driver. For there is really no place in Russia for the weary traveler to stop. A traffic cop in the city of Dzerzhinsk (one of many hundreds of Soviet towns named after the founder of the organization known today as the KGB) had warned us that sleeping in our cars at the rest areas along the road was not recommended by the police.

"And what if we do?" Liberman asked pertly. He likes fighting for his rights. This time he was doing it just for its own sake, because we were not going to stop overnight anyway.

"That's what!" The cop grinned wickedly and swiped the edge of his hand across his Adam's apple.

You may have already guessed that for the ordinary public there are no Motel-Sixes or Holiday Inns in our country, nor are there any in sight for the foreseeable future. Only in the resort areas, in the Crimea or the Caucasus, may one come across a motel for drivers. But even during better times, they would only accommodate foreigners for hard currency, or Soviet people with *blat*.

"Shall we eat?" I proposed, remembering the chicken legs and potatoes that Alexandra prepared for our journey.

"Don't worry, I'm not hungry yet," he answered, stretching until his bones cracked. "I'd rather talk about something to make the road shorter."

To talk about something means talking about politics, but even I am already sick of politics. We cannot talk about women, for the only woman Liberman knows is his wife, and we do not discuss wives in our country.

"Look, we drove out of the rain!" I informed my companion, but he had dropped off.

Our car had an additional gas tank of monstrous dimensions, which Liberman found in a junkyard and installed in the trunk. I do not discount the possibility that it was one of those suspended fuel tanks that are dropped by MiG-21 interceptor-bombers in the air after the fuel runs out. In lines for gasoline, our car always provoked about the same reaction as the appearance of a man equipped with a root of life of extraordinary dimensions in a Soviet public bathhouse. All it would take was for us to open our trunk with feigned indifference during "refueling" and start pumping gas into this additional reservoir, as a crowd would immediately form accompanied by the ironic and envious humming of standard-tank owners.

Including its factory-supplied ten-gallon standard tank, the car had a capacity of about thirty-five gallons of gas. With the carburetor and engine ideally adjusted by Liberman, our car could make about nine hundred miles on one fill-up, which cannot be overestimated in the last frontier of our socialist *oikumena* (civilization), given the permanent shortages of gas in our provincial cities. One of the drawbacks of this additional tank was that it occupied too much space in the trunk and was an additional strain on the axle.

I looked at Liberman's sleeping form with respect and started slowing down for an early breakfast at the side of the road.

3

"What is Chuvash for 'Glory to the Communist Party!'?"

If you ask a foreigner who knows anything about the Russians what the most common name is in the Soviet Union, he will confidently answer "Ivanov." That is undoubtedly the right answer. But even the Ivanovs themselves are probably not aware that their last name is also the most common one among the Chuvash people, which is the result of their having been forced into the Russian Orthodox Church. All new converts were given Russian names when they were baptized, a process that began in the sixteenth century, when the last remaining faction of the kingdom of the Kazan Tartars collapsed, overrun by the army of the victorious Czar Ivan the Terrible.

To commemorate this event, Ivan built St. Basil's Cathedral, the church with the colorful onion-shaped domes in Moscow's Red Square. Some unpatriotic tourist guides have been known to mention that the thankful monarch blinded and cut off the hands of the creators of this architectural masterpiece, so that they would never be able to re-create the design for anyone else.

While chewing on my chicken and drinking my lukewarm tea, I was excitedly telling all this to sleepy Liberman, who also held a piece of chicken in his hand but would forget to take it to his mouth, as he was not fully awake yet. It was 1:30 A.M., and the empty central square of the town of Kstov, where we were having our early breakfast, floated in a haze.

We arranged our food on the hood of our car under the only functioning streetlight in town, and ate standing up, as though we were at a reception *à la fourchette*. We failed to notice several silhouettes emerge from the cold fog. They turned out to be four teenagers of different sizes, dressed in quilted jackets secured with wide military belts with stars on their buckles. One of them looked like a girl. They stopped at some distance, regarding us like naturalists examining fauna, and then the eldest croaked, "Hey, what are you turkeys up to?"

Liberman and I glanced at each other. The best thing we could do was to escape from their nocturnal turf as soon as possible. We had no idea how many more of them might be hiding out there in the fog. But we had to do it calmly, so as not to provoke an attack. Besides, it would be a pity to leave behind the food that my wife had cooked for us.

"Come on over, guys," I said in an overconfident voice, and waved my hand invitingly. The sarcastic remark by my wife, that my dark green jacket made me look like a young NATO general during military exercises, crossed my mind. The hoarse-voiced guy passed his cigarette to his friend and came closer.

"Help yourself," I said. "How about you, guys? Come on!" I continued, pretending to be the host of a picnic, and hoping with all my heart that there were no more guests than these four.

"What's this stuff? Chicken?" my guest inquired as he reached out his hand for food. In the dim light I saw dark blue tattoos like rings around his fingers. It meant that he had spent several years in jail for juvenile delinquency. Judging by his old-looking facial features, he had probably done time as an adult, too.

"It's turkey," said Liberman in an unexpectedly high-pitched voice. He deliberately reached his hand into the side pocket of his black jacket. Well done, Vova! His mingling with racketeers who had their cars serviced free of charge at his auto service co-op was paying off. Putting his hand in his pocket that way telegraphed that he had a weapon, a handgun or a knife.

"Why aren't you guys in bed yet?" I inquired, genuinely curious. We knew in Moscow that gangs of such teenagers, ranging from a handful like this to several dozen, arrive in Moscow by train to ply their trade, and then try to leave Moscow on the same day in order to shake the police. It is not that difficult, since Moscow police have a hard time controlling their own robbers, rapists, and killers. Our guests could be such visitors from Moscow, just returned home on the night train after a hard day's work.

"Okay, see you later!" The old-faced teenager said through his clenched teeth after a short pause and backed away toward his silent companions, holding the chicken leg in his tattooed hand. The main force of their gang had apparently left, and he had decided that we were not easy enough prey for the remaining foursome.

Toward daybreak the fog began to dissipate, and driving became easier. Judging by the fact that road signs, scarce even around Moscow, had disappeared altogether, and that several countrified trucks we had seen had the letter *C* on their license plates, I deduced that we had reached the territory of Chuvashia, proud recipient of three honorary orders.

In the Soviet Union, all the republics were decorated with orders. Another strange, narcissistic fancy of the Communist state was to give awards originally intended for people to its own property and its component parts: administrative territorial units, cities, collective farms, industrial organizations and enterprises, and quasi-public organizations like the puppeteers' trade unions, say, or the singing and dancing ensembles.

The final surrealistic effect was achieved by the party apparatus when it finally decided to attach the names of inanimate phenomena to concrete objects. The names of the following Soviet organizations sound odd enough in Russian, but translated into English they must be positively bizarre: the Central State Barber Shop Named After the Twenty-fifth Congress of Trade Unions and Decorated with the Order of the October Revolution; or Decorated with the Order of the People's Friendship, the State Seaquarium Named After the Fiftieth Anniversary of the U.S.S.R. and Dedicated to the Four Hundredth Anniversary of the Voluntary Entry of the Kazan Kingdom into Russia.

Before entering Cheboksary we were stopped again, this time at the permanent checkpoint of the State Automobile Inspection. The standard SAI checkpoint is a large, glass-fronted building, where the staff of the local highway division carries out its duties. Around Moscow such checkpoints appear every five or six miles, but the farther you are from the capital, the fewer and poorer they become. An elevated platform with crushed cars that were wrecked in accidents, stained if possible by the blood of their passengers, is considered a very important educational tool at these places.

When the cop at the checkpoint saw our Moscow license plates, he asked us to get out of the car and checked our papers thoroughly. First, our car registration, the model, color, license plate number, and place of registration along with the name of the car owner. Second, our driver's licenses, and third, passports with our residence permits. Not finding anything suspicious, the cop asked us where we were going in such troubled times. We explained that our goal was to visit relatives in Novocheboksarsk. Of course, this was only part of the truth, but he did not ask us about the rest of our trip. We drove off and left the cop, short, sleepy, and discontented, looking after us, tapping his boot with a striped traffic baton.

Liberman was behind the wheel to drive us into the city of Cheboksary; the ceremonial entrance into Novocheboksarsk was his prerogative. He already knew his way, as he had driven it before. What made this time different from before was that he would usually leave Moscow early in the morning and arrive at night. This time it was just the reverse.

Cheboksary is a large city; it is not very friendly. The city is the site of the military-related chemical industry, which does not make life there pleasant. Unlike many other cities on the Volga, the capital of Chuvashia was not an important city before the Revolution, and thus its architecture is not very interesting. During the Soviet period, like so many places, ecologically disastrous industrial plants and gloomy barracks were built around the city, and around them have proliferated the standard boxlike, multistory apartment houses. And since it is a typical Russian provincial industrial city, that means that in the center of the town there was a bronze statue of Lenin in a coat and tie, cloth cap in his hand, standing like a stuffed dummy. Behind it was a pompous building, the headquarters of the regional party committee. In the depths of the country, the regional party committee in 1990 was still considered the supreme and incontestable authority.

The Chuvashes, just like their neighbors, the Maris, Mordvins, and Udmurts, are patient, modest folk. In more than seventy years of totalitarian rule, they have never grumbled about the troubles inflicted upon them by the ingenious Bolsheviks. All the evils of life in the Soviet Union, from the forced collectivization and mass famine in the twenties and thirties to the poverty and moral degradation of recent years, came down in full measure on the good-natured Chuvashes. As the reward for their exemplary behavior and as an example to other ethnic minorities, about twenty years ago the party selected a Chuvash man named Adrian Nikolayev to be one of the first cosmonauts. Today the young generation of Chuvashia have organized themselves into gangs, and they have new heroes. Their greatest hero at the moment is Arnold Schwarzenegger.

Just as many little towns in California have a street called Sunset Drive, in every Soviet city is a major street bearing Lenin's name. As we were driving down Cheboksary's Lenin Avenue, I asked Liberman to stop for a moment at one of the ugly three-story houses. It was built in the sixties and had the typical design of the Mature Socialism style, which is to say, no style at all. Liberman looked at me with displeasure: "What kind of people go sight-seeing at five o'clock in the morning?" But I got out of the car anyway and went up to the dark brown wall to look at the unfinished memorial plaque. On my last visit, the plaque was not on the wall yet; the man to whom it was dedicated was still alive.

Yakov Ukhsai was an amazing old man who resembled Hemingway in his old age, even though he did not have a beard. In Chuvashia, which has always been considered inferior in many respects in the family of Soviet republics, Yakov Ukhsai has always enjoyed special privileges. Several years ago he won the State Prize of the Russian Federal Republic in literature, and thus became the first, and for the foreseeable future the only, Chuvash recipient of this award. By Soviet criteria, he was honored with this award not so much for his literary contributions as for the cultural progress that all of Chuvashia had achieved.

The tradition of allowing the country's official cultural establishment to lead a quality of life equivalent to that of the low-level party bureaucrats goes back to Stalin's time. They were given good apartments and dachas (country houses); they had access to the special distribution stores, shops that were off-limits to the ordinary person where they could buy food and merchandise; they could use special hospitals and sanatoriums where they were treated with imported medicines not available to the public. In other words, they were bought.

In return, they were expected to serve the government by glorifying it and brainwashing people who lacked even the basics of life, by lying to their countrymen that the party does everything "in the name of the people, and for the benefit of the people." For one reason or another, the authorities especially prefer to feature this slogan in dirty supermarkets, where cockroaches on empty shelves seem to be the only interested parties. In Moscow, the slogans were taken down, but they are still around in the outlying reaches of the country, a reminder of the good old days.

Yakov Ukhsai took full advantage of his position, but, to the horror of the local authorities, he not only refused to glorify Communism but also refused in every way to abide by the rules of the game.

I first visited Chuvashia in the early eighties. Vadim Dementyev, the cheerful son of the influential secretary of the Writers' Union of the Russian Republic and my immediate supervisor then, was my companion. I had just started my career in publishing, and one of my tasks was to publish Russian translations of ethnic writers. Dementyev was showing me the ropes, introducing me to the local writers, editors, and authorities. Some time later, when perestroika was in full swing, he had an excellent party career, became a part of the ruling party elite, and was made a section head in the Department of Ideology of the Central Committee of the CPSU. But in the early eighties Vadim was just a young literary critic with a promising bureaucratic career. In literary circles he was laughed at because he would write articles only about official celebrities, winners of State and Lenin Awards, many of whom were friends of his father.

Yakov Ukhsai was in the last years of his life when Dementyev introduced me to him. By then he had almost completely stopped hiding his disloyalty to the regime and terrorized the local literary officials with his scandalous behavior. The chairman of the Writers' Union of Chuvashia of those days, a novelist named Anatoly Yemelyanov, almost cried when he complained about Ukhsai.

Ukhsai began his day with a glass of cognac. After his drink, he would come to the Writers' Union, kick the office's doors wide open, and start cursing at his ideological bosses. "Hacks! Cowards! Corrupt creatures!" Passersby outside could hear him screaming through the open windows of the bureaucrats' offices. The victims of Ukhsai's spleen could not complain, for they did not wish to wash their dirty linen in public. If he had been an ordinary Chuvash, he would have been curbed long ago. To punish the "national pride" of the entire republic was not worth the trouble, for many of the local officials would probably have lost their comfortable positions in the aftermath of the scandal. Therefore, they gritted their teeth and tolerated the old man.

Ukhsai liked me for some reason, perhaps because I am not Russian (although Russian is my mother tongue). I liked old Ukhsai, too. The last time I visited him, he was in his office, redolent of tobacco and old age, in the house on Lenin Avenue. He was dressed in warm, light blue sweatpants and an undershirt. Over his shirt he wore an old sleeveless, fur-lined jacket. A winter snowstorm was howling outside the window, which was covered with frosty patterns, and he poured each of us a glass of Armenian cognac so that we could get warm after the cold outside. I gave him one of my books. He began searching his bookshelves, and then suddenly he handed me a book by the blind medieval Arab poet Abu-Ala ibn al-Maari, which had been translated by the patriarch of Soviet intellectual poetry, Arseny Tarkovsky.

"Take a look. A good translation, even though copied from a literal transcript," he said with a sly grin. He was taking a dig at our methods at the State Publishing House. Most of the minority authors' books published in Moscow were in fact not translations from the original work but rather poor editions of word-for-word literal translations. Russian translators did not know the ethnic languages of the U.S.S.R., and minority authors were therefore required to submit their works translated word for word. If the original poem was like a lively embarrassed girl, ready to surrender to her insistent lover, this word-for-word translation was a one-armed, bandy-legged plaster-cast dummy with a crooked nose, whom the translator-Pygmalion was supposed to revive with his mercenary kisses.

Then Ukhsai told me something that shook my impression of the Chuvashes as complacent, law-abiding citizens of a totalitarian state.

In the late thirties, when the next campaign of terror, like a gigantic meat grinder, had started once again to grind up millions of

Soviet people, those who were the most talented, independent, and eccentric were, as usual, the first to die. They were the ones whom envious, malicious, or simply foolish people, brainwashed dead by the Communist dogma of class struggle, reported to the NKVD, later renamed the KGB. Such information was sent about the young and talented Ukhsai. He, as well as many others, was facing a torturous death from his own government simply because, in the opinion of some half-witted investigator, he was not stupid and obedient enough. But unlike the majority of his brothers-in-misery, the future State Prize winner conducted himself not like a whipped dog but rather like the hero of a romantic adventure story.

Two NKVD agents arrested him in his native village, to which he had come from Cheboksary on personal business. They had followed him in a horse-drawn carriage from the city that night. One of them took out a handgun, while the other slowly, syllable by syllable, read the arrest order to him. Then they tied him up, smoked the cigarettes they had confiscated from him, and lay down for a night's sleep. One of the agents had diarrhea and had to go outside several times during the night. At sunrise they were going to set out for the return trip; they were planning to travel in their carriage, while he was to follow on foot, tied to a rope. They were so used to the humble obedience of their victims that they were absolutely dumbfounded when they discovered not only that he had disappeared, but had even taken their only gun with him.

Upon their return to the city, the unfortunate agents were executed for incompetence, and Ukhsai was on the run. He was wanted by the authorities, but he managed to escape to Moscow somehow, where he found the first secretary of the Writers' Union, Alexander Fadeyev, who had been compelled more than once, because of his high position, to sign death warrants issued for disgraced members of the Writers' Union and their families. Otherwise, one of his deputies could sign his death sentence. This system of repression was merciless and never failed, but something went wrong with it this time. Whatever happened, the iron-willed Fadeyev, in a moment of unforgivable moral enlightenment, most likely felt sorry for the truth-seeking Ukhsai. Instead of calling the NKVD, he sent the unruly runaway to his state-provided dacha, where he spent nearly half a year.

By that time Stalin had again executed the head of the NKVD, after having denounced him as the people's enemy, so that people would not forget who their real friend was. The incoming head of the secret police had his hands full with new problems, primarily to replace the blades in the nightmarish human meat-grinding machine. Fadeyev in this situation had Ukhsai pardoned relatively easily.

In 1956, when Khrushchev in his secret address to the Twentieth Congress of the CPSU lifted the veil which had hidden from the whole world the horrors of the "final victory of socialism in one isolated country," Fadeyev committed suicide. But he had saved Ukhsai, and hopefully it would count on his Judgment Day.

"What kept you? Come on, let's go!" Liberman was impatient for his reunion with his family. He looked at his watch. "My, it's already half past five!"

"The home stretch," I said, getting into the car and slamming the door. "Our lunch, our fresh bed sheets, and your rejoicing family are all awaiting us."

Amazingly, his rejoicing family was indeed already awake and waiting for us. When we arrived, they were looking down at us from the eleventh floor. The building in which Liberman's Chuvash in-laws got their two-bedroom apartment several years ago was on a lot along the road, part of a residential district that belonged to the Novocheboksarsk Chemical Industrial Complex. A residential complex in the U.S.S.R. is a tight cluster of nine-, twelve-, and sometimes even eighteen-story concrete apartment buildings, typically shaped in the form of an L, H, T, or E. People call them "towers," as they look like gigantic matchboxes standing on end.

Dancing with impatience and happiness, Liberman waited while I got out of the car, and then he rushed into the building like a hurricane. I grabbed my bag and hurried after him. The elevator, its unlubricated wire cables squeaking, took an age to drag us up to our floor.

Liberman's father-in-law, beaming with delight, opened the door. The whole family was standing behind him, including Liberman's wife with the two children in her arms and the eighty-year-old grandmother. They all had kind and friendly faces.

I went straight to bed and slept until about 11:00 A.M. The door to the balcony was open, and the hubbub of children's voices could be heard from outside. I recalled that it was Sunday, and looked a little more closely at the room I was in. It was the grandmother's room, which probably explains the idyllic dreams I had had here. Could these dreams have been called up from the prerevolutionary Chuvash village? Some kind of windmill at the river, some clouds up in the sky...A wasp, which had lost its way, flew through the window into the room from outside. I got up, dressed, and went to chat with Liberman's family.

By Soviet standards their apartment was a mansion. It consisted of two small rooms and one slightly larger room, an entry hall, a bathroom, kitchen, and two balconies. Liberman's father-in-law had gotten it from the state just before his retirement from a lifetime of work at the chemical plant. His job was justifiably considered to be hazardous. Workers in industries officially classified as unhealthy receive certain fringe benefits. For example, people who work in hazardous places get a free pint of milk daily. More importantly, they can retire five years earlier than everyone else, though it comes to the same thing, since the retirees from such industries die sooner. Yet it is the free housing that is the most attractive inducement for voluntarily destroying one's health.

"Otherwise, who would work at these chemical plants but jailbirds?" Liberman's father-in-law frankly wondered.

"How about inmates? Don't they get apartments?" I knew that prisoners could receive a conditional parole if they agreed to work at a hazardous industry and be paid much less than other workers.

"No way, they must live in the barracks." He laughed at my naïveté.

The scale of industrialization accomplished in the U.S.S.R. in the thirties amazed leftist European intellectuals. They were even ready to close their eyes to the fact that it was carried out by the unpaid slave labor of tens of millions of the Soviet prisoners. But those who were considered "free workers" did not even suspect for many years that the major portion of the fruits of their labor had been illegally appropriated by the hierarchy of the Soviet "partocracy" on behalf of the so-called people's state. Capitalists, who were declared "sharks" and "blood-suckers," had held for themselves approximately a quarter of the value produced, but the Communist rulers in the Soviet Union even today continue to take away from their citizens up to 80 percent of what they actually produce, all the while posting slogans like "Long

Live the CPSU!" and "The People and the Party Are One!"

"There are no such slogans left in Moscow," I informed him. "At least not on the major streets."

He hopelessly waved his hand. "But we'll have them here for a long time to come. Take a look at yesterday's newspaper." He handed the paper to me.

I quickly scanned the front page of the newspaper, which was called *Path to Communism*. At the top was this slogan: "Proletariat of the whole world, unite!" The date: May 19, 1990. The lead story was an interview with the deputy chief of the city police, Nikolai Makarov, who opined, "The principal line of our party is correct; the party protects the interests of the people."

Right under the interview with the policeman was a conversation with the metalworkers' team leader, Vsevolod Makov: "What we need is to strengthen the party. I myself would personally vote for the one-party system. With five to six parties in business, there would be a fight over vacancies, and we would have anarchy again." Next to it was another contribution, from N. Mourigina; judging by the style of the article and its title, "A Search for Truth," she is probably the local ideologist:

"The party's discipline has been weakened; those ideals to which the party called the people have become eroded. All this undermines the credibility of the CPSU.... The cultural deficit is so enormous that it is no match for the shortages of soap or sugar...." And, of course, the reason for all this is world imperialism and Chinese revisionism.

"What a funny paper your city has!" I told Liberman's father-in-law and gave him back his newspaper. "But then again, you have the television schedule for the whole week on the third page. How many channels do you have?"

"Two," he said proudly. "Sometimes daytime programs, too."

"In Moscow we have five," I bragged. "So, how many years did you have to wait until you got your apartment?"

"My whole life," he answered cheerfully. It appears that the apartment is free, but that is actually not quite true. So many deductions are made from a worker's pay toward the future apartment throughout his lifetime that it would actually amount to enough to buy five such apartments. Not to mention the cost to his health. Americans who curse the tyranny of their landlords have no idea what happens when the landlord is the totalitarian state, free of any responsibility for its citizens' welfare.

You can forget about mortgage loans for building or buying your own house in the former U.S.S.R., for all the land here belongs to the state; even if you built your own house, you would still be paying rent on the land it was built on. Even if you simply wanted to rent or buy an apartment in a city, you could not do so legally under any circumstances. There has been a permanent housing crisis in Russia from the very first day of Soviet rule, which is responsible for the nationalization of the housing construction industry and everything related to it in the Soviet economy.

Then there is the residence permit, which makes Soviet citizens slaves, completely dependent on the state as far as housing is concerned. The residence permit deprives people of their right to live where they wish in their own country. Originally, this measure was designed as a means of controlling migrational processes in the country—for instance, to prevent people from leaving their jobs and looking for better positions elsewhere in the country.

Today you have the right to live only where you were born and currently have a residence. When you are sixteen, you must report to your district police precinct, where you receive an internal passport with this sinister message: "You are registered at Such-and-Such Address." From then on you are only allowed to change it when you get married and move to your spouse's address, when you get a new apartment, and when you work your way up through the *nomenklatura,* the rigidly structured bureaucracy of the party.

A person who is found living at a place other than his official domicile is a criminal in the eyes of the state. First, he is fined, then put into prison. When he gets out, he cannot get a job without his residence permit, and he cannot get his residence permit until he has a job; thus he winds up in jail again. It is a Catch-22. It was that way during Stalin's times, and it is happening now, with Gorbachev in charge. Without your residence permit you have no place to live, and you cannot get medical care. You are not allowed to travel on an airplane or to open a bank account without it. You cannot buy groceries in a store, and above all, you can never get a job.

"Stop boring them with your dull stories," commanded Antonina Pavlovna, Liberman's mother-in-law. "To the table, everyone! Sveta, wake up that man of yours."

Antonina Pavlovna works in a grocery store, which is a privileged position, for those who work in the grocery stores will never die of hunger. My instincts were right: the table was laden with good food. Liberman and I tucked in with gusto, eating slowly, relishing every bite.

4

The Knight in the Tiger Skin

Muscovites are hated by the whole country, because non-Muscovites mistakenly assume that they are the elite. All of Soviet society has been categorized, and those who are lower hate those who are higher. First-class people have unlimited access to first-class privileges; people of the second category are happy because, although they do not have the privileges of the first class, they still have much more than the third category, and so forth.

These gradations are not based on material wealth. People of the fifth category see and understand it all, while those in the fifteenth category can only guess at what is happening. The twenty-fifth category honestly believes that Stalin would not allow such a mess if he were still alive.

Over the course of seventy years, the image of Moscow as the summit of the state pyramid became so deeply imprinted on the public consciousness that in the Russian provinces and the ethnic territories nearly any Muscovite, irrespective of his social status, became associated with the universally hated authorities, who care only about themselves. These feelings are also fortified by the fact that the regime at one time tried to turn Moscow into a showcase of socialism by supplying it with agricultural products and industrial goods of better quality than those given other cities, and at their expense. The capitals of republics and regions in turn received better supplies than surrounding, smaller cities for the same reason. But if the small towns and settlements could at least get tiny bits of the pie, the rural population had to further tighten their belts. Most of the rural stores simply went out of business because they had nothing to sell, and the remaining few had only about a dozen items to offer. I have been in such stores, where there was nothing to buy except kerosene for household lamps; cheap flannelette for foot binding, shirts, and shrouds; and salt and matches.

But Moscow residents had long since lost their former privileges and during the years of perestroika became almost as destitute as the rest of the population of the superpower. To buy you must have a passport with Moscow registration or food cards like the ones used during World War II. Most goods are distributed at work nowadays.

"In America," Liberman said pensively, taking a long, inquisitive look out the window, "you can buy in any country store the same stuff as in New York. And if it's not available in the store, they will order it for you by mail."

"You're pulling my leg," said Shlupkin, distrustfully shaking his head. "By mail? I can't believe that."

"You can ask someone who was there." Liberman, eating mushrooms, pointed a fork at me.

Shlupkin himself gathered mushrooms in the forest. Then Liberman's mother-in-law, Antonina Pavlovna, marinated them, using her great-grandmother's recipe. The latter was sitting at the table but did not participate in our conversation. Whenever America was mentioned, however, a slight cloud of disapproval would show on her face. All her life she had believed the propaganda, and honestly thought America to be a bad word, probably a curse. She, therefore, felt embarrassed that her only granddaughter's husband would use such words at the family dinner table.

For the first course, we had an excellent mushroom soup. Stewed potatoes with meat and mushrooms were served for the second. May turned out to be a rainy month, and there was an abundance of mushrooms in the forests of Russia. Sveta was feeding three-year-old Motya and looking at Liberman with anxiety and love; he had his one-year-old daughter Ksyusha sitting on his lap. They made a touching picture.

What kind of future will their children have? Sveta's parents were trying to persuade the Libermans to move to Novocheboksarsk. This proposal was discussed at every visit.

"Of course, we would have to live with the parents again." Liberman sighed. "But this apartment is bigger. The chemical plants poison the air, but who said that the air in Moscow is fresh and clean?"

"That's true, but how about your Moscow residence permit?" Liberman's parents would reply, appealing to his common sense, when he called them on the telephone from Novocheboksarsk. "If you lose it once, you will never, you hear me, never, ever again have the right to reside in Moscow."

Shlupkin tried to persuade Liberman. He doted on his grandchildren and wanted them to grow up near him. "Though I'm drawing a pension, I still work at the same place as before. We have good food distribution, and you can even sign up for furniture. And once you start working, you'll get an apartment, and all kinds of stuff."

"Vyacheslav Afanasievich, what kind of business do you want Vova to get into?" I interrupted.

"It should be the chemical plant," Shlupkin answered, as if he did not fully understand my question.

"What does it produce?" I asked again, politely. I was curious, because at the moment we had a catastrophic shortage of rubber products, from automobile tires, which are prized, to condoms, even more desirable. A silence fell over the table. Sveta's hand froze with a spoon of hot cereal halfway to Motya's mouth. Motya, in turn, could not decide if he should close his mouth or keep it open, and looked at his mother for an answer.

"Don't be afraid, Shlupkin. Tell the truth. It's glasnost time!" Liberman teased him and gave me a sly wink.

I winked back mechanically, though I did not understand what he was driving at.

"No, I can't say. Our plant is secret…" Shlupkin was in doubt, but I could see that he wanted to tell me.

"Don't do it, don't!" Antonina Pavlovna said in a subdued voice in Chuvash. Her life experience told her that it was safer to keep your mouth shut. She loved Shlupkin and respected him, and as a member of their family Security Council, she put her veto in her delicate way, softly in Chuvash, so that their guest did not feel embarrassed. Suddenly I got it. I looked at Liberman, dumbfounded. He tapped his head with his fist and laughed his head off:

"Yes, you got it. They manufacture chemical weapons! That's what they do!"

The entry hall of Shlupkin's apartment was decorated with a homemade copy of the painting *The Knight in the Tiger Skin*. In his present incarnation, Shlupkin, unfortunately, was not a great primitivist like Henri Rousseau or the Georgian lumpen sign-painter Niko Pirosmani, who both lived a hundred years ago. But he was involved in his new hobby with no less fervor and devotion than his great predecessors. The catalogue of his finished works was modest: a couple of still lifes of field flowers and, unheard of in this area, fruit, a couple of winter landscapes with hunters, a yellow moon emerging from behind the clouds; and a picture of Avtandil, the great hero of the medieval Georgian poem, fighting a lion with his bare hands. Shlupkin grew up in the late Stalinist era, when illustrations of the poem "The Knight in the Tiger Skin," by the Georgian genius Shota Rustaveli, were printed in all textbooks, and copies of these pictures could be seen at all public places. Stalin was himself from Georgia, of course, and thus the mass depictions of the Georgian knight were a form of homage to the noble roots of the leader.

Many Soviet people still do not know that Stalin was the illegitimate son of a laundress. Besides, his mother was not exactly Georgian but rather an Ossetian. But Russians are not very well versed in the nationalities of the Transcaucasus and the northern Caucasus. For example, my Moscow neighbor is a Tat, or Daghestan Jew, sometimes called "mountain Jew." But the residents of our co-op apartment house keep calling him a Georgian because of his sheeplike bulging eyes and full head of grayish hair. It is no wonder that Stalin, who completely rewrote his biography, became for millions of Russians a Georgian, whose cradle was gently rocked in turn by Karl Marx and Friedrich Engels. By the way, the identity of the father of "the leader and mentor of all the peoples" remains unknown, though rumor has it that the honor belongs to the Russian traveler and ethnographer Nikolai Przhevalsky. A species of wild horse in Central Asia was named after this famous scientist.

Our meal turned into a lengthy tea ceremony with homemade

pirogis and a remarkable cherry preserve, cooked according to a traditional family recipe. The number of participants in the conversation began to dwindle. First, Sveta put the children to bed, then her grandmother minced quietly to her room, then Antonina Pavlovna relocated to the kitchen, and then Shlupkin at her call joined her to wash dishes.

The evening was young, so I decided to leave Liberman in the bosom of his family and took a bus to Cheboksary. I walked for a while through empty, dreary streets until I found what I was looking for. A clumsy picture of Rambo wearing a machine-gun cartridge belt hung above the door. Except for his blood-covered torso and huge muscles, Rambo looked just like an ordinary, peaceable Chuvash. The sign above his head proclaimed, in red and black letters, "Sputnik Youth Video Club." A handwritten notice of the shows, full of errors, was attached to the door. The videos were shown from early in the morning till late at night. First on the list were karate films, then an endless string of commando and ninja exploitation movies, and by evening, low-quality, hard-core porno flicks, which would make *Emmanuelle* an award-winning classic, worthy of the Young Communist League's prize "for the ideological education of the young generation in the spirit of the current Congress of the CPSU."

I produced a three-ruble note and entered. Strangely, nobody in the crowded hall was smoking. It made me happy; I quit when my daughter was born. In our country, the rule against smoking in public places is violated so often that nobody pays any attention to it. That is how I easily recognize my former countrymen driving cabs in New York, who light up cigarettes without even bothering to ask passengers if they mind. Yet the absence of smokers in this place did not mean that they were following rules; it simply meant that the hall was occupied by a gang of weight-lifters. The young usher took my money and pointed at a vacant chair in the last row. The theater was actually nothing more than a large room in a first-floor apartment, with bedspreads covering the two small windows. About a dozen broad-shouldered teenage boys dressed in identical quilted jackets were sitting on plain office chairs staring at the screen. I felt a slight cold inside my stomach, an instinctual warning of danger.

Meanwhile, the color television screen shattered with violent explosions. A huge fellow in a knitted sports cap sitting in front of me was twitching with excitement, slapping his neighbor's back with a giant fist. In Moscow his knitted cap is called a "rooster," because it looks like a cock's comb. At one point, when the hero cut his arch-enemy's stomach open in a particularly elegant manner, the fellow in the cap, in his desire to share his excitement with everybody present, turned round to me. When he saw my face in the darkness, he was stunned. Both my foreign appearance and my age made me an obvious outsider here.

"Hey, guys!" he cried in a high-pitched voice. "Look at this dude!"

"Don't bother," another boy, apparently the gang leader, barked at him. "We'll check him out later."

"What's wrong, guys?" the administrator asked. "Let the man watch the movie he paid for."

Over the last ten years, the Volga Basin has become the center of a new social phenomenon in the U.S.S.R., officially dubbed "criminal youth gangs." I saw them first in the capital of the Tartar republic in the early eighties. I was driving through with Renat Harris, then edi-tor-in-chief of *Lights of Kazan* magazine, whose book I was preparing for publication in Moscow. Suddenly I saw an excited crowd of teenagers coming out of a side street. They were dressed in oversized quilted jackets, shabby shoes, and bell-bottom trousers that had gone out of style in Moscow about eight years before. The pedestrians ran away from them almost in panic, but the hooligans did not pay any attention to anyone. They were moving, almost running, as one noisy group, waving their hands in the air, carrying on a hysterical discus-sion.

"Who are they? Why are they dressed like that?" I asked.

Renat Harris looked at me with his still blue eyes and answered casually, without any sign of surprise, "It's a youth gang. Nonfor-mals."

In Moscow, there were many youth groups—hippies, punks, and their rival skinheads and rockers. But the Moscow youths' clothes were almost fancy compared with these young Tartars, who were dressed like a team of prisoners.

"They fight with iron rods, one gang against the other," added our young driver from the front seat, eyeing me in the rearview mirror to see the effect of his words. I thought he seemed almost proud of this local oddity.

We did not have enough time to talk more about it during our dinner in the restaurant, which had the same name as the magazine my companion worked for, Lights of Kazan. Renat was one of the candidates for the position of chairman of the republic's Writers' Union. The Tenth Congress of the Tartar writers was approaching, and I was more interested in talking to Renat about literature and everything connected with it than about some youth gang in bell-bottom pants. At those times censorship would not allow the press to report on disturbing new social trends, and with the exception of criminologists nobody had any idea of how ugly and frightful this new movement of provincial youth in quilted jackets was. It was not until several years later, in the epoch of perestroika and glasnost, when an epidemic of mass crime among youth started taking over other cities, that the press sounded the alarm to a frightened public.

Only bits and pieces of information about the youth gangs were then available to me from my Kazan friends. My close friend Z. (I must withhold his name), who abandoned writing for a large-scale free-lance business, told me a lot of interesting stories about the sinister and terrifying customs of these youth gangs. To protect his business from racketeers, he was compelled to hire a team of "gopnicks" (Kazan slang for professional criminals) and thus he had firsthand information.

Like the majority of the Soviet entrepreneurs who have attempted to set up private businesses, Z. found himself in a dangerous position: on the one hand, he had to pay protection money to the criminals, who in return would allow him to conduct his business operations more or less unscathed; on the other hand he had to bribe the corrupt local authorities and the police, who can accuse and convict private businessmen of "economic crimes" almost at will. Soviet legislation can be interpreted very ambiguously; it allows malicious bureaucrats to turn the life of any businessmen into a nightmarish balancing act on a wire over an administrative abyss. Extortion, blackmail, and bribery by Soviet officials are among the most widespread ills of the Soviet economy. But Z., like so many of his colleagues around the country, long ago accepted such "inconveniences." First, he is his own boss; and second, his business profits, especially illegal profits, are much greater even than the salary of a Politburo member. The significant difference, however, is that the latter can get a thousand times greater value for his money in goods and services. And that is not even to take into account what the MP gets in the way of freebies—a private plane, for example.

The film was over. Someone turned on the light. Everybody looked at me. I took out my international driver's license, which I received ten years ago in Iraq. It looked very impressive—it was almost a little book, as the text was duplicated in about twenty languages. The first page with my photograph, and, most important, the tattered blue cover, were without any doubt in Arabic. In the entire city of Cheboksary I knew only one person who had studied Arabic in the university. I wished he were here.

"I am an Arab journalist. My name is Murad," I said, attempting a slight Arab accent, and trying to sound as free and easy as I could.

"Give me that," an older ruffian ordered roughly. His round cheeks made a strange contrast with the powerful chest of a heavyweight wrestler. After having checked my Iraqi license with a puzzled look of disapproval, he carefully looked me over. My clothes must have looked exotic to him: a German sweater, gray stone-washed jeans from Tunisia, a hundred-dollar pair of high-top Reeboks I had bought in the United States. Then he looked at my photograph and birthdate. "Hey, check this out!" he cried. "Born in 1948. An old fart! Look guys, he's as old as my old lady." They stared at me with unfriendliness in their eyes. There were about twelve of them; they all had beardless, boyish faces.

"The dude's all dressed up!" one of them yelled, evaluating my combination of casual wear with hostile approval. "Look at this motherfucker's shoes! They're worth two grand on the street," said his buddy in the "rooster."

I knew that many of the youth gangs in the Volga Basin cities cultivate a contempt for good clothes. Their basic reasoning is simple: if it is not available to them, it must be bad. But, the main reason is the aesthetic influence of the prison subculture. The tattoos, the slang, their contempt for women—all have been borrowed from the criminal world. Intellectual and spiritual things have no value for them. Their parents have been breaking their backs in sweatshops all their lives for

peanuts. Therefore, any intellectual profession, such as that of a computer programmer or a political scientist, or any artistic occupation, is
considered to be either fraudulent or pretentious. One more peculiarity of their character is their xenophobia. Their fatherland, as they
understand it, is not Russia, and not even Chuvashia, but rather their
district, their street, even their block. No one they could identify with
has ever traveled abroad. Their cheated parents have spent all their
dismal lives in Chuvashia, and they know that they themselves will not
be able to see anything of the world. In order to do that, as to do anything in our country, one needs not only money but also *blat*. Could
that not be the reason these youngsters so openly hate the unattain-
able West?

"Well, raghead, what do you need up here?"

"I would like to write about your people for *National Geographic*."

"Get outta here! You must be kidding!" The musclemen were
buzzing with excitement.

"Shut up, guys!" the older guy, the gang leader, shouted. His
brain seemed to be working hard at the basic choice: either to let his
thugs finish me off right away, or to postpone the fun until later on.
After all, they had the whole Sunday night at their disposal with no
particular entertainment but the disco at the local club.

"Ask the 'author,'" I said, demonstrating my knowledge of their
jargon. "Author" is short for "authority," or the adult leader, in their
lingo.

"Where did you learn Russian, you Arab shithead?" my interroga-
tor inquired, still holding my driver's license in his hand.

"I studied it in Tashkent, and my wife is Russian," I answered
without thinking, because both statements were true.

"Okay, let's go to the 'office.' We'll see," he finally said, putting
my license into the pocket of his oversized quilted jacket.

Everybody moved to the exit. I managed to catch the administrator's eye, but he turned away. He did not want to have anything to do
with it.

The "office" turned out to be a large, clean basement in a multistory residential tower, located several blocks from the video club.
The ineradicable smell of sweat, dirty clothes, and God knows what
else was overwhelming here. Somehow the smell reminded me of the
transient nature of human life. The "lads," as the members of youth

gangs call themselves, spent most of their time on the premises. They had turned the basement into a sport facility, with homemade equipment for bodybuilding, karate, and kung fu. They had subordinated themselves to the rough criminal hierarchy and professed a cult of brute power. Yesterday they were children; today they were mutants from a Saturday night horror movie.

Razors, brass knuckles, metal rods, clubs, knives, and homemade handguns—all these are issued to youth gang members on the order of the "author," who is usually a person with a criminal past and labor-camp experience. All gang members, including their girlfriends, ritually urinate on the helpless, bloody bodies of their victims. According to official statistical data, one-fourth of the teenagers in the cities of Kazan, Cheboksary, Naberezhnye Chelni, and other cities of the Volga Basin are members of youth gangs.

Of course, there are other young people who do not wear quilted jackets with bell-bottom pants and the heavy shoes called "shit-walkers," who do not "work with instruments," that is, subject a helpless victim to torture and violence. The "lads" contemptuously call them *chushpans*, the Russian equivalent for "geeks." The "geeks" must pay the "lads" a daily tribute, ranging from twenty kopecks to five rubles and up, depending on the wealth of the victim, a system which grimly resembles the progressive income tax imposed by the Soviet state on its citizens.

But the lads have their own code of honor. It is simple, including only two items: they are fearless and they have no interest in money. They are proud that they rob and cripple people for somebody else, the organized criminals. The money and the loot they collect goes to the "cashiers," who sort it all out and give it to the "authorities." It is all used to cover wages for the authors' operational expenses and what they call the "pot," for material assistance to their kin in prison, lawyers, bribes for prosecutors, and for fancy funerals for those who lost their lives while "on duty."

At the moment, the spheres of influence of the different groups have been established, and there are no longer mass battles for territory. Each gang takes care of collecting regular taxes from teenagers and small businessmen in their mandated region. However, either for the sake of simple terror or just to stay in shape, from time to time the lads decree a "killing month" or a "rape month" in their city, during which time it is unwise to go out in public.

From the conversation of the youth gang member who surrounded me, I gathered that it was now a "rest month," a cooling-off period. They were heading for a discotheque in the local club. "Hot babes" from the local vocational schools were expected to come. The only thing I could not understand was the reason for the lads' wild laughter; apparently, they were planning some sort of "check-up" at the dance hall entrance.

"We'll take you to the disco, okay?" the author told me. "You'll get your stuff to write about. Unless you're a snitch. If you are, we'll take care of you. Vityok and Lyokha, keep an eye on him."

The lads laughed heartily, first envisioning me dancing, then after I had been "taken care of." They thought it was all very funny; for by their standards, at forty-two I was an old man who had lived too long anyway.

"Hey, Murad, take off your sweater. I want to trade with you," said the one called Lyokha. "You can't have all this stuff for yourself. I'm gonna give you my jacket and my cap, almost new, okay?"

I tried on his stinking jacket. It was too large, even for me.

"And I want your sneakers and pants," Vityok happily demanded.

"Forget it!" I growled indistinctly. I stood paralyzed, anticipating a blow. I was suddenly glad that I did not have my cameras with me, and no more than 150 rubles in cash. Then the lads and I headed into the night to go partying.

5

The Equalizer, Chuvash-style

Judging by its shabby façade, the Palace of Culture was probably built in the thirties. If we could look at it from above, we might see that it is in the shape of a five-pointed star, or a tractor, or some other fanciful form. The Soviet constructivist architects were in the habit of designing their projects in this way during the decade prior to World War II. The heroes of the Soviet motion pictures at that time kept informing each other and their audience that they were building a bright future life for their children and grandchildren. Could it be that the chaos of the present day was what they had in mind?

I was sitting between Lyokha and Vityok in the club hall on three squeaking chairs that had been welded together and seemed to be as old as the building itself. After having served a long life in the auditorium, and polished by several generations of human behinds, they seemed inseparable, like aging Siamese twins (or, in this case, triplets). Now they were being stained, cut by knives, covered with four-letter words, and abused by cigarettes, but still they would not break, living out their last days by the violet wall next to the ladies' room.

"Say something in your language," ordered Lyokha, the boy in the rooster cap who was the first one to notice me in the video club. He was bored. His real name turned out to be Gataullah, which meant that he was pure Tartar, although he could not speak a word of the language.

"*Lyan yusibunna illa ma kataba llahu lena*," I said, hopefully. It was a verse from the Koran, which I instantly translated for him: "Nothing shall happen to us except what is predestined by Allah."

"He's full of shit," said Vityok, with a friendly blow on my shoulder. Every now and then he looked at my Reeboks. I promised to give them to him as a present after the party. "You shouldn't have come here, wimp. You should've stayed in Istanbul and smoked grass in a hookah. You Arabians wouldn't understand our life, anyway. Not a damn thing."

"It looks like he's getting it," Lyokha suggested with some doubt in his voice.

"You know, Vityok, Istanbul is in Turkey," I said with a sigh.

"No shit!" Vityok was surprised. Then he said to Lyokha, "See what he learned from those 'monkeys' in Tashkent. They just got down from their palm trees not long ago."

I looked at these degenerate descendants of a once-great people with sadness. Ten centuries ago, when Istanbul was called Con stantinople and was the capital of the Eastern Roman Empire, Vityok's forefather was attaching his shield to the gates of this eternal city as a sign of his victory. A few centuries later, the Byzantine Empire collapsed, and its double eagle flew over to the Russian state seal. In 1917 it was replaced with the hammer and sickle. It looked as though it was these people's turn now.

"Hey, check it out! Our lads are taking care of the chicks!" My guards brightened up, watching the commotion at the entrance.

"What are they doing?" I did not understand. "Are they searching the girls?"

"Sure they are," said Lyokha. He and Vityok giggled happily. "They're making sure that not a single one slips through."

"What do you mean?"

"What a dummy!" Lyokha became indignant at my stupidity. "The ones in pants are not allowed in at all. And those in dresses must come without their panties. Otherwise, the 'lads' take 'em off right at the entrance."

"Otherwise, they won't clear 'quality control,'" said Vityok, laughing. "Our guys check them all by hand, quick feel, one-two-three, ready, clear! You got it, Istanbul?"

I bit my lip, regretting that I did not have a machine gun like the heroes in the movie I had seen at the video club. But what good would that do? There are hundreds of thousands of such bastards all over our country.

"Don't feel bad, old man! The girls are used to it. Look, they are laughing themselves." The observant Lyokha turned to the doors again. "How're you doing, Galchonok," he said to a fifteen-year-old girl in heavy makeup, with bleached yellow hair in fine curls. Then he told me confidentially, "We've been screwing her in the basement since she was twelve. Now she won't do it with fewer than three of us."

The ball began. The loudspeakers roared, the lights started blinking, hundreds of pairs of feet in dirty shoes shuffled across the old parquet floor, blackened with age. A disk jockey in white trousers and a red, gold-embroidered shirt looked especially absurd against the dreary sea of quilted jackets. He talked nonsense into his microphone, and executed a few intricate steps with his short crooked legs. He also paid his dues to the lads, so that he would be allowed to come here with his equipment twice a week for dancing parties. The lads even protected him from any stray, out-of-town hoodlums.

"Let's go. Sitting around here won't turn our balls to gold!" My companions led me into the dance hall. After half an hour it was worse than a gas chamber. The dust kicked up by dancing feet mixed with the smell of the sweat and dirt of hundreds of young perspiring bodies. I was standing against the wall, watching these unfortunate boys and girls who defied all the official values of their state having fun in their natural environment. At times they were tramping in a circle, clapping their hands and cheering at those who could twist their bodies in the ugliest manner inside the circle. Then they would disperse into smaller groups, or by twos. In the darkest corners something obscene was happening; squeals, screams, and moans could be heard. Every now and then short fights would erupt; someone would fall down and, kicked by dancers, crawl away, leaving dark wet prints after him. During one of those fights something heavy and ribbed came rolling to my feet. I swiftly bent forward and picked it up. It was a lead knuckle-duster. "Give it to me!" Lyokha ordered, squeezing through the fighting crowd.

"Here you go!" I answered and hit him hard on the head. He silently slumped to the floor. My dishonest knockout was unnoticed in the violent atmosphere of the ballroom and the hypnotic twinkling of the lights. The older fellow, Igoryosha, was nowhere to be seen. He might have gone to his "author" to inquire about me.

"Ladies' dance," the disk jockey announced in a husky voice, and put on the Beatles' "Yesterday." I knew that the lads hated Western music, but every city has its own exceptions. The lights became colorful and subdued.

A small round-faced girl with traces of squeezed pimples on her chin approached me. "Would you like to dance with me?" she asked me in the voice of a child. "Why did you come here tonight? You might be killed."

"I don't know why," I answered breathlessly, moving slowly toward the exit at the same time.

"I saw you on TV!" she exclaimed, and said my name.

"You must be mistaken," I said. I was so surprised that I even forgot my Arab accent.

"Oh, no! It was in winter and you were doing that show from the youth library on Preobrazhenka in Moscow. My aunt lives not far from there, and I was there during my holidays. I have a book of your poems..."

"Then what are you doing in a place like this"? I asked her, trying to make it through the crowd to my freedom.

"Where are you going, Arab?" All of a sudden their chief was in my pathway, coming out of nowhere.

"He wants to have a good time with me," said the reckless fan of my poetry. I did not even know her name.

"Okay, let's go!" The young Hercules grinned. He grabbed her by her short hair and dragged her to the women's room. I burst in through the dancing crowd after the whining girl and her torturer, squeezing my newfound weapon in my pocket.

He kicked the door open so that it almost came off its hinges, and rushed into the room with his victim. Then he threw her toward the window.

"Get out of here, little fuckers!" he bellowed at the legitimate users of the women's room. "No, wait!" he ordered one of the frightened girls. "Go get me Vityok! Go fast!"

She disappeared, moving backwards.

"What do you want, Igoryosha?" the little girl murmured in a zombie-like voice, trembling with fear and sniffing with her smashed nose. "What do you want from me?"

She was thrown against the windowsill, and her entire face was covered with blood.

"Don't you know?" He leered at her and said, "Pull up your dress and bend over."

I made a step toward Igoryosha.

The girl obediently complied. My heart ached with pity when I looked at her bare skinny behind, with fine, downy hair standing up on her thighs.

"Go ahead, journalist, you're first!" Igoryosha invited me with his hand and grinned.

I hit him on the face as hard as I could, and he fell on his knees with a moan. His body pounded heavily against the wall. The middle finger on my right arm was burning with unbearable pain. I must have broken it with the brass knuckles. I hit him again, awkwardly, on the chin. He fell on his side and lay there, breathing hoarsely and heavily.

The girl came up to him, looking distrustfully at his smashed face, then stood over him with her legs apart and urinated all over him.

"You have amusing customs here," I said, trying to subdue my shaking body. I did not have time to spare. I locked the door, went through his pockets, and found my driver's license. Then I took off the hideous quilted jacket I was wearing, applied it to the window, and pushed out the entire rotten window frame. The girl hurriedly put her dress in order and washed her face.

"I'll go with you," she said resolutely.

"Only as far as the next intersection," I said even more resolutely and led her through the crushed window.

Our departure from Novocheboksarsk took place the next evening. It was a shock for Liberman, who had planned to spend at least a week with his family.

"What's the rush?" he said, understandably disappointed, but he would not violate our gentlemen's agreement. He was responsible for the car, and everything else, including the itinerary; the lengths of our stays were my responsibility. Of course, he could back out of our agreement. But I knew that he had already given the money I had paid him in advance to his wife, so he could not go back. Still, it would have been too cruel to pull poor Liberman away from his peaceful family without any warning or moral preparation. So the evening departure was a sort of compromise on my part between my desire to leave immediately, early in the morning, and Liberman's desire to stay there forever.

Shlupkin did not have a garage, and so our car was parked in the open, near the next building.

In order to protect our car, Shlupkin spent the night inside it under my blanket, surrounded by knives, hammers, and hatchets. A passenger car with a Moscow license plate would likely attract the attention of the local riffraff, especially if Igoryosha and the lads were smart enough to look for me not in the central hotels but in this god-forsaken town, a satellite of the Chuvash capital. In Moscow I also park my car under the windows. Every time I forget to take off my windshield wipers or the side mirror, somebody else does it for me.

Irritation over the loss turns into despair, as it is almost impossible to buy wipers in Moscow. But this is nothing compared with the feeling of despair a Soviet car owner feels when he finds that the wheels are all gone, the front and back windows have disappeared, the trunk has been opened, and his car stereo torn out, a process known as "undressing and unshoeing" a car. It happens every day, and the reason is as old as the Soviet system: shortages. Teenagers are usually responsible, but they are working for adults, not for themselves. After they become skilled hands at this, they move on to an even more profitable business: they steal cars, dismantle them, and sell spare parts. The price of the spare parts sold separately is much higher than the price of the entire car, even at black market prices. The truly daring thieves finally advance to the most sophisticated auto racket: armed with firearms, they go out in small groups onto the big intercity highways and steal automobiles by force from their owners, *tchainiks*, who sometimes get careless and forget about the dangers on the roads. They kill the owners and dismantle the cars to sell the parts. Newer cars are especially valued. There are many reports of such crimes in Soviet newspapers.

We were barreling down the road toward the town of Tsivilsk, about twenty miles south of Novocheboksarsk, or so we hoped.

"Hey!" I stuck my head out the window and yelled at some farm girls who were sitting with their backs to the traffic on the back of a truck. We were passing it on the right, driving almost on the roadside, for it was a one-lane road. "Is this the exit to Kuibyshev? The exit to Kui-by-shev?"

"Go there, if you want to!" The girls laughed cheerfully, shaking their toil-hardened fists at me. Their unexpected reaction was caused by the unintended pun arising from the close phonetic resemblance of the prepositional phrase "*na Kui-by-shev*" to the common Russian street expression equivalent to the American "Go fuck yourself!"

With the one second we had left to consider the matter, I decided to exit the Nationally Important Highway M-7 or M-8, perhaps forever.

A-151 was a dusty, bumpy road, which forced us to decrease our speed and enjoy the country landscape. Soon we came to a little village. "Look," I cried, "it's Ryndino village, and the geese are standing on one foot beside the road! Did you ever hear the story about Nasretdin, Tamerlane, and the geese?"

Liberman sighed. "Who's Nasretdin?" I had told him about Tamerlane during the first night's drive to Cheboksary.

"Nasretdin is a medieval Central Asian folk hero," I answered. "He always gets himself in awkward situations, but he always pulls through somehow. Everybody thinks he's a dummy, but he is a wise man."

"What about the geese?" Liberman wondered. "Is this a joke?"

"It is, but not exactly. Listen," I said, and jumped with the car over a pothole. "Nasretdin decided to express his loyalty to Timur the Great, who had just finished conquering his country. He asked his wife to fry a goose, and took it to the palace. It was quite a long way, and he became hungry. So he stopped and ate one of the goose legs. When he got to the palace, Timur accepted the humble present, but he laughed when he saw that there was only one leg. 'Why are you laughing?' asked Nasretdin, offended. 'All the geese in this area have only one leg. Look out the window if you don't believe me.' It was getting dark, and all the geese outside were sleeping standing on one leg. Timur ordered his prized harquebus to be brought and mounted it on a tripod near the window. The crowd of courtiers and guests stood still. Timur quietly loaded the weapon, took aim, and fired at the geese. The geese cackled and flapped their wings, scattering in different directions. 'Can you see now?' the satisfied commander said. 'They all have two legs.' Everybody smiled with relief. 'If they fired at you with such a terrible weapon, you would also have run away on your four!' the wise man quickly replied."

When I was a child I heard dozens of such stories about Nasretdin from my grandmother Hadia. At times it seemed she had known him personally. The events of the night before seemed to be a horrible dream, but the pulsating pain in my tightly bandaged finger was very real. I wished I could forget the terrible image of the girl at the windowsill, her dress awkwardly pulled up. What was going to happen when Igoryosha came to his senses and recalled what happened to him?

"I think we'll move to Novocheboksarsk, after all," said Liberman, again pondering his family. "No matter how you look at it, Sveta's parents' apartment is bigger, and you have fishing and mushrooms here."

"And what will happen to Motya and Ksyusha there?" I asked sadly.

The landscape gave way from a steppelike wilderness to birch and fir forests. We crossed the Chuvashia border at about 9:00 P.M. and drove for no more than ten minutes on the territory of the Drozzhanov region of the Tartar republic. This region is like an appendix sandwiched between Chuvashia and the Ulyanovsk regions of the Russian Federal Republic. It is shaped like the Italian peninsular boot, shrunken after long hours of rain. When complete darkness fell, the drizzling rain increased. By nine, the rain was coming down in torrents; the windows of heaven opened wide. Our good old Lada successfully cut the water with its blunt prow, but the windshield wipers could not keep up with the flows of water streaming down the windows. Liberman got drowsy from their cozy squeaking sounds. There were no cars in sight. The only real things were the drone of the engine and the noise of the night rain, surrounding our car with a solid wall of water.

The invisible forest stretched on for many miles, drowning in the millions of gallons of water falling from the skies. It seemed boundless, and I felt as though we were lost in timeless space, like disorganized astronauts aboard an archaic spaceship. In order to return safely to earth, I started converting the kilometers of our journey into miles.

We covered 405 miles from Moscow to Cheboksary in nine hours. Now we still had 140 miles of driving to Ulyanovsk, and about 200 miles from Ulyanovsk to Kuibyshev. If we had driven from Moscow straight to Kuibyshev by the Nationally Important Highway 5, the distance would have been only about 670 miles. Because we included Chuvashia on our itinerary, we had had to cover 745 miles, or about 75 more miles.

Just before Ulyanovsk, formerly Simbirsk, I almost lost my way because of rain and darkness. Then my headlights, which Liberman had transplanted from a tractor, picked out through the rain and fog a police motorcycle with a sidecar, right in the middle of the road. The cop was standing there in his raincoat, the hood over his head. I was relieved that I had not hit his motorcycle; then we would have had a very serious problem.

I woke Liberman, took a two-dollar New York umbrella and Liberman's and my documents from under the seat, and went out into the deluge to greet the authorities. There was also a police car with several cops sitting in it on the roadside.

"What does he want?" Liberman asked with irritation when I got back. He had to shield his eyes from the sudden flash of the police flashlight on his face.

"He wants to find out who you are," the cop said, opening the door and shoving his head inside the car. Under his wet hood he was wearing a police cap.

"They're looking for someone," I answered. "They want a yellow Moskvich."

"But we are driving a red Zhiguli," Liberman began, exasperated. The water from the cop's cap was dripping on him.

"We might have put new paint on it," I said in a loud whisper.

"Does everybody in Moscow joke like that?" the cop asked, looking at me unfavorably. "Try it again and we'll detain you until we find out who you are. You'd have a nice rest till morning in jail. Decent people wouldn't roam around the roads at night."

"We're not smart enough to stay at home," I said, lifting my hands helplessly. "Would you tell us what's the best way to road A-151?"

"So this is what Lenin's native land looks like," said Liberman, annoyed that the Ulyanovsk cops had interrupted his sleep.

All Soviet people learn in their childhood that Ulyanovsk is an old Volga city, formerly called Simbirsk, renamed after Lenin. Lenin was his secret party name, but his real name was Ulyanov. Therefore, while St. Petersburg was renamed Leningrad to honor Lenin's political achievements, Simbirsk became Ulyanovsk after his entire family.

"Vova," I asked Liberman, who was tossing about on his seat-turned-bed in discontent, "how do you like the idea of Novochebok-sarsk being renamed 'Libermanovsk'?"

"I didn't do anything wrong," said Liberman, taking offense. "I never killed or jailed anyone! I never even praised Soviet power."

He must have been referring to the city of Gorky, renamed in the thirties after the founder of the socialist realism genre of official Soviet literature and art. It is odd that the city of Gorky, like so many of the renamed cities, gave up its ancient name of Nizhny Novgorod not for the writer's real name but rather for his assumed name. The Russian writer Alexei Peshkov, who became famous at the turn of the century, gave himself a meaningful name: "Gorky" means bitter. His fate was tragic. Lenin, who had once had a friendly relationship with Peshkov, called him in one of his articles "the storm petrel of the revolution." This label would eventually become the writer's official title. Stalin (the jail nickname of Iosif Djugashvili) lured Gorky from his self-imposed European exile to Russia. The writer, popular in liberal European circles, became a sort of courtier to official Soviet literature. In exchange, Gorky, who was an old man then, had to glorify the slave labor of prisoners in the Soviet labor camps. He called the process "reeducation." The unfortunate "storm petrel" was never allowed outside the country anymore. When he became insistent, his grateful boss, it is said, sent him a box of poisoned chocolate.

"Vova, do you know how Gorky chose an apartment for himself in Moscow?"

"No, but I wouldn't be surprised if he got himself four or five rooms," Liberman was quick to answer.

"Go higher." I looked back at him. "Old killer Joe allowed Gorky to pick up any mansion in the center of Moscow for free."

Liberman got angry. "My grandfather was a composer, but he never got any mansions! Why Gorky? He must have called the Moscow city council and got whatever he wanted."

"No, it was much more ceremonial," I said. "He was driven in a convertible, complete with chauffeur and bodyguards, all over Moscow until he finally made his choice: the former palace of Savva Morozov, the famous millionaire and patron of arts before the revolution."

"Oh, my goodness!" Liberman whistled. "Where is that?"

"At the Nikitsky Gates," I said, "right across from the church where Pushkin was wed. At that time the Goslit, now called the Khudozhestvennaya Literatura Publishers, was located there. But it did not stop Gorky. Goslit had to move out, while the 'storm petrel of the revolution' moved in right away to enjoy the millionaire's palace."

"I've never heard anything about that," Liberman said. "At school we were told that Gorky was a very poor man. And the six of us are crowded into a small two-room apartment, even with my mother a Candidate in Science!" A Candidate in Science is the Soviet equivalent of a Ph.D.

"Which science?" I asked, because I happened to know his mother. Mira Mordukhovna was a very kind person, but like many Moscow women, she possessed the iron will of a life-hardened person.

"Economics. She could have become a Candidate much earlier but for the party bosses. They would die one after another, and her dissertation couldn't be defended."

I was surprised by the relationship between his mother's dissertation and the unfortunate deaths of the party's General Secretaries. What a mysterious connection!

But it turned out to be very simple. As Liberman explained, his mother had her dissertation ready as far back as 1980. According to unwritten law, any research work submitted for a doctoral degree must be dosed with quotations from Marx, Engels, and Lenin. But the main thing, she was told, was to make references to the speeches and reports of the General Secretary of the CPSU, who is the main successor and promoter of the above-mentioned classics. No candidate for a Soviet Doctor of Science degree could get around this rule, not even those who later dedicated their lives to the struggle against the stupid system that created such rules.

But Mira Mordukhovna was fighting not against the educational system but rather for decent living conditions for her family. There was a regulation that provides Candidates of Science with additional living space, although it was applied quite selectively. Still, it was a possibility, and Liberman's mother hoped that her degree would help her family to get a better apartment.

On the very day set for the defense of her dissertation, Brezhnev died. Not that it happened absolutely unexpectedly, but as Liberman put it, "the old bastard picked the wrong time." Then KGB chief Andropov assumed the vacancy, but he was mortally ill. While Mira Mordukhovna was feverishly rewriting her work, doing away with Brezhnev's quotations and making references to the new General Secretary, Andropov died. It saved the country from being turned into a vast hard-labor camp again, but what a price Mira Mordukhovna had to pay! Her dissertation was returned to her for corrections and clarifications. When the new General Secretary Chernenko was shown on television, the country started laughing cynically. The new General Secretary appeared to be trembling with senile infirmity and suffering from incontinence. Even the retirees and veterans of the GPW (Great Patriotic War), who most vehemently support the gerontocrats, knew that this one would not last long. But Mira Mordukhovna gritted her teeth and set to work again. Everything was ready; even the restaurant was reserved for the occasion, but then Chernenko, too, checked out.

"But Gorbachev, on the other hand..." I wondered, looking at Liberman.

"Forget about it!" Liberman shrugged his shoulders with disappointment. "She did defend her dissertation successfully, no doubt about it. Only by that time all privileges for Candidates were canceled. Nothing! Zilch! Stagnation, depression, that's all!"

We were so deep in conversation that I almost missed our exit. I planned to drive to Kuibyshev and farther down through the western and southern areas of Kazakhstan, past the dying Aral Sea, to Tashkent. In Tashkent I wanted to replace the car, as I did not want to attract too much attention with our Moscow license plate. It would be too noticeable in the Central Asian republics, torn by ethnic violence, and especially in the war-ravaged Caucasus.

"Caucasus?" screamed Liberman. "No way! I wouldn't go there even for a million bucks! There's a war going on there, don't you know that? You can take your desire for adventure and stick it. If those

Moslems catch you, you're dead meat. They would kill us instantly!"

"Where did you get these strange ideas?" I asked indignantly. I did not anticipate this mutiny on my ship. "We'll have local license plates. We're not blond, so we won't look alien. And my friends will accompany us, anyway."

"I don't want to hear about it!" Liberman was daring me fearlessly. "Of course I will go with you to Central Asia. I want to see Samarkand; I've never seen a live camel in my life. But no farther, no way! My folks were right about this trip. If it were not for the money, they would never let me go."

6

Pushkin in Basra

That night we rushed through the city of Togliatti, formerly Stavropol-on-Volga (not to be confused with the Stavropol in the south of Russia, the home and political cradle of President Gorbachev) but renamed in honor of the quiet leader of the Italian Communist Party, Palmiro Togliatti. In the sixties, the Italian automaker Fiat built a huge automobile assembly line in Stavropol-on-Volga, which even today is the primary producer of Soviet private automobiles.

The closer we approached the Volga, the more insistently did apprehensions about crossing it arise in my mind. Someone had told Liberman in Moscow that there was only a ferry at this point, but the map promised a bridge. We would only know the answer by seeing it with our own eyes. To my great joy, this time the map coincided with reality. Over the dark waters of the river hung a massive, brightly lit bridge, utterly devoid of people. Accelerating to seventy miles per hour over the course of several minutes, I flew across the Volga, humming "I Left My Heart in San Francisco." Funny, I recalled, last spring while crossing the Golden Gate Bridge with my American friends, I was singing "Volga, Volga, mother dear…"

About three-thirty in the morning we drove into the sleepy, deserted city of Samara, located where the little Samara River flows into Mother Volga. I previously referred to it as Kuibyshev, because for the last half century that is what it was called. It is now reverting to its prerevolutionary name. Listen to the melodious sound of the word: Sa-ma-ra...To the Russian ear it is associated with a warm and comfortable feeling. One of my earliest recollections is the sight of curtains fluttering in the breeze, and a radio playing a song popular at the end of the forties, "Oh, Samara, little town, I am troubled..." And now, forty years later, thanks to a strange combination of circumstances, I was entering for the first time this city from a half-forgotten song, heard in childhood.

Before the revolution it was a large mercantile city, and many buildings of that era have been preserved here till now. In the thirties Samara was renamed Kuibyshev in honor of one of Stalin's henchmen, who was responsible for creating the military-industrial complex, and who died under questionable circumstances. During World War II Kuibyshev was for some time the capital of the U.S.S.R. All the foreign embassies were transferred here temporarily. After the war, the city expanded to one million inhabitants and became one of the centers of the Soviet aviation and space industry. It remained a closed city for a long time, due to the spy mania of those years, and foreigners are still denied access to it. But times have changed, and judging from the fact that the city's old name is about to be returned, there is reason to hope that soon it will be open to foreign spies.

The moon emerged from behind the clouds and illuminated a man walking along the road. It was around 3:30 A.M. Where could he have been going so early? Approaching closer, I rolled down the window a little. Before me a heavyset, fair-haired, robust-looking fellow stood, rocking slightly, in pajama pants with sandals on his bare feet. He was rather tipsy and had no shirt on, in spite of a cold drizzling rain, or perhaps just because of it.

"Howdy, bro!" He answered my greeting in prison jargon. When I asked him where the nearest gas station was, he looked me in the eye for a long time, knitting his brow and scratching his immense head with a powerful hand, as if he were trying to decide whether or not to disclose the location of this secret place to a stranger.

"Gas station!" I repeated. "Where do they sell gas?"

"Oh, the gas station," he repeated happily, enjoying the word, and suddenly he seemed to have a breakthrough. He began to explain in a passionate but muddled way how to get there, but he quickly forgot what I had asked him, and he stopped. Evidently it was beyond him. At first it seemed to me that he was about to tell me the story of his life. Then I thought that perhaps he was talking about sudden reversals during the last soccer match of the local team, Wings of the Soviets, against the Armenian team Ararat. The clearest part of his speech was the powerful curses that supported his communication as concrete piers support a bridge.

Russian-Soviet profanity is a "thing unto itself," as the old German philosophers said, though it is true that they were talking about something completely different. What is especially surprising to researchers (and some users) is the prodigious number of denominative verbs formed from the words for genitals and the variety of their semantic possibilities. Individual virtuosos can convey practically any information purely through the use of profanity. Our Virgil, however, was either profoundly inarticulate or just dead drunk. In any case I did not hear any helpful information, only boring constructions like "Fuck this, dicking straight, afterwards cunt to the left." I glanced at the slumbering Liberman, turned off the engine, and got out of the car. Then, stating my name, I heard in response that my nocturnal companion was named Anatolii.

"Anatolii, won't you drink to our acquaintance?" I said. Soberly assessing the situation, I proposed the traditional Soviet opening line, and began to feel in my bag under the rear seat for a soldier's flask filled with liquor. Liberman and I do not drink, but we took a supply of vodka on the road. That which cannot be bought for money can sometimes be exchanged for booze.

"Uh...we don't have any..." He threw up his hands in distress.

"But we have some!" I declared triumphantly, holding up the flask. An enameled mug was at hand, and I generously splashed into it six ounces of Shlupkin's home brew.

"Top quality?" he asked, noisily sniffing with his cavernous nostrils.

"Absolutely!" I answered, although I did not have any idea what quality it possessed.

"Are there snacks?" he asked.

I unwrapped a sandwich of greasy sausages.

"Great, bourgeois!" It was not clear whether Anatolii meant that positively or negatively, but at one gulp he emptied the contents of the cup down his throat and quickly ate the sandwich. Then he found a crumpled unfiltered cigarette in his half-empty pack. While he smoked, I sat on the edge of the sidewalk. Momentarily losing me from view, Anatolii began to look in both directions. Peering into the car, he paused over the snoring Liberman, probably trying to recognize in him the missing me.

"Hey," I called, scared that he would tumble down onto Liberman, who could get a fright from a dream and think that bandits were attacking us. "'Did you lose someone?"

"Yes, my wife," he unexpectedly answered, looking around. Then, in several motions, panting, although not without a heavy grace, he sat down beside me.

"I sympathize," I muttered, thinking he meant that he was divorced. I kept tactfully silent, guessing that no line of questioning would work out.

"I lost her at cards!" he announced in a flat voice and put his shaggy head in his huge hands.

"And what did your opponent put up?" I asked, having lost my sense of tact from surprise. "His own wife, eh?"

"Money!" he answered in a businesslike way and glared at me.

"Where has he come from?" asked Liberman sleepily, breaking away with difficulty from his dreams of Novocheboksarsk, when I got back into the car.

"Probably from his beloved woman," I supposed, based on my own life experience, and started the engine.

"But perhaps he was repairing a car for a friend," disagreed Liberman, undoubtedly having in mind the facts of his own biography.

"Perhaps," I said obligingly, in order not to get involved in a useless argument. Liberman was again snoring, and I continued my surreal excursion through the city from an ancient song: "Oh, Samara, little town..."

Our Lada slowly rolled downhill through wet, deserted streets, dimly lit by luminous street lights, fluorescent cockle shells perched on swaying water plants. In their pale, deadly light the damp foliage of the trees looked black, and the drizzle seemed to flow up from below us. From the Moscow highway I entered Aurora Road, then on to Aerodrome Street, through Industry Street and Gagarin Street, and returned to Aurora Road, named after the cruiser that in 1917 fired a blank shot at the Winter Palace in St. Petersburg, thus launching the October Coup. It would indeed be strange if this pretty little street were called by the name Aurora in honor of the eternally youthful goddess of the dawn.

Fortunately, the system of ideological control did not know how to distort all the street names in our country. Even in the very center of Moscow, you need only take a few steps off the beaten track to find a pleasant jumble of roads whose names evoke genuine antiquity. Not far from my apartment in Moscow there is a street called Seaman's Silence. It has been called that nearly since the time of Peter the Great. It was named that in honor of a prison, an almshouse, or a cemetery. The patina of time poeticizes even the most prosaic words. Will our furthest posterity be charmed by names like Twenty-second Party Congress Street, Aircraft Motor Boulevard, or Cosmonauts' Prospect?

It would soon be dawn, and we needed to decide what to do next. Of course, we could rush through Kuibyshev without stopping, in order to get to Central Asia before a great conflagration separated it from the European part of the U.S.S.R.

However, in Samara lived two reliable contacts, Aleksandr Pokrass and Sergei Dobrynin. Pokrass was my recent partner in publishing. The previous winter he had tried to start publishing the Bible, and I led him to some solid financial circles in Moscow that agreed to support this project. He was the president of the local scientific production cooperative Sigma, which in addition to everything else was also involved in a computer business. Pokrass, by the way, had good connections with the municipal and regional authorities, so he could also help with a room at the hotel.

Sergei Dobrynin was quite another story. Twelve years ago we had known each other in the city of Basra, in southern Iraq. I went there as an Arabic interpreter on contract to the Iraqi National Oil Company, where he had been working for two years as an engineer. We worked together for about a year and became rather close friends.

In Basra at that time there were several thousand Soviet specialists, mainly oil-industry workers doing exploratory drilling and pipeline builders. Although the Soviet government confiscated a substantial part—usually four-fifths—of our pay, even before deducting taxes, the remainder was nevertheless immeasurably higher than what our countrymen received at home. Thus the Iraqis could not understand at all why their Soviet colleagues, in spite of the infernal heat, were economizing on each bottle of Pepsi for their children.

The Soviet personnel, knowing that for the same work the Italians or the Japanese were pocketing five times more than them, thought that it was the Iraqis who were fleecing them, not their own Communist Party of the Soviet Union. But people were largely satisfied even so; in Iraq in those times it was possible to buy not only decent food, clothing, and appliances, but also many other things that the inhabitants of the U.S.S.R. in general had never heard of, like VCRs—and all without ration cards or lines. However, it did not take much for them to feel as though they had been elevated to the elite circle of Soviet society. The bosses also supplemented their incomes by petty swindling: after the death of Brezhnev, some of the Soviet officials, including the representative of Tekhnopromeksport in Iraq and the president of this company, were shot for hard-currency embezzlement in large quantities.

Sometimes Sergei and I argued about Pushkin, who was not only a poet but also a prose writer, a historian, and sometimes a philosopher: in a word, a humane genius, who knew how to link the introverted culture of his native land with Europe in the era of the Enlightenment. Many of my foreign friends do not completely understand why we call this whole period of Russian history the Pushkin era. Nevertheless the fact remains: the names of the rulers and great generals of that time are well known today only to specialists and the intelligentsia, but everyone in the Soviet Union knows the name of Pushkin. After his death in a duel, he was transformed into a national superstar. Soviet children are very fond of Pushkin's charming fairy tales, but as early as the eighth grade, upon hearing his name they begin to experience an undercurrent of irritation that haunts them for the rest of their lives. It is not so much a matter of teachers teaching Pushkin wretchedly as it is the too grandiose treatment of his work and personal life. The party has never understood that in our country it is only the people whom the party praises whose reputations suffer.

This lingering resentment of Pushkin finds its reflection indirectly in the form of a rather strange habit of speech. When a mother, herself an embittered former student, scolds her child for a missed lesson, she will gruffly say, "And who do you think will do your mathematics, Pushkin?"

I do not remember whether it was Sergei or I who proposed a public discussion of our argument, but we agreed on the spot that our thoughts about the poet must be heard. Pushkin's birthday was nearing, which in our country is always marked with quite a bit of pomp, so Sergei approached the party bosses, with whom he had good contacts, who regarded the idea favorably. About 1,500 people gathered on a hot, humid night in the Soviet cultural center on the outskirts of Basra. A crowd of children romped on the playground, raising clouds of dust around centuries-old palm trees, decorated with multicolored lights. Enormous rats darted about. Sergei and I ascended to the stage of the summer movie theater, turned on the microphone, and performed an hour-and-a-half improvisational show.

Blond Sergei was dressed in light colors and spoke very positively about Pushkin, seriously expounding theses from Soviet school programs and raving about Pushkin's struggle against czarism and the reactionary nobility. I played the role of his antithesis, appearing as the brunette villain, dressed all in black, speaking in a frankly seditious way. For greater dramatic effect, we seated a beautiful young woman between us in a bright red blouse and long brown skirt, and we directed our speeches to her. Holding a small blue volume of Pushkin's collected works in her hands, she read his verses, some to the point, some not, as illustrations of our arguments. The spectacle horribly recalled the medieval arguments between scholastics of various factions of Christianity, and, as a result, choking from restrained laughter, we continued arguing until we had come to agree that the historical Pushkin had nothing in common with that collection of ideological clichés that had been drummed into us since childhood. For the Soviet intelligentsia that is an established fact, but most of our audience perceived our argument as one of monstrously daring frankness. At all times, citizens of a totalitarian society have perfect command of a servile, Aesopean language of hints and things left unsaid; therefore, everything that was said that evening about Pushkin could easily reflect our whole lives at that time. But it is one thing to have such conversations with friends over tea in the kitchen; it is another to speak of them publicly in the presence of the authorities. It was 1979, and it seemed to us at the time that we would never live to see freedom of speech.

As a result, all copies of Pushkin's works were taken out of the cultural center's library, and our Basra ideological overseers made notes on Sergei and me. However, everything was soon resolved, inasmuch as Sergei and his family soon thereafter left for home, and I was transferred to Baghdad.

Then Iraq started a war with Iran, and only smoking ruins remained of the city of Basra. Afterward, when I had to return there on business, I went back for a look at the old places. The communal villa that I had shared with several families of Soviet specialists, as well as all the homes surrounding it, were empty, ransacked by marauders. But still more horrible was the picture presented by the cultural center. It looked like the dusty, neglected scenery from some old-fashioned horror movie. The surreal effect was reinforced by the brandnew asphalt road that had been built right through the auditorium, leaving a piece of stage left intact. Whether it was someone's malicious whim or the result of a real engineering requirement I do not know to this day. But the dirty palm trees, strung with garlands of broken lights, and the childrens' playground with piles of roadmakers' dried shit in the sandboxes were still there. Also left intact, by some miracle, was the torn banner with the slogan "Long live the indestructible Soviet-Iraqi friendship!"

I had not seen Sergei since that time. In the middle eighties, when my books began to be published in Moscow, I received a note from him, and since that time we had called each other only rarely; somehow we were just too busy to get together.

Now it was four-thirty in the morning—not the most convenient time for a visit. I drove onto a dark, vacant lot between two houses, turned off the engine, and, following Liberman's example, reclined the seat back all the way down and fell asleep.

7

Good Samaritans

We were awakened at eight o'clock by a knock on the windshield. A furious woman shook her fist at us and went away, seething with indignation.

"Vova, look, we are at a crossroads!" I exclaimed in amazement, seeing that the rush of people hurrying to work went right around our car. The open space I had taken to be a vacant lot a few hours before had proved to be a pedestrian thoroughfare. I had parked the car at the intersection of these paths. The car's wheels had played havoc with the unpaved paths, turning the ground after a night of rain into a nearly impassable swamp.

"Shit!" Liberman shook his head disapprovingly. Usually rosy-cheeked, his face was yellow and flabby.

"Relax, everything will be fine," I promised, and turned the key in the starter. The car skidded from its spot.

"Stop!" Liberman shouted. "The rear wheel is loose!"

As we soon discovered, it was not loose; it had been slashed. We had two spares in the trunk, and Liberman, cursing, quickly changed the tire.

Partisans Street, where Dobrynin lived, turned out to be right next to where we were. He was not home, but his oldest daughter let us in.

"Liubava!" I was astonished, seeing what a beauty the little girl who used to hang onto me in Basra had become.

"Uncle Marat!" she squealed joyously. "Mama, Anya, look who's here!"

"Well, you have come to the right place," said Sergei's wife, Alla, standing on tiptoe and holding me in a warm embrace. "Couldn't you have told us you were coming?" Behind her towered her younger daughter Anya, red-haired and freckled like an Irish girl.

"I am not alone," I said, smiling euphorically at them. "I have brought a friend."

Liberman had been skeptical that anyone could have friends whom he could burst in upon without warning after a separation of eleven years at eight o'clock in the morning, and still expect to receive a warm welcome.

"Glad to meet you!" all three said to him in unison, and they invited us in. I proudly looked back at Liberman and made an inviting gesture with my hand.

After a festive, noisy breakfast, I called Sergei at work. During the time since I had seen him, he had succeeded in a scientific and administrative career and had become the assistant director of research at the All-Union Scientific Research Institute of Development and Utilization of Oil Industry Piping.

"Welcome!" he said to me on the telephone as if we had last seen each other only a short while ago. "This evening I'll make pilaf," he promised. "Do you remember teaching me how in Basra? Now it's our family holiday meal."

The family supper at Dobrynin's somehow reminded me of the festive dinner at the Shlupkins'. Perhaps it was simply the aura of a happy family, a subtle reminder that true happiness is something that flourishes when people do not even know that they are happy. To paraphrase the famous beginning of Tolstoy's novel, guests are welcomed in the same way by all happy families.

Sergei's pilaf had acquired an unlikely Kuibyshevian flavor, only faintly recalling the original recipe, but I recognized it nonetheless. It was as if I had left the upbringing of a curly-haired lad to Sergei, and I saw him again now, grown up to be a bald old man: he was altogether changed, yet surely it was he.

Genghis Khan's cooks invented pilaf. They cooked it at night, so that at dawn they could feed the soldiers before battle. There are more and more pilaf lovers throughout the Soviet Union, and in spite of problems in getting fresh produce, pilaf remains one of the main holiday dishes in many Moslem republics. There are dozens of variations, but they are all related to two main types: Central Asian and Transcaucasian.

In the Transcaucasus, women cook pilaf, and the main ingredients of the dish are prepared separately and combined on the plate. In Central Asia, men prepare pilaf, and while it has many variations, the ingredients are always combined in the caldron, where they are transformed into a completely new entity. Needless to say, I belong to the Central Asian school of pilaf-masters, more particularly to a sect of my own invention, the *choikhanali oshpozlar,* which may be translated as "cooking pilaf for a group of close friends in a winter teahouse on the bank of a frozen irrigation ditch." Even this translation does not convey the essential nuance, which is only comprehended by those who are fully versed in the cultural background. One must try to imagine the gentle Central Asian winter, and the weeping willow bending over the irrigation ditch, as its branches freeze into delicate ice formations, calling to the wind. While you are making the pilaf, you glance at these weeping willows once in a while, and the humble landscape mysteriously influences the final result of your labors, bringing the taste of this dish to absolute perfection.

Those are the basic features of this special pilaf. Not counting the spices, there are five necessary ingredients: vegetable oil or sheep tail fat, white or purple onions, mutton, yellow carrot, round white or pink rice, and spring water. They must go in precisely that order into the cauldron, which should be swinging in the open air over a wood fire. Pilaf is an artistic production, and therefore it can turn out or not turn out. Out of ten pilafs I have attempted, nine have turned out. Professional masters succeed ninety-nine times out of a hundred. The most important condition of success is that the cook must love the people for whom he labors.

Sergei Dobrynin loved us, and therefore, even at an ordinary gas range, his pilaf was a culinary miracle. In honor of our arrival, Liubava canceled a date with her boyfriend, Anya promised to return early from someone's birthday, and Alla prepared half a dozen salads, baked pies, and roasted chickens. Liberman, astonished by their hospitality, hugged all the Dobrynins in turn for the fifth time, while offering to fix their car for free. He was used to the Moscow custom that all human relationships must be based upon an exchange of services, and he did not want to be left owing. But the Dobrynins only laughed lightheartedly in response, because they do not own a car.

The next morning, while Alla was at work and her daughters at the institute, I slept for a while on the enormous folding sofa, the fulfillment of my recent dream about a broad bed with bedsheets dazzling with cleanliness. In the afternoon Liubava arranged an excursion for Liberman and me along the Volga River. The old city center seemed to me like a decrepit silent movie star who has miraculously survived till now, maintaining traces of her former beauty. But architectural antiquity is more attractive than that of people. The shoreline of the Volga, reconstructed in the years after World War II, looked imperial and immense, but neglected. The cafés and newsstands, despite the fact that it was daytime, had obviously been closed for a long time. Liubava told us that even several years ago flower beds were filled with flowers, and that by the beginning of the summer everything here was alive with fragrance.

The weather on this day was windy, and the species of seagull known as Viktor Ivanov circled over us with heartrending cries. The water in the river was rough, and the city beach hopelessly flooded. I took a photograph of the gentle Liubava and dashing Liberman as a keepsake. More than anything I was surprised by the dormitory of the medical institute, where Liubava was studying. In czarist times this building was the municipal prison. Now future doctors live in what used to be the prisoners' cells. The Lenin museum, like all Lenin museums in large cities, was very impressively located. Liubava said that recently the whole city had been shocked when someone wrote in the museum's visitor's book "Lenin, Hitler and Mussolini were triplets!"

"But what of it?" Liberman asked, although for him, as for every normal Soviet person, such a remark just a few years ago would have sounded like a slanderous blasphemy. And today as well. When people have their god taken away, and they are trained to worship idols, they give them up even more unwillingly than the true god.

Liberman had been in a vicious mood ever since this morning, when he had managed to start a political argument at the service station where he had gone to buy gas. One of the other customers turned out to be the secretary of the party organization at the local valve factory.

"Imagine!" raged Liberman. "He said that it is impossible to eliminate the party committee at the factories because it would introduce a destabilizing element. They say that the function of the CPSU is the social protection of society! Imagine, in the legislative system they combine the post of first secretaries of all levels with the presidents of the Soviets of all levels, and now all by themselves they will protect us. Now, where on earth is there any justice, I ask you?"

Liubava turned a frightened look from Liberman, who was almost crying, to my sour face, not comprehending how he could consume his health over such trifles. We strolled past a newsstand where records were sold.

"Oh, look!" I was surprised to see a new album by the Soviet pop star Mikhail Muromov. Among his hits was a song that was set to one of my poems. The tune was hugely popular. It had first seen life as a video on television, then it had been performed a thousand times in concerts, and now it was out in record form. I had never once been paid for my contribution, which did not surprise me in the least. I bought a copy and gave it to Liubava.

In the evening, after dinner, we put a weary Liberman to bed on the sofa, and, following an old Soviet custom, we relaxed by drinking tea in the kitchen. Soon Dobrynin and I were at it again, deep in conversation, trying to unravel the mystery of the Russian soul.

"I am a technocrat," he proclaimed, "and therefore I think that it is stupid to take offense at things that are eight hundred years old. Yet, even so...I am sure it was your two-hundred-year Tartar yoke that produced in the Russian people some kind of ingrained gift for submission to a higher administrative power."

"What do you mean?" I was astonished. "What is this, as you say, notorious Tartar-Mongol yoke? Up until the conquest the Russian princes gathered tributes and taxes and kept it all, and then afterwards they had to pay tribute themselves to the Golden Horde. But there had been no occupying force in the territory of the Russian princes, no organs of ideological oversight. Just once a year the princes sent cartloads of goods to the Horde—they paid the tribute, basically, in kind. And when was that? How long was that before the discovery of America?"

"About five hundred years," Sergei said, not very confidently. "But we were talking about the national character, not the fall of the Russian empire," he said, graduating from tea to vodka.

"But Russians have reason to be proud of the military might of a great power!" I remarked with incomprehensible pride. "For the past two centuries all attempts to use force against the Russian empire from the outside have ended in failure. Well, that is if you don't count the Russo-Japanese War at the beginning of this century, or the Crimean War in the nineteenth century."

"I'm not talking about external enemies of the Russian empire or about its military might. Who needs this might if the people have nothing?" answered Sergei. "The main enemy of the Russian people is themselves. You have noticed how devoted the majority of Russians are to their state? However stupid or cruel a decision of our leaders, they only had to lift a finger, and every time the Russian people sub-missively gave in to them."

"What's so surprising about that?" I said, shrugging. "The found-ing fathers of the U.S.S.R. did not do badly with the human material they inherited from czarism. The best people were either killed in the civil war or escaped by emigration. Then followed decades of terror and prison camps. How could that not infuse the people with fear and submissiveness?"

"But how could that alone succeed in developing in our people such a high level of resignation in their relations with the state, if the people themselves were not already predisposed to it?" Sergei lightly tapped the table with his fist. "No, say whatever you like, but there is some kind of feminine principle entrenched in the Russian people; they are accustomed to submit to the administrative phallic force."

"Just wash the dishes, Sergei," said Alla, sweetly interrupting him. Sergei started washing the dishes, none too happily, and Alla and I continued a leisurely conversation about her daughters growing up so quickly, and about how it has become more and more difficult to buy clothes and shoes for them, and about how they would soon marry and turn their young parents into grandma and grandpa.

At a moment's lull, I again pressed Sergei: "Perhaps the real issue is the huge expanses of Russia." He stood in his apron in front of the sink carefully washing the dirty plates with a soft sponge. "In order to create this enormous state, the main thing is to hold it together; the Russian people had to give up all power to that state, and all of their history. Isn't this why the Russians are not a joyful people? Wasn't it Berdyaev who said that the Russian soul is injured by the wide-open spaces?"

Sergei replied, "In my opinion, the only consequence of the huge expanses of Russia is the monstrous centralization of state power. This damn power from the beginning repressed interests, personality, and society. For us everything, including people's lives, is subject to the interest of the state. Yet the immensity is not external but internal; it is not material, but a spiritual factor of the Russian soul."

Alla made another pot of tea with some Indian leaves she had saved for a festive occasion. The girls, bored, had gone to their bedroom to sleep, while Sergei and I continued to swim across the ocean of a typically Russian argument about the power of geographical spaces over the mysterious Slavic soul.

"Where do you think our or the Russians' deficiency of initiative comes from, indifference or laziness?" Sergei sadly asked me, returning to the table. Concealing his keen, melancholy eyes behind the smoke of his cigarette, he answered his own question: "National character can be developed within and without. That is, intensively and extensively. The gigantic expanses of Russia did not require intensive development of the Russian national character. The German soul, after centuries of being crowded, could not exist in the Slavic boundlessness. For the German, everything is the opposite; development is directed inward. His life is self-discipline and responsibility. He has everything placed on little shelves; there are definite precise boundaries for everything. His soul is closely packed and everything is determined for his whole life to come. But the Russian was never organized that way. The organization was always imposed from outside."

"From the Western point of view, it is dreadful," I said, "that Soviets do not know how to arrange their lives, do not know the arrangements or places for anything, that they do not try to do the obvious in order to save themselves and their country."

"Let the Western person save his country, and Russia herself will save the Russian!"

"Yes, yes, tell me more. What is Russia? Is it a spiritual continent that will save the world?" I sighed, knowing there was no answer.

"Read something from your verses," Alla asked. Short, warm, and very lively, she had almost not changed at all during the past eleven years.

I looked around at my friends. What happiness that, in our country, which was beginning to look like Atlantis sinking into the profound depths, such islands of goodness, mutual respect, and love have nevertheless survived. Then I remembered that Chuvash girl with the blood-covered face, against the windowsill in the ladies' room.

8

The Golden Teeth of
Marilyn Monroe

A few hours after we left Samara, we rattled across the bridge over the Talovaya River. Thus, without much ado, we crossed the border between the Orenburg Province of the Russian Republic and the Ural Province of Kazakhstan. The distance from Kuibyshev to Uralsk, the center of the province, is only 160 miles, but beyond us for many thousands of miles stretches Kazakhstan, the first ethnic republic we had come to that is not part of Russia itself.

"Farewell, unwashed Russia, country of slaves, country of lords..." I quoted the classical lines of Lermontov, another Russian literary genius of the last century, first exiled to the Caucasus and then, like Pushkin, killed in a duel. In Russia geniuses were always first banished and then killed. Under Soviet rule this custom has spread to the other republics.

"Kazakhstan is the only republic of the union where the indigenous population is outnumbered by the other ethnic groups."

"How is that possible?" asked Liberman. "Where did they go?"

"They didn't go anywhere," I said. "Look out the window. What do you see?"

"I see nothing!" he responded. "A black Volga car is behind us.

Otherwise, there is absolutely nothing. From horizon to horizon, emptiness."

"All right, then," I said. "Let's play a game: 'What Do You Know About the Soviet Union?' To begin, tell me: Which is the biggest republic after Russia?"

"The Ukraine?" Liberman's forehead wrinkled with effort.

"That's right, in terms of population. About 150 million people live in Russia, and more than fifty million in the Ukraine. Uzbekistan is in third place, with about twenty million people living there now. But in terms of territory, Kazakhstan is the second largest republic, after Russia. Its territory is several times larger than the territory of the largest European country, while its population is only about seventeen million. A little more than six million of them are Kazakhs."

"And how many Russians?" Liberman asked, calculating something.

"A little less than seven million."

"What about the other four million?"

"Oh, as everywhere, it is hard to say who doesn't live here. Ukrainians are in third place, almost one million. They live mainly in the north and northeast parts of Kazakhstan. There are also more than three hundred thousand Tartars."

"There seems to be no place where you Tartars don't live," Liberman remarked.

"Yes, indeed," I agreed. "Tartars feel themselves at home everywhere. Incidentally, I think there are about three million Tartars in the Tartar Autonomous Republic. The other three million are dispersed throughout the Soviet Union."

"Why is it that there are so few of you?" Liberman intrigued.

"Well, among the 130 ethnic groups of the as-yet intact Soviet Union, the Tartars hold fifth or sixth place in terms of population," I replied. "But even more Tartars have been Russified. It was considered to be stylish by Russian gentry to able to count some Tartar princes, murzas, or beks among one's ancestors. That somehow confirmed the antiquity of your pedigree, for in the period of the Tartar yoke, Russian princes tried to strengthen and improve their position with the help of Mohammedan in-laws. But the ethnogenesis of the ordinary Russian people has been even more affected by Russians intermarrying with Tartars. Don't you know that not only the Chuvash people but Tartars as well were baptized by force, and thus lost their ethnic identity?"

"That was under Ivan the Terrible, wasn't it?" Liberman asked, having heard my conversations with Shlupkin.

"And under Peter the Great, too, and later. And to differentiate the converts, the Tartars, when baptized, were given names of animals for their last names. That is why there are so many Medvedevs (Bears), Konevs (Horses), Gusevs (Geese), Vorobievs (Sparrows), and Zhukovs (Beetles) among contemporary Russians."

"And what about Jews?" Liberman inquired pensively.

"Why Jews?" I asked, bewildered.

"For instance, Katz? You know that means cat!" Liberman cried triumphantly. "Do you think that that is a Tartar name, too? And Fischer, the former world chess champion? 'Fish' in Yiddish means fish!"

"Okay, but what about Karpov (Carp)?" I said, choking with laughter and almost driving into a telegraph pole.

Ten minutes later we went on with our conversation about the different peoples of Kazakhstan.

"There are still many Germans here," I said, feeding Liberman the next bit of information. "But because they have finally been allowed to emigrate to Germany, they are leaving the country en masse. On the whole, though, the assemblage of nationals here is rather exotic: for instance, there are some Uighurs, emigrants from Sinkiang..."

"What is this Sinkiang?" Liberman interrupted me nervously. "Isn't it Chinese or something?"

"It's the northern province of China," I confirmed. "So, what was it we were talking about? Okay, there are also Chechens from the Caucasus. Poles have been stuck there since the same time, World War II. Even Koreans managed to end up in this place. Kazakhstan was always considered to be a place of exile. But while the czarist government banished individuals, the 'world's first state of workers and peasants' began exiling whole peoples."

"But where did all these Germans come from?" Liberman was completely lost.

"The Germans were forced to resettle from the Volga, where they had lived since the eighteenth century. Until World War II they had their own autonomous republic."

"That is strange—I never heard about it," said Liberman.

"The Germans who had to resettle here came from the Volga, almost next door, but the Koreans were deported from 6,000 miles away!"

"Hush!" Liberman's face suddenly grew concerned. "Do you hear a strange sound in the right rear wheel? Move to the right side of the road and pull over."

I obeyed his order, and we both got out of the car at the same time.

"That's that!" Liberman banged his forehead with grief and anger, as he opened up the trunk.

"What happened?" I asked, frightened.

"What? Can't you see for yourself? An axle box is leaking!" Liberman snapped at me in distress as he pulled some greasy overalls over his clothes.

The black Volga sped by with a whistle and caught us for a moment in a dense wave of air. A sparkle of sunlight shot at us from the chrome of its telephone antenna.

"They would never stop to ask if, perhaps, someone needed help!" Liberman nodded in anger toward the speeding car. Oh, damned partycrats!"

"But maybe they are from the KGB," I said jokingly. "Chasing spies!"

Having jacked up the car right on the dusty side of the road, Liberman completely dismantled the right rear half axle, replaced the axle box, and adroitly brought everything back to normal. All this took him approximately fifty minutes. While doing this he kept sighing and mumbling awful curses, but at last he came up with an undeniably valuable observation. He said:

"One hundred percent of the rubber products made in the U.S.S.R. fail to conform to standard."

This phrase was coined with such precision that I duly inscribed it in my notebook.

Within half an hour we were driving into the town of Uralsk, which by some fantastic luck has kept its old name. It is true that the River Ural where it is situated was formerly called Yaik. But it was renamed not by Stalin or Brezhnev but by the Empress Catherine II (who was German by birth). This took place after the suppression of a bloody rebellion of the Yaik cossacks in the second half of the eighteenth century. In Soviet schools this event is interpreted as a harbinger of the October overturn of 1917. But for some reason the students are not informed that the rebels were routed by the famous Russian commander Alexander Suvorov, who voiced one of our most oft-quoted and idiotic phrases: "A bullet is a fool but a bayonet is a good fellow!"

In honor of this bloodthirsty old man, the high point of whose career was to lead his troops in a successful crossing of the Alps, a multilevel Order of Suvorov was established during World War II. But why did Russian troops have to storm the Alps, which are thousands of miles away from Russia? Even the most bespectacled nerd in the U.S.S.R. cannot explain that. Since then, the river that springs from the mountains of the Ural range is called the Ural, while the formerly rebellious Yaik cossacks are now called Ural cossacks.

The story of the Yaik rebellion was beautifully explored by Pushkin, who wrote two works about it from directly opposite viewpoints. One of them is a charming tale, a genuine masterpiece of Russian literature, *The Captain's Daughter.* Emelian Pugachev is presented there almost as a Santa Claus who settles the fate of young lovers. The second version of the same horrible event is presented in Pushkin's historical essay *The History of the Pugachev Uprising,* in which Pugachev, the leader of the rebels, stands out in his truly horrifying incarnation. Which story do you think was written first?

After Samara, Uralsk was rather upsetting to me. Several dozen large apartment buildings made of reinforced concrete stood in the center, and the rest of the town was a warren of dusty streets with cheerless one-story private houses. That exhausts your sight-seeing in the town, unless you include the plumes of smoke pouring from numerous industrial enterprises. Residence permits and the force of habit restrain the inhabitants of such towns from migrating, while a lack of experience with other places on the globe makes even thinking about moving improbable.

At the entrance to the town we were stopped as usual by a traffic cop. This time it was a Kazakh. The farther south we went, the more exotic our license plates looked, so we had to get used to the inevitable checking of our documents by every passing patrol. The most difficult was answering the question of the purpose of our journey. To introduce oneself as a writer in such a situation would be dangerous and preposterous. Besides which, Soviet writers and journalists always act with the permission of the authorities. They have special credentials confirming that they are sent by a certain organ of the mass media. All I could do was mumble something about driving this car to my relatives in Tashkent. That sounded unusual, since in the Soviet Union old cars are more often driven from the southern republics to Moscow, to be sold on the black market at exorbitant prices. But this traffic cop turned out to be young and even benevolent, although he scared us by warning against picking up hitchhikers and making unplanned stops on the road. We promised to be on the alert, and then asked him to explain where spare parts were sold in the town.

He laughed. "This isn't Moscow, you know." We laughed, too, as his ideas about Moscow were about as realistic as Liberman's ideas about New York. But he did tell us where we could find an auto-parts shop in this town of half a million. After that we parted in peace.

We went directly to the automobile dealership, where no car had ever been sold, but where at least theoretically some spare parts could be found. I let Liberman go inside and I stayed to watch the car. At the entrance, right on the steps, a couple of swindlers were cheating people at cards. I turned on my radio, which picked up a German language broadcast from Alma-Ata.

"Hey, guy, sell me your radio!" said a man with a beard, from somewhere behind my back. "Or would you like to play a game of cards?"

"This is a family relic," I said proudly. "Can't you tell? It's an antique from the end of the nineteenth century. I can't sell it or lose it in a game of cards. I might consider trading it for a collection of the works of the poet Marat Akchurin."

"Never heard of him!" The goateed man looked at me wildly and plunged back into the noisy crowd.

Liberman came out in a minute.

"No good," he said ruefully. "Let's get out of here."

"The main thing is to hold on until we reach Tashkent," I said determinedly.

"Well, I don't know..." Liberman was shaking his head, making me shiver with foreboding, although the day was as sunny and warm as summer.

After driving for several hours along an empty highway, a lonely string across the steppes, we stopped near the turnoff to the *kolkhoz* Lenin's Way. We decided to change places, as I was beginning to nod off at the wheel. Before going any farther, I persuaded Liberman to take a bite of the leftovers from our Moscow, Novocheboksarsk, and Kuibyshev meals. On the menu there was tea from the thermos, some gray bread, potatoes boiled in their jackets, hard-boiled eggs, and a chunk of sausage that Dobrynin had given us as a farewell present. While we were chewing our lunch a truck, coming from the direction of the *kolkhoz*, pulled over near our car. It braked sharply, spraying us with dust. Two Kazakh women climbed out of the body of the truck, dressed in shapeless men's jackets over their drab frocks, heavy work boots, and kerchiefs striped with glittering metallic threads over their heads. The truck drove back onto the highway and sped away toward Uralsk.

"Let's give those women a lift," I suggested to Liberman.

"Sure, let's give them a lift, if it's on our way," Liberman agreed, although before that he had flatly refused to take hitchhikers, scared after our conversations with traffic cops about bandits and killers.

Liberman pulled the car up and stopped in front of the women, who were squatting in a pose of patient waiting.

"Where are you headed?" I asked in Kazakh, opening the door of the car. To my surprise, they did not move, pretending not to see us. "Hey, don't you hear me?" I addressed them again, but their faces kept the same completely blank expression.

"Such fools!" Liberman said angrily. "Are they afraid of us, or what?"

"Of course they are afraid," I answered, feeling pity. "It would seem they have talked to the same traffic cops. Is it true that the roads are so dangerous? All right, let's go! They have enough trouble without us. And you know, Vova, those were their best outfits they were wearing. Maybe they're going to the district center, or even to the center of the province, to Aktyubinsk."

"But why are they so afraid?" Liberman went on, bristling. "Do they really think that we would…"

"Make attempts at their virginity?" I prompted with a ferocious air.

"But they are so ugly!" Liberman protested naïvely.

"Everything is relative, Vova," I said. "Of course, we will hardly see them on the cover of *Playboy*. But that doesn't say much. To you or to the editor of *Playboy* they may not look attractive, but for all that they may be the top beauties and the most fashionable women in their village. American women prefer to have white teeth, but in the Soviet Union among the indigenous populations of Central Asia and the Caucasus gold crowns are in vogue. In Africa there are tribes where a woman is considered to be perfect only if her front teeth have been sawed down into triangles and painted black."

"That sounds awful."

"When I served in Egypt in the early seventies, I witnessed a funny scene once," I told him. "With a driver named Abdel Fattah who was from Upper Egypt—that is, as we would say, from the depths of the country—we pulled over to a building where some Soviet specialists lived with their families. Just at that moment a beautiful young blonde came out of the entrance. I looked at Abdel Fattah to see his reaction. To my surprise, he covered his eyes with his hand and turned away."

"Perhaps because she was without a veil?" said Liberman, intrigued by my story.

"Oh, no. They haven't worn veils in Cairo for a long time," I responded, recalling with a smile Heliopolis and the good-natured, mocking Egyptian women. "It's just that in his village women with 'white' hair were considered to be witches. Can you imagine Marilyn Monroe's or Madonna's surprise if she found out that her hair can terrify a whole Egyptian village!"

"But that is savagery!" Liberman laughed. "And who is this Maliryn Munro?"

"It's not Maliryn, Vova, it's Marilyn," I corrected him. "But why do you think that other viewpoint is savage? Americans would probably think that you are a savage because you have no idea who Marilyn Monroe was. And an intellectual friend of mine, a woman from Berlin, believes that it is savagery that all America knows Marilyn Monroe."

Seventy miles before Aktyubinsk, Liberman's fears came true: the right rear semi axle started leaking. His grief was boundless.

"Vova," I said, unable to share his sense of the immensity of our misfortune. "Why are you so grief-stricken? Do you really think that because of this broken half axle we have to commit hari-kari?"

"You just don't understand a thing about cars," Liberman whined. "Four things are impossible to replace on the road: engines, the gear box, reducing gears, and semi axles!"

"Keep calm!" I yelled at poor Liberman, who was on the verge of hysteria. "Aktyubinsk is the center of a province. They must have a Zhiguli shop. It can't be impossible to find this stupid piece of metal without which you'll end up with a duodenal ulcer, and I with a heart attack."

"We'll get nothing there," Liberman said, trying to regain his composure. What he meant was that we would not be able to buy a semi axle at a price he would accept.

Amazingly, we dragged into Aktyubinsk while it was still daytime. We had driven three hundred miles from Samara in eleven hours despite all our stops. At the entrance to the town, we were stopped by a traffic patrol. Judging by the remarks of other drivers, the cops were looking for some bandits who had been marauding on the roads of northwest Kazakhstan. When they found out that we were driving in the direction of Tashkent, the policemen exchanged glances and said that the gravel road beyond the Irgiz River up to the town of Aralsk was completely impassable.

"But isn't M-32 a Nationally Important Highway?" I asked, recalling what Liberman had told me. "That means there must be asphalt."

"That's right, there *must* be, but there *isn't!*" The cop shrugged his shoulders. "It's being repaired. Perhaps, in about five years they will have it fixed. Better drive through Chelyabinsk or Kustanai if you have a bee in your bonnet to go somewhere."

"Don't listen to him, Vova," I whispered to Liberman, who was taken aback by this news. "We'd better go and find some place to spend the night. Or still better, let's go straight to the car place. We'll make an appointment for tomorrow, and then try our luck with hotels."

Fifteen minutes later, Liberman had found two Kazakh mechanics. They gave me an unfriendly nod and leaned over the trunk that

Liberman had flung open before their alert gazes. The sight of our huge backup gas tank melted their professional hearts, and after a fastidious inspection of the spare parts that Liberman offered to trade, they struck a deal. Liberman swapped two brand new ball bearings bought from Moscow dealers at my expense during the preparation for our departure, plus twenty-five rubles and a bottle of vodka. We received in exchange an old semi axle acquired God knows where, how, and by whom. But we had no choice. This apparently criminal semi axle was stashed at one of the mechanics' houses, so we had to go there to get it.

"If I'm not back in half an hour, raise the alarm!" the mechanic told his friend in Kazakh while taking his place in the backseat next to our bags and bundles. The friend curtly nodded. I judged from his moving lips that he was trying to memorize the number on our license plate.

"And will we be back in half an hour?" I asked in Russian when we drove away.

"Of course, we'll be back! I live close, on Lenin Prospect," the fitter replied cheerfully, then cut himself short. He realized that I had understood what he said to his colleague. "You know Kazakh, don't you?" He smiled, tensely, looking at my face in the mirror.

"Just a little," I said and smiled back at him.

In the Soviet Union, with its 130 ethnic groups, all with unequal rights, the first question one asks a person after his or her name is ethnic origin. Nor is this always an idle question. In certain situations your fate depends on your answer. Your ethnic origin is asked in all kinds of questionnaires that have to be filled out from the day of birth till the hour of death. No matter whether you are trying to get your child into a nursery or find a place at the cemetery for a deceased grandfather, to buy an antediluvian radio in installments, enter college, or get a job—everywhere and always you must answer the question of your ethnic identity. And it is a critical issue on the person-to-person level, as well. I recall with a smile even now how, in the far-off fifties, I got into a day-care center for preschool children (its name was something like "Fifteen Years of Red Uzbekistan"). I was completely stunned when two boys, one of them Russian and the other Jewish, both of whom later became my friends, said with contempt upon first meeting me: "We do not play with Tartars." Then they put their arms around each other and proudly walked away. Where could they have learned this except from adults? Yet I had also guessed their nationalities immediately and correctly.

"I am a Tartar," I replied to the unasked question that was evidently tormenting the mechanic, and his face cleared a bit. Tartars and Kazakhs, like Uzbeks, Kirgiz, Azerbaijanis, Turkmen, and quite a few other peoples of the U.S.S.R., belong to the ancient family of Turks. Their total number is about fifty million. In the U.S.S.R. with its population of 280 million, it is the second largest group after the Slavs. That is why "Pan-Turkism" is an obscene word in the Soviet political lexicon. The languages of the Turk peoples are rather similar to each other, especially within each of the three groups into which they are subdivided. It is only a slight exaggeration to say that a Tartar, an Uzbek, and an Azerbaijani can understand each other no worse than, for example, an Australian, a Canadian, and an Irishman, all of whom speak English in their own fashion.

"What is this plane standing in the middle of the street?" exclaimed Liberman in surprise, poking his finger towards a real IaK-40 airplane, sitting as if quite at home on a low pedestal in the middle of the square.

"We have a school of civil aviation here," the mechanic answered indifferently.

"What about perestroika here?" Liberman asked curiously, in the condescending manner of a Muscovite. "Does one feel it?"

"Ah, that is all a lot of bullshit!" The Kazakh grinned and showed me where to pull up the car. He took the ball bearings, wrapped in a plastic packet, and left, promising to come back in five minutes.

"And what if he doesn't come back?" said Liberman nervously after ten minutes had passed.

"He'll come back," I said with certainty. "Here he comes now!"

9

"A Horse! A Horse!
My Kingdom for a Horse!"

Hydraulic jacks! Semi axles! I was fed up with the dreary words that kept peppering Liberman's conversation. Finally I said resolutely, "Let's postpone our repairs until tomorrow. It's time to take care of our lodging for the night."

Here we came up with some incredible luck. In the very first hotel we tried, the receptionist, a heavy woman with bleached yellow hair, reacted with interest to the banknote that had somehow found its way into the pages of my passport. Which is to say, she let it fall into the drawer of her desk. The omnipresent line was jammed in front of her little window; this inhospitable hostess had plenty of offers to choose from. Other candidates for a bunk in the hotel poked their heads through her window in their turn, as if through a guillotine. I wondered how we appeared to her: perhaps like mechanical cuckoos, endlessly popping out of a huge clock. In all Soviet hotels, ticket offices, post offices, banks, and information booths, a client must bend way over, almost doubled in two. Only in this posture, humiliating even to a monkey, can the applicant address his entreaties through the small aperture in the glass barrier. Behind it, like a piranha in an aquarium, the official bubbles about with an air of importance.

Our rivals in the line gave us looks of envy as the receptionist handed us questionnaires.

"Sorry, comrades, sorry! We were here before," I said pompously. After filling out my form I made my way through the crowd back to the little window, and signed the standard form obligating us to leave the hotel whenever the management might request it.

"No, wait a minute," said a puny, one-eyed man in an old green felt hat and seedy raincoat, bristling at me. "I am the senior officer of a group of blind people. We have a conference here and they have lost our reservations. Let her first contact the province's Party Committee."

"For one day only!" the receptionist warned me sternly, postponing for a moment the pleasure she would derive from driving the one-eyed man crazy. For the next fifteen minutes, with a sadistic slowness, she busied herself writing out for us a receipt saying that we had paid for a double room for twenty-four hours. Documents in our country are almost always written out by hand.

With our bags in hand and our guest cards in our teeth, we rushed to the elevator. The hotel had three of them, but only one was working, and it did not stop on our floor. "Maybe it stops only at even numbers," I theorized, correctly. Instead of the seventh floor the elevator let us out on the eighth.

This was Cosmos, the best hotel in town. A little boy, about five years old, was sitting at the desk of the *dezhurnaya,* the woman who oversaw all the guest rooms on the floor. He was trying, without success, to dial a number. When he saw us, he handed me the receiver and ordered peremptorily: "Call my mother, get her to come!"

"And what is the number?" I asked this nice if somewhat dirty child in my questionable Kazakh. It seemed that the *dezhurnaya* had no place to leave her son, and so she brought him with her to work.

"I don't know," the boy said in Russian, and started to cry. We put down our bags and tried in every possible way to amuse him. A twelve-year-old girl who had heard all this noise appeared from a service room at the corner. She turned out to be the boy's sister. She did not know where their mother had gone either. Or maybe she did not want to tell. Or maybe she had been ordered not to say anything.

"Well, all right," I said, taking the initiative of opening the desk drawer, where the *dezhurnaya* usually keeps the room keys for the floor. "Tell your mother when she comes that some new guests have arrived in room 713."

Our room was furnished with the asceticism common to all Soviet hotels. Two beds like those in an orphanage, covered with flannelette blankets, a shabby table with an empty three-liter jar posing as a decanter, two rickety chairs, a stinking closet, and a bathroom with no light bulb but at least containing a sink and a shower stall (although, it is true, there was no hot water). Yet was it worthwhile to pay attention to such trifles as hot water, when there was a roof over our heads and we were reasonably sure we would not be robbed that night?

"Look and rejoice," I told Liberman, pointing to a piece of paper, bleached with age, pinned to the inside of the door with a tack. The text read as follows.

Services available in the hotel Cosmos:
Electric kettle—20 kop.
Electric samovar—20 kop.
Iron—5 kop.
Fan—20 kop.
Humidifier—25 kop.
Alarm clock—5 kop.
Booking a cab—10 kop.
Tea caddy (china)—10 kop.
Brushes for footwear and shoe polish—5 kop.
Spoon, fork, knife—2 kop.
China dishes—5 kop.
Laundry basin—10 kop.
Use of refrigerator on the floor—10 kop.

"What kind of prices are these?" Liberman asked. "What kind of damn china would rent for five kopecks?"

"These prices were set before you were born," I answered him. "And maybe before I was born. Now any service on this list will cost you a ruble. Unofficially. And I'm sure that half of the services enumerated here are long gone. There's no competition, and therefore anything will do. Do you know how much I paid to get us in here? Fifty rubles. What can you do? State monopolies!"

"Let's go now and park the car," Liberman said gloomily.

We walked down to the sixth floor and pushed the elevator button, but, as it turned out, it could not be used to go down.

"All right, we aren't lords," I told Liberman. "Let's go on foot."

When we reached the first floor, the senior officer of the group of blind people was screeching heartrendingly at the receptionist; it sounded like he had got his head stuck in the little window and was trying to yank it out.

Our car was parked in a small parking lot in front of a restaurant, which was blasting loud music. At the entrance some seedy-looking characters were cursing each other in loud voices.

"Let's eat in our room," Liberman said, trying not to look in their direction.

"Yeah, let's," I agreed. However, room service has not caught on in our country. By dinner in our room he meant eating what we had brought from Samara: tea in a thermos, boiled potatoes, hard-boiled eggs, and remnants of the sausage the Dobrynins had given us.

When we approached the parking lot, a guard in a military cap came out from his sentry box and yelled sternly, "Your documents!"

"Please," Liberman responded, handing him a ten-ruble banknote. I felt somber and bored. Leaving Liberman to find a place for the car, I returned to the room and lay down on the bed right in my clothes, thinking, "How are my wife and little daughter, in far-off Moscow? I need to call them."

There was no telephone in the room, but there was one at the *dezhurnaya*'s desk. In most Soviet hotels the automatic telephone service is inaccessible to the guests, so that the management can control whom you talk to and how much you pay. It is more convenient for everyone if guests go to the post office or the long-distance office, buy a coupon for a certain length of time, and then come back to the hotel to order a call with this coupon.

In the Soviet Union, it is always expected that one will pay cash on the counter for any service. Most Soviet people have never even heard of credit cards or checkbooks. When I tried once to explain the system of electronic cash transfers to my mother, who had worked all her life in Soviet business, she was terrified. In her view, all those myriad electronic transactions would have to be handled by accountants in satin oversleeves. Yet even the young and restless Liberman did not believe me when I told him about automatic teller machines giving out cash twenty-four hours a day. All this ignorance and waste because half a century ago some party dignitaries, conceited idiots, whose education was completed in primary school, announced to the Soviet people that computer science was the handmaid of imperialism. Everything that was beyond their understanding they declared a handmaid of imperialism.

"Is that you from 713?" the *dezhurnaya* asked me in a melodious voice, when at last I found her at the shabby desk in front of the elevator. Like the receptionist on the first floor, she was portly, but in contrast to her arrogant superior she impressed me as a talkative and agreeable woman. All her life, the receptionist had had to deal with aggressive people trying to gain access to the hotel, while the *dezhurnaya* only encountered the lucky ones who had succeeded in getting in and were already considered "one of us." "Store up some water," she cooed protectively. "You'd better put some water in glass jars. If you want, I'll give you some. Tomorrow there won't be any water at all."

"There is no water today, either," I pointed out.

"No, today there is no *hot* water." She smiled with an affectionate, almost maternal expression on her puffy face. "But tomorrow there won't be any cold water, either."

"That's nice. But how can we wash?" I asked. "Or shave, for that matter?"

"Would you like me to give you an electric kettle and a wash basin?"

"I would like it very much," I replied. "And besides that, I want to call Moscow."

"Oh, that's easy!" she cried. "Go to the long-distance telephone office. And now, I'll give you some linens and you can take a basin, a kettle, and some jars."

"And is the buffet open?" I asked, just in case we might be in luck.

"Oh, you're so cunning, you Muscovites," she said, tenderly wagging a finger. "The buffet is open in the morning and during the day. But in the evening it's clo-o-sed."

Liberman came back and we dined silently, having laid out our cold supper on a table covered with old newspapers.

The sausage had garlic in it and I tried to open a window to let some air into the room. But it was tightly sealed for the hotel's central ventilation system—which did not work. I turned on my orange transistor radio to listen to the news. A local station was broadcasting a survey of views, entitled "Let's Listen to the Voice of Reason." I listened a little and almost choked.

"I am a veteran of the Great Patriotic War," a man read bitterly from a text, "and the question of the unification of the two German states worries me as much as it worries any other Soviet man. Certain forces will use the open borders between West Germany and East Germany, West Berlin and East Berlin, for undisguised interference in the internal affairs of East Germany, for the purpose of its destabilization. The government of West Germany is not ready to give up its claims on the territory of Poland and the Soviet Union. I completely support the declaration of the All-Union Council of Veterans of War and Labor and the Armed Forces of the U.S.S.R. in connection with the process of the unification of Germany that has, in fact, begun. With great concern for the fate of the world, the veterans have called on all public organizations of the U.S.S.R., the states of Europe and of the whole world to protest against interference in the internal affairs of East Germany and to support the process of building 'a European house' with the participation of both German states. With a feeling of deep pain in my soul I ask: why is it that such global questions have not been submitted to the approval of our people, of veterans who bore the full brunt of World War II?"

"My God," I said sadly to Liberman, "how cruelly brainwashed were our fathers' and grandfathers' generations. What morons they've been brought up to be. It doesn't occur to them at all that the Germans themselves do not want any East Germany! And that West Germany has paid us several billion dollars in compensation!"

At the long-distance office there were many people in line, even though it was so late. One line had formed at the window where they changed money, and another, longer line at the window where one could order a telephone call. A third line, the longest one, was crowded in front of several booths with intercity telephones.

"Leninabad, third booth! Semipalatinsk, second booth!" the operator announced loudly when she got a line through to a certain town. An express order was filled within an hour, a standard order had to wait for several hours. I decided to buy three express orders and to call from the hotel. To call from here meant that my conversation with my wife would be listened to and commented on by all three lines, because no other entertainment was available to all these people, who had been waiting for hours. And if I called from my hotel, at least I would be heard only by those who are entitled to listen to such conversations.

After I left the long-distance office, I looked back and took a photograph of the line with my flash. That was a mistake, one which could have cost me my life. Ordinary Soviet people cannot stand it when a stranger takes aim at them with his camera, but for Gypsies, photographing them is considered tantamount to attempts on their lives. An enraged young Gypsy virago with golden teeth dashed at me from the line, accompanied by a pack of Gypsy children.

"What are you doing? What right do you have to take our picture?" she shrieked at the top of her voice, trying at the same time to snatch the camera out of my hands. Her hysterical howling inflamed the crowd, which darted at me in a fury, obviously intending to tear me into pieces. My first reaction was to leave the battlefield shamefacedly and run as fast as I could to the hotel, but I quickly conjured up an image of the scene that would have resulted if the crowd had followed me there, breaking the hotel windows and demanding the right to lynch me. Even if I extricated myself, the KGB or militia would put Liberman and me under observation, and no real journey around the Union would then be possible. So out of this fear I made a spontaneous decision.

"Hold still...KGB!" I cried in a squeaky voice. I ruthlessly wrestled the Gypsy woman over my thigh and stepped forward to meet my other stupefied attackers. They instantly believed me; the KGB is the one governmental organization that people are still afraid of. Had I told them I was from the militia they would have beaten me up all the same. The crowd rapidly disintegrated. "Come with me to the car!" I commanded the Gypsy, forcing her hands behind her back and pulling her from the steps of the entrance into a shadowy alley. Gypsy children, breathing heavily, attacked me from all sides at once, forcing me to let go of the screaming virago. She began limping in the direction of my hotel, tripping over her numerous skirts.

The children ran after her. Deciding not to tempt fortune twice, I also dashed along the badly lit street as if I were chasing them. When I was a good distance from the damned long-distance office, I quickly turned into a dark passage between some tall apartment buildings. Looking over my shoulder for the last time, I saw a yellow-and-blue patrol car speeding with sirens blaring toward the site of our incident. Since the time of Brezhnev, who had set Andropov, the head of the KGB, against Shchelokov, the head of the Ministry of Internal Affairs, relations between these two departments had been far from idyllic.

After an hour, having heated up some water in the electric kettle and washed the unpleasant adventure off myself, I changed my clothes and went out to the *dezhurnaya*'s desk. To my delight, she was not there. Using the coupons that I had bought I ordered three calls—to Moscow, Samara, and Tashkent—and sat in a broken armchair to ponder the situation. The bad news was that I had received several scratches and bruises, my clothes were torn, and my Minolta had been pierced through by some sharp object. The good news was that my scratches and bruises would soon heal, I had plenty of clothes with me, and I still had two cameras in working condition.

My connection with Samara came through first. Alla answered the phone. Something in her voice struck me as unusual. She asked over and over again whether we had gotten to Aktyubinsk safely, and how Liberman was, but she was apparently depressed about something. To change the subject I asked if Liubava liked the record.

"Oh, we've had no time to listen to it," Alla said with a sigh. "And now we have no record player. Now we have almost nothing left. Our apartment was burglarized."

"What? I can't believe it!" I exclaimed, stunned. I knew that the rate of crime in our country was spiraling up and up, seemingly without end. Holdups, murders, apartment burglaries, all kinds of rackets have long since become the commonplace realities of our life. But the Dobrynins, the honest and peaceful Dobrynins! Who would want to break into their modest, two-bedroom apartment on the first floor of an old house? Professional criminals are not interested in trifles. They are on the lookout for large sums of cash, diamonds, expensive fur coats, videos, and especially personal computers. The official price for computers in the U.S.S.R. is incredibly high, second only to foreign cars. Even my daughter, Mary, in first grade at elementary school, knew perfectly well that she should not tell anyone that we had a computer at home. It is better to keep mum even about ordinary VCRs. The newspapers are full of stories about garrulous video owners who were murdered right in their own apartments. Yet the Dobrynins had neither VCR nor PC nor mink coat.

"How did it happen?" I asked Alla in a depressed voice, but she burst into tears and passed me to Sergei.

"This is how things are going," he said calmly. "After we saw you off, Alla and I went to work and the girls left for the institute. Anna was the first to come back. You can imagine how lucky we are that they were already gone."

"Thank God, thank God!" I mumbled, trying to drive away the unsettling images from the Moscow-Leningrad television show "Criminal Chronicles" that had crept into my mind. "But what on earth did they hope to find at your place?"

"That's what is so strange. There was nothing special here to take." Sergei sighed. "A couple of gold and silver chains, which we brought back for the girls from our long-ago stay in Iraq, our old JVC record player—you remember, the one I bought in Basra. And some clothes. The girls are crying, even their perfumes were stolen. It's so stupid! Can you imagine, they just broke the lock and came in. We are just lucky no one was home."

After that came my connection to Tashkent. In April, after many years of moving slowly through up the line at the District Executive Committee, my Tashkent relatives were at last eligible to receive a coupon to buy a new Zhiguli, the car I was counting on to continue my journey around Central Asia. But in April they were told that new cars would not arrive until the end of May. On the phone I found out that because of supply problems, the cars would not arrive until December at the earliest. Yet another hitch!

"Somehow I don't feel that you're glad to hear my voice," said my wife on the telephone, when eventually they got me through to Moscow. "Well, what's up? I'll never forgive you for not taking me with you. We've always traveled together, you know, to Africa, even to America. And now you've left me to sit in rainy, hungry, angry Moscow while you enjoy yourself alone."

"Why alone?" I rejoined. "Liberman is also here enjoying himself. Although I have the feeling he's ready to ditch me at any moment."

"Finish your conversation!" commanded the operator after a few minutes' chat; she evidently did not find our talk interesting.

"Everything is fine with me," I said cheerfully. "Soon I'll be in Tashkent. I love you. Bye-bye!"

"Take care," my wife said in English, and the line was disconnected.

In the morning Liberman went alone to the auto repair shop. He did not want me there, and with that I easily agreed. We arranged that if he was unable to get to a jack, he would call me. But Liberman did not call, which meant that he had succeeded in penetrating and putting down roots at the shop—or that he lacked a two-kopeck coin for the pay phone. I washed up with the water stored the day before, and breakfasted upon a boiled potato and cold tea. There was another woman on duty in the hall, much less agreeable than her colleague of the day before.

"It's time for you to move," she informed me without looking in my direction, absorbed in her book.

"What are you reading?" I asked in an interested voice, pretending that I had not heard her command. In cases such as this it is important to establish an informal relationship as soon as possible. She was reading a third-year high school textbook of the Kazakh language. After talking with her for only a few minutes, I already knew that she was Russian and that the prospect of compulsory study of Kazakh seemed to her dreadful. Many Russians living in Central Asia and Kazakhstan have been shocked and discouraged to be told that they must learn the local languages, which were overnight decreed to be state languages.

On the one hand, many Russians living outside Russia still find it difficult to get rid of their colonial attitude that the languages of the Union republics are second-rate and unnecessary. That point of view has a long-standing pedigree: In 1938 a decree was issued by the party and the government, entitled "Regarding the Compulsory Study of Russian Language in Schools of the National Republics." It gave three reasons why everyone should know Russian: for the sake of communications within the confines of the U.S.S.R., to help introduce the national cadres to science and technology, and to fulfill their military duty in the Red Army. For several generations of Soviet people it was quite enough to know Russian to live in any part of Soviet territory. And then, suddenly, on top of their other problems, millions of people were being forced to learn a local language under the threat of losing their jobs. A remote analogy might be to suppose that California had declared Spanish its state language. The problem is especially painful in those Soviet republics where the root ethnic population constitutes a minority, such as Kazakhstan, where Kazakhs make up only 40 percent of the population.

On the other hand, it is not a simple matter for the republics to transfer all business, technical, and scientific documents into the languages of their ancestors. No decree can overturn at once a linguistic reality that has been evolving for decades. For example, consider the languages of the Turkic group: During Soviet rule their alphabets were forcibly changed twice. At the end of the 1920s the Latin alphabet was substituted for their original Arabic characters; and then in 1940 they were compelled to replace Latin with Cyrillic. That meant that millions of Uzbeks, Tadzhiks, Tartars, Kazakhs, and dozens of other ethnic groups were suddenly unable to read a line of their own languages. All of Turkic culture, fifteen hundred years old, as well as the even more ancient Persian culture, which had used Arabic letters for the previous ten or twelve centuries, was in one blow transformed into a vast graveyard of unintelligible scribbles. Can you imagine if, by the decree of some political party, all Anglo-Saxon and Middle English literature was transcribed first into Cyrillic and then into Japanese characters? And that anyone who protested was declared to be a bourgeois nationalist and sent to die in a concentration camp? That is precisely what occurred in many southern republics of the Soviet Union several decades ago. Now, trying to repair the injustices done to their native languages, the governments of the republics are hastily mandating that these be the official state languages. However, good intentions do not always turn out to be a benefit for all. A friend of mine once asked someone standing next to the ticket puncher in a streetcar in Tashkent to have her commutation ticket punched. The person responded crossly, "Say the same thing in Uzbek and I'll do it."

"And how would one say it in Uzbek?" my friend asked, furious, although she speaks Uzbek. At this point the whole streetcar began to argue the question of how to translate the words "punch" and "ticket" into Uzbek. The problem was that the Uzbek equivalents were loan words, identical to the Russian from which they were borrowed! Never mind the fact that in Russian they were borrowed directly from English.

There are a few wonderful exceptions to the rule, such as Nadezhda Miroshnikova, a well-known author who performs traditional Kazakh folk tales, accompanying herself on the dombra, an ancient Kazakh instrument. But that example would hardly console the *dezhurnaya,* who in her old age had to learn a new language. Maybe to reward me for giving her moral support in her linguistic problems, she warned me not to waste my energy on the receptionist on duty.

"She's such a bitch," the *dezhurnaya* said of her chief, "that unless you have influential friends she won't let you stay here even a day longer. The more so as tomorrow the Congress of People's Deputies of the province starts in Aktyubinsk."

"And what about cash?" I asked. I am an idealist: I believe in the mystical force of money.

"Connections only!" the *dezhurnaya* said. "She has a rich husband."

"Perhaps we can arrange it between ourselves?" I asked politely. "We plan to leave this evening, in any case."

"What am I going to do with you?" The woman smiled coquettishly, giving me a flash of her steel crowns.

Apparently my flattery had paid off, for she did not take my room key and allowed us to leave our suitcases in the room until evening.

I took a taxi to the auto repair shop, where I found the gates padlocked. To enter I had to crawl through a hole in the wire fence. I quickly found our car, standing alone, off to the side, looking like a child who had just recovered from an illness. Liberman himself, surrounded by the local auto mechanics, was rummaging through some other car's intestines. By all appearances, it was by no means the first or even the second car he had fixed that morning. From time to time he straightened up and with wild gesticulations tried to get something across to his listeners, who respectfully listened to the guest celebrity with impassive faces. "Dr. Liberman, new exploits are awaiting you," I said to him. "It's time for us to hit the road!"

10

A Meteorite on the Road

We went southward, a cloud of steppe dust trailed us, the wild
grass was smoking; grasshoppers played about..." Translation
does not really render the mood of these lines, which are as nerve-
racking and thrilling as a conversation with a woman who is not yet
yours. Arseny Tarkovsky, the crippled poet who wrote these lines,
seemed to me in the seventies to be the best among his contemporaries. He died recently, having outlived his own son, the great film
director Andrey Tarkovsky, one of the few Soviet directors known
outside Russia. Not to annoy Liberman, I restrained myself from
reciting aloud. My heart was full of song: we had managed to break
free from Aktyubinsk!

It was four hundred miles across the naked steppe and near-desert
to our next stop, the town of Aralsk. We had begun to traverse the
exotic Asian lands that Liberman had dreamed about in anticipation of
our journey. Had I really succeeded in overcoming all of Liberman's
doubts and hesitations about continuing on this expedition? I felt the
change in his mood and had some alternatives ready. For example, if
he refused to continue on this leg of our journey by car, I could put
him on a plane to Tashkent, where he could wait for my arrival by car
at my relatives' home there. Yet now it seemed that everything would
turn out all right, because, damn it, we were moving!

The road was totally empty; only occasionally did we meet trucks with Aktyubinsk license plates, most probably shuttling from Aktyubinsk to the town of Khrom-Tau (which in Kazakh means "Chrome Mountain").

Unlike Liberman I was in a hurry. First, I wanted to make it at least halfway across the two-hundred-mile span of unpaved road that awaited us. Second, I was rushing to get as far away from Aktyubinsk as possible, in order to cut off all possible retreat in Liberman's mind. In other words, if something went wrong, let it happen closer to Aralsk than Aktyubinsk so that we could go forward instead of backward.

"Vova, would you like to look at the notice in *Aktyubinsk Week?*" I asked Liberman, in order to distract him from gloomy thoughts. That morning I had bought several issues of this four-page weekly paper. The print quality was atrocious enough to challenge that of the underground Bolshevik proclamations calling for the overthrow of autocracy in 1905. Under the heading "Miscellany" was printed the following matter-of-fact information:

"On the 29th of April two young horses ran away in Aktyubinsk: one of them is a three-year-old chestnut mare, with legs all white up to her fetlocks, a distinct white spot on her forehead, and the other is a bay foal, one year old. Please report their whereabouts to this telephone number: 3–33–04 or 3–51–15. Reward."

Liberman silently read the notice, folded the newspaper four times and returned it to me. I looked at him askance.

"Well, Vova, keep looking out the window, maybe we'll spot the lost Houyhnhnms. Imagine the reward we'll get!"

Passing a truck that was raising all kinds of dust from the road, I honked in greeting to the driver.

Our conversation made the time fly, and it seemed that we reached Khrom-Tau rather quickly. Just as there was no white hill in Aktyubinsk ("Ak Tube" means in Kazakh "White Hill"), so there was no chrome mountain in Khrom-Tau. I supposed it had been razed to the ground. One does not meet bears in Moscow outside the zoo, although the name of the capital could be translated as "the bears' watering hole."

The first thing we saw of Khrom-Tau, towering above the town, was a gigantic Ferris wheel. "What do you think, Vova, shall we give it a try?"

"But it's not working," Liberman said with certainty. "It was either not completely put together or not completely dismantled."

"Like socialism," I said.

"Huh?" grunted Liberman, and spat out the window.

We drove through the whole town in just a few minutes. It was not even a town, but a big village which had grown up around an enterprise for extracting and processing chrome ore. There was no one in the little side streets, no grown-ups and no children, only a brood of scrawny chickens, digging at the dusty road in search of fossils, and a couple of stray dogs which chased our car. I wanted to stop at the gas station to ladle out a little more gas but it was closed.

Gasoline in the Soviet Union, outside Moscow, Leningrad, and some provincial capitals, is not clear but of a nasty red color. "What kind of gas is this with blood in it?" I asked Liberman with surprise, when I saw it for the first time when we bought gas somewhere between Kuibyshev and Aktyubinsk.

Liberman laughed at my naïveté. "It's full of lead, that's why it's red. The Ministry of Health has forbidden the use of this kind of gas since its exhaust is carcinogenic. Yet in our country they don't know any other way to increase the octane level of gas. But it doesn't matter—after all, it's a big country, and we won't all be poisoned for at least twenty years! It's not Chernobyl, you know; it's not even Semipalatinsk."

Yes, Soviet people were terrified by the Chernobyl catastrophe, but there was an equally horrible ulcer on the body of Kazakhstan, although people knew much less about it and spoke about it even less frequently. Since 1949 nuclear weapons tests have been conducted in Semipalatinsk Province, and until 1963 bombs were exploded directly in the air or on the surface. The state could not have cared less about the people of the area. As far back as 1957, medical researchers from the Soviet and Kazakhstan ministries of health knew that certain parts of Central Kazakhstan had been exposed to intensive radioactive contamination. Sources of radiation were found in the soil, the food, the water, and in human and animal excrement. But even when the tests were transferred underground, the health of people living in the adjoining areas continued to deteriorate alarmingly. Malignant tumors, cancers of the blood, a mounting death rate among children, congenital anomalies, psychological problems, and suicides—even all that is not the full price that the local Kazakhs had to pay for the nuclear might of the empire. While our leaders, puffed up with pride, enjoyed the cardboard models of nuclear-armed ballistic missiles that they observed from atop Lenin's tomb during military parades, the infant mortality rate in the Semipalatinsk Province had grown to 34 percent. The military had occupied nearly eighty thousand square miles of land, but no one uttered a word about some form of compensation to the local authorities. The state of Nevada reportedly receives nearly one billion dollars in compensation, which is why so many of its residents support nuclear testing. Until recently in the U.S.S.R. it did not even occur to anyone that it is possible to protest. It is better to die slowly in freedom than to die quickly in the torture chambers of the KGB. In the epoch of "developed socialism," there was no question of holding mass protests or creating public antinuclear organizations. The fear of bloody reprisals, inculcated from the first days of the Soviet regime, was too strong.

All that was allowed (or, more correctly, prescribed) in the way of demonstrations was to participate in protests against the nuclear tests conducted by other countries, marches organized by the party bosses themselves. People were taken away from their workplaces to buses to halls and stadiums, where they sat, bored to tears, while official ora-tors recited the usual diatribes against world imperialism.

But times changed, and in the end of the fourth year of Gor-bachev's rule someone from the local establishment publicly con-demned the nuclear tests of the *Soviet* military-industrial complex. The someone was Olzhas Suleimenov, a renowned Kazakh poet who writes in Russian. I am calling him a poet out of habit, yet he now has other occupations which probably seem to him much more important than poetry: he is a deputy of the Supreme Soviet of the U.S.S.R. and head of the Writers' Union of Kazakhstan. A release of poisonous sub-stances into the atmosphere by nuclear tests in February 1989 started a panic. Olzhas Suleimenov made a special announcement on televi-sion, which was not sanctioned by the authorities. Within a month a public antinuclear movement had arisen; it was later transformed into the movement Nevada-Semipalatinsk, which was made up of corre-sponding groups in the United States and the U.S.S.R., focused on ending nuclear weapons testing at the Nevada and Semipalatinsk test sites.

However, some people in the Soviet Union firmly believe that all this antinuclear movement has been inspired by the Soviet military and KGB themselves in order to create a respected formal pretext for reducing unbearable arms race expenditures. Otherwise, how to explain the fact that all leaders of this movement belong to the high-ranked Soviet hierarchy since Brezhnev's time?

Fifteen years ago Olzhas Suleimenov had raised a huge scandal when he published a book of literary criticism entitled *Az and I* ("Az" was the first letter of the Russian alphabet before the revolutionary reforms, and "I" is the last letter of the Cyrillic alphabet). The book, so innocent from a contemporary perspective, was by the standards of those times a dangerous example of encroachment on the ideological foundations of the state. Its principal sedition was the cautiously worded notion that history must not be the handmaid of ideology. It discussed this idea only with regard to very remote historical occurrences, and touched only indirectly on the imperial myth of the superiority of "the elder Russian brother" over the wild and unsophisticated juniors of the peaceable family of peoples.

But Olzhas Suleimenov's career was developing with much greater success than his numerous adversaries and zealots could envision. First, he became the chairman of the State Cinematography Ministry of Kazakhstan. Then, under Gorbachev, he became the first secretary of the Writers' Union of Kazakhstan. Both positions are rather high up within the *nomenklatura,* and Olzhas Suleimenov is now an established statesman and politician.

Despite all that, his book was not in fact forgotten. On the one hand, it became extremely popular among the intelligentsia of the Turkic peoples of the Soviet Union. Among my acquaintances in Uzbek, Azerbaijani, Tartar, Kazakh, Altaic, Kirghiz, Bashkir, Turkmen, Balkar, Nogais, Uighur, Kumyk, Karakalpak, Karachaev, and even far-off Siberian, Yakut, and Tuvinian literature and culture, there was no one who had not read or at least heard about this book. On the other hand, rank-and-file Russian patriots (or Russian chauvinists, to use a general term) reacted violently whenever this book was even mentioned. "Don't you know that he's married to a Jew!" they would assure each other at meetings and behind the scenes. "And he, himself, quite possibly, is the offspring of those Yids. It's known for certain that that book was written under a commission from the Jews and Masons." None of them had any idea what this book was about, as none of them had read it. But at least one ideologue from the Russian party had read it, the late prose writer Vladimir Chivilichin, who wrote two books in response to Suleimenov. They were both published under the title *Pamyat' (Memory)*. Later his title was taken up as the banner of the Russian chauvinist organization Pamyat', today known as the National-Patriotic Front.

"Do you know who Olzhas Suleimenov is?" I asked Liberman, who was dozing.

"Sure, I know. He's a deputy of the Supreme Soviet!" Liberman snapped. "Look, we're already to Bogetsai. Soon we'll cross the Or' River, and the next river will be the Irgiz. There all our troubles will start."

I shrugged my shoulders absentmindedly, having no way of knowing that Liberman's nagging doubts would soon prove to be an accurate forecast. An hour and a half later, while our Zhiguli was driving at full speed, a hellish noise suddenly erupted from beneath the chassis. The car careered as if it had rolled over a mine.

"Now we're done for!" Liberman cried. "That's it! Brake! Brake!"

"Oh, no!" I mumbled in shock, jamming on the brakes and trying to control the car, which was convulsively jogging along the road. "What now?" We had driven almost halfway to Aralsk. Was I victim of that Gypsy woman's sorcery?

The car jolted several more times with a terrible crashing sound and finally came to a stop. "Are you blind, or what?" Liberman shouted, raising his hands. Sobbing, he got out of the car and flung himself underneath.

His anger was limitless, but perhaps just. The asphalt had ended, but the road had still seemed to me quite drivable. I had been driving faster than I should have, veering like a slalom skier around the big stones, like meteorites fallen from the sky, which were scattered on the road. One of them, the size of a small asteroid, had scratched the belly of the poor vehicle, and, most appalling, bent the massive grill which protected the oil pump.

"What now?" I asked Liberman indifferently, getting out of the car. The oil pump had turned into a metallic oddity, tied with a knot.

It looked like a huge ravioli. I understood that this time we really were kaput. The odds seemed to be stacked against Liberman accompanying me on this trip.

"It's all screwed up!" Liberman said loudly, reiterating his favorite words. "That's it."

"Aren't you exaggerating?" I asked, hopefully. "Is it really irreparable?"

"Do I exaggerate?" Liberman said angrily. "You just ask anyone whether a car can go without an oil pump."

"And is it impossible to replace it?" I asked curiously, feeling certain that this was possible.

"Where will I get you an oil pump? There is an even greater deficit of oil pumps than of semi axles!" Liberman wailed. "They don't exist in all of creation. Only if I return to Togliatti and get hired at the auto plant there. But who will hire me without a residence permit?"

"Okay, let's go back to Togliatti," I agreed peacefully. At that moment, all I wanted was to box the guiltless Liberman's ears.

"What Togliatti are you talking about?" Liberman's head drooped all of a sudden as if someone had deflated him. "Look around, where are we? Either wolves will eat us here, or bandits will cut our throats!"

We were towed back to Aktyubinsk. The driver, a former prison lumberjack with the inevitable rings tattooed on his fingers, one for each year he had served, had passed us by the first time, but then for some reason he returned. Perhaps he could not get the pathetic face of the unfortunate Liberman out of his mind; it might have been that he was intrigued by the image of the roll of ten-ruble banknotes that I was furiously waving in the air. In any case, we were very lucky to have his services, if it is appropriate to speak of luck in such a situation.

It was already after midnight, when, in a heavy silence, we drove back to Aktyubinsk. A mile before the hotel the driver stopped and ordered us to unhitch our car. We were already in the center of town, and he was scared of traffic cops who might see that he was towing Muscovites and ask for a cut of his fee. I paid him generously, for if it had not been for his passing by on his way to Irgiz, we would surely have spent a night in the steppe.

Silently, panting, each of us steeped in his own thoughts, we pushed our car to the Hotel Cosmos, locked it, and paraded past the receptionist, who had fallen asleep at her military post with an extinct cigarette in her teeth. The most incredible thing was that I found the key from our old room in my jacket. Despite the massive plastic club attached to it, on which the number of our room was imprinted, in the haste of departure I had forgotten to give it back to the *dezhurnaya*. We opened the door of our former room without any obstacle and discovered to our surprise that nothing had changed. Even the towels and linen were the same. The deputies of the Provincial Congress, for whose sake we had been so rudely kicked out of the hotel, were nowhere in evidence.

"Time for all to sleep," I told Liberman, who fell onto his bed in his clothes, not even needing my announcement, and immediately plunged into sleep.

"And who will brush your teeth for you—Pushkin maybe?" I asked and followed his example without delay.

At six-thirty the next morning we were awakened by an impatient and angry knock on the door. Cursing all early callers, I dragged myself forward to open the door. I had left the key in the lock, so that it was tricky to open the door from the outside.

"Who are you, and how did you happen to get here?" a strange face yelled at me spitefully, thrusting her mop at my forehead.

"We're guests, we're peaceful people," I mumbled. "And you seem to be a maid who has come to clean the room for our comrade deputies. How do you know that *we* weren't deputies? But, unfortunately, no, we're not from this hospitable province..."

"You can crack your little jokes to the militia!" the maid shrieked, and then tried to throw the sleeping Liberman out of his bed and onto the floor, prying at his body with her mop.

"What the hell are you doing, you bitch?" Liberman howled, only half awake, attempting to jerk the weapon from the hands of his enraged enemy.

"Vova, stop it, you are wrong!" I wagged my finger at him in what had become a standard parody of the famous hard-liner Ligachev, who was eternally threatening Boris Yeltsin at the Party Conference a couple of years ago. At that juncture no one could know that Ligachev would be disgraced, while Yeltsin would become President of Russia. If this maid, angry with life itself, succeeded in provoking a fight, we really could end up in the hands of the militia. A turn of events less favorable to my plans simply did not exist in the whole realm of the possible. Fortunately, yesterday's *dezhurnaya* heard the noise and ran in. Instantly comprehending the situation, she took hold of the maid's broad waist and threw her into the corridor.

"Don't get cross with her," the kind woman pleaded, inhaling and exhaling deeply to catch her breath. "The other day her husband was taken to jail by OBHSS [the agency of financial control]. She's always had a dog's life, and now she's close to hanging herself: she has to support three children and a sick mother who only gets a small pension from her *kolkhoz,* and she herself gets only one hundred and forty rubles a month."

"Oh, yes, we understand," I answered for Liberman and myself. "We'll go downstairs now and pay for yesterday. Or, perhaps, we can stay here one more day?"

We did not succeed in getting to stay longer. Fortune, in the guise of the stone-faced hotel receptionist, turned its back on us.

"I suggest we leave here," I told Liberman when we found ourselves, finally and irreversibly, out on the street in front of the hotel. "First let's persuade someone to tow our car to the auto repair. You can try to get an oil pump there, and I will go look for another hotel."

"It's useless," Liberman answered in a grim voice. "All this is useless."

"What is useless, Vova?" I asked, trying to make my voice sound as neutral and calm as possible. "Are you talking about the oil pump or the hotel?"

"All is useless," Liberman repeated desperately. "I'm not going anywhere."

"Let's postpone this conversation till this evening," I said, putting my hand on his shoulder. It is a stupid gesture, but sometimes it works. "First we'll have breakfast, then we'll go repair the car and find a place to spend the night. And then we can go on to solve a few global problems."

"And what's there to postpone? There's nothing to postpone." Liberman turned his eyes aside. "We can't drive this car anymore. Do whatever you want, but I'm going back."

"How?"

"In my car!" Liberman replied in a dull voice.

For five seconds I was thinking about what to do next. To appeal to such notions as "honor," "your word," or "responsibilities" would be useless.

"All right," I said. "Go ahead. But it's farther from here to Moscow than from here to Tashkent."

"That's not the point!" Liberman answered, raising his voice. "I don't want to pay for some adventures with my ass. I'm tired. I can't do it. I have a family, children…"

"That's right," I said. "Just don't yell at me. If you don't want to, you don't have to go. But the car. Why on earth did you talk me out of driving my own white car and suggest this one? You knew perfectly well, didn't you, that I was going beyond Cheboksary?"

"I didn't think everything would be like this. I thought it would be more…*humane*. I don't want to shake with fear anymore. I don't like these squinty-eyed people. You know better than I do about Eastern perfidy. You never know what to expect from them. If something happens, who will take care of my children?"

"But then leave me the car. I gave you everything you asked for. Or give me back my money."

"I left my money with Sveta in Novocheboksarsk."

"Then repair the car and go back home by train or plane."

"It's impossible to have it fixed here. Here I can only jerry-rig it so that I can get the car back to Togliatti and replace the oil pump there."

"I don't believe you."

"Then get it fixed yourself."

A three-second pause. Liberman went white from tension, because he understood that I wanted to hit him. I wanted to just turn around and go away. The hell with him and his car! Let him do with it whatever he wanted and go wherever he wanted. But I could not afford even that. He did not have money for getting the car fixed, for gas and meals. According to our unwritten contract, I was to pay for everything. So until he repaired this damned oil pump, I could not leave him alone in a strange city.

"Here's money," I told him dryly. "Take care of the car, and I'll go look for a hotel. Toward evening, let's say at six, we'll meet here."

11

"In the Land of Earless Dogs"

The notorious Eastern perfidy that Liberman so feared is, by and large, not present in the Kazakh national character, provided one can speak of national character as some constant, not subject to the impact of such powerful factors as economy, politics, and ecology. But even decades of Communist terror have not erased from them the straightforwardness, friendliness, and hospitality that the Kazakhs inherited from their steppe ancestors. The nomad code of behavior, about which Liberman had no idea, and the ethos of urban Eastern civilizations, which he had possibly gleaned from the stories in *The Thousand and One Nights*, were miles apart. Let us project ourselves back a century and compare the simple-hearted son of the steppe with the sly resident of cosmopolitan Bukhara. This Persian-speaking city, with its tangled streets and solid clay fences, with its noisy rows of traders and marketers, with its courts, harems, and mosques, has for centuries taught its inhabitants cunning, resourcefulness, and the skill of double-talk; when someone says "I will" and then does not, without giving it much thought, no one is surprised, because it is so easy to get lost in a crowd of many thousands. But who would a nomad living in a lonely yurt on the enormous steppe try to outsmart? His kith and kin who sleep next to him in the yurt, on the same piece of felt? His herd of horses and his flock of sheep, guided by brave sheep dogs with cropped ears and tails?

"What?" you ask, indignantly, "they cut off the poor animals' tails and ears?"

"But their ears are the most vulnerable part of their bodies, and steppe wolves can bring them down catching their ears in their teeth," a steppe resident would answer, surprised by your slow-wittedness. "And their tails are cropped so that the dogs won't hold them between their legs or wag them in front of a pack of wolves. You know that among the wolves and dogs a weakling always wags his tail before a strong one, and if they have nothing to wag with, then they have to fight..."

In the Soviet Union it is impossible to stay in a hotel without connections. This is an axiom that won't be overturned by the signing of a thousand SALT treaties. While I knew no one in Aktyubinsk, it would be quite simple to activate my Moscow or Alma-Ata contacts over the phone. But because of some idiotic obstinacy I wanted to make do without anyone's help. We had to begin this day with breakfast, since Liberman and I had not eaten since the day before.

That might not prove to be so simple to arrange. We did have a gas stove, and some earthenware pots and spoons in the trunk of Liberman's car. But whether I would see Liberman again was not altogether clear to me. Perhaps he would replace the oil pump and leave without bidding farewell? No, he would not do a thing like that, if only because my belongings were still in the car.

To buy some foodstuffs in a shop was out of the question, for the staples of the Soviet table have long since been sold by ration cards only. The cards are handed out to residents by local authorities based upon their residence permits, or by trade unions at their jobs. The monthly per-person ration established in Aktyubinsk for basic foods and goods was as follows:

Butter—100 grams
Sugar—1 kilogram
Soap—100 grams
Vodka—0.5 liter
Laundry soap—one box, about four ounces, for a quarter of a year
Meat and sausage—no rations guaranteed

Nor is Aktyubinsk at all unusual in having such ascetic allowances; most Soviet towns live in just the same state of deprivation. In those places where the climate is better and the land has not been absolutely contaminated, many goods—meat, potatoes, and apples, for example—can be bought at the market. But the vast majority of Soviet citizens can do nothing but express themselves in impotent rage at the market prices. Every day one can observe the same nerve-racking picture at Soviet markets: old ladies, crippled from decades of excessive labor, mumbling curses at the laughing faces of speculators-traders. Why are they laughing? Because the price of a mid-sized melon in the beginning of summer is equal to the average monthly pension of a state worker?

The government recently determined that 80 percent of Soviet people live at or below the official poverty level. But as soon as newspapers announce a strike of British miners, a flood in India, or an earthquake in California, old Soviet ladies, half-famished pensioners, drag themselves to the post office as if obeying some invisible command and stand in line to send contributions. All their lives it was preached to them that the lives of the working people in "the countries of capital" were unbearable, and that the whole world looked to the great land of Lenin with pride and hope. How could they refuse to help those people who were not so lucky as to be born in the country of Great October? So they voluntarily part with a portion of their miserable pension, sending it to yet another fund from which will be paid the salary and traveling expenses of some cynical party bureaucrat, the head of the fund.

And what of their grandchildren and great-grandchildren? They do not go to the post office, for they think the values of their grandmothers and great-grandmothers are ridiculous. *Moskovskii Komsomolets,* a popular newspaper for young readers, asked the seniors of a Moscow high school this question: "What profession do you think is the most prestigious?" The majority of the nation's future wives and mothers answered, quite seriously, "Hard currency prostitute. They can marry foreigners and leave this country."

"Isn't this a national catastrophe?" cry soapbox orators in Pushkin Square. Yet the majority of people do not hear them. They are standing on the other side of Pushkin Square, in a line stretching for miles, to get to the Canadian McDonald's, the solitary oasis of civilization in the Soviet Union accessible to all layers of society. They are standing in this line not because they are dying to get a Big Mac, as Western correspondents report with a condescending smile. They stand in line because they hope to spend at least half an hour in a world where no one bullies them while taking their money, where no one reminds them sneeringly about which layer of Soviet society they belong to.

In Aktyubinsk, though, there is no McDonald's. There is a buffet in the hotel but without a guest card they will not let you even cross the threshold. In some big Asiatic towns like Tashkent, Samarkand, Frunze, and Dushanbe, it is still possible to eat in the street without difficulty, although it is not advisable to inquire too closely into the question of the quality and wholesomeness of the food. Yet Aktyubinsk and Uralsk, although they are the provincial centers of Kazakhstan, are more reminiscent of joyless, colorless Siberian towns than of their enterprising and resourceful southern neighbors. One of the explanations may lie in the fact that here, as in many other regions where Russians represent the majority of the population, private enterprise is not held in great esteem.

According to my Slavophile acquaintances from the Central House of Literati, a striving for personal success is considered to be shameful by Russians. Perhaps for this reason, the partocracy has succeeded in inculcating in the credulous citizens of older generations a false public ideal, proclaiming asinine patience to be the main virtue of the Soviet man. Certainly not everyone has been satisfied with resigning himself to poverty and to faithful service to the party-state apparatus. Some people, inclined to private enterprise by nature, made money under all Soviet regimes. But, unfortunately, it is safer even now to steal from state businesses, from stores, shops, cafés, and restaurants (regularly delivering a share of the loot to whoever must be paid off), than it is to open a private venture.

It is a shame that foreign tourists are not shown the ceremony of the carrying-out of stolen goods from the Soviet public catering system instead of the changing of the guard in front of Lenin's mausoleum. The first is every bit as impressive and picturesque as the second. It does not matter where you go—to the back entrance of the Central Committee café or some fancy restaurant, or to the backyard of a dirty canteen for the dregs of society. Just wait patiently and at a certain hour you will see people from these enterprises carrying bags with stolen victuals. "What is left to cook, then?" you might ask, struck by the vast amount of booty. So far science has been unable to answer this question, but what the Soviet public catering systems do offer their customers even a stray tomcat would turn up its nose at. If the czarist prison administrators had dared to serve our usual garbage-borscht, or the modern cutlets made out of stale bread and fat, which impudently claim to be meat, to their Bolshevik inmates, the latter would surely have undertaken a hunger strike.

My forays into all the hotels in town—and there were just four or five of them in all of Aktyubinsk, with a population of 500,000—were a fiasco. Finally, a vendor of carbonated water, recognizing a homeless stranger, advised me to head to Oleg Koshevoi Street where, she had heard, a new cooperative inn had recently been opened. After a long, tiresome search and interrogations of local residents I managed to find out that the cooperative inn Damolis, which means "rest" in Kazakh, did in fact exist, but it was not quite a hotel. To be precise, it was not a hotel at all, just several rooms on the first floor of the workers' dormitory of the Aktyubinsk iron alloy plant.

Opening the entrance door I saw two women arguing with animation. One of them, an elderly, wrinkled Kazakh woman with smart, shining eyes, was sitting right in front of the entrance at a shabby table. Judging by the keys hanging on a board behind her and the register book on the table, she worked here as the receptionist. The other one, who was standing, arms akimbo, facing her, was much younger. She had curlers in her hair and wore a motley gown, negligently wrapped about her, under which one could see hairy, white, muscular calves and unexpectedly tiny feet in worn-out slippers. Her bossy tone and the grandeur of her posture betrayed her association with the administration. She was probably a commandant of the dormitory and, therefore, the boss of the first woman. I greeted them cheerfully, but neither of them even turned around to look at me. After several minutes of waiting I got out a Dictaphone and put it on the table between the two arguing women. Both continued yelling, from simple inertia, for about a minute and a half, and then they stopped and stared at me with surprise.

"What are we arguing about?" I asked serenely, and smiled the most pleasant smile of my repertoire.

"Who are you, comrade?" the commandant asked. She obviously considered herself to be Russian but, judging by her faded blue eyes and the Finno-Ugrian features of her face, she was probably a Russified Mordvinian.

"I am a correspondent from the journal *Crocodile*," I said with a sigh. "I have been assigned to write an article about your inn, the Damolis."

"What inn? There's no inn! Folks keep coming here and asking for the inn! Give me a break!" the enraged commandant exclaimed and went away, slamming the door. The Kazakh woman looked at me and laughed. She understood that I had nothing to do with *Crocodile*.

"I need a deluxe room," I said seriously.

"All our rooms are deluxe," she answered in the same tone and laughed again. I looked at her with increasing sympathy, and it seemed to me that it was reciprocal. We introduced ourselves and I found out that her name was Zakiya Manasypova.

"Are you a Kazakh or a Tartar?" I asked, following the Soviet custom, as her first and last names sounded Tartar rather than Kazakh.

"Half and half!" she smiled cunningly. "And I saw at once that you were a Tartar."

I shrugged my shoulders, as there was no reason to deny it. Zakiya turned out to be a retired high school teacher of mathematics. Working here as the receptionist was a much-needed second vocation for her: her husband had died long ago; her son, a geologist, had perished in an expedition; and her grown-up daughter was divorced and raising three children in almost total poverty. Zakiya's pension, in its American equivalent, was twenty dollars per month. She had worked at her full-time job for thirty-five years, and had been awarded the medal "For Valor in Labor" for her excellent work.

While she was registering Liberman and me as guests of the Damolis, I asked her about the establishment in more detail. In the four-story dormitory building lived several dozen families of workers from the iron-alloy plant. Each family, including those with one or two children, was allocated one room of about seventy square feet. There was one kitchen for each floor, one toilet and one shower for each block of four rooms—in other words, to be shared by four families.

In the previous year, when the first floor was in a state of crisis because everything was falling apart, the administration of the plant took a revolutionary step. It decided to lease it to people who would repair and maintain it by themselves. These daredevils were a young couple, Polat and Bataghoz Urambesimov. Zakiya had no idea how they communicated with the plant administration, nor what kind of agreement they had signed. The only information she had was that one of them worked as a doctor. Or, possibly, both of them. And because doctors, nurses, and other medical workers belong to one of the lowest-income professions in the U.S.S.R., it is quite understandable that such a couple would decide to run a hotel on top of their primary jobs. After enduring several months of trouble with the repairs, Polat and Bataghoz had finally re-equipped some rooms and rented twenty bunks at rates comparable to those at state hotels. Even the numerous insolent cockroaches could be neglected, for in the long run they were just another element of the environment. The only thing that depressed me was the sharp smell of chlorine bleach, which literally paralyzed the breath and burned the eyes. According to the sanitation inspector's request, all toilets and shower rooms had to be profusely dusted with chlorine powder. Probably the leasers had not accumulated enough money to bribe the regional sanitation inspector, and so had to comply with this rule.

"So, what were you arguing about?" I asked again, eating the homemade noodle and vegetable soup that the hospitable Zakiya had warmed up for me on the electric cooker.

"Sveta is jealous because I get paid in two places," Zakiya explained to me. "My principal job is guard here at the dormitory, you know, and she is my boss. My responsibilities are quite simple: I sit at the door and turn away strangers. But Urambesimov's inn is on the first floor. So Polat and Bataghoz suggested that I could register their guests and hand out room keys, so as not to hire another person to sit here. Of course, I agreed. And Sveta is enraged about it. But I have a right to combine jobs according to the law. Moreover, I do not have to leave my post—I just sit and ask to see entrance cards and hand out keys. But you know it's hard to argue with the bosses. Sveta wants to sack me, no matter what, and therefore raises some kind of hell twice a day. But if I lose this job, who will look after my grandchildren? So, I tell her: 'Just try to sack me! I'll go all the way to Gorbachev himself! Are you against perestroika or what? Are you against the guidelines of our dear Communist Party?'"

Zakiya and I laughed.

Liberman had softened somewhat by evening, and seeing that I was not going to fight, he relaxed completely. After we met at the entrance of our former hotel, we went to the Damolis. The car was running again and, according to Liberman, it could make the distance to Togliatti without a problem. He intended to get a new oil pump there, after which he could go back to his family in Novocheboksarsk. In giving him money for the return trip and for an oil pump I was indirectly giving my consent to discontinue our contract. But I couldn't afford to completely break off our relationship since, after I returned to Moscow, I couldn't do without an auto mechanic. There was an extreme shortage of them, just like everything else. Besides, no matter what, Vova was one of the best of that breed and, undoubtedly, the most honest.

After he saw what kind of hotel I had found, Liberman soured again. It was almost evening, and there was no prospect of any kind of entertainment. The only choice was to walk the streets and find some-one to pick a fight with. But this sort of sport attracted neither Liber-man nor me.

A new leg of my journey was to begin tomorrow, and I wanted to have a good night's sleep. However, I did not succeed, because at about two o'clock in the morning I was awakened by the wild groans of Liberman.

"I'm going blind! I'm dying!" he cried in despair, as if it really were the last moment of his life. When I turned on the light, a grotesque vision met my eyes. Liberman's face was monstrously swollen, and tears were pouring from his eyes. He was sitting on the edge of his bed, swinging his body back and forth, and his hands were moving crazily in the air. Cockroaches! He had been bitten by flying cockroaches! The awful thought flashed through my mind, but I gave that up at once.

"Vova, you have an allergy!" I said, rushing to him. "This is from the chlorine bleach, the gas, and the smell of a foreign land. What a dreadful combination! Let's go outdoors at once. You need to wash and recover your breath. It will go away: don't worry, you won't go blind."

"I can't walk! I can't see anything!" Liberman was convulsively sobbing and groaning while I carried him on my back like a fireman.

At last we got to the street. The night was cold, and there were a hundred times more stars in the sky than in Moscow. Leaving Liberman on a bench, I ran to the dormitory to fetch some boiled water I had providently left in a big electric kettle, borrowed that evening from Zakiya.

"Well, Vova, let's wash ourselves," I said to Liberman as people speak to sick children. "Look, there is some clean water. Bend down lower, so you won't splash yourself."

I left him to recover in the fresh air and went to gather up our things. So it was settled. I would go by train to Aralsk, and there I would see what happened. I was desperate to get out of Aktyubinsk as soon as possible.

At dawn he brought me to the railroad station and went to Novocheboksarsk. Good-bye, Vova Liberman, unsuccessful lover of Asiatic exotics, Mozart of auto service, and fine family man. God bless you and all your remarkable family.

Despite the early hour, Aktyubinsk's railroad station was noisy and full of people, recalling the crowd scenes from Soviet movies about the Civil War of 1918. Even several computer games, installed in the waiting room by some cooperative businessmen (it would be interesting to know how much they pay the authorities and how much they pay the racketeers for allowing them to do this), did very little to make the scene seem more contemporary.

At the ticket office, I was told that there were no available tickets for the next train to Aralsk. That in no way meant that there were really no tickets.

I went out to the platform to wait for the train. It was supposed to come at 4:59 A.M., but it was half an hour late. More than half the people in the crowd waiting for the train were, like me, hopeful stowaways. The main thing is to choose a sympathetic conductor and to strike the right chord with him. My train would stop in Aktyubinsk for ten or fifteen minutes, which was more than enough time to find a compliant conductor.

In an hour I was lying on the top berth of a stuffy four-berth compartment of an express train, mulling over my plans for the future. Having parted with Liberman, and temporarily left without a car, I could of course have stayed another week in the cockroach-infested, chlorine-poisoned Damolis, on the outskirts of Aktyubinsk, sipping kindhearted Zakiya's homemade noodle soup. During that time I could try to find a car going to Aralsk and hitch a ride. But judging by the information that had influenced Liberman so deeply that he deserted me, I would likely not succeed in this. That damned span of unpaved road between Khrom-Tau and Aralsk had always enjoyed the same reputation as the Bermuda Triangle, and now, because of armed robbery on the roads, the area had become completely devastated and depopulated.

I swore and turned to the wall. What was to be done, then? In the majority of countries in the world cars can be rented. But in the U.S.S.R., with its ruined economy and overall deficit, it is impossible even to think about that. It is true that in some big cities there are places where one can get a car. But there are three important conditions: they are foreign cars, they must be paid for in hard currency, and they are rented exclusively to foreigners. Two of the three points were clearly dangerous; I have already explained that driving a foreign car was to court disaster, and that having hard currency in hand was a crime for a Soviet citizen at that time. In any case, even if I were a citizen of the Ivory Coast, with piles of cash, desiring to rent a Mercedes, it would have been impossible in Kazakhstan at the end of May 1990, for no such services existed.

Suddenly I noticed the aroma of pilaf, which was coming through the crevices in the door, which creaked to the accompaniment of the wheels. Was somebody really cooking somewhere nearby or was it just a hallucination? I got up and went out into the corridor. Several men were standing by the open windows, and they looked at me with curiosity. They were on the train for the second day, and they were totally bored with the sight of the deserted steppe outside the window. "I smell pilaf!" I said to the guy standing closest to me in the corridor.

"Ah! It's the conductor, cooking down the hall!" he said, laughing cheerfully. "He'll sell it. But there won't be enough for everyone!"

And he laughed again. He was about forty years old, and despite the hot weather he was dressed in a crumpled, light brown polyester suit, a synthetic shirt, and a necktie which seemed to have been tied when it was manufactured, once and for all. He wore only sandals on his bare feet. I smiled back at him, politely but with some concern.

Most of all I wanted to eat and then to fall into bed. I could have done the same things in reverse order, but then I risked missing the pilaf.

In the train carriages built by East Germany for the U.S.S.R., there is a small coal oven, used to boil tea, which is installed in the corridor next to the guide's compartment. The conductors from Central Asia cook their pilafs there, violating all rules and regulations, but feeding those passengers who can afford their prices. When I walked into the conductor's compartment, I cried to him in Uzbek: *"Ergash-aka! Biza'am oshdan yeilyu?"* ("Uncle Ergash, would it be possible for the likes of us to try your cooking?").

"Albatta, Maratzhon!" ("Sure, Marat-soul!"), he said agreeably. My Tashkent dialect had won his sympathy as far back as the platform of the railroad station in Aktyubinsk. While we were negotiating, I got to know that he had worked for twenty-five years as a conductor, and had raised four children. Naturally, his miserable salary was not his only income. The majority of conductors carry on what is categorized in Soviet law as petty speculation. In fact, it is merely the same occupation that merchants, leading their caravans laden with goods, were engaged in for centuries. That is, they bought goods where they were available and brought them to where they were needed. Until recently, when Moscow was still "a model Communist city," and supplies in Moscow were the best in the country, it was really possible to buy something there and sell it at the numerous train stations along the way to Tashkent. But if Ergash's ancestors were bringing silk from China to Europe, now they had to buy cheap candies by the ton in Moscow and sell them in Uzbekistan, where they were in a constant state of deficit. In keeping with Uzbek customs, they are distributed in great numbers during such events as marriages, circumcisions, or wakes, where hundreds or sometimes thousands of people gather.

At this point we were rushing along the Kazakh steppe in a train consisting of a dozen old carriages with the air-conditioning out of order, dirty bathrooms, loose doors, and shabby berths. To say nothing of the thieves den-cum-restaurant, and the train's radio station, which, in railroad newspeak, was broadcasting for the twenty-fifth time that day the rules of behavior for passengers. "And now, respectable citizen-passengers, listen please to the Moscow deputy procurator of transport speaking on the topic 'Sobriety is the Norm of

Life for Every Soviet Passenger,'" said the unctuous female voice, against the background of a military march. It seemed she was a reasonable woman, aware of the stupidity of what she was saying.

"In trains, such behavior as the consumption of alcoholic beverages, which is incompatible with the moral code of the builders of Communism, is absolutely intolerable." With these words the deputy procurator of transport began his talk; I fell asleep immediately, and woke up half an hour later, when Ergash-aka brought a large plate of pilaf to me in my compartment.

12

On the Coast of the Perishing Sea

I was the only passenger in a four-berth compartment, but people could board at any upcoming station. My berth seemed to be one of those places that the conductors keep for stowaways, or "unofficial" passengers, who pay them under the table because tickets are unavailable at ticket offices. This practice entails a certain risk, as trains are checked periodically by teams of inspectors. But it was clear that Ergash, who had worked as a conductor for more than a quarter century, could take care of them.

I went out into the corridor. A middle-aged woman with small pockmarks on her tanned face was standing by an open window. I started a conversation with her. It turned out that she was a German named Catherine from Kazakhstan who worked as a biologist on a wildlife preserve on an island in the northern part of the Aral Sea. The management of the preserve was in Aralsk, about one hundred and fifty miles from the island, which bore the name Barsa-Kel'mes.

"I can't believe it!" I exclaimed. "Is it really the legendary island of Barsa-Kel'mes, about which I have heard so many strange stories since I was a child?"

Translating from Kazakh, Barsa-Kel'mes means "If you go there, you don't come back." Most people believe it got this name because

of rumors that there was a hospital for lepers on the island. My interlocutor just shrugged her shoulders and smiled vaguely.

"The island is easily visible from the coast. Long, long ago, before
Russians conquered Turkestan, several Kazakh families, fleeing from
intertribal feuds, decided to seek shelter on this island. Driving their
cattle before them, they moved to this island in winter, when the bay
was covered with ice. The temperature there sometimes drops to
minus thirty [Centigrade; more than –20 Fahrenheit], so the ice is
rather firm. They survived the winter, so they decided to stay for the
summer, too. And in summer the temperature rises to forty degrees
[over a hundred degrees Fahrenheit]."

"And they were stranded without drinking water?"

"Yes. The reservoirs were filled with water from melted snow, but
when they dried up, everyone perished, people and cattle alike."

"That's an awful death—to die from thirst, when one is surrounded
by a sea of salt water. And they could probably see the coast of the
mainland..."

"But the island was actually discovered in 1848, by a Russian
expedition there. And do you know who made the first landscape
drawings there?"

"I know." I smiled. "Taras Shevchenko."

"That's right." The biologist was surprised. It was clearly not the
first time she had asked this question about Taras Shevchenko, and
she was not accustomed to people connecting the name of the famous
Ukrainian literary genius of the last century with this semi-legendary
island in the Aral Sea. In good old imperial style, the great poet was
called up for active service and sent to the end of the universe. At that
time, people in Russia were drafted for twenty-five years, so that Taras
Shevchenko came to be on that island for quite a while, and involun-
tarily, not as a world traveler like Lord Byron.

"And what about the leper's hospital?" I asked.

"It's near Kzyl-Orda, about forty kilometers away in a village
called Taldy-Kurgan. I know that there are about two hundred
patients there. In all of Kazakhstan there are about fifteen hundred
lepers. However, these statistics are not available to the public. Treatment is mandatory; therefore, the patients actually try to hide on the
islands in the Aral Sea. Unfortunately, this disease is still not complete-

ly understood: it is always endemic in certain regions and never occurs in others."

"What about the children of patients?"

"The children are born healthy, but then they become infected by their parents. Therefore, immediately after birth, they are taken away to an orphanage."

I talked to Catherine for about an hour and learned a lot of other interesting things. It turned out that Central Asia and Kazakhstan are regarded as one not only by the national separatists that the Kremlin is so afraid of, but also from the standpoint of physical geography as well. That science, indifferent to social cataclysms, treats this area as if it were a separate continent, which stands apart in the central part of Eurasia, far from any oceans and without access to open seas from its rivers. Its territory is more than 1.5 million square miles, 17 percent of the territory of the Soviet Union. According to physico-geographical mapping, this area embraces nine geographical countries and thirty-eight geographical provinces—divisions that have nothing to do with the usual administrative-political divisions. If Central Asia and Kazakhstan are represented on today's political map by five Union republics (Kazakhstan, Uzbekistan, Tadzhikistan, Kirgizia, and Turkmenistan), the geologists and biologists still refer to this area as Turkestan, which may be translated as the land of Turks (or Turkic peoples). Among the indigenous population of this area, only Tadzhiks and some small nationalities of mountainous Badakhshan are not Turkic; they have their roots in ancient Persia.

Another interesting thing is that until recently Kazakhs were called Kirghiz-Kaisaks, in contrast to the Kirghiz themselves, who were called Kara-Kirghiz, *i.e.*, black Kirghiz. Both groups are nomad Turks, the difference between them being that the Kirghiz encampments were situated in the Tai Shan mountains and valleys, while Kazakhs wandered mainly along the spacious plains of Central Asia, which in medieval manuscripts were called Deshti-Kipchak, the Kipchak Steppes.

Our peaceful conversation was interrupted by some noise from the adjoining compartment. Although all of my previous life experience in the Soviet Union would urge me to pretend that nothing was happening, I did not follow the wise example of the biologist Bauer, who excused herself and returned to her berth, leaving the corridor empty.

In the neighboring compartment were three young women. A young Kazakh man of about twenty was with them. Probably they were students from Aktyubinsk, headed for a weekend home, to Chelkar or maybe Shillikty. Our car was next to a dining car, and crowds of disheveled demobilized soldiers, who had not been completely sober from the moment they embarked on the train, were strutting along the corridor. Three of them, who had probably been without the company of women for a long time, spotted the students through the open door, and broke into the compartment without invitation.

According to the law of compulsory military service, all males have to serve in the army from the age of eighteen. The culture of the military barracks is known for its extreme cruelty, since all the "relations not covered by service regulations" are traditionally based on the violence of "old servicemen"—soldiers in their second year—toward first-year recruits. The barracks code orders the "greenhorns" or "pricks" to endure all oppression silently, and then in their second year they in turn may vent their anger on the newcomers. This kind of thing, which plagues the army, is called *dedovshchina*, the rule of old servicemen, literally grandfathers. From a sociologist's viewpoint, it is a clear case of the reproduction of criminality, the same that governs Soviet jails and labor camps.

The bewildered women at first tried to make fun of the whole situation. But the uninvited guests had quite serious intentions. The young Kazakh fellow, who was at first discouraged by the onslaught of the enemy forces, finally took heart, cleared his throat, and suggested to the intruders that they leave the compartment.

"What did you say, louse?" said the former glorious defenders of the motherland, rejoicing. "Let's go out to the end of the car!"

"He's not going anywhere!" said the women, really frightened. They knew that the demobs would not likely force themselves on them in earnest. The drunks would swagger, paw them a little, perhaps hit them a few times, and in the worst case vomit and piss in the compartment. But if they dragged their friend to the platform, he would really get hurt.

"What kind of a guy are you, if you hide yourself behind women's skirts!" said the drunks, egging the poor lad on, relishing their sadistic entertainment by prolonging it. "It's clear that you didn't serve in the army!"

"Okay, let's go!" said the student, in whom the heart of his nomad ancestors had leaped up, making him change his mind, to the surprise of his attackers.

The whole group—the victim, red from tension, and his young executioners with sly smirks on their drunken faces, resolutely walked in a procession past me down the corridor, leaving after them a reeking wave of wine and tobacco, mixed with the smell of leather and boot polish—and, perhaps, also of the blood they anticipated. They were lurching along toward the end of the car, occasionally catching its walls to keep their balance. They seemed to be just a normal company of drunken friends, returning to their compartment from the dining car. Recalling my adventure in Cheboksary, I turned to the open window with an indifferent air, but at the last moment I could not help following them with my eyes. Just at that moment the student opened the door at the end of the car and looked back. His face expressed such despair and terror that my heart sank. Our eyes met and a shadow of hope passed across his face. The demob behind him shoved him angrily, then the others got there, too, and the door closed after them.

Swearing and cursing myself for my feelings of faintheartedness, I ran to the door and flung it open as hard as I could. As I had planned, the unexpected blow from the heavy door had thrown the man who was standing behind it to the wall. Fortunately, it was one of the executioners.

"Sorry," I said, walking in and pretending that I had no idea what was going on, while I hit, as if by chance, one of the demobs, who was standing behind me, in the solar plexus with my elbow. To the victim I said, "Your friends asked you to return to the compartment."

"I'll be right back," he replied, and suddenly hit the stomach of one of his tormentors, who groaned with pain and bent down. "Come on, come on!" I said, hurrying the student, shivering in a sudden fit of rage, and we left. He silently shook my hand and retreated to his compartment, where the women surrounded their hero. Fifteen minutes later, when the train arrived at the Chelkar station, all four of them got off, and disappeared into the hot haze of the Aral outskirts.

I had to move to another car, as the ensuing course of events could easily be predicted. The demobs would come to their senses, call for assistance from their friends, and return for revenge. And I would not be likely to catch someone's compassionate gaze in the empty corridor.

"Well, all right, let's suppose that Gorbachev will really renounce the Russian imperial idea and try to carry out a transition to a federation, or even a confederation," said Zhankuzha Aliev. Like many other Kazakhs he spoke Russian without any accent. He drank one glass of black tea after another, without pleasure. Kazakhs like to add hot milk to their tea, but where can one get hot milk on a passenger train, lost somewhere on the boundless steppe?

"Oh, sure, and who in the Kremlin is going to let him renounce the imperial idea!" Shinali Baidil'daev interrupted, pouring me more tea from a teapot with a broken spout, which was state property. "Russia has governed us for so long that it is easier for Moscow to replace the General Secretary than to get out of the habit of owning one-sixth of the earth's surface."

In Soviet trains people always drink tea from glasses in glass-holders (a nineteenth-century tradition) and have endless conversations about life, politics, and family problems.

I had found asylum in Zhankuzha and Shinali's compartment, in the farthest car from the one where the skirmish with the demobs had taken place. My companions were middle-aged, young-looking Kazakhs, who, despite the heat, wore suits, neckties, and green felt hats. "What a strange predilection for official clothes they have in this area," I thought, tucking my black T-shirt into my jeans. When we introduced ourselves I found out that my new acquaintances were high school principals, one of them a director and the other his deputy. When I told them that I was from Moscow, they started interrogating me about the future state structures of the Soviet Union.

"My knowledge is your knowledge," I could only answer, quoting an Arabic proverb, which meant that I knew no more about the future of the country than they—or Gorbachev. "Federalism, with its divisions between the ethnic republics, is one of the major shortcomings of our state," I continued, pouring oil on the fire. "The division of the country into national republics was an awful mistake."

"What?" The Kazakhs expressed their indignation simultaneously. Like the majority of the intelligentsia in Kazakhstan and Central Asia, they adhered to a moderate point of view, that the national republic must be turned from a colony into a "sovereign national state," yet remain part of the Soviet Union.

"In genuinely civilized societies," I continued, "the interests of the citizen are held above the interests of the nation. So long as we live in a state, what difference does it make to which ethnic group each of us belongs? I would say that a nation has no higher interest."

"But the right of republics to self-determination is written in all our constitutions: Lenin's, Stalin's, and even in Brezhnev's constitution!" Shinali exclaimed, becoming impassioned. He taught history and political theory (*obshestvovedeniye*—literally, "the science of society").

"And so what if it is written there," I rejoined with a Muscovite's cynicism. "It's just a slogan, isn't it? A usual bit of Soviet showing off? There are many other multinational states in the world besides ours, but nowhere is it written in their constitutions that ethnic groups living there have the right to secede and proclaim their own states. Because all this can only lead to bloodshed. But it would never have occurred to the founding fathers of our state that the day would come when almost all of the national minorities in the country would demand in earnest to realize their 'right to self-determination up to complete separation.'"

"Well, yes, our bosses are used to the fact that laws written on paper have nothing to do with reality," wise Zhankuzha agreed with me cautiously.

"Does it follow, then, in your opinion, that national movements are altogether negative phenomena?" asked Shinali, trying to corner me. He had intuited my spontaneous cosmopolitanism, something it is better not to disclose in our country. For Communists and nationalists, cosmopolitanism stands out as a dreadful ideological infection, a kind of political AIDS. It is not for nothing that all Soviet emigrants are still widely (although now not officially) talked of as "traitors" and "betrayers of their motherland."

"Are you talking about nationalism?" I asked again, pondering the answer. "If you ask me whether nationalism might be used as a means of destroying empires or doing away with dependency on the center, the answer is yes. But just picture nationalism unleashed in our country. It would bring about nothing but social despair. And, okay, what comes next, after the big blast? No one ever succeeded in creating a democratic civil society in a state based on ethnic principles. Look at Lebanon, Sri Lanka, India, Ethiopia, if examples from our own country do not suffice."

"What do you suggest then?" Zhankuzha asked.

"Let the Kazakh nation die!" Shinali answered for me.

"If we are talking about Kazakhstan only, why do you think that only Kazakhs are dying? What about all the others? Are they in a better situation?" I was growing angry. "And why do you think that your 'own' Kazakh national partocracy oppress and exploit less than non-Kazakhs? What if they do it to a greater extent than Russian party bosses?"

"Yes, he is right, regionalism, paternalism, connections between relatives and members of a clan still play a great role in this area," Zhankuzha said placatingly, patting Shinali and me on the shoulders. And then he added in Kazakh: "Don't get too excited, Shinali, we don't know who this person is; maybe he is from the TV show 'Vzglyad' ('Glance'). One guy on their staff looks exactly like him."

"It's not me," I said in Kazakh, with an Uzbek accent, and my interlocutors started smiling, caught by surprise.

"Oh, you speak our language," Zhankuzha said with an exaggerated jubilation in his voice. "What is your nationality?"

"I'm Tartar," I said gloomily. If I told them that nationality, unlike ethnicity, is just a social acquisition, they would probably fight me again.

After a long pause, Shinali asked me, "Have you heard that two fictitious hospitals were discovered in Taldy-Kurgan?"

"I have heard about fictitious diplomas for doctors," I said, bewildered. "I have also heard about people giving bribes to enter a medical college, but fictitious hospitals are something new."

"Well, there's a region called Akakul, right, Zhankuzha?" Shinali turned to his friend for confirmation. "All the former authorities in this region were corrupted."

For ten years there existed on paper, according to fictitious documents, two hospitals, complete with staff, wages, material, and financial expenditure. But in fact, there was nothing, no hospitals. And the party bosses got all the money through their stooges."

I turned to Zhankuzha in disbelief and asked, "Is it really so?"

"Oh, yeah," said Zhankuzha, "there was a whole mafia down there." All of them were connected, the whole gang. There was a lot of noise around the republic. Even an attempt at one of the local mafiosi. His name, it seems to me, was Seurbayev. He was the director of a *sovkhoz* [government-owned farm], and his accounts were in bad order because he stole too much. Probably the mafia decided to ditch him so that word wouldn't get out."

"Who will saw at the branch on which he's sitting?" Shinali said, smiling joylessly. "If you pull a rope, Allah only knows what's on the other end!"

We started to talk about traveling abroad. "In America there are quite a few noncommercial and public organizations interested in Soviet life," I said. "It's also true, of course, that Moscow has been palming off some phony peace activists, who were mainly KGB agents and wives and children of high officials from the *nomenklatura*. In Moscow, you know, there is a whole Ministry of the Struggle for Peace, on Prospect Mira, Peace Avenue. It's called the Soviet Peace Committee, and it's a state-funded organization. Naïve old ladies from America have taken it to be a popular organization. But times change, and you have a real chance to collect a group of people and go with them to that very same America. And then invite back here those people who invited you."

"Huh, do you think that our *obkom*, our Province Party Committee, would ever allow us to invite them?" Zhankuzha shook his head in grief.

"Don't ask them, then." I gave some silly advice.

"Are you a Martian or what?" Shinali was annoyed. "They would sack him at once for doing that."

"What does the *obkom* have to do with your school?" I asked, a bit disingenuously.

"Perhaps in your Moscow it has nothing to do with schools," Zhankuzha sighed, "but here everything is still just as it was before. By the way, I am a member of the bureau of the regional Party Committee myself."

After rummaging around in my notebook, I found the address of an American organization called Beyond War. Two years ago, as the editor of a Soviet-American poetry anthology called *Double Rainbow*, I was invited—it seemed by mistake—to take part, with my wife, in a Soviet-American peace cruise on the Volga River. Before that I had never taken part in such a thing, but a friend of mine was a member of the organizing committee, and he was the one who got me the invitation. The tickets were fairly cheap, but without his help we would not have had access to this remarkable spectacle, for it was completely closed to ordinary people. By Soviet standards, this was a tourist cruise of the highest class. To be sure, it had nothing to do with the peace movement, for at least on the Soviet side the delegation consisted of the kind of people that I mentioned before. But the Americans were not ringers; they were quite real, and they came from all corners of the United States. Among them was one delightful and very energetic older woman from Los Angeles named Flora Murai, who especially attracted our attention. She was an activist of Beyond War, whose address I gave to the astonished Zhankuzha and Shinali.

"Write them a letter," I said. "Just don't lie about anything. They are good and credulous people. And very benign."

"We're getting close to Aralsk," Zhankuzha informed me, having written down the address accurately in his notebook. We looked out the open window. The windows in Soviet train compartments are supposed to be closed for the air-conditioning, but the air-conditioning is never turned on: either it is broken, or, if it does work, the conductors will not turn it on for reasons of economy. But because Zhankuzha and Shinali served in a boarding school for children of railroad personnel, the conductor allowed the window to stay open. He opened it with a special key that fits all windows and doors in the train.

"And in what language shall we write this letter?" Shinali asked.

Then the door opened with a jerk, sliding along its grooves, and a couple of familiar faces poked inside.

"Here he is!" yelled one of them joyfully, as if he had found his brother after a long separation.

I jerked the sliding door closed, almost cutting off the head of the bawler. I locked the door and looked at flabbergasted Zhankuzha and Shinali. The attackers started kicking and tapping on the door. A woman in the corridor started yelling.

"Write the letter in English. I think I will leave," I said, trying to remain calm. "Help me get out the window!"

"Where do you think you're going? What are you doing! The train hasn't stopped yet!" My new acquaintances grew fearful, but I did not listen to them. I stood on the table under the window, threw my bag, zipped and locked, outside, and then crawled through the window myself, groaning and swearing. The train was approaching the station, very slowly. After hanging outside a couple of seconds by my hands and getting my jacket covered with soot from the dirty side of the train, I unclenched my fingers and jumped, managing not to break anything.

I had to pick my bag up rather hastily, lest it be chewed by a shabby, two-humped camel watching me curiously from his enclosure near the tracks.

It might be said that I had safely reached the coast of the Aral Sea. Once, in my childhood, I was there with my father, and one of my brightest memories of that time is of huge smoked fishes the size of human beings hanging from huge hooks like those used in the Inquisition. Now there is no fish and no sea here. What is left of the sea has rolled back more than sixty miles from its former coastline, leaving souvenirs of itself—rusted structures of fishing trawlers, the wooden corpses of boats—scattered across the desert. The sea is dying, and the reason for it is predatory man. Or, to be more precise, the Communist state, which has treated nature as inhumanly as it has treated its own citizens.

I had to decide what to do. Best of all would be to try to move eastward to Kzyl-Orda, where lived some relative of a friend of mine, the famous poet and playwright Iranbek Orazbaev. Along the railroad there were some shacks where people lived from birth to death. The light smoke of *kiz'yak,* pressed dung, was coming out of the chimneys in curves. Barefoot children were strolling in wire-enclosed yards, and hens and dogs were peacefully coexisting with the children. At the curb stood a truck with wooden sides, and several rams, resigned to their fate, were crowded onto its bed. Judging by their sad faces, they knew that soon they would be eaten. A Kazakh driver went out of the house and headed for the cabin of the truck.

"Hi!" I said, coming closer. "Will you give me a lift to Aralsk?"

"And where do you need to go?" he asked, taking my measure from head to foot. Hitchhikers in our country look suspicious.

"To the bus station," I said and made a vague gesture with my hand, which could signify either the supposed direction of the trip, or a careless attempt to check my hair, or a desire to drive away a fly, since hosts of them were swarming in the beams of the evening sun.

"Will you pay me five rubles?" the driver said with a frown.

"Three!" I replied, not to arouse suspicions.

"Well, get into the back!"

I stood on the wheel and threw my bag inside, and then stepped over the side of the truck. The rams bleated with disapproval and crowded to the opposite side. The driver finished his cigarette, exhaled smoke through his iron front teeth, and spat. Then after looking critically at me and the rams, he said resolutely, "Okay, get in the cab."

We did not drive together for very long, but because of his tense silence the road did not seem to me to go by very quickly. The driver kept looking at me askance, trying to understand who I was and what evil spirit had brought me to this place. I was also looking at him tentatively time and again, trying to decide whether it was worth my while to start a conversation with this gloomy fellow. At last he coughed and grunted inquiringly:

"Are you from Alma-Ata or what?"

I said no, and he immediately lost all interest in conversation. It seemed he was not interested in anything that happened outside Kazakhstan. There are many people on this planet who are not interested in what goes on outside the confines of their states.

13

Disposable World

He drove me to the bus station, and after about three hours on the tour bus, I reached Kazalinsk, covering another ninety miles of my journey. I sat next to an ordinary-looking man in a dark crumpled suit with a checked cotton shirt that used to be red. Or maybe purple. I could not see his feet, but he must have worn the inevitable worn-down sandals that most Soviet men wore in dry weather. Only his lively, roguish eyes and the complete absence of a decorum that would have befitted his age betrayed that all was not as simple as it seemed. Kazakhs highly value portliness and pompous dignity in a man over forty, but my seatmate, though he looked to be in his early fifties, was as scrawny and cocky as a teenager. The latter quality, how-ever, could be explained by the fact that he was drunk.

Suddenly my seatmate laughed so loudly that he startled the other passengers, and the bus driver almost drove into a ditch.

"I am an *akyn*," he said proudly. "Do you know what that means"?

"I know," I answered. "'*Akyn*' means improvisational poet, a storyteller. And in general, beloved of the gods."

"Eh, well done," he said, approving of my definition of *akyns*. "What's your name?"

We introduced ourselves. His name was Esenbai.

"And where is your *dombra* [fiddle]?" I joked.

"At home," he said with a laugh. "And how do you know? You are a dangerous man! You know too much."

"No need to exaggerate," I said with a satisfied smile. "I am interested in Kazakhstan, that's all. In 1985 in Moscow I published a collection of poems called *Sunlight on the Steppe*. It contained verses by Russian poets about Kazakhstan and works of Kazakh poets and *akyns* about Russia."

"Was Abai in your book?" asked Esenbai.

"Of course," I assured him.

For Kazakhs, Abai, son of Kunanbai, held the position occupied by Pushkin for Russians, or Goethe for Germans, or Walt Whitman for Americans. In our country literature has always been seen as a state matter; therefore, the state always treated prose writers and poets far more seriously than lawyers or dentists. In Kazakhstan many city streets were named after Abai, as well as schools, theaters, and libraries. After all, he was lucky—he managed to die a natural death, not in a concentration camp, like many of his followers and students.

"But didn't you know that he died on his birthday, precisely where he was born?" asked Esenbai, as if guessing what I was thinking.

"No," I said, astonished. "Is that really true?"

"The day he died he turned fifty-nine," said Esenbai. "Now there is a nuclear test site there. Every time an explosion underground is heard, the birds sitting on his tomb take wing with cries of alarm. But who hears them in Moscow?"

"Well, why," I asked uncertainly, "do they write about the Semipalatinsk testing ground so often in the newspapers?" Previously, before glasnost, it had never occurred to me that in Kazakhstan's province of Semipalatinsk twenty thousand Hiroshima-size bombs were exploded!

Esenbai looked gloomy. "They say that Abai foresaw the dreadful future of the ancient pastures of his tribe when he died," he said. "Do you know that he died from drugs?"

"No!" I answered, amazed. This in no way correlated with the stereotypical image of the death of a great poet. Duel, exile, insane asylum, transfer to a job in the party apparatus—any of those makes sense. But to die from drugs? It seemed to me that only poets and musicians of the beat or the hippie generations could allow that to happen, not a Kazakh writer canonized by the Soviet state.

"Both him and his sons." Esenbai nodded his head. "At first they played around, then they died."

"What did they use?" I asked. I knew that people in Central Asia smoke marijuana. In the local lingo it is called *plan,* and people who are addicted to it are called *planakesh.*

"They were drinking an infusion of poppy stems," Esenbai explained. "*Kok-nar,* as we call it. Have you tried it?"

"No. Interesting idea. But where did they get it?"

"What do you mean, where?" He was in turn surprised. "Dealers brought it in from Sinkiang. At first they gave it to them to try, then they began to sell it. And then the Russians closed the border with China, and caravans were stopped. But for Abai and his sons, withdrawal had begun, and they died. But they had everything—fame, wealth, and universal love—what more could they want?"

"So who is guilty of their death?" I asked, remembering the paranoid talk of Russian chauvinists about the Yid-Mason conspiracy against Russian culture. Maybe the Kazakhs also think that there is a conspiracy against them? "Tell me, Esenbai, who is guilty in the death of Abai and his sons? Kashgar dealers, the lords of the narcobusiness? Or the Russian Cossacks who closed the border?"

By the time we reached Kazalinsk, it was quite late. Knowing that I had no place to stay, Esenbai proposed that I spend the night at his friend's house. It turned out that he himself was here on some kind of business, which he did not think necessary to discuss in detail.

"It's not right to come without an invitation," I said. "Maybe it would be better to call him first?"

"Call?" Esenbai roared with laughter, scaring half to death a stray dog that was tagging along behind us. "What do you think, that we are going to the home of the regional party secretary? There are so few phones here that the numbers usually have only three digits."

"Right," I said tiredly. "Well, then, let's go."

The friend in fact turned out to be a sweet young woman by the name of Rosa. She could have been the daughter of the *akyn,* but in fact she was his beloved. I was startled by the joy that sparkled in her black, narrow eyes when she saw Esenbai. That whole evening she did not take her devoted gaze from him, only rarely looking proudly in my direction, as if offering to share her admiration for the poet who for her pushed the whole world into the background. For them absolutely nothing mattered—what political party was in power, or what millennium was occurring outside their door. By Western or even by Muscovite standards they were horribly dressed. The food they ate was harmful to their health. There was no water in the house, and the toilet was outside in a cesspool. But for them all this had no significance. Something else filled their harsh existence with meaning. The human spirit triumphed over their dark everyday life, even if only for the moment. For the first time since Cheboksary, I thought that to be born a man was perhaps not so bad.

We slept on the floor in different corners of the room, and I hope that my powerful snore did not disturb the lovers very much. When I awoke, Rosa was already gone, and the half-dressed Esenbai, smiling, was sitting on a thick piece of felt at a low table, eating *kazy,* a sort of colt sausage, and drinking his tea with milk. Rosa probably bought *kazy* at the bazaar, or perhaps her relatives sent it from the village.

"Come and eat breakfast," he invited.

"Right away," I said and walked out to the yard.

On the outside of the doorway hung a washstand. Under it stood an empty garbage bucket. Making my hands into a ladle, I washed myself and wiped dry with a handkerchief. Sparrows chirped on the fence, and the sun already shone summer-hot. I needed to stay here for a long time or quickly go on my way.

When we had eaten breakfast, Rosa returned. She was wearing a deep-blue dress with white polka dots and a white scarf on her head. According to Kazakh custom, only unmarried girls could walk around with their heads uncovered. In daylight she was as beautiful as the night before. It seemed to me that even the fastidious Liberman would approve of the absence on her fresh face of cosmetics.

As I understood it, Rosa worked as a nurse in the registry of a children's clinic. Someone from her work planned to go by car to Dzhusaly, and she made arrangements for them to take me with them.

"For money," she said, obviously embarrassed that she could not arrange it for free.

"Well, that's wonderful," I said, rejoicing. "When are they planning to go?"

"In an hour they are stopping by here," Rosa answered. It seemed to me that there was slight irritation in her voice that she had had to waste time conversing with me instead of turning the whole force of her soul to her lover.

"I am going for a walk," I said cheerfully. "Are there any museums here?"

"There are, right next door, on Karl Marx Street," answered Rosa and turned to speak with Esenbai in Kazakh.

The museum, surrounded by old trees, was located in a huge single-story frame house. It was dedicated to a local figure in the Union of Communist Youth, one Gani Muratbaev. It appeared that he was an extremely capable young man. In any case, after the October coup of 1917 he had absolutely dizzying success as a politician, fighting his way up to the highest *nomenklatura* of the country. This proved to be his undoing, because in the thirties, like many powerful people, he was shot, or they killed him somehow in a camp. In the worst traditions of Soviet historical science, the museum maintained complete silence about the circumstances of his arrest and death.

Returning to Rosa's house, I gave the *akyn* a farewell embrace, bid good-bye to the beautiful Rosa, and stepped out onto the street in a very philosophical mood. The car arrived without delay. I greeted the driver, threw my bag into the backseat, and got into the front. It was about two hundred miles to Kzyl-Orda, about five hundred to Chimkent. Only after Chimkent, returning to the road to Alma-Ata, could I finally part with road M-32, as endless as the Great Silk Route itself.

Kairulla Esdavletov, my ride, was too cheerful for a pediatrician. In any case, he created the impression of a man of smiles and gaiety, which in no way matched the subject of our conversation. Looking at the young, round, smiling face of Kairulla, it was difficult to suppose that he seriously grasped what he was talking about. But unfortunately, he was not joking.

"The Aral has died!" he told me when I asked him if there had been any improvement after the U.S.S.R. Council of Ministers passed a resolution about improving the situation around the Aral Sea. "What happens now is agony. Do you think if two dozen old bureaucrats write a memo ordering the sea to live, that it will listen to them?"

"You do not fully appreciate the magic of bureaucratic papers," I retorted. "In our country a piece of paper with a seal on it can influence even the fate of a sea."

"It can destroy it, perhaps, but not heal it," Kairulla said with a shrug of his shoulders.

The car we were in was a Zhiguli, which knocked, squeaked, and choked going uphill, and howled going down, as if pleading with its cruel passengers to change course to the junkyard, where its tired body would find its final resting place, and its soul could await its next incarnation, in a child's toy car or tricycle. But Kairulla paid no attention to its screeching complaints. Perhaps he was professionally accustomed to someone else's pains.

"They ruined the sea a full thirty years ago," I said, "and it could hardly be returned to life sooner than half a century from now."

The story of the death of the Aral Sea is inextricably connected with the sick megalomania of the "builders of Communism" who were obsessed with the idea of "conquering nature." Sometimes it seems to me that even today, the poster that several generations of Soviet people grew accustomed to—"We cannot wait for the favors of nature. It is our task to take them!"—still hangs in our schools. The state invented dozens of methods of perpetrating large-scale violations of nature, but one of the most effective methods of violence was undoubtedly the construction of reservoirs. In this region they needed huge areas in the steppe and desert for cultivation, which, since the end of the fifties, had been planted with cotton crops. For decades Soviet propaganda exalted these so-called handmade seas, which had destructive consequences for the environment fully comparable to the Chernobyl catastrophe.

Into the Aral Sea flow the two largest rivers of Central Asia, the Syr-Darya and the Amu-Darya, which in the works of ancient historians were called the Seikhun and the Dzheikhun. The basins of these rivers, as well as the space between them, became the cradle of several of the most ancient agricultural and herding civilizations in the early history of mankind, including Sogd, Bactria, Khorezm, Chach, Parkan (from the sixth to the fourth centuries B.C.), Tokharistan, Kushan (from the first to the fourth centuries A.D.), the kingdom of Eftalit (from the fifth to the sixth centuries A.D.), the Turkic khanate (from the sixth to the seventh centuries A.D.). Then the Arab invasion occurred in the eighth century A.D. and the Tartar invasion in the thirteenth century. The states flourished, they declined, and they perished; scarcely a century passed without invasions and destructive wars, yet the land remained fertile and the water supply remained plentiful.

Then, in the middle of the twentieth century, when the state dug the "handmade seas," the rivers became shallow, and the sea began to dry up, just like in a fairy tale. The sea withdrew over the course of ten years to a distance of sixty miles! In the space of one generation, the climate had sharply deteriorated. Moreover, salt, rising from thousands of square miles of exposed sea bottom, began to fall on the coastal regions. According to official figures the winds annually disperse from fifty million to eighty million tons of saline dust in the region surrounding the Aral. Agricultural productivity began to fall sharply. In the Soviet system, the party leaders were responsible for the productivity of the regions, provinces and republics. Not wishing to leave their armchairs, they began an uncontrolled increase in the use of chemical fertilizers. As a result, they began to introduce into the soil twenty times more fertilizers than in the country as a whole. You see, the former U.S.S.R. is the champion of the world in the use of chemical pesticides. In Moscow foreign diplomats, journalists, and businessmen are allowed to shop in special stores that sell only imported vegetables, fruits, and greens, for there are too many nitrates in the Soviet products.

Thus the Aral, deprived of its water influx, began to die of thirst. But what about the lands irrigated at its expense? Did the efforts of the transformers of nature benefit these lands? No. The only thing they managed was to turn the healthy soil into a dying drug addict. The soil already could not produce without chemicals, and in order to support productivity, the "dose" had to be increased in an arithmetical progression. But the plan for state purchases of cotton also steadily rose with each passing year. Moscow demanded ever more millions of tons, and the local party bosses willingly doubled and tripled their efforts. "On behalf of the workers" they took on more and more "socialist obligations" and, like extraterrestrial conquerors, pitilessly destroyed the land that until very recently had been considered so fruitful.

Recently an item appeared in the Soviet press, saying that the herbicides used in the cotton fields contain dioxin, the same toxic material in the defoliant Agent Orange, which the American army used in Vietnam. The difference is that Agent Orange was scattered in regions where the enemy was located, while we use it on our own territory, against our unarmed countrymen.

Moscow never tires of reminding the republics that their economic activity as a whole is basically unprofitable. How can it be otherwise with prices for cotton that were established almost in the time of Lenin! My friend Sabit Madaliev somehow calculated that modern state slaves, called Soviet collective farm workers, must strike the cultivated ground 159 times in order to receive for their labor in the broiling sun remuneration equal to one kopeck. In other words, in order to earn one ruble a peasant must raise and lower his hoe, weighing a couple of pounds, almost sixteen thousand times. And he receives for this the equivalent of four cents. That is, for a working day from dawn to dusk the state pays him three rubles, which in current buying power is equal to twelve cents.

"You will see what animals' lips turn into when they eat pasture grass strewn with sea salt," said Kairulla, breaking an extended silence. "Continuously bleeding ulcers."

"And the people?" I asked.

"What people? Do you know that the death rate among adults and children is twice as high as, for instance, in Alma-Ata? Of course, there are illnesses here that you will not find even in Moscow."

"Is there leprosy?" I asked with veiled horror.

"Bubonic plague," answered Kairulla.

"Where do they catch that? This is not the Middle Ages. Well, cholera—that is still here and there. I myself once ran into a cholera quarantine. But where does the plague come from?"

"Ask the top brass in Moscow." Kairulla smiled evilly.

"Are you saying that..."

"That's just the point." He broke off my question.

The day had grown hotter and hotter. Hot air blasted in the open windows of the car, and I wished I could put on a respirator, because this was not the kind of air that can be breathed deeply. But I immediately felt ashamed, thinking of those three million people whose native land surrounded the Aral Sea. Their own government is the agent of their death; every eighth child here is born deformed.

"Is there really nothing that can be done?" I asked not of Kairulla, but of God.

"It is possible," the pediatrician answered with a crooked smile, "that there is only one solution: to drop an atomic bomb on us, to stop the torment."

We parted in Dzhusaly. He refused to take my money, and continued on his way to Zhanakala. After hitchhiking in front of the local marketplace for about forty minutes, I finally managed to stop a passing car and made arrangements that for twenty-five rubles the driver and his friend would take me in their old clunker to Kzyl-Orda. Their names were Akylbai and Mukhtar, and their car was an old Rafik, the Soviet version of the mini-van, with thick metal walls and a solid partition separating the front seat and the remaining space in the vehicle. For a person suffering from claustrophobia, the only place more congenial than the metallic maw of this car would be a bathysphere sunk in the Marianas trench. On top of everything else, it was stifling inside, smelling like moldy rags, urine, and dust. I had no choice, and climbed inside.

I found a seat on a bench along the side of the van's interior, and underneath I stowed my traveling bag, which had aged during these last few days. Across from me sat another passenger, whom Akylbai and Mukhtar had barely mentioned. I figured that the upcoming journey of a hundred miles would take about four hours; I even had hopes of getting to Kzyl-Orda in daylight.

"Greetings!" I said politely, trying in the gloom to see my companion. After the bright daylight, it was as dark there as inside the belly of a whale.

"He is an instrument of Satan!" answered the man with an unpleasant croaking voice.

"Who?" I winced with surprise. But the man was silent. The gloom seemed threatening to me. I felt in my pocket for matches and struck one of them. In its uncertain flickering light an emaciated old man, dressed in a dark robe which looked like a hospital gown, looked at me indifferently from the opposite bench. "Oh, God, a real psycho," I thought, trying to quell my fear and at the same time trying to remember how to behave with insane people.

"While they prepared him, he went through some reincarnations," the old man told me when the match went out. Judging from his monotonous voice, he was not planning to attack me in the next few minutes. Of course, it was possible to knock on the wall and ask Akylbai to stop. Damn them, you would have thought that they would warn me about their other passenger! But the car had already left Dzhusaly, and the prospect of walking back on the deserted road M-32 (and where to spend the night?) was not very attractive. I was getting so angry that at that moment I wanted to attack my fellow passenger and strangle him slightly, just as a warning. That startled me, and I burst out laughing. Why not associate even with a psycho?

"But is he or is he not a genius?" I asked the man across from me, falsifying my voice to imitate his nonexpressive intonation.

"Well, no! Genius, genius," squeaked the old man in the darkness, and then he laughed. Or was it a cough? "He is not simply a genius, but a universal genius...yes! A universal evil genius, but the forces of light did not fully make way for the dark force lodged in him to be manifested."

"Who are we talking about?" If I was to participate in this pastime, I needed to try to understand who it was about. Tamerlane? Napoleon? Lenin? Tutankhamen? Or a water worker from the housing office who did not come when the broken lavatory flooded his neighbors' apartments during the night?

"Who, who! We know who!" The old man again started to giggle violently, and it seemed to me that he threatened me with his finger in the darkness. "But they don't know how to do the most important thing—they did not cut the energy umbilical cord that connected him with the anticosmos. All the great prophets predicted his appearance! He already appeared on the earth several times; he was even born in Russia twice. But the great demonic plan of establishing a world tyranny he must accomplish only in his last appearance!"

I understood that he was not talking about a water worker. It would be interesting to know what this man worked at before his illness. Judging from the planetary scope of his ravings, he could definitely have been in the humanities.

"So you think that the course of world history is directed from somewhere outside of here?" I tried to reorganize our strange exchange into a dialogue.

But none of this, nor any of my subsequent attempts to establish rational contact, had any effect, since the old man did not listen but only spoke. Realizing that he was harmless, I decided not to pay attention to him and tried to focus my thoughts.

The car was going rather fast, bouncing over bumps, its tires squealing on turns. From behind the metallic wall came the voices of Akylbai and Mukhtar, muffled by the straining drone of the engine. Tiring of listening to the monotonous chatter of my neighbor, I began to get sleepy. And then, in that wavering moment between sleep and wakefulness, all at once, as if in a flash of lightning, a picture of the world suddenly opened up to my internal vision, the world that my insane fellow passenger had painstakingly and incomprehensibly tried to describe. Despite its grotesque deformity, it seemed to me surprisingly authentic.

As I understood it, the crazy old man's basic idea was very similar to the bizarre world view of the Russian philosopher Daniel Andreev, who believed that some titanic combat of cosmic forces of good and evil had selected our planet for its battleground. What for us was the history of the earth was for them only an episode in their eons-long struggle. All leaders of the peoples on earth, from King Solomon and the ancient Chinese emperors to Saddam Hussein and President Gorbachev, were not simply people but fully conscious instruments in this struggle. Each of them had passed through several reincarnations, which had prepared them for their predestined participation in the bloody combat for power over humanity. These earthly leaders had entered into communications with the highest demonic forces, which inspire them through their subconscious to fulfill the tasks set for them. They were like pieces in a planetary chess game, charged with the energy of their dark overlords. But unlike chess, the dark forces fought not only with the white ones but also among themselves. Like, for example, Stalin and Hitler.

At the level of cosmic demons, it was a battle of the dark hordes of evil with the still blacker hosts. And human life was ruined in this earthly war, as the more powerful became the forces of evil. But even those forces had freedom of choice. World War II was just such a test, in which the antithesis of Demiurge, sitting on his infernal throne, decided which of the two doctrines, fascism or Communism, would become the basis for enslavement of the entire planet and its subsequent death.

Hitler's doctrine in the eyes of the prince of darkness lost out to the Communist vision, above all because it was nationally and racially limited. That is, if Hitler had been victorious, then his conception of racial supremacy of the Germans over everyone else would have remained an object of abhorrence and disgust for the abject majority of the peoples of the planet. But this meant that they could again unite for battle.

The Communist doctrine is another matter. It seemed at first glance so attractive to many peoples of the earth thanks to its pseudo-science, universality, accessibility, and ethical degradation. The world did not immediately comprehend that in any country where this doc-trine, bathed in blood, is victorious, what unavoidably reigns is hatred, fanaticism, and violence. At first this occurred in Russia, where the dictatorship, proclaimed in the name of a classless society, turned into such a horrific historical drama that even today it is still unclear how to end the insane agony of Russia's body and soul.

"But why Russia, exactly?" I asked with parched mouth the prophet in the hospital gown.

"Don't you know that Christ's mission on earth was interrupted? And Russia was his favorite, and therefore defiled by darkness, deceived earthly sister. He whose name is cursed through the ages grasped her with his tentacles and began to fumble with them far behind her back, trying to grasp other countries on the planet."

It followed that a country profaned by a metahistorical monster gave birth in torment to a new social formation which must become a prototype of universal, absolute tyranny. The Church was crushed, and its place was occupied by the false Church of the New Doctrine. Its demonic character was noted even when they took the brain from the dead body of the first leader and forced the people to bow down before his embalmed body.

I recalled how in the summer of 1956 my younger brother Tahir and I, when we were young children, stood in line for half a day at the mausoleum, where our muddle-headed Muscovite uncle had brought us. He had just been demobilized from the navy. Thousands of the same kind of simpleminded new visitors from the ends of the country crowded in line, wishing to behold the mummified stuffed animal of two Soviet leaders, Lenin and Stalin. One was supposed to worship them for the fact that they brought so many uncountable miseries to their people, and confused tens of millions of people in other countries. But to wait five hours with respectful, pious faces was more than we could do, and my brother and I earnestly competed to see who could eat more ice cream. In my mind are forever combined eleven portions of Eskimo pie on a stick and the frightful two bodies under glass. They were so little that it seemed they belonged not to people, but to dwarfs.

Yes, it was easy to demoralize children, whom it costs nothing to inspire, to teach them that meanness is a heroic deed, inhumanity is heroism, a lie is truth, and war against all humanity is a struggle for peace. The main task of our education was to create a nation of spiritless fanatics, who imagined that they lived in the best state ever created, that its people are more talented and farseeing than all other peoples, that its ideology is the only infallibly true one, and that everyone who thinks otherwise must be pitilessly destroyed.

But the Most High did not abandon us, and therefore the forces of light continued to struggle for human souls with those who tried to eradicate our normal intellect. In love, in family life, in friendship, in everyday life, in our way of life, the human spirit continued to resist, deriving strength from a random glance at the stars, or at a tree, or a flock of migrating birds in the autumn sky, or an inspired human face from some old picture.

And what about those whom the Doctrine irretrievably devastated spiritually? I could ask the prophet. There are tens of millions of such people in our country; for a long time they have made up a majority. Nature for them is dead, and art and literature boring. They understand only vodka, cards, spectator sports, and movies on television. They fear silence, because in silence it is possible to guess about their spiritual poverty. Being alone with themselves is stupefyingly boring for them. And is it not monstrous that it is precisely they who are exalted before humanity, as the model, as the most important class in human history, to whom the future belongs?

They are not to blame, the sad old man could answer me, they themselves do not understand the horror of their situation. But their karma needs to be fought for. Because there are interwoven inspirations of a much larger scale, which pursue much more grandiose goals than a seventy-year zigzag in the history of the country chosen for these fearful experiments.

But he said nothing because his whole body suddenly twisted in wild cataleptic rigidity, and his face was contorted by such an agonizing convulsion that I lost all self-control from horror, and with all my strength I pounded my fists on the partition.

Akylbai immediately stopped the car, and Mukhtar, who was a nurse, gave the old man a horse-sized dose of chlorpromazine. Then he and Akylbai tied the patient with dirty checkered towels and strapped him to the bench so that he would not hurt himself if he suffered another convulsion.

"Who is he?" I asked them fearfully.

"A former political officer, a major," Mukhtar said, and reluctantly recounted the biographical particulars of the patient. He spat near his feet through yellow crooked teeth. "Every year we take him to the provincial psychiatric hospital. You need not fear; he's not dangerous now."

14

A Laurel Wreath for the Major

After spending a few hours in the stuffy confines of the van with the raving political officer, I wanted more than anything a good gulp of fresh air. However, nothing of the sort happened, since the residential area where we stopped was covered by a stinking miasma of mold and decay.

"What is that smell?" I asked Akylbai when I paid him for the ride, trying not to wrinkle my nose and offend his patriotic feelings.

"Oh, we have an open sewer system," he said angrily and, looking at me, he added derisively, "This ain't Moscow, pal. People breathe this kind of air their whole lives."

"You were in Moscow?" I asked Akylbai, remembering the Garden Ring at rush hour. Because of unregulated exhaust gases from millions of automobiles, it resembles nothing more than a battlefield during a gas attack. Exhaust gases eat away the leaves on the trees and shower toxic soot on the neighboring houses—not to mention the lungs and hearts of the people who live in them.

"I wasn't there, he was," answered Akylbai, pointing to Mukhtar. He angrily shrugged his shoulders and turned away. That means Moscow at some point did not welcome him too warmly. I pictured Mukhtar on Kalininsky Prospect at rush hour, a part of the city where there are always swarming crowds of visitors. They ask each other how to get to this or that place, but clearly no one else knows anything, except that they do not want to be recognized as visitors. Thus they walk by each other with stony faces, not responding to questions from poor wretches just like themselves. Then they return home and remember with hostility the hard-heartedness of "Muscovites."

I waved to them, and the car drove away. I was getting used to the smell, reminiscent of the canals in Basra, the Venice of Iraq. Basra, too, had open sewers, for the residents used the canals crisscrossing the city for throwing out sewage, garbage, and waste water. In Kzyl-Orda, thank God, it was not as hot as in Iraq, where a humidity of nearly 100 percent combined with daytime temperatures well over one hundred degrees Fahrenheit. Yes, it is good that instead of canals filled with slops, which generate health crises, here there was only one lake of sewage, invisible to me.

Dusk was gradually closing in, and I needed to think about lodging for the night. Stopping a merchant, I told him the address of Iranbek's relatives. However, my luck, it seems, had ended, because no one was home there. Having located, not without difficulty, the main telephone switchboard, I called Iranbek in Alma-Ata.

Newspapers usually call Iranbek Orazbaev one of the outstanding Kazakh poets of the middle generation. He is also a well-known playwright; his play *Genghis Khan* had been presented in Moscow the year before at the Friendship of the People's Theater. Why "outstanding," and why the "middle generation"? In the pre-breakup Soviet Union, without noticing it, we long since got used to thinking in hierarchical categories. There is nothing unusual in this, since any totalitarian state trains every cog in the mechanism to know clearly the place assigned to it from childhood. Literature, like any other type of human activity, was no exception. "Equating the writer's pen to a bayonet," the state even established a table of ranks for poets. Hence the "titles" of Soviet poets used by the press. For instance, "well-known" or "eminent" are regarded as lower than "outstanding" or "remarkable," but higher than "popular" or simply "young." Many of my friends have entered their forties or fifties, but are still considered "young" poets, for under socialism, just as under feudalism, it is very complicated to transfer from one class to another. But time is cruel to the state's conditional evaluations. Dozens, even hundreds of state laureates have sunk into oblivion as if they never existed, while ordinary people readily give up their week's wages on the black market for a book of formerly disgraced authors.

As for the title "great," artists receive it only posthumously. The term "genius" (with the exception of general secretaries and "classics of Marxism-Leninism") has been used in recent years to refer to those figures in art and culture who received from state or society a martyr's death.

"Greetings, Iranbek!" I began conversation in our usual half-joking manner. "Do you know that I plan to be your guest?"

Audibility, as always on a long-distance call, was abominable, and I had to shout like a military telephone operator under artillery fire.

"Of course, come on!" he said, his usual answer. Yet in fact only the words were usual. The intonation and timbre sounded as if I was talking with a telephone answering machine. I realized that some great misfortune had befallen him.

"What has happened, Iranbek?" I yelled with alarm. "Is someone ill, or is something wrong at work?"

The last several years he had worked as an editor at the *Kazakh Literary Gazette,* where they had constant troubles for publishing unsanctioned materials.

"No, nothing!" he said in a shaky voice. "Not on the telephone. We will talk when you get here. When will you arrive?"

"In about two days," I answered, disheartened. "And where are your Kzyl-Orda relatives?"

"What is this? You're not in Moscow?" Iranbek was alarmed.

"No, I am right now in Kzyl-Orda."

"They are here in Alma-Ata," he said, not explaining anything, "but they are going there tomorrow. Do you have a place to stay?"

"Well, that is, not really…" I mumbled.

"Wait, I will give you an address," Iranbek said in a colorless voice, as he evidently began to leaf through a notebook. "Here it is, one of my half relatives lives on Gani Muratbaev Street. You can spend the night with him. His name is Alibek S. By the way, he is a policeman."

He gave me the address and telephone number.

Iranbek and I had become friends at the beginning of the eighties, when I translated a large volume of his poems entitled *Tsar-slovo* for the Moscow publisher Sovetskii Pisatel (Soviet Writer). Since that time he and I had gotten together from time to time, sometimes in Moscow, sometimes in Alma-Ata, talking not so much because of business as out of respect and affection for each other.

What the hell had happened to him there? Why couldn't he talk about it on the telephone?

"Come to Alma-Ata; you can also help me," he answered, and we said good-bye.

Iranbek's countryman Alibek S. turned out to be a very representative, portly gentleman about fifty years old. The excited state in which I found him was probably unusual for him. I sensed that he was probably hiding confusion or mental trauma. Judging by his powerful manner, he was accustomed to giving orders. But at that moment there was no one to give orders to except his own wife, who obviously did not approve of my unexpected appearance.

When he found out that I was a close friend of Iranbek's, and, even more important, a writer from Moscow, Alibek S. jumped up almost to the ceiling with joy, which did not fit his portly sedateness.

"No, there is an Almighty God after all!" he cried, turning to his wife. They both stood at the doorway ready to leave for the city of Turkestan, and had I arrived ten minutes later, we would have missed each other. I heaved a sigh. Would my simple plans—to wash up, to eat whatever dinner God might provide, and to get to sleep as soon as possible—again be frustrated? And why was he so happy? It had no personal connection with me: he decided that I represented some Moscow newspaper. Did he have a conflict with his manager? It seemed that this was exactly the issue. Unfortunately, I was only too well acquainted with that half-insane spark of hope in the eyes of people who have been offended by the authorities. This spark of hope arises every time a "correspondent from the capital" appears on the scene.

For simple Soviet people, the Moscow newspapers were always something like books of complaints and proposals on a union-wide scale. But where could they complain of the tyranny and oppression of the local authorities? In those years not many people realized that the local partycrats paid their central bosses a tribute that gave them virtually unlimited power over people. In the first years of perestroika some kinds of materials began to trickle through to the pages of the Soviet press, which exposed specific republican party leaders giving large bribes to workers of the central party apparatus. But the tracks led so high that the fire had to be put out immediately.

Nevertheless, the local authorities had really been afraid of articles about their affairs in the central press. According to unwritten laws of the party mafia, the low-level and in certain cases even the middle-level *nomenklatura* did not have complete immunity and had to be careful themselves in order not to perpetrate a scandal. Moreover, in order to show the people that individual executives were guilty in the misfortunes of society, and not the system as a whole, one of the small fry was usually sacrificed. In such cases a column in *Pravda* or *Izvestiia* signaled the end of a party or state career for its hero, and often also his being sent to prison. But in recent years the partocracy stopped fearing the newspapers. First, the newspapers stopped being the state mouthpiece, and subsequently everything printed in them was no longer a guideline that had to be followed. Second, so much shocking truth was published in the press about the crimes of that very system that its functionaries no longer needed to hide its true face. They stopped concealing the fact that their main priority was to keep power in their hands no matter what people thought of them.

"We must go," Alibek's wife reminded him, letting me know once more that she did not much share his joy at meeting me.

"Yeah, yeah, we must go to Turkestan. I'm going to the hospital," confirmed Alibek. "If you wish, go with us and spend the night there with our relatives. There's room in the car. What's the problem?"

"Fine," I said, trying thoughtfully to figure what kind of man this was, and why he would drive one hundred and seventy-five miles to a neighboring city to lie in a hospital. "But we won't arrive there till almost morning."

"We'll get there in five hours," he answered, rubbing his hands.

After all, it would be possible to sleep in the car, I thought to myself. From Turkestan it was just a stone's throw to Chimkent. And from Chimkent to Alma-Ata it is always possible to take an intercity taxi or to make arrangements with a private driver. I knew that a journey from Chimkent to Alma-Ata in a car would run me about five hundred to seven hundred rubles, which for a distance of four hundred and fifty miles was then a fair price.

We left the city and headed south. While Alibek and his wife discussed their household matters in Kazakh, I started thinking about how to decline politely the role of advocate for Alibek. Helping him get rid of his enemies by writing an article for the central press no way fit into my immediate plans.

In the Soviet Union there are hundreds of thousands, perhaps millions of people who use hundreds of tons of paper writing complaints to various departments and editorial boards of newspapers, losing years of their lives and the last scrap of their health in fruitless attempts to find truth and fairness in a society founded upon tyranny and lies.

All the same, many old people still consider the Central Committee of the Communist Party of the Soviet Union to be the bulwark of truth and fairness, and so they direct to it tens of thousands of letters with pleas for help and heartrending complaints. Usually the letters are returned for examination to those very bureaucrats about whom the petitioner was complaining. As a result the complainer gets into an even worse situation, and if he continues to resist, he is often put in prison for making a false accusation.

Several years ago I myself ran into a typical case of tyranny, some local authorities who were bullying a helpless old woman. That story took almost half a year of my life, and probably half a million horsepower of energy, since it occurred in the suburbs of Moscow, about an hour's train ride from the city center.

There were two sisters by the name of Karavai. There had been ten brothers and sisters in their family, but by the end of their lives only they two remained. Nina, the elder, was eighty, and Matilda was seventy. Both were teachers, and during World War II they had worked as laborers in a defense plant. The pension, as usual, was paltry, but they did not complain, because throughout their long lives they had become used to burdens and deprivations. Each of them had a tumbledown shack, which, according to American standards, was not fit for habitation. Yet by Soviet standards, these dumps were perfectly tolerable, since millions of citizens who are useless to the state while away their old age in such dwellings in our rural areas. Nina lived in the Ukraine and Matilda in the village of Kryukovo, in the Solnechnogorsk district, a suburb of Moscow. Nina's husband died in the war, while Matilda's had died recently. Nina had two grown children, but they lived in other cities for a long time and were busy with their own problems. Matilda had no children, and, without her loving husband, she did not want to go on living. One day she fell seriously ill. She lost the use of her legs, and then Nina sold her shack in the Ukraine and moved to Kryukovo to be with her sister: someone had to be there to carry water from the well, to cut wood for the stove, to shovel snow, to carry meals to the patient.

Then, unexpectedly, Matilda's turn in line came to get a one-room apartment in one of the high-rise buildings built in the neighboring town of Andreevka—what she and her husband had waited for all their lives. "This will be wonderful," the sisters rejoiced, "because in a high-rise there is running water and hot water, as well as gas and a full bath!" But in order to receive the apartment, first Matilda had to turn over to the town Soviet the house she was living in. Matilda was sorry to part with her old home; however humble, she had spent her whole life there. Before the war, she and her husband had built it with their own hands, log by log and brick by brick. Through almost a half century of life in this house, she had grown accustomed to the squeak of every one of its floorboards and to the sight of each crack in the low ceiling. But there was nothing else to do; she needed to move. However the local authorities told her that they would never register Nina in the new home. They had never registered her even in her sister's old house; for a simple Soviet person to receive a residence permit (*propiska*) in Moscow or the Moscow province was as difficult as for a homeless person in Grand Central Station in New York to buy a palace in Pebble Beach, California. Yet a head of the local militia, for whom Matilda was once class monitor, had simply closed his eyes to the illegal residence of Nina in the home of her younger sister who was confined to her bed.

The next winter Matilda stopped getting out of bed. It was harder and harder for Nina, who had passed her eighty-first year, to cut firewood, to carry coal from the yard for the stove, and to carry water from the well. She decided on the move. "Maybe everything will turn out all right," she soothed Matilda. Although all her life experience testified to just the opposite, she reasoned, "It is impossible that the authorities would treat badly someone who worked honestly for them her whole life." The two women gave the house to the town Soviet; they transported their embroidered napkins and flower pots to the new apartment on the second floor of a large nine-story building at the edge of the forest. And then in the spring Matilda died. I was at her funeral. I found out there that they had already told Nina to vacate the premises. She was being evicted.

"Where will they evict you to?" Stupidly, I was surprised. "What can they do, return you to the house which you and Matilda turned over to the town Soviet?"

But the chairman of the town Soviet had already sold their home to other people.

"I will write to the Central Committee; I will write to Gorbachev!" the old woman cried. She was angry, and she still maintained, as did many people of her generation, a naïve faith in the kind ruler. She still did not imagine that she was entering into battle with a powerful system that had ground into powder tens of millions of her countrymen.

I will not begin to describe our entire journey through purgatory. One of the most influential and popular weeklies in the pre-breakup U.S.S.R., the *Literaturnaia Gazeta* (*Literary Gazette*), was and still is published in Moscow. This newspaper for many years ran a great number of stories about the victims of tyranny and cruel repression. Against this background what is the fate of an eighty-year-old teacher, whom the bosses of the Solnechnogorsk region stubbornly tried to throw out on the street? I went to the *Literaturnaia Gazeta* and told the deputy editor-in-chief, Yurii Poroikov, whom I knew well, about Nina. He treated me to good coffee, puffed on his pipe, and said:

"It's impossible to do anything. Don't waste your strength in vain. It is a grain of sand in a gigantic sandstorm."

He looked at me with a wise, "state" gaze. He was a charming, extraordinary man. I was sure that his career would continue. And no one will throw him out on the street when he is old.

But this story after all had something like a happy ending.

The general chaos of perestroika broke out in our society, and Nina, apparently, was forgotten or had just been deleted from the list of top priorities of the local party bosses. Or maybe they would say it is all right to let a granny live without a residence permit. After all, this person, well into her ninth decade, will probably die soon anyway. Yet Nina is still alive and healthy, and loves to watch television and read the liberal press. She does not approve when top party bureaucrats begin to spout about socialism with a human face, because everyone in the Soviet Union knows the true meaning of these words. She no longer says that evil Uncle Stalin distorted the ideas of kind grandpa Lenin. Finally she dared to understand that no one distorted anything. It was simply that some replaced others. Yet the essence up till now remains as before.

Alibek, it turned out, really was a policeman; moreover, he was a major in the militia, a rather high position for a regional company. Right now he was in civilian clothes, although his squeaky brown leather jacket would immediately distinguish him in any crowd. Real leather jackets in our country are considered a luxury item and are primarily the uniform of urban film directors. Racketeers have their own style, preferring "batwing"-style leather jackets.

Alibek S. was not simply a policeman but also a former traffic officer. He had some deep disagreements with the oblast (provincial) leadership about the management of internal affairs, and they had rather unceremoniously sent him into retirement. He seemed obsessed with getting even with his tormentors in the central press, although he persistently avoided telling me any details. "Fine," I said, "but what if I really write about you, and publish this—not in Moscow, but in New York?"

"Wh-where?" Alibek laughed nervously and threw a disbelieving glance my way. He drove the car himself, and I sat next to him, leaning my shoulder against the closed window. All I wanted was to sleep and eat, yet neither desire showed much promise of being satisfied anytime soon.

Alibek's nameless wife began to toss and turn uneasily on the backseat.

"What did he say?" she asked in Kazakh.

"Sleep, woman!" he snapped, not turning around. However, remote control did not work, for Alibek's wife loudly asked again, "Why in New York?"

"Yes, why?" Alibek chimed in. "In America, eh? What do Americans have to do with the management of internal affairs in Kzyl-Orda?"

"What happens in our country is interesting to them. They hope that Gorbachev's reforms will change our life for the better."

"Gorbachev's...what?" Alibek disapprovingly wrinkled his nose.

For a moment he looked just like Toshiro Mifune. "There are reforms for you there in Moscow and Leningrad, but we have the mafia, and it still remains."

"What mafia? Get a hold of yourself, Alibek, what nonsense are you talking," wailed the frightened woman from the backseat. "Think of the children if you don't want to think of yourself!"

"What is this, 'What mafia?'" Alibek yelled at his wife, and violently stomped on the gas pedal. "The party mafia! And you don't know! If Yeltsin doesn't crush this nest of vipers, consider what it was like before perestroika."

"Don't listen to him! They shamed him; they sent him into retirement before it was time. That's why his tongue is loosened." The poor woman grasped my arms. "Don't write his last name. For the sake of the children, don't write his last name!"

Alibek suddenly stepped on the brake, and the car squealed in protest.

"It's okay, it's okay," I said, soothingly patting Alibek's wife's hand, as little as that of a frog, with which she now clutched the back of the seat.

The car stopped, and Alibek, breathing heavily, his jacket squeaking, unsuccessfully tried to turn toward his wife.

"Everything's fine, *Amake*," I said, calling him uncle in Kazakh. "Calm down. Maybe your wife is right. Do you think that a newspaper article can change the system? 'The dog keeps barking, but the caravan keeps coming.'"

"No, I want you to write it." Alibek obstinately pounded on the steering wheel with his fist. "Let the whole world know that the changes have occurred only on the pages of the liberal Moscow newspapers! Gorbachev has deceived us! Why, oh, why do they praise him so much in the West?"

"Because now the Soviet Union doesn't push atomic bombs in their faces! Because he gave Eastern Europe freedom of choice!" I cried. "Isn't that enough?"

"But we, we are so much worse! Why doesn't he give us freedom?"

"What kind of freedom are you talking about? Freedom from what? Or freedom for whom?"

"There is freedom, and there is freedom," Alibek said with a weary wave of his hand, "only what's the use of talking for nothing. If you say 'halva' a hundred times, your mouth doesn't become sweet."

He restarted the car and abruptly took off. For some time we drove in pained silence; then he unexpectedly said, "By the way, I am the laureate of the Second All-Union Festival of People's Arts."

"And do you in fact wear the laurel wreath on your head?"

"Do you think that the word 'laureate' and a laurel leaf have some connection with each other?" Alibek knitted his brow.

"In the most direct way," I affirmed. "It's not just for making soup. What kind of art, if it is not a secret? Amateur filmmaking?"

"Why film?" Alibek was hurt. "No kind of film. I have no patience for film. No, I play the *dombra* and sing. That was why the leadership came to hate me. The head of our internal affairs management, Commander Demesinov, never gave me a chance. No advancement, not in title, not in position. But before last May Day he swore at me and dismissed me from the operations conference. 'Go into retirement,' he says. 'Starting today.' How am I going to retire if I'm only forty-eight! In order to earn a full pension, I need two more years. I have six children, three of whom are in school."

"How many years did you serve in the militia?" I asked Alibek.

"Since 1966," he said proudly. "And a member of the Communist Party of the Soviet Union since 1969! I was head of the division of the oblast state automobile inspection, head of the militia for the airport, and head of the regional state auto inspection. That was where my unpleasantness with the oblast leadership began."

"Alibek!" his wife again spoke up.

"Stop bothering me," he snapped in Kazakh. And, turning to me, he continued in Russian: "Beginning May 5, I lay in the hospital for almost a month with my blood pressure at one ninety. However, they wouldn't admit me in Kzyl-Orda, so I had to drive to Turkestan. We have friends in the hospital there who didn't listen to Demesinov, and they let me retire for medical reasons and not have to be fired as my bosses were trying to do."

"What did it do for you?" I asked with weary interest.

"A 10 percent addition to my pension," he said. Strangely, I expected that this time his wife would answer instead of him. But it seemed that she had fallen asleep. Following her example I, too, drifted off.

Among the old cities of Turkestan (i.e., Land of Turkic peoples), the city of Turkestan occupies a highly esteemed place with an ancient history. Up until the tenth century it was known as Shavgar, and from the tenth to the fifteenth centuries historical chronicles called it Yasy. Only at the end of the fifteenth century, after becoming the capital of the southern Kazakh khanate, did the city receive its current name. Today its main claim to fame is that it is the site of the majestic mausoleum of Hadji Akhmed Yasavi, a widely revered Sufi holy man. The mausoleum was erected at Timur's command in the fourteenth century right over the existing tomb, which had become dilapidated.

Iranbek once told me about a gigantic caldron, with a capacity of sixty buckets, a diameter of two and a half meters, and a weight of two tons. Six centuries ago it was smelted from seven metals: copper, silver, gold, iron, zinc, lead, and tin. In antiquity clergymen gave believers sweetened water from this caldron after Friday prayers. Fifty-four years ago, during Stalin's reign, this unique caldron, considered a local holy shrine, was packed up and carried off to "temporary storage" in the Leningrad State Hermitage. Only recently the Kazakh museum directors managed with great efforts to grab it back. Now this priceless antique, cast by the command of Timur the Lame, again stands in its rightful place in the mausoleum of Hadji Akhmed Yasavi.

Hadji (that is, "pilgrim") Akhmed Yasavi is widely known and esteemed in countries of the Moslem East as a holy Sufi sheikh, who lived and preached in this city in the twelfth century. He left a *divan* (collection) of philosophical lyrics, *Khikmat,* a name that may be translated as "Wisdom" or "Secret Knowledge." In accordance with Sufi tradition, it is thought that each line of Sufi poetry contains a second and sometimes even a third meaning, since the concepts and forms of usual speech in the language of the Sufis have another, allegorical interpretation. For example, a cup of wine signifies merging with the absolute world spirit, a black curl belonging to your beloved symbolizes the dialectical spiral of development, and the pink flower of her tender cheeks is the happiness of knowledge.

Even now I remember how surprised I was when, as a student preparing for a seminar in medieval Eastern poetry, I discovered a passage in an ancient poem in which the poet delights in the depth of his beloved's navel. Even from kindergarten I considered myself a connoisseur of feminine beauty, but it never occurred to me that the contemplation of a feminine navel could lead anyone to such indescribable delight. From remote antiquity this proud, fortunate man communicated to his readers how many ounces of nut oil there was room for in the navel of his beautiful slave. How could he calculate it? Is it possible experimentally? Even more astounding, the verse may also be interpreted as an allegory of astrophysics.

After this example I became interested in Sufi symbolism, and even tried to translate into Russian some verses of Bobo Kukhi Shirazi, a medieval Sufi poet of the tenth century. I translated each couplet twice: as a strictly lyrical poem and as a decoded philosophical and religious cipher. By the way, the great Omar Khayyam, whose verse has become so widely read in English in the excellent translation of Edward Fitzgerald, was also a Sufi. This explains one serious discrepancy that cannot fail to attract the attention of anyone who stands with one foot in Europe and the other in Asia. Why does the West consider Khayyam a charming drunk and philanderer, while in the East his grave is a place of religious worship? Those who interpret the *Rubaiyat* too literally, delighting in all those voluptuous discourses about cups of red wine and moon-faced Persian beauties, are missing the hidden mystic text, which is completely different.

I scarcely even approached the strongholds of esoteric Sufi wisdom before I acknowledged my defeat. Sufi knowledge, even in abbreviated form, for all its attractions, at a certain moment seemed to me threatening and frightful. Above all, against the background of its stern revelations, the conditionality and even falsehood of many ordinary values of life became too obvious. The well-being of loved ones, my studies at an elite Oriental institute, a future career and work abroad—in comparison with the abysses of eternity, all that lost meaning. The starry sky over one's head and a moral law in one's heart were reference points too dangerous for Soviet reality. Any youth choosing to follow them into adult life in our country would land himself directly in prison.

I decided that it was possible to wait a little for Sufism. If I am disappointed in the joys of life, then it will be better to reject them, based on my own true experience, and not under the influence of the borrowed wisdom of medieval philosophers. Especially since they actually measured the depth of real girls' navels.

15

Two Bullets for a Ride

Although my journey resembled nothing less than an Intourist-arranged vacation, as I got closer and closer to Turkestan I could not help dreaming of a short excursion to the ruins of the town of Otrar. Even back in Moscow, while planning my itinerary, I was divided on the question of whether to visit Otrar or not. To leave highway M-32 and head up some unpaved steppe road seemed dangerous even for Liberman's Zhiguli. Because this forty-mile road was not indicated on the map at all, to drive it was no doubt possible only in a four-wheel-drive vehicle—or on the back of a camel in one of the caravans that traversed the Great Silk Route ten centuries ago. Yet Otrar still called to me, for it was the first town in Central Asia to experience the prowess of Genghis Khan's troops. Later, Tamerlane, too, often went there, as we shall see.

"I'll go!" I finally decided when I woke up in Alibek's car. The general mood inside the car was already different. While I was sleeping, Alibek had been driving, and now he looked tired and gloomy. His wife was silent, but I felt that she was awake, too.

"So, are we driving up to Turkestan?" I asked a little bit louder than necessary, to cover up the indecent rumbling in my hungry stomach. "Is Otrar far from here?"

Alibek was silent, trying to figure something out, and then answered: "It's next to a village called Shaul'der."

"Shaul'der..." I repeated after him and rolled this word in my mouth as if it were a plum pit. No, this name did not tell me anything.

"And how one can get there?" The idea of seeing the ruins of a legendary town seemed more and more appealing to me.

"By train!" Alibek's wife answered for her husband in a strict voice. "At night an express train from Moscow to Tashkent comes through Turkestan."

"At what time?" I asked her. After all, it is possible to sleep in a train, too. Of course, it might not be possible to arrange a ride with a conductor. At night they are much less compliant than in the daytime.

"I don't remember, about three o'clock in the morning," the woman answered with a disgruntled sigh, letting me know that she was the wife of a boss (even if he was only a former boss), not an information office. I understood that these people had serious problems themselves and it would be impolite to abuse their hospitality.

"And does the train go through Chimkent?" I decided to ask the last question.

"No, it goes through Arys'," Alibek informed me.

When we arrived in Turkestan, two hours before dawn, the black cupola of the warm sky was studded with such huge stars, as only happens in summer, that I felt like giving up my present career and becoming an astronomer. However, all of a sudden I remembered the sad fate of the medieval astronomer Tycho Brahe, who died at a royal levy from a ruptured bladder because he was too shy to ask where the toilet was. Well, as Lenin once said: we'll take a different road!

At my request the owners of the car dropped me at the railroad station, where we parted with somewhat vague good-byes. Alibek S. was obviously annoyed with me for not volunteering to speak out in the Moscow press against his illegal dismissal. His wife, on the contrary, was really nervous, for she understood that I was not joking when I talked about a book that would be published in New York. But I kept my promise to her: the last name of her husband has shrunk to an initial.

The railroad station in Turkestan did not strike me as a masterpiece of architecture, and the benches in the waiting room could have been softer. The train toward Shaul'der had already gone, which was bad news. But the good news was that it went from Turkestan to Arys' without stopping, since it was an express train. So I had to wait till morning and take the mail train. I put my bag under my head and plunged immediately into a deep sleep. But in a minute a cop woke me up, his attention probably attracted by the ribbed soles of my Reeboks, which look from a distance like the footwear of an astronaut. And since Baikonur (the town where our spaceships take off from) was rather far from here, he decided just in case to check my documents. Seeing a Moscow residence permit in my passport, he arched an eyebrow in disapproving surprise and asked me where I worked.

"I'm a writer," I said in a sleepy voice, putting my feet down onto the spit-covered floor. Talking to cops while lying down is not recommended. Unless, of course, your aim is to get fifteen days at hard labor. The cop looked at me in overt disbelief, and then he suddenly smiled.

"All right, don't give me this crap!" he said, patting me on the shoulder. "Writers are never as huge as you are. One could cart water on your back."

Unexpectedly he sat next to me and offered me a pack of cigarettes: "Have a smoke!"

He was quite young and could have been a country lad. Probably he had recently finished his military service, and he decided to stay on in the town as a policeman, for there were few other ways to get a residence permit even in such a modest town as Turkestan.

"Thank you, I don't smoke," I answered politely, and then broadly yawned, almost throwing my jaw out of joint. Then I reached into my side pocket for a copy of my most recent book, which I had taken with me as a gift for Iranbek Orazbaev.

"What's your name?" I asked the cop, who was watching my actions with interest.

"Zhumabai!" he answered coyly. "So what?"

"Here we are, Zhumabai, it's my book with an autograph—as a token of our meeting. Are you married? Maybe I should write it for your wife, too?"

"No," Zhumabai answered with a sigh. "How can I marry if I don't have an apartment? You can't bring your wife to a dormitory."

"Well, yes," I said uncertainly. "Can we talk about this later? I need to sleep a little. It's already the second day that I haven't been able to get a good night's sleep."

"In general, one may not sleep here lying on a bench," Zhumabai said, inspecting my face on the book cover. Everything checked out to his satisfaction: the same name on book and passport. His face grew brighter. "So you really are a Moscow writer? In that case, sleep tight. I'll see to it that your belongings are not stolen."

"Yeah, it's not for nothing that literature in our country is a state business," I thought with pride, adjusting my bag comfortably, as though it were a pillow.

"Perhaps you'd prefer to go to the room for mothers and children?" Zhumabai asked respectfully. "There's a bed there."

"Oh, well, that's all right," I mumbled, my eyes closed. "And anyway, who will let me in there without my mamma?"

In the morning, I loaded myself aboard the train with Zhumabai's assistance and reached Shaul'der in a few hours. The ruins of Otrar, like any ancient town, presented a rather sad picture. The wind, lifting whirlwinds of dust, the stems of some steppe weed, a hawk making circles in the Asiatic sky, whitish from the heat—is that really all that is left of one of the richest Turkic towns on the Great Silk Route?

In the beginning of the thirteenth century, Otrar was a border town of the state of Khorezm, in Central Asia. The ruler of Khorezm, called Khorezmshah, succeeded in uniting several independent provinces of the Central Asia river valley, including such famous city-states as Samarkand and Bukhara. He fancied himself a second Alexander the Great and cast greedy looks toward China, where the Tsin dynasty ruled.

But while Khorezmshah was laying his plans, a new dramatis personae appeared on the political arena of the world. As early as 1215 Khorezmshah heard rumors that a barbarian named either Temuchin or Genghis Khan, so far unknown to anyone, had seized northern China and even overthrown the powerful Tsin dynasty that had ruled the country for almost one thousand years. Later it became known from the merchants, who combined intelligence-gathering with their mercantile occupation, that this impostor had acquired in China some novel weapons of siege and gadgets that threw liquid fire, as well as craftsmen who knew how to make and handle these technologies.

Greatly annoyed, Khorezmshah sent a caravan to Genghis Khan, assigned, of course, to learn what it could about these marvels. Genghis Khan gave the ambassadors a warm welcome and even bought their goods at a decent price. It is true that there was initially some misunderstanding between them, as the merchants first tried to ask three times as much as usual for their goods, mistakenly supposing Genghis Khan to be in the dark about world prices. But everything turned out all right, and both sides parted contentedly.

After a while Genghis Khan sent an envoy caravan, loaded with gifts and goods, to Khorezm for a return visit. He appointed as his head envoy a Khorezm deserter, the rich merchant Makhmud Ialavach, who later became his governor-general for all of Turkestan, including the lands of the former Khorezm state. Khorezmshah received this turncoat in Bukhara, one of the richest and most arrogant cities of his kingdom. At the gift-giving ceremony, Makhmud Ialavach told Khorezmshah that Genghis Khan had heard that Khorezmshah was a powerful sovereign, and desired to conclude a peace treaty with him.

Some of the historians of the thirteenth century, such as the Persian historian Juveini and the Turkic historian Nesevi, described how the Khorezmshah proudly stroked his black beard, touched with gray, and threw a triumphant glance toward his mother, Turkan-Khatun, who stood surrounded by her fellow tribesmen from the Tangly tribe, of the Kipchak.

"Well, yes, a peace treaty." The Khorezmshah nodded his head in a grand manner, and then suddenly his eyes darkened with fury. He grasped the sense of the words with which the placidly reverent ambassador had completed the oral message of Genghis Khan: "And he regards Mohammed Khorezmshah as among the best of his sons."

Genghis Khan had called Khorezmshah not brother but son! In the idiom of Eastern diplomacy this choice of words signified that Genghis Khan believed that Khorezmshah should consider himself a vassal of the Tartars.

That night Khorezmshah secretly sent for the ambassador and suggested that he become a double agent. Because of fear or possibly because he had been set up to do so, Makhmud Ialavach agreed. The historian Nesevi, who wrote about these events in the first half of the thirteenth century, believed that Makhmud Ialavach told Genghis Khan much more about Khorezm than he told Khorezmshah about the Tartars. Anyway, the Khorezmshah let the ambassador go and ordered him to tell Genghis Khan that he agreed to conclude a peace treaty. Perhaps he wanted to gain time, in order to prepare for war with the hateful upstart.

Contented, Genghis Khan sent Khorezmshah a second huge caravan, which consisted of 450 people and 500 camels, that same year. For the time being, he was much more interested in rich China and fairy-tale India than in still-unknown Central Asia. After seizing India he intended to move through ancient Iran to the flourishing lands of the Baghdad Khalif.

But this time Genghis Khan's caravan, which was headed for Urgench, the main city of the Khorezm state, was not fated to reach its destination. Here, in the town of Otrar, before the ruins of which I was standing now, in need of sleep, dirty and hungry, the caravan was stopped. What happened here 772 years ago? Why did the commandant of the fortress of Otrar, whose name was Inalchik, order the pillaging of the whole caravan and the murder of all its people? What would the history of Central Asia have been if that war had been avoided? What people would inhabit these lands today? And what would stand in the place of the ancient ruins of that mosque?

I tried to imagine that dreadful night, the bleating of frightened animals, the glowing embers of torches on the ground, the clinking of steel, the cries of dying people. As it happens, several people managed to escape. They reached Genghis Khan's headquarters and informed him of what had happened. The ruler was at first infuriated, but then he thought that perhaps the destruction of the embassy had resulted from a decision by the hotheaded commandant of the fortress. In a totalitarian regime the military always consider themselves to be cleverer than the civil authorities. And if the decision was taken by Khorezmshah himself, perhaps he was unaware of the devastating circumstances of this step?

Genghis Khan sent a new envoy to Khorezmshah, a man by the name of Ibn-Kefradj Bogra, with a request to punish those who were guilty of the killings and to turn over the commandant Inalchik. But the Khorezmshah ordered the execution of Genghis Khan's ambassador and sent his retinue back, having first pulled out their beards.

Now there was no doubt about it. All this meant that Khorezmshah wanted war. Perhaps none of the participants of this conflict that ultimately grew into the world war of the Middle Ages had any idea what colossal transformations were in store for the many peoples of Asia and Eastern Europe as a result of this clash of the Central Asian and Tartar-Mongolian superpowers. Instead of invading India the troops of Genghis Khan moved into Central Asia, and from there to the Middle East, Russia, and Eastern Europe. But in 1218 no one could really envision the genuine relation between the forces which originated the conflict.

Khorezm, weakened by internal tensions, was a colossus with feet of clay. Otrar was taken and ruined, and the same fate followed all the other big cities of Khorezm's state. The entire political map of Turkestan, the Volga valley, the Transcaucasus, and even the future Russia, which consisted at that time of a dozen rival princedoms, was decisively reshaped as a result of this war.

Khorezmshah himself left his throne and went into exile. For half a year he managed to hide from the chase on a small island of the Caspian Sea, where he caught cold and died ignominiously from pneumonia. Genghis Khan's best commanders, the red-bearded Jebe and the one-eyed Subedei, lost track of Khorezmshah, but continued to fight triumphantly through all the Trans-Caucasus and arrived unexpectedly, for themselves, at the southern borders of Russia. Here Russian detachments, together with Polovtsy, gave battle to the Tartars on the Kalka River, in 1223. All high school students in the U.S.S.R. know about this event, but no one can answer who won and who lost this battle. But if it had been a Russian victory, the students would undoubtedly know about it.

In the local museum in Otrar there is a whole exposition dedicated to that ancient defense of the city. The siege continued for six months before the town fell. But no word was said in this exposition about the cause of the war. Inalchik, ordered to murder the embassy and pillage the caravan, stands out as a national hero, and the murder of the envoys is not even mentioned. Such revisions are nothing extraordinary: if even our recent history has been heavily altered and fabricated to fit into present ideological concepts to such an extent that it is impossible to recognize it, what can one expect of events from seven centuries ago? For the sake of so important a task as the upbringing of patriots, historical truth may be "edited" as need be.

But I did not harangue the museum guides. After all, they live and work under the laws of the society to which they belong. The main thing is that here, in a godforsaken place like this, such an archeological museum exists in the first place. I got acquainted with a local man named Bakyt, who had worked for several seasons as a field worker in archeological expeditions. He told me that a few years ago some scholars had come here to excavate a monument. When they returned to their universities to defend their dissertations, they left the monument unprotected, open to the winds, rains, and scorching sun, which destroyed what time had not succeeded in destroying.

As far back as the thirteenth century, a mausoleum was erected on the grave of Arystyn-bab, an ancient thinker, and it became a site of pilgrimage for Moslems for centuries. Under Soviet rule, this tradition almost disappeared, but in recent years it has begun to reappear. However, there is no hotel, and no services are offered to the pilgrims, except for a few wagons that the local authorities have set up near the museum, so that pilgrims will not have to spend the night on the damp ground.

At the bus stop, several women were selling the Kazakh national dish, *kuzhe-ochitpa*. It is something like cooled weak rice or barley soup, diluted with fermented kefir or sour milk. It is offered to customers in big round bowls, ladled from a bucket sitting on the ground. Next to it sits another bucket with water, where the dishes are rinsed when they are returned.

While I was diligently making short work of my first bowl, the women were driving flies away from their buckets and looked with curious smiles in my direction. I bought another helping and praised their cooking. When I asked for the recipe they laughed. I took out my notebook with a pen, but they said that there was nothing to write down. The recipe was very simple.

"What is it?" I asked innocently.

"A good wife!" they answered and giggled, covering their scant-toothed mouths with tanned palms.

In Chimkent, where I arrived toward evening, I at last got lucky with transport. Right in the railway station square a young man came up to me and asked where I was going.

"I need a cab," I said, surreptitiously looking him over, trying to understand what kind of a person he was. The Soviet man is always alarmed when people offer their services to help him. He was burly and stern, with closely cropped hair, looking more like a good guy from the movies, an Afghan war hero perhaps, than a shady cab driver from the gang that works the intercity highways.

"So what do you need, a nice yellow taxi or a ride?" he asked with a mocking smile, understanding perfectly well why I hesitated. Something in his manner was quite appealing, his sense of humor perhaps, and I decided to take him up on his offer.

"I need to get to Alma-Ata," I informed him.

"Possible," he said, "if we find some other passengers."

"No," I said, "that's just what we don't need."

"And can you pay eight hundred rubles?" he asked. "Usually passengers pool money, two hundred rubles each."

"I'll pay six hundred," I said, "but we won't take anyone else."

"Seven hundred," he said with a tense smile.

"Let's go!" I laughed. In the inner pocket of my black bag there was a small but heavy pack of banknotes with a portrait of Lenin on each of them. Now it would lose seven more banknotes. Well, I thought, money is for spending.

But when I saw that he had a Moskvich-412 I was a bit upset. Like every other Soviet Zhiguli owner, I was biased against Moskviches. When a country produces just two brands of cars, the customers inevitably fall into two parties—those who like to eat their boiled eggs from the top, and those who eat it from the bottom.

I rubbed my earlobe and looked at my new companion, who was driving his Moskvich in a professional manner. It was still quite light out, and long-tailed magpies were perched on the telegraph poles that flashed along the highway. All other manifestations of earthly life seemed remote. The boundless hilly steppe, so far unspoiled by man, looked like an otherworldly landscape, but I knew we were still on earth because I could see the familiar, far-off evening star, which has been known to people for so many centuries.

"Can it be that I will make the next four hundred and fifty miles without great misfortunes?" I thought, trying to relax in the uncomfortable seat of the Moskvich. I reached for my calculator and made some calculations. From Moscow through Cheboksary to Samara I covered 755 miles. From Samara to Chimkent, about 1,420 miles. Thus for the first ten days of my wanderings I had gone already 2,175 miles—farther than the distance from San Francisco to Chicago.

"Well, how are your incomes and expenditures going? Do they-match?" the driver asked with curiosity, bored by driving in silence.

"I'm counting the mileage," I explained, putting the calculator back in my pocket.

"What's there to count? By tomorrow morning, God help us, we'll be in Alma-Ata!"

"Aren't state cabmen mad at you for cheating them of their incomes?" I asked, stretching out wearily. It would be fine to relax on the backseat and to wake up already in Alma-Ata. But the driver had asked me not to sit there.

"Ah, the devil knows them!" he said irrelevantly, and looked at me with curiosity again. Unshaved and rumpled, I could pass for a doubtful personality myself. Law-abiding citizens nowadays do not travel from one town to another in private cabs. I wondered what he made of me.

"You are, perhaps, a journalist," the driver said, grinning. "Probably from Moscow."

"Exactly right," I said, shrugging my shoulders in disappointment. "But how did you guess?"

"By your eyes," he said. "They don't dart back and forth across your face. I can't afford to take risks with my passengers. Although once I made a mistake…"

"And what happened?" I asked, intrigued.

"Oh, no!" he brushed me off carelessly. "I'm not keen to remember."

"All right, then, why do you have a Moskvich?"

"I had a number six before." He heaved a sigh.

The "number six" is the sixth model of Zhiguli, which was considered to be the best Soviet car during the fifteen years it was manufactured.

"The single drawback of the Zhiguli," the driver, whose name was Polat, continued, "is that many of its breakdowns you can fix only in the shop. But you can get a Moskvich fixed, provided of course that you can tell a hammer from a screwdriver, right in your own garage."

"Is that why you sold your Zhiguli?" I asked, trying to suppress a yawn.

"No, I didn't sell it," he said. "It was taken away from me."

"Someone took it away from you, or drove it away?" I asked, suddenly feeling an unpleasant sensation running through my stomach.

"I was killed," he said calmly, "then thrown into a ditch, and my car was taken away."

"What do you mean—you were killed?" I asked, flabbergasted.

"Two bullets from a pistol," he said, and then calmly unbuttoned his white shirt and turned to me. Two scars that had been made by bullets reddened his young chest.

"So, did it happen quite recently?" I asked.

"This year, on Monday, on the third of March," he said, buttoning his shirt with one hand and steering with the other. "They also got in the car at the railroad station in Chimkent, only they wanted to go not to Alma-Ata but closer—to Lenger. As soon as we drove out of the town, they asked me to stop so they could take a leak. And then they pulled out a gun and fired two times, right in the chest."

"And what happened then?" I asked, imagining with a pain in my heart the horror this boy must have felt when the bandits pointed their weapon at him.

"Then someone picked me up. It turned out that I have nine lives, like a cat. Although there is some complication with one lung. I'll probably be certified as some kind of an invalid."

"Did they find the bandits?" I asked, thinking in advance that they did not.

"Yes, they did," Polat answered. "Or to be exact, they presented themselves. On the very same day."

"What?" I exclaimed. This I could not believe.

"Because they crashed the car. They drove too quickly, swerved over onto the wrong side of the road and ran into a truck coming from the opposite direction. And both men were immediately killed. The car was totaled. So after I got out of the hospital I had to swap for a Moskvich."

"A nice story," I said darkly. "It's good that one of my friends does not hear it. If you are tired, would you like me to drive?"

"Do you have a license?" Polat smiled.

"You bet!" I said. "Even an international license."

"Okay, maybe later," he promised.

"Later I will be sleeping." I laughed and pointed with my hand to the backseat. "Back there."

"All right, then," he agreed and pulled up at the curb. It was still about fifty miles to the town of Jambul, and the traffic on the highway was rather intense.

"And in general, how is it to live in Chimkent?" I asked after I took the wheel. After the restless and brisk feel of a Zhiguli, the Moskvich seemed like a heavy, clumsy invalid. The gears were switching with a crank, the engine was howling, the back axle of the car was clinking suspiciously, but all the same the car was moving rather speedily. Polat, who at first was watching how I drove, soon calmed down.

"Well, it varies," he said. "Of course, it's dull here. The young guys have no place to go. In the restaurant there are mainly criminals, and the discotheque is for kids fifteen or younger. Even guys who are twenty years old are old folks to them. One can only go to the movies, and even there it is dangerous to go with a woman. You might be beaten up. Sometimes, the guys are smoking right in the movie, then someone raises hell, and there's a fight. No, I'm not interested in all that."

"What are you interested in, then?"

"When I make more money, I'll get married, then I want to buy a house and have children."

"And who will you marry?"

"I don't know yet. There are plenty of nice girls."

"That's right," I agreed with Polat. "How are the air and water down there?"

"As everywhere," he answered. "That is, bad. We have a huge lead plant here. The acid smell one can endure, but it's better not to breathe the lead dust. Besides that, we have a phosphorus plant."

"You don't by any chance have a Green party in this town?"

"We have the Communist Party of Kazakhstan!" He laughed. "And the 'black battalion' to keep order."

"Isn't that basically something like a detachment of internal troops? For keeping order? Whenever something goes wrong, you get it with a rifle butt on your noggin! It's very convenient to use against demonstrators. But they are also used to round up groups—to arrest the criminals who carry guns on them. Have you heard about that?"

"Ah, the devil knows them!" Polat shrugged his shoulders. "People say a lot of different things about them."

"And what about the national question?"

"So far, more or less okay. Although the Kazakhs and Chechens in Jambul couldn't share anything among themselves. There was even some shooting. And in December of 1989 in Chimkent the Meskhetin Turks received an ultimatum: either you leave before the first of May or it will be the same as in Uzbekistan."

"A slaughterhouse, huh?"

"That's right. So all of them left. They sold their houses and stuff for half price—they were rich, you know—and left."

"What do you think, is it right when people are made to leave their old haunts and flee under threat of death?"

"Let them go to their Meskhetia!"

"But no one will let them go there. They are Turks, as you know, and the Georgians think that this is a Georgian land from time immemorial. When Stalin resettled them, there were thirty thousand Meskhetin Turks, and now there are ten times as many. Where should they go?"

"I don't know," Polat answered nervously. "We have lots of our own troubles. Have you heard about Aral? And that the Kazakh language is dying out?"

"I know all about it," I said. "Three alphabets plus a mass Russification. The drying out of the sea and the massive degeneration of all species."

"And do you know that we're governed by the mafia?"

"I heard about that, too," I said.

"All right, what shall we do now?"

"I would like to go to sleep after Jambul," I replied. "Listen, wouldn't you like to give me a lift from Alma-Ata to Issyk-Kul'?"

"To give you a lift?" Polat grunted. "Are you a millionaire, or what? Or maybe...?"

Once more he measured me up appreciatively with his eyes.

"Or maybe what? Mafioso?" I laughed with a certain effort.

"No, I won't go." Polat grinned. "The times have changed."

16

"The State...Is You!"

For some reason, I always used to think that Alma-Ata and San Francisco had something in common. I knew, of course, that Alma-Ata is surrounded on three sides by mountains, not by water. And that San Francisco's skyscrapers are higher than Alma-Ata's. In fact there aren't any skyscrapers in Alma-Ata, and those buildings that are referred to as skyscrapers are actually just a couple of administrative and apartment buildings having, say, eighteen to twenty-four floors, and a few hotels of the same height. I was also well aware that in Alma-Ata there is nothing like the Golden Gate Bridge, or Chinatown, or the City Lights Bookstore. And it was true that in San Francisco one would not find a great many women of Kazakh-Russian descent (so beautiful!), or apple orchards, or a concert hall in the shape of a gigantic felt hat (the Kazakh national headgear, vaguely reminiscent of Napoleon's tricornered hat). But all the same, I always felt that these cities were somehow similar. And finally the day came when I saw San Francisco with my own eyes. Oh, yes, it was quite beautiful: elegant, exquisite, extravagant. But there was no resemblance to Alma-Ata whatsoever.

Then some time passed, and my recollections of San Francisco got dim, and—strangely enough—the idea of Alma-Ata made me think of that faraway city of the Golden Gate. What a mirage, I thought with surprise. How can I persist in thinking there is some similarity when I know perfectly well that there is no physical resemblance? Why do they hang together so stubbornly in my imagination? Is it just their ability to invoke in a stranger that mental state Ernest Hemingway once called "a moveable feast"?

I went to Alma-Ata for the first time as a little boy in the early fifties, with my parents. It was my first journey to another city. Moreover, it was the first time in my life I had ever traveled by air. I remember even now the old prop-engine passenger plane with its uplifted nose and its drooping tail directly over the wheel. Churchill must have flown on board such planes to the Yalta Conference during World War II.

When the plane landed, it was ignored for a long time; nobody brought the stairway for us to descend. It was stuffy in the plane, and a crew member opened the door. As if casually, I walked up to the open door and cautiously looked down. The ground proved to be unexpectedly close. Without thinking, while someone screamed, I jumped down and plunged up to my ankles in a thick layer of a hot summer dust.

Later I visited Alma-Ata many times, and each time, as long as my exotic great-aunt Mayra was still alive, I stayed with her. She and her husband had no children, and their house had an apple orchard, which seemed enormous to me at the time. The street where they lived faced mountains, with fir trees and larches growing thickly on their slopes. They seemed strange to me, craning my neck, all those countless trees, climbing the steep sides of mountains almost halfway to the sky.

Mayra forbade me to call her "great-aunt," and because of that I always regarded her as my aunt, though she was in fact my mother's aunt. Mayra's husband was a passionate hunter and fisherman, and he kept several hounds in the house, mostly setters. Mayra always walked around the house in flowing Chinese dressing gowns with fiery yellow dragons and, without fail, some health-giving mask on her face. She adored jewelry, velvet dresses, and journeyed yearly to resorts. She was the only person I knew who did her morning exercises with unfading enthusiasm to the accompaniment of the pseudo-cheerful plunking of a piano on the radio. Even more odd at that time was the fact that she had her own car. To have a private car in the Soviet Union in those days was approximately the same as having a private jet plane nowadays in America. Even more bizarre, she drove it herself. A woman driver provoked the same kind of contradictory feelings on the part of a majority of Soviet people as would the first woman astronaut, Valentina Tereshkova, fifteen years later.

When I was studying at the university in Tashkent, Mayra often urged me to move to Alma-Ata. But in those years, compared with Tashkent, with its population of a million and a half, Alma-Ata seemed like a dull place. Now, of course, everything has changed, and the capitals of the republics, having awakened after a long sleep, are trying to figure out where to put foreign embassies. After I graduated, I decided that the only place I could get something worthwhile was Moscow. The capitals of totalitarian empires, with their proximity to the highest echelons of power, always attract both the best and the worst citizens. Can you imagine a supercapital that would combine Washington, D.C., New York, Los Angeles, Boston, Chicago, San Francisco, Detroit, and Las Vegas all at once? Because of the myriad opportunities that it offered to the Soviet people, Moscow was just such a supercity. And I decided that I would only live in the capital of the empire.

Mayra once told me that in her youth she had been a girlfriend of Kunayev. That was in that prehistoric time when the future first secretary of the Central Committee of the Communist Party of Kazakhstan was just beginning his career, at the Balkhash copper complex. But even many years later, already at the top of a hellish political mountain, the old man remembered his former sweetheart and cautiously patronized her.

"It's a shame you decided not to move here," she told me when I saw her the last time. It really seemed to her that I had missed the chance of a lifetime. But I was not so much upset by the lost opportunities as bewildered by the fact that she had a close relationship with Kunayev. Over the course of several decades, without interruption, that man had been Moscow's governor-general in Kazakhstan, and he was even related to Brezhnev himself. That was a strange epoch, when the fates of hundred of millions of people often depended on whether the biochemical processes went well in one worn-out, ancient organism on a given day.

Later, after my aunt's death, I made some friends in Alma-Ata, and when I visited the city, I never went to a hotel. Usually I stayed with Iranbek and his family, who had a relatively comfortable life. The Kazakh writers' union provided him with a nice three-bedroom apartment in a huge building with central heating, hot water, gas stove, telephone, and the other joys of civilization, right in the center of the city. In the Soviet Union living in the center of the city is very prestigious. Iranbek was already forty-three years old, and his wife, Fatyma, was slightly younger. Thanks to her efforts their home was always kept in a state of incredible order and cleanliness. Like many other wives of Soviet literati, Fatyma had taken on herself everything concerning housekeeping, thus freeing her husband to create. They had three daughters, of whom Iranbek was very fond, and then, in their middle age, they had a fourth child, a boy. The youngest was, of course, the pet of the family. The last time I saw him, he was a junior high school student, but now he must be fifteen years old. Other people's children always grow quickly.

I rang Iranbek's doorbell, rejoicing in the imminent encounter and trying to figure out what kind of trouble could have befallen my friend. Fatyma opened the door.

"Hello, Fatyma!" I said with a smile which I cut short at once, seeing her tear-stained eyes and her careworn face, which seemed much older than the last time I had seen it.

"I greet you on your arrival," she said in a suppressed voice and led me to the familiar guest room. A photo portrait of her son hung on the wall, in a black frame with a mourning band.

According to the official version, it was an accident. But the boy did not drown, nor did he fall from the roof, nor was he run over by a car. He was shot. Or, probably, he shot himself. How it had happened no one had discovered. It seemed the boys had found a pistol. Found? One cannot buy arms legally in our country. So it would be impossible to find a pistol in the drawer of a bedside table, and even more impossible to find one somewhere in the street. However, it must be said that arms have become quite accessible on the black market nowadays, especially in the last few years. But where would the teenagers have found that enormous amount of money? The inconsistent evidence from the boy's friends explained nothing. The cops were still trying to clarify the matter, and no final decision on the case had been made.

Iranbek and Fatyma were so devastated by this tragedy that at first they had no stamina for the investigation, nor even any desire to find out what had happened. Their child had died, and nothing else mattered.

"When we came to our senses, I understood that nothing could be done about it," Iranbek told me. "God had taken my son from me and there was nothing I could do about it. I wanted to die myself. But then I thought about my daughters. Who would take care of them if I was gone? They're not even married. I decided to go on living."

He was talking in a quiet, calm voice. But it was a dead voice. It gave me the creeps. There was nothing left of the former Iranbek, joyful, amorous, and reckless. His apathetic attitude reminded me of the Kazakh steppe, burned from beneath by a nuclear blast.

I feel ashamed to say it, but I wanted to leave. The feeling of helplessness, that nothing could be changed, was terribly stressful. I felt something like that once at a Moscow market when, by chance, I saw an armless, drunken man with a cigarette, trying to light a match with his stumps in the wind. The efforts of Iranbek and Fatyma to be hospitable presented an even more awful sight. Iranbek understood how I felt.

"Don't go away!" he said. "I told you on the phone that you must help me."

"How? What can I do?" I asked in a strained voice.

"Stay with us a couple of days. Don't you understand that when we care for a guest, it distracts us from constant thoughts about our son? When Fatyma and I are alone, she can't talk and she only cries. So, tell me, what are you doing now? Are you writing a book? Or an article for *Ogonyok?*" he asked, referring to a journal published in Moscow.

"Why *Ogonyok?*" I forced myself to smile. "What if I'm writing for a foreign publication?"

"Oh, really?" Iranbek showed a flicker of interest. "But they're not interested in anything but the Baltic republics, or perhaps Armenia."

"But that only makes sense," I said, getting a bit involved in the conversation. "For instance, in the United States there is no Kazakh community, but there are considerable Lithuanian and Armenian communities. And that is important, because they are voters, and politicians listen to them."

"No, that's not the main reason." Iranbek waved his hand in

protest. "Moscow is trying all the time to make the West understand that the Islamic threat comes from our part of the world. That if Moscow weakens its grip on our neck, an Islamic revolution like the one in Iran in 1979 will immediately flare up here."

"And *won't* it flare up?" I asked slyly.

"Of course not!" Iranbek got angry. "In any event, not in Kazakhstan. Kazakhs are nomads, and Islam is an urban religion, a religion of merchants. For Kazakhs the Moslem customs are a tradition, embedded in everyday life, rather than a militant ideology."

"But didn't the very first uprisings against the ruling ideology in our country take place right here in Alma-Ata?" I said, hinting at the events of October 1986.

At that time, over the course of two days, December 17 and 18, the army and the internal troops crushed a demonstration on the central plaza of Alma-Ata, Brezhnev Square. The demonstration had been organized by the local population, protesting the appointment of a Russian party functionary as first secretary of the Communist Party of Kazakhstan. The genuine scale of this tragedy will, in all likelihood, be covered by a mist of secrecy for a long time to come. According to information from TASS, which no one believes except the White House, the glorious troops scattered a gang, thirty thousand strong, of drunk ruffians and drug addicts. But according to the data of a Kazakh organization called Kairat, it was a political demonstration, and for participating in it 185 people were brutally killed, about two thousand were wounded (four hundred of them soldiers), and almost three thousand were arrested. More than one hundred among those arrested were sentenced as criminals; three women from the Porshen' piston plant got ten to fifteen years at hard labor, and two were sentenced to death.

"That's right," Iranbek said, looking pensively out the window. "That was really the first open collision of local national forces with the ruling party. Or, to be more precise, with its central apparatus. Kunayev was forced into retirement, and in his place a Russian was sent here. How was it before? Whoever Moscow appointed became our ruler. But at last the people dared to challenge that. You know, many people believed in Gorbachev, believed that now with perestroika everything would be different. Do you know what slogans the demonstrators carried? 'Long live Lenin's ideas!' And they were attacked with bludgeons, boots, shovels, and water cannons."

"At first the authorities kept saying that criminal elements were wreaking havoc on Brezhnev Square," I responded. "But three years later a commission for the investigation of the December events was established. Does that mean justice was restored?"

"Your traveling abroad didn't do you much good." Iranbek grinned. "You reason like some Englishman and not like a Soviet man. What f—justice can there be in this country? First of all, the commission was dismissed, and then the requests and complaints of the victims were forwarded for consideration to the republican Ministry of Internal Affairs, the KGB, the procurator's office, and the Supreme Court—in other words, to the very people who organized the massacre."

"Is that why you decided to give up politics and take up literature exclusively again?" I asked. "But who needs literature today? Can it change anything in our perverted society?"

"And what about spirituality?" Iranbek clenched his fists. It appeared that I had managed to bring him back to life, if only a little. "Not all people are screwed up by our pitch-dark life, without one gleam of hope. You say books are read less and less? Well, let people stop reading altogether! But if literature exists, then it will act. Invisibly. We Kazakhs have a legend: A poor woman was milking her sheep and she looked at her landlord, her *bai*, looked him straight in the eye and asked him when he would marry his daughter to her son. The *bai* grew almost speechless from such insolence. How could some trash dare to desire to become his relative? The poor thing wouldn't stop: 'Marry your daughter to my son. You must!' But the *bai* was a smart guy; he turned it over in his mind many times and guessed what it was all about. He ordered his servants to dig into the ground under the poor woman's sheep. And they dug out a treasure—an ingot of gold as big as a horse's head. You understand?"

"Yes," I nodded. "The gold was radiating such power that even a pauper, when caught in its energy field, dared to ask the *bai* to give his daughter to her son."

"The same thing happens with literature." Iranbek stood up from his armchair. "It allows people, even the poverty-stricken, to feel its power. Let's go eat. Fatyma is calling us to the table."

"That means that literature is not a reflection of being but a natural phenomenon?" I said with a laugh. "Something like the sun or the moon, which causes the ebb and flow of the tides?"

"And earthquakes, too!" Iranbek smiled.

I had not been to Alma-Ata for several years, and during that time many of my friends and acquaintances had made considerable progress in their official careers and their creative work. Some entered the *nomenklatura,* others went in the opposite direction. It is interesting that in the ethnic republics, the ranks of the national partocracy, as well as its adversaries—the nationalist and separatist movements—are mostly replenished by former journalists, writers, and scientists. But one should not try to explain this phenomenon by inferring that national leaders belong to the humanities, or that they are broad-minded. The explanation is quite different.

I began calling my friends, and I was lucky enough to catch Rustem Dzhangushin at home. It has not been easy to find him in Alma-Ata lately, for he has been going around the country as a member of the Coordinating Council of Nevada-Semipalatinsk. But Rustem is also interesting in another respect. He is regarded as one of the leading unofficial Soviet experts on the national question. Back in Moscow, I was told that he is considered to be one of the main theorists and ideologues of the movement for the unification of the Turkic peoples of the U.S.S.R. The Turks make up the second largest national community in the U.S.S.R....

"...which in reality doesn't exist!" Rustem rejoined with restraint. We had been sitting in Iranbek's living room for two hours already, trying to clarify the prospects of Pan-Turkism as a political force in the U.S.S.R. Even Fatyma got interested in this talk. Or rather in Rustem's statements. Rustem is youngish and as lean as a professional tennis player, but his soft, ironic manners betray his intellect. Unlike the other Pan-Turkists I have met, he did not grit his teeth or roll his eyes, but, on the contrary, he was quite careful in his expressions and gestures. It was clear at once that he had studied in St. Petersburg and earned his Ph.D. there. Rustem worked for about fifteen years at the Kazakh Institute of Philosophy and Law. Now he was a senior research associate in the Center for Sociological Research, affiliated with the Kazakh Institute of Economics.

"Well, if a 'unified Turkestan' is impossible in principle," I asked Rustem, "then what is Moscow so afraid of?"

"Unified Turkestan is possible," he answered in a calm, even voice. "At least, theoretically. And Moscow is right to beware of Turkic unity. Otherwise, why does it exert such efforts, trying to separate us and set us in opposition to each other?"

"Divide and conquer!" I said. "Formulated long ago but for all times. Given, of course, that undemocratic societies will always exist."

"And what's your prognosis?" Iranbek asked.

"Well, our prospects are bleak," I responded. "To be sure, we won't see the dusty old Soviet Union as a free and democratic state. Perhaps, our children..."

And I almost choked, seeing how Fatyma and Iranbek immediately paled. "So is it possible to restore Turkic unity, or not?" I asked Rustem.

"Possible?" he repeated. "Certainly! I've been talking about it for a long time. It's not enough just to give up your Kazakh, Uzbek, and Tartar 'belongingness.' You ought to start thinking of yourself as a Turk again. And that's it. All problems are eliminated at once."

"With regard to culture," I retorted. "But what about the administrative division into Union republics and autonomous republics?"

"All this will be solved. There was no Uzbekistan, nor Kazakhstan, nor Tadzhikistan, nor Turkmenia until the Bolsheviks seized power. This division is for the most part artificial and doesn't reflect the historical settlement of the peoples."

Rustem was right. I myself was pondering how strangely the borders between the Central Asian republics were drawn. Big compact groups from different nationalities were left within the confines of other republics: Uzbeks left in Tadzhikistan, Tadzhiks in Uzbekistan and Kirghizia, Kirghizes and Kazakhs in Uzbekistan, and so forth. I recalled my friend, the Tadzhik intellectual Safar Abdulayev, with whom I planned to meet later in Dushanbe. He always felt very strongly about the enforced, as he put it, Uzbekification of the Persian-speaking population of the cities Samarkand and Bukhara. But when I met him the last time in Moscow, he finally told me something that he said he had known since birth: namely, that Uzbeks and Tadzhiks had always been a single unity, which was cut into two parts under Soviet rule.

When I related this to Rustem, he rejoiced.

"At last Safar has seen the light!" he said. "I've been telling him that over and over again for ten years. When was it that Uzbeks and Tadzhiks lived on opposite sides of a border? When Tadzhiks say that Samarkand is their city, that is true, and when Uzbeks say that it's theirs, that is true, too."

"Does it follow, then," I asked incredulously, "that abolishing all the borders between the existing republics of Central Asia will solve every problem?"

Rustem smiled. "Of course not, Perhaps it would be better not to give up the existing borders at first. The twentieth century has given us some awful examples of the consequences of such attempts. Perhaps it must be some sort of confederation, to begin with, although it's not necessary to transfer all existing structures onto future wholes. Life itself will suggest the forms unification might take."

"And what about the Turks of the Transcaucasus?" I roared. "And the Turks of Siberia? And the Turks on the Volga River? Please, don't forget that in Central Asia religious allegiances were always the substitute for ethnic allegiances. That is why Sunni Islam, with a stretch of the imagination, might be considered here as a formal unifying idea. But Azerbaijanis are Shiites! And Chuvashes are Christians! And Iakuts and Altais, for that matter, are idol-worshipers!"

"That's right," Rustem confirmed, cold-bloodedly. "That's why whenever people talk about Islam as a parallel structure for the Pan-Turkic unity, I am always troubled, for it has more minuses than pluses in this regard."

"Kazakhs can't come to an agreement among themselves," Fatyma said, "and you are discussing the unity of all Turks."

She was referring to the rather complex relationships among the three historical branches of the Kazakh people, the senior *dzhus,* the middle *dzhus,* and the junior *dzhus.* Until recently, a lady from the junior *dzhus* could not marry a gentleman from the senior or middle *dzhus.* Now, at least in the cities, that practice is gradually disappearing.

"And does it reverberate through the democratic movement and in the new parties?" I asked.

"No," Rustem replied.

"What about the party-state apparatus, Kazakhstan's top authorities?"

"Oh, yeah," Rustem said.

"Who's ruling now?"

"The senior *dzhus*."

"They say here," Iranbek said, "give the senior *dzhus* a staff for grazing, give the middle *dzhus* a pen for writing, and give the junior *dzhus* some arms for fighting."

"All right, then," I said impatiently. "Let's say that the Turks will be able to come to an agreement about everything. But they need to have a capital, don't they?"

"Of course," Rustem answered confidently. "It's clear that Tashkent must be the center. It is conveniently situated. And it never was a purely Uzbek city. Kazakhs, Tadzhiks, and Karakalpaks regard it as the center of all the Central Asian region."

"It used to be called Shash or Chach," I informed everyone. I love the city where I was born. "The Great Silk Road from China to Europe went through it."

"Do you remember the ancient proverb, 'In Chach a cat can run along the rooftops without ever getting down'?" asked Iranbek, smiling.

"And what about the democratic movements, like Azat?" I asked. "Azat, as far as I remember, means 'liberty.' Does it have legal status?"

"Oh, yes," Rustem said, "it's already registered and even has its own newspaper. But in general it's more like a People's Front than a party. Communists also infiltrate it quite actively."

"How will it all end up?" asked Iranbek pensively, without addressing anyone personally. "How many years must we live under perestroika? Isn't this the fifth year? In my opinion, this whole undertaking reeks of a hoax. There has been a lot of talking, but the essence of power remains the same."

"And what did you expect?" I inquired, struck for the umpteenth time by the pure-hearted credulity of my compatriots. "The main purpose for which it was designed has been realized."

"What do you mean, glasnost?" said Rustem.

"Or the disintegration of the socialist camp?" Iranbek asked.

"Those are all side effects," I responded. "The main reason was for the former second layer at the top of the party *nomenklatura* to be promoted and become the first. The fifty-year-olds have superseded the eighty-year-olds."

"But at what price!" Iranbek was terrified. "They have ruined the whole country."

"Nothing of the sort," I stated. "It was ruined by those who were in power before that. The new ones aspire to save the system. They are even ready to change its name. If you don't want Communism, all right! There won't be any Communism. The main goal for them is to preserve power in their own hands. All the rest is unimportant."

"You're a cynic," Iranbek said. "All Muscovites are cynical."

"Don't go around spouting such clichés," Rustem said. "You might just as well say that the Russians are to blame for all our troubles."

"Now, many people believe that!" Iranbek retorted. "Before all this, Kazakhs loved Russians and trusted them. But now they don't. The elder brother has brought us a lot of troubles with his 'bright future.' But I respect Russians for their great literature."

"And I think," I interjected, "that it's not a dislike of Russians themselves but a dislike of their regime that is in the minds of many national minorities. The Russians have probably suffered from the Communist terror more than anyone else in the U.S.S.R."

"But at least they have kept their language," Rustem said, "while in many national republics no one wants to speak his own language. For instance, in northern Osetia almost no Osetian schools are left, because people do not let their children go there."

"It could end up like that here, as well," Iranbek observed. "Or rather it could have been like that."

"And not only here!" I agreed. "That's why many national republics are hurrying to legitimize their languages as state languages. But I think that is more a political than a cultural fact. How can one make millions of people switch from one language to another by decree?"

"Now a homeless cosmopolitan is speaking through your mouth!" Rustem laughed.

"People no longer respect each other!" Iranbek said with bitterly. "I wonder whether it is like that everywhere, or in our country only?"

17

The Steel Wings of an Engineer
of Human Souls*

It takes almost no time to go by air from Alma-Ata to Lake Issyk Kul in the high mountains. As the crow flies, they are separated only by the high ranges of the northern Tien Shan mountains, which rise 15,000 feet above sea level at their highest peak. You can get to Issyk Kul by land, too. The map suggests two routes, from the west and from the east. The western road goes through the city of Frunze and is about 400 miles long. With a bit of exaggeration it could be called a highway. After Frunze the road starts to climb up and dodges along steep slopes, reminiscent of California's Highway One between Big Sur and the Carmel Highlands.

The eastern road is a hundred miles shorter, but it takes twice as long to drive it as does the western road. In America such roads would be traveled only by four-wheel-drive vehicles. And it turned out to be more difficult than I had imagined to find someone in Alma-Ata who would drive on this road. Moreover, in general, people refuse to go to Issyk Kul by automobile, and not just because it is safer nowadays to stay at home. Even in the most troubled times, it is possible to find

*A translation from the Soviet Newspeak of the thirties: "A Soviet writer flies by plane."

people ready to set out for an adventure, adventures even more daring than a simple car journey along a mountainous road (albeit with some risk of being robbed or killed). They do it either for money or because of a weakened instinct for self-preservation.

The main reason for people's refusal to go over dry land turned out to be much more pedestrian: the lake Issyk Kul is closed to car owners who do not have reservations at state boardinghouses or rest homes. Police ambushes on the roads are quite common, and it is impossible to bribe everyone. One more state monopoly, this time on recreation. Rooms in rest houses are yet another deficit item, and it is impossible to just go and rent one; they must be reserved in advance—provided, of course, that you have some strings to pull.

In principle, one can understand the authorities' ban on "unorganized autotourists," as they are called, meaning people who have no reservations at the state rest houses. On the one hand, God has created this wonderful salt lake, in fact a real little sea in the mountains, which are themselves beautiful beyond description. On the other hand, the Communist dictatorship has a phenomenal ability to turn whatever it touches into shit. The beach areas of the lake, which would have flourished under other economic systems, attracting hundreds of thousands of tourists from this country and abroad, have remained at the level of a decrepit provincial backwater, where there are no hotels, no food, no transport—indeed no services of any kind. But there are luxurious palaces, built in closed compounds on the southern bank of the Issyk Kul for the *nomenklatura* and their families.

The whole life of the Soviet people from cradle to grave consists of a variety of bans, because the Communist regime knows of no other ways to react to the variability of being. "But why do you put up with all that?" a freedom-loving Western reader might ask. "Isn't it better to die with a proudly raised head than to live squatting on your knees?"

"No, it's not better!" the no-less-freedom-loving author of this book would roar back in response. "Because in Soviet concentration camps they won't *let* you die with a proudly raised head." First they turn you into an animal, and then they make you work until you croak from emaciation and the weight of unbearable burdens. And you'll know that at the same time your kith and kin are going through the same hellish tortures. Including your children. Have you ever heard of the MFTM camps? The abbreviation means "members of the families of traitors to the motherland." The dictators adore representing the betrayed motherland. And, by the way, there were many MFTM camps on the territory of Kazakhstan. Tens of millions of Soviet people went through the grindstones of the Soviet punitive machine and their lives ended in the ravines.

That expression must be understood quite literally. It refers to ordinary ravines that are filled with corpses by bulldozers. In the Soviet Union dozens of such burial sites have been found, piled with thousands—or tens of thousands—of skulls with a characteristic bullet hole in the back of the neck. This is what is left from those who did not want to live on their knees in the thirties and in the forties. And how many such burial sites have not been discovered? Is it really surprising, then, that the Soviet people are in no hurry to revisit the route to the ravines, bringing along their next of kin, babies included. Even if there were no more threat of reprisals, the genetic fear people have toward the totalitarian state can only be done away with in several generations. But no Soviet man has any doubts, even for a moment: all that can be repeated any time because the same criminal organization is in power, and the same punitive machine is at its disposal.

If you want to understand what is going on in the Soviet Union today and what you can expect from it tomorrow, you have to know what happened to it yesterday and the day before yesterday. People make a joke in our country: the U.S.S.R. is a unique state having an unpredictable past. The only thing that has not changed in the past seventy years is the most perfect machinery of violence in the world. Every time the Communist regime spots a real threat to its power, as, for instance, in Tadzhikistan or Azerbaijan, it will immediately and repeatedly come down upon the heads of those who are trying to get up from their knees. And it will do so without any self-doubt and with all its repressive might still at its disposal—no matter how enthusiastically Westerners root for the Soviet leaders.

But let us return to cool Alma-Ata. Of course, it would have been possible to relax and spend another week here, enjoying the approximation of civilization's comforts, such as a hot shower—until the hot water was turned off in Iranbek's apartment building for what they call "summer prophylactics." Or conversing by telephone with Moscow—until the authorities pulled the plug on them, something that has happened in some cities in the Baltics. Or to stare at well-dressed women—until martial law was announced and curfews established, as they have been in dozens of major Soviet cities.

But I was already impatient to get to Issyk Kul, which seemed to me some kind of Shangri-la, where one can distract oneself for a few days from the endless stresses of an ugly society and feel oneself a part of indifferent nature. Golden sand, blue water, green mountains, and the golden sun above your head...at least until you encounter your first line to get into a canteen, or a store, or a ticket office.

But how to get to Issyk Kul? Since land transport seemed to be so difficult to arrange, I decided to fly, and headed cheerfully for the airport. I waited in mile-long lines at the ticket offices, and all I could find out was that there are no tickets to Issyk Kul, there never were any tickets to Issyk Kul, and there will not ever be any tickets to Issyk Kul. But it is not so easy to break down a Soviet person.

"Iranbek, help me get a ticket to Cholpon-Ata through the Writers' Union," I said resolutely.

"Are you going to leave or what?" Iranbek asked. "We were going to take you to Medeo."

Medeo is an open skating rink with a vast stadium in the high mountains, not far from Alma-Ata. When I was there last time, I liked most of all that many people there were skating in their bathing suits, thus combining sliding on the artificial ice with sunbathing.

"No, I have to move along," I said.

"Okay, but it can't be done earlier than Monday," Iranbek responded. "Now we won't find anyone in the Union."

I had forgotten; it was indeed Friday, and the end of the working day besides.

"Although there is another way," Iranbek said, and his slight smile echoed with the mysteries of *The Thousand and One Nights*. "If you are really in a hurry we can try it."

"All right," I replied without giving it much thought, guessing that even if it was not a flying carpet it could be nothing less than a cashier acquaintance who could sell me a ticket, for a surcharge. Disgusting, but I was used to it. The only alternative was to stay at home and be quiet.

"No, it's not what you think." Iranbek smiled, putting on an even more enigmatic air.

"Come on, enough taunting of the poor wanderer," I entreated him. "What's up?"

"We'll go and buy a ticket right before takeoff."

"Who will sell it to you?" I grew indignant.

In the Soviet Union tickets are sold forty-five days before the day of departure, but there are no discounts, even for roundtrips. Sometimes one can really buy a ticket in the airport on the day of the flight, but that does not apply to tickets to resorts or major cities.

"They'll sell it to me!" Iranbek said self-assuredly and looked at me with cunning eyes.

"Ah!" I drawled, disappointed, as I finally got it. In Moscow that trick stopped working long ago. Sometimes a writer can use it: he comes up to the ticket office, bends over to poke his head into a little window, and proudly announces: "I'm the writer so-and-so!" About thirty years ago, it worked without fail. Even if a cashier had never heard the name, the very fact that a live writer, whose books are published by the state, stood in front of her made her tremble with delight. She would sell a ticket immediately, the more so as in those times people did not travel much, and there was no shortage of tickets.

On the next day, Iranbek and I went to the airport early in the morning to try our luck. On the way there we had an argument when I carelessly said that Russia has a legitimate claim to the northern and northeastern provinces of Kazakhstan, which are predominantly populated by non-Kazakhs.

"Nothing of the sort," Iranbek said, grinding his jaws. "In fact, Kazakh lands are even more extensive than just Kazakhstan's territory. The Orenburg province, the Omsk Province, and Altai, too, if it comes to that, were never Russian lands. The Russians took them from us by force. There was never any voluntary joining of Kazakhstan to Russia!"

"But will you agree that from the point of view of the ratio of Kazakhs to non-Kazakhs, Kazakhstan is not Lithuania or Georgia, where the majority of the population belongs to the local nationality?"

"But it's our trouble, not our fault, that there are fewer Kazakhs in Kazakhstan than people of other nationalities."

"Yet perhaps in that case it would be better to think about an alliance with Russia rather than about a restoration of Turkestan, would it not?" I asked. "Suppose it were an alliance not with the former 'center' of Gorbachev, but with a partner with equal rights—Yeltsin's Russia. Let everyone who wants to secede from the Soviet Union—the Baltic states of Lithuania, Latvia, and Estonia; the three republics of the Transcaucasus, Georgia, Armenia, and Azerbaijan; perhaps Moldavia, too, which wants to go back to Romania. But might other republics want to stay in an alliance with Russia? Not with an empire, but with Rus' proper."

"Where do you see this Rus' proper?" Iranbek got stuck. "Today Russia consists of colonial territories, three-fourths of it, if not more. The Volga area, the Urals, Siberia, the Far East—all these are conquered lands where other peoples are living."

"Well, first of all, they were seized even before the eighteenth century," I replied. "If it comes to that, compare the political map of the world in those times and now. Who would agree now to redraw the borders of the states to make them fit into the eighteenth-century map? And second, it's a question of whether those peoples that survived would like to secede from Russia. Fancy that there is no more Communism in Russia. It means that the hope of having a normal economy, with time, comes immediately to the fore. And if so, people will gradually begin to live like people. Why then, should the smaller ethnic groups leave Russia if every single citizen, whatever his nationality, would be able to live a normal human life?"

"That's a utopia!" Iranbek waved his hand. "Why should we wait until the Kremlin deigns to give up Communism? Gorbachev will procrastinate for one hundred years, and are we to writhe with pain all that time?"

"Then it follows that the peoples of the U.S.S.R. have rushed to secede not because of secession as such but to get rid of the vampire's embrace of the Communist system. It's clear to everyone, down to the last camel, that this system is not viable. And imagine that it would be dismantled in Russia first?"

"That will never happen!" Iranbek cried. "These rascals will never voluntarily give up their power!"

"They've been stinging us like bugs, and they can't get enough of our blood!" said a man entering our conversation all of a sudden, a guy who looked more like an agent-provocateur from the KGB than a peaceful *paisano* or cattle breeder.

People from the crowd that had gathered around us began to applaud.

"Break it up, break it up, comrades!" a young cop commanded, holding a hefty walkie-talkie crackling with interference.

Iranbek and I exchanged glances and began to make our way energetically through the crowd.

"Here we go!" Iranbek exclaimed, bumping into a pretty young Kazakh woman in an Aeroflot uniform. "That's who we need!"

"What's the matter, comrade?" she asked with a businesslike air, obviously going to push him away with her hand. "Haven't you been in a jail for a long time?"

"I'm Iranbek Orazbaev!" Iranbek announced solemnly in Kazakh, looking as though he was going to pound himself on the chest like a top gorilla. I almost started shaking with laughter, but then choked and gaped with amazement. The woman evidently reacted to his name—and how! It was not the fear or obsequiousness with which people greet bosses whom they have failed to recognize at once. And what kind of a boss could Iranbek be to her in any case? The miracle was that suddenly her face took on a human expression, as if she had met a close relative.

"May I help you?" she asked Iranbek in Kazakh with a kind smile, and I looked around in amazement to see if anyone else had heard this magic phrase.

"Give me your passport and money and wait for me here!" Iranbek said to me proudly, leaving with the Aeroflot woman for the office.

In about fifteen minutes he returned with the plane ticket and a bouquet under his arm, a bouquet, it seemed, of chamomile.

"I'm speechless!" I shouted, heedless of the dangerous presence of the cop with his walkie-talkie. "The people know and love their heroes!"

"I'm surprised myself, take my word for it," Iranbek said, smiling from ear to ear for the first time in several days, and we embraced while parting.

Coming in for a landing, the plane hung for a second above the turquoise vastness of Issyk Kul, which suddenly reared slantwise, covering itself with an image of half the sky. In fact everything was just the opposite: it was the plane that banked over the transparent waters of the mountain sea and started landing with a roar, gobbling up thousands of gallons of the pure oxygen produced by the local forests, miraculously spared despite all the monstrous perturbations attendant to the building of a new socialist life.

Issyk Kul is an unfreezing salt lake occupying one of the hollows of the northern Tien Shan at the height of 5,270 feet above sea level. Its is 112 by 37.5 miles, with a maximum depth of 2,303 feet. Even in the coldest part of the year, when everything around is covered with snow, the temperature of the lake does not fall below thirty-nine degrees Fahrenheit. Hence, its name, which means "hot lake."

The swimming season is not very long, running from mid-May through the end of August. During this time the temperature ranges from sixty-five to seventy-five degrees Fahrenheit. Of course, one can swim before May and after August, but rubber wetsuits are unknown in the U.S.S.R. Some bathers swim in bikinis, while others go in wearing old-fashioned canvas frocks. Even nude bathers are not unknown, although one never encounters them on public beaches.

There are frequent summer thunderstorms on Issyk Kul, but more often they occur in the evening and at night. However, in the middle of this scorching day, sunset appeared to be no more than a theoretical possibility. The sun had reached its zenith and generously poured its fierce radiation over the earth, but the sky was of such a virgin cobalt color that talk about ozone holes seemed like the habitual lies of the local party press.

The town of Cholpon-Ata, which is near the airport, occupies the northern bank of the lake. On this side of Issyk Kul there are mainly tourist boardinghouses and rest homes, which were built in the sixties and seventies by the big industrial factories of Central Asia. The southern side of the lake was considered to be for the elite; accordingly the boardinghouses and rest homes there were more chic.

After I soberly estimated the situation, I decided not to poke my nose into the southern side. Yet it is practically impossible to get room and board even at a tourist place for Soviet plebes on the northern bank. The *putyovki*—special certificates that give you the right to spend a certain amount of time at a hostel (usually for twelve or twenty-four days)—are distributed among state workers and employees by the trade union committees of their workplaces, long before the tourist season opens. To get an opportunity to buy them, people pull strings, intrigue, and try to become "winners of socialist competition."

Dragging behind me my hateful black bag, I set out to travel on foot along Cholpon-Ata's streets, which climb up into the foothills that girdle Issyk Kul along the coastline. To rent a room turned out to be not an easy task. I was knocking on gates, looking into yards, talking to local residents and "wild" holiday-makers, and only two hours later did I succeed.

It was a small house in the midst of an apple orchard. The landlords themselves lived in the main house, whose fortresslike fronts overlooked the street. When I knocked politely on the high window with open shutters, a red flowery curtain was drawn, and an aged Russian mistress in a white kerchief looked at me from behind a pot filled with geraniums. Studying my face, she poked herself out through the window in a manner more conducive to further negotiations. Trying to keep the same positive expression on my face that had induced her to talk with me in the first place, I asked whether she would agree to take me temporarily as a lodger.

"Well, it depends on how long you stay," she said, trying to look from on high into my breast pocket, in which was conspicuously visible a wad of bills, encircled by a thin rubber band.

"However long it takes," I answered with a diplomatic smile, for I didn't know myself how all would go in the future.

"No less than thirty days, and all money in advance," the mistress said, frowning in the manner usually employed for such negotiations. "And show me your passport! You know what times are like now."

"Oh, sure!" I nodded respectably, trying to figure out which of my passports to show her, the domestic one or the passport for traveling abroad. I showed her the domestic one to escape tedious inquiries. And then I asked, "And what does one pay nowadays for a cot?"

"As you know…"—she halted for some reason—"ten rubles."

"Per day?" I feigned surprise to be polite.

"Not for a whole year, you can bet." The mistress joyfully smiled. "And why are you so serious?"

"I want to eat," I told her truthfully.

There were two rooms in the small house, separated by a thin board partition, but each having its own entrance. My trestle bed was in a smaller room, more reminiscent of a half-built clothes closet, although it had a big window. The main furniture consisted of a single nail driven into the wall and an old coat hanger made of twisted wire. A basin could be seen under the trestle bed, which judging by some remains of enamel had once been blue.

"When it rains, the roof leaks. But you can use the basin there," the mistress explained affably, having grasped my interest in the basin. "The linen is fresh. I've done the laundry myself, but I had no time to iron it as the electricity was off for some reason. The iron and the samovar are on the veranda. The outhouse is at the end of the yard. And you have seen the running water yourself. It's in front of the summer kitchen."

"And who lives in the other room?" I asked curiously.

"Oh, don't worry, they are cultured people, also from Moscow," she said. "They spend the whole day on the beach, although they quarrel at night. But they don't fight!"

"The sweethearts are arguing just for fun," I mumbled, already an official neighbor.

The "wild" beach, the beach full of unofficial visitors, seemed to me to be rather crowded, although it was not as crowded as the beaches on the Black Sea. There are probably no statistics on holiday-makers coming to Issyk Kul without *putyovki*, who they are and how many of them arrive each year. According to my cursory observation, the majority of them are Russian-speaking residents of the Central Asian republics and inhabitants of the large industrial cities of Siberia. It's easy to recognize men and women from Siberia because of their red sunburned skin, peeling as the result of too much sunbathing. But all the same one could say that they were contented and happy, having come to this beautiful place after a long, sad winter in their smoky city barracks.

The contradictions of human nature are revealed in a quickie way. Many Russian women, light-skinned from birth, try to burn themselves, lying in the sun, so that they become completely brown, while their swarthy sisters from Central Asia have always considered white skin to be a sign of beauty. Despite all selectionist efforts of the ruling ideology, which attempts to breed in our country "a new historical community, the Soviet people," one can see the differences between the folks of different nationalities with an unaided eye. Unlike Russians, Central Asian people do not fancy the idea of lying naked in the sun near water. Offer the head of a patriarchal Eastern family a chance to take his family some place thousands of miles away, so that his respectable wife and unmarried daughters can denude themselves in broad daylight to the amusement of complete strangers, half-naked good-for-nothings and gapers. You will get a polite but unbending refusal. And if you ask why, you'll not hear references to religious or ethical considerations. Most probably, the motivation will be business or someone's sickness or other unexpected circumstances. The Asiatic soul is no less mysterious than the Slavic soul or, for that matter, the Russian soul.

In rural Central Asia the bathers are mostly boys. Sometimes they are joined by girls, usually no older than twelve or thirteen years old, who swim in their dresses and long wide trousers. I once saw a group of young people swimming near an Uzbek village in the Chimghan mountains. Boys and girls were jumping into a noisy river feet-first from a huge boulder hanging over a dam in the mountains. The sky seemed to be burned out from heat, the yellow heads of St. John's wort were heavily scented. Meanwhile, boys with close-cropped hair, in white homespun underpants that came down to their knees, and girls in their wet red dresses, and hair woven into forty pigtails, climbed the rock, stretched their arms wide, and jumped with closed eyes into the foaming water. They plunged in slowly, as if in slow motion, up to the waist and then submerged their heads in the water with an iridescent splash.

Of course, as they are everywhere else in the world, the inhabitants of the big cities in Central Asia differ considerably from the country people. Until recently, the thirty- to forty-year-olds in the cities aspired to be exactly like Russians in everything, but in the last few years the pendulum of public fashion has swung back sharply toward traditionalism. Rejecting the official values of socialism, the intelligentsia throughout the U.S.S.R. are calling upon the people to return to the ancient customs of their forebears.

I left my clothes in a pile on the water's edge and dashed into the cool salty waves of Issyk Kul. After swimming about thirty meters in a crazy crawl, I almost knocked a hole in the prow of a life-saving dinghy. "Where are you going! Are you crazy, man?" a tanned sailor from the lifesaving service yelped cheerfully over his megaphone, his other hand lying lazily on the shoulder of a girl in a white felt hat, proudly looking back at her girlfriends on the shore. "Now go back to the shore!"

Smiling happily, I swam back, doing the breaststroke. My rest and relaxation on the seashore had begun.

18

A Tea Ceremony
in an Apple Orchard

For the past five or six years I have managed to arrange regular visits to the sea with my wife and daughter. People in the Soviet Union usually go to the Black Sea or the Baltic Sea. On the Black Sea it is always hot, damp, and crowded as Coney Island. On the Baltic it is much cooler, and more respectable, too, rather like Carmel on the California coast. In the Soviet Union there is also the Caspian Sea, which is much less popular because its coastal facilities have not been developed to receive large crowds of vacationers. Besides that, the desert steppes surrounding it with their sharp continental climate cannot compete with the lush subtropics of the Black Sea or the sandy banks of the Baltic, surrounded by pine forests. But on the Caspian Sea, despite the lack of a resort tradition, there are also quite a few beautiful, well-equipped places, where you can pass a delightful week or two, and improve your health at the same time—provided that you have good friends among the local residents. The problems involved in taking a seaside vacation in the Soviet Union are far greater than simply choosing the right place and having enough money to afford the journey. In a country where every aspect of life hinges upon personal relations, the main condition for the successful realization of any plan—from the purchase of sausage to one's summer vacation—is not so much money as it is having good friends and useful acquaintances.

To my wife and me it was especially important, for we never bought *putyovki,* preferring to arrange accommodations on the spot with the help of our friends. Fortunately, I had plenty of them in almost every Soviet republic, including on the shores of all the Soviet seas. As a result we could vary the geography of our itineraries, and thus not become a burden on our *kunaks,* good friends, by visiting too often. Quite naturally, we tried to be useful to our friends in turn during their habitual raids on Moscow. There is no other way to survive in our phantasmagoric world, where instead of succinct laws the whims of the state reign in all spheres of human life.

My sojourn on the shores of Issyk Kul did not have the usual beneficial effects of a seaside vacation. Neither the primordial landscape of the mountains, nor the bright sun above my head, nor the monotonous pounding of the surf aided my yogilike attempts to escape to another dimension and be rid, if only for a moment, of my sad reflections on the unfortunate destiny of my motherland and murky forebodings about my own fate.

While I lay on the beach, I wondered if some of the other people on the beach were my neighbors in the small house in the apple orchard. Some people were simply lying in the sun, eyes closed and arms outstretched, completely oblivious to the hateful life of society; others were noisily playing volleyball and occasionally trying to roust the dozers with the ball. Some folks were nibbling on boiled potatoes and hard-boiled eggs; some were flirting quite openly, showing off all their natural endowments; and the couple sitting next to me was quarreling, quietly but rather fiercely. Unfortunately, squabbles in public places do not astonish anyone anymore. Yet one is advised not to act as peacemaker, and especially not to take sides, in the Soviet Union.

Cholpon is the ancient Turkic name for the planet Venus. One might venture a guess that the name of the town Cholpon-Ata migrated to the local signs from an ancient star atlas. In winter it is probably very quiet here, but in summer, the tourists make the town look like a disturbed beehive. There is a prevailing mood of anxiety and nervousness that would seem to be out of place in a resort town. But the Soviet people, especially those who have come here from big cities, have many reasons to be fussy and nervous. Like their brothers in misfortune from the country, city dwellers have gotten used to doing without many basic commodities during the decades of Soviet rule. But unlike the provincial residents the city dwellers never became genuine stoics. We are still hurrying somewhere, we are still afraid to be late or not to succeed, to be deprived of some of life's goodies—or rather, the leftovers from the lordly table of the *nomenklatura*. Diogenes, the stoic who lived in a barrel, was never the hero of the Soviet people.

I had long been accustomed to the sight of lines. In Moscow it was possible for me not to stand in lines, but in Cholpon-Ata the prospect was inevitable. If I wanted to eat at the canteen, with its trashy food and bullying treatment of customers, I would have to stand in line for several hours a day just in order to get to the counter. There was a bazaar in Cholpon-Ata where at least I could buy something to eat. But there was little alternative to the line at the long-distance telephone office. Of course, I could write a letter and send it by mail instead of calling Moscow. (My telefax at home was useless in Kirghizia in the summer of 1990. If I had tried to explain to the aged, extremely stern woman who was taking telegrams what Genie or CompuServe meant, I would probably have been sent to a mental hospital as a person who came to the post office to send a cable to the planet Jupiter.)

But if I could escape *some* lines in Cholpon-Ata, how could I avoid spending days of standing in line for a return ticket? Only one who has experienced it can know the feeling of helpless fury at the sight of a crazed, thousand-strong crowd surging toward the two little windows at an Aeroflot ticket office that are actually open—out of the twelve that should be open.

Soviet people associate their recreation in summer not only with crushing onto the beaches and waiting many hours in line to get to the canteens, but also with daily roll calls at the lines at railroad and air ticket offices that occur in the evenings, the search for their names among the lists compiled by voluntary organizers, the sobbing and crying when their names suddenly get crossed off, but also the incomparable happiness verging on a heart attack when you get your return ticket at the end of your holiday.

For the third night in a row I fell asleep early and slept straight through the night, waking up in exactly the same posture in which I had plunged into sleep. It was probably the result of exhaustion and an overflow of impressions during the previous weeks. It is true that living in Moscow I got used to meeting dozens of people every day, discussing countless topics and answering endless phone calls. But I was mixing with different people now, and life itself had become altogether different. And then I had an awful realization. I understood that I would never be able to return to my former normal life. What I had seen and what I was still to see about my country could not pass through me without leaving a trace.

It was not until Wednesday morning that I got acquainted with my neighbors. At first I heard their nervous voices through the thin plank partition. It sounded like the beginning of any marital squabble.

"I told you, we should have gone the Baltic," the young woman on the other side of the partition said. One could tell that the scenario had been well rehearsed over the past few days, and that both sides had already lost some of their interest in the topic.

I closed my eyes and turned onto my other side.

"It's not quiet in the Baltic," a confident male voice answered with a habitual-sounding irritation. People use this kind of intonation to repeat something that has been said many times before. "Besides that, all the beaches are closed because of a cholera infection. At least, that's what they are saying in the newspapers."

"Then we should have gone to the Black Sea!" his wife said, apparently trying to get at some as yet unclear point. "Give me a light."

"Why is it better?" The male voice got indignant, and the metallic springs of his bed squeaked furiously with his motions. A lighter clicked quietly and the familiar smell of a burning Dunhill reached me. "The Georgians are fighting on the Black Sea with the Abhazians; in Sukhumi they fire machine guns for nothing. Don't you watch television? If so, don't you know that the Black Sea is dying? It's permeated with hydrogen sulfide, in which not only fish but even all the seaweed has died! Life is preserved only in the upper layers, the top fifty meters."

"Well, that would be enough for us," the woman replied angrily. "And in general I don't believe anything I read. All this is fabricated by the newspapers to distract us from our own difficulties. Why did I listen to you and come to dreary old Issyk Kul? There's nothing here:

neither a decent hotel, nor a restaurant, nor society. Why did I bring my high-heeled shoes? And I brought five evening dresses, like a fool! Here there are only mountain tourists from Siberia and those frightening Kirghizes!"

"Quite ordinary Kirghizes," the man replied wearily. "Typical minorities, that's all. They ride horses, graze sheep in the mountains. Why don't you like them?"

"It seems to me he stopped snoring," the woman said, distracted from the main subject. "Maybe he woke up."

I smiled. It seems that the last statement referred to me. Fumbling in the side pocket of my black bag I pulled out my radio to listen to the news. The batteries were not yet dead, and the radio started crackling with atmospheric interference.

My radio was broadcasting the news from Frunze. Kirghiz is very similar to Uzbek, so for variety I could listen to the news in Kirghiz as well. Then I heard something that made me shiver with fear: martial law had been announced in Osh Province of Kirghizia three days earlier. That would play havoc with my plans: martial law and curfew meant that all roads were blocked by military patrols. Damn! I had intended to drive to Frunze after Issyk Kul, and from there move through Osh Province to Tadzhikistan. If I had known that events would turn out this way, I could have planned that leg of my trip through Central Asia. How was I to get out of here? There are thousands, perhaps tens of thousands of vacationers at Issyk Kul, and a constant deficit of tickets for any kind of transportation. And suppose that the insurrection were not just "a small group of irresponsible extremists," as they like to say in the official organs, but something much more serious? As soon as the genuine scope of the problem made itself known, a real panic could start. Everyone would try to leave, and the only way to do so was to go through Frunze. It was not quite clear why martial law was established, for the information on the radio had obviously been cleared by censors. The announcer spoke in a worried voice about collisions of hooligan groups. I turned up the sound. There were wounded and killed. Administrative and apartment buildings were damaged.

My neighbors across the wall first whispered something to each other and then delicately knocked on the partition.

"Hey, man," the male voice said sternly, "make your radio quieter! You are not in your own yurt, you know."

"War has begun," I said angrily. "So you may want to go to the White Sea, it's safer there now."

"And where is it, the White Sea?" the woman asked her companion.

"On the north, in the Arctic Circle," the man said impatiently, and then addressed me again. "Excuse me, I thought you were...a local. What happened? What war are you talking about? Could it be just some pogroms, as in Sumgait or Fergana?"

"I believe it's something awful," I answered, tuning my radio. "Wait, maybe I can find something in Russian... Do you have return tickets?"

"No, we don't have anything," the woman intoned with evil mockery. "Thank you, Kolen'ka, for this remarkable holiday."

They invited me through the partition to join them for a cup of tea and asked me to come in an hour. Thanking them for the invitation, I went to town on a reconnaissance mission and returned rather worried. There was already pandemonium at the bus station, while the beaches and the bazaar, on the contrary, were almost empty. The newspapers only repeated what had been broadcast on the radio. There had been no telephone connection with Moscow since the day before—"for technical reasons," they told me at the post office. The local police were patrolling the streets by twos and threes, although soldiers with machine guns were not to be seen as yet. *Uzun kulak* had already brought the bad news here; although no one knew the details, everyone agreed on the main points. What was happening in Osh Province was the beginning of an ethnic war between Kirghizes and Uzbeks.

"Yes, and what about Turkic solidarity?" I thought, remembering my recent talks in Alma-Ata with Rustem Dzhangushin. Then I tried to create a working hypothesis of a Kirghiz-Uzbek conflict. There were a little more than two million Kirghizes in Kirghizia, which amounted to nearly half its population. The next biggest ethnic community was Uzbek. As the result of a confused Moscow demarcation policy, it turned out that almost half a million Uzbeks live in Kirghizia, exactly in the territory of Osh Province. Uzbeks are one of the most numerous nationalities in Central Asia. There are almost fourteen million of them in the territory of Uzbekistan alone.

The conflict between Kirghizes and Uzbeks flared up in the Fergana valley, the same region where there had been clashes between

Kirghizes and Tadzhiks a year earlier. The Fergana valley is one of the most densely populated regions of Central Asia, about nine hundred people per square mile. (For comparison: there are five people per square mile in Australia, sixty-five in the United States, 260 in France, and 595 in England.) When the Soviet government drew the border lines between Uzbekistan, Tadzhikistan, and Kirghizia, none of them had ever been separate national state establishments before. How did it happen that such towns as Osh and Dzhalalabad, populated predominantly by Uzbeks, ended up in Kirghizia? And what about the Tadzhik-speaking cities of Uzbekistan? To continue this logically one would have to remember the crazy major from Kzyl-Orda Province.

Could it be that the founding fathers of our utopian state-prison were so farsighted—indeed, such geniuses? Could it be that they had divided the rich Fergana valley in this way not because of the illiteracy of the "red governor-generals" but for one purpose only—to push parts of the once unified Central Asian ethnic groups into conflict every time the imperial power of the Kremlin was at stake?

The conflict in 1989 between Kirghizes and Tadzhiks had occurred because of water for irrigation. And what was the reason for this row between Kirghizes and Uzbeks? A living standard below the poverty line, overpopulation, the highest level of unemployment in the U.S.S.R., and a complete lack of prospects for the younger generation—in such a strained situation it is easy to provoke civil disorder, using any pretext, thereby keeping power in the hands of those to whom it already belongs.

I went through the gate and crossed the orchard to my temporary asylum. Trees and plants, birds and insects lived their own life, without any suspicion of the tragic farce of human society. Or maybe they just pretended.

"Come in, come in!" my neighbor answered in a purring voice to my knock. I entered and was caught by surprise: a living version of a Barbie doll was sitting in front of me, albeit with a burning cigarette in her hand. Even ten years ago smoking remained a symbol of emancipation for many Soviet women. Now it is merely a bad habit.

"Good morning," I said, trying to conceal my astonishment at the sight of such an extraordinary resemblance. The young woman could have served as an advertisement glorifying the stupid doll.

"Please, sit down, Kolya will come shortly," Barbie said. "Our stuff is in the hostess's refrigerator. My name's Lara. What's yours?"

She looked like she was in her twenties, but the expression of conventional wisdom on her beautiful face testified to the fact that she had no illusions concerning humankind. Young women living with fifty-year-old husbands often have such faces.

"It must be your first time at Issyk Kul," I said in a half-inquiring, half-asserting tone after introducing myself to the lady.

"And the last time, too," she responded in the voice of a woman who knows exactly what she wants. Her ways were soft, but her claws were sharp.

"A few years ago I might have advised you to go to the Caspian Sea." I smiled politely. "But after what happened in Baku in January, it's better to miss that season there. Although there is also Makhachkala."

"Is that in Daghestan?" Lara-Barbie asked with a bit of interest, and shivered. "No, it's even scarier to go there!"

Young Russian women, especially Muscovites, are absolutely sure that all beautiful blondes would meet with unspeakable dangers in the Transcaucasus. Perhaps with good reason. At any rate, persistent glances and even harassment on the beach are considered to be common occurrences in such places. Even plain women who are not used to such signs of attention are transformed as soon as they arrive on the shores of the Black or Caspian seas. Their gait and facial expressions become somewhat royal, which gives evidence one more time that, first, there *are* no plain women in this world, and second, that not only kings but queens as well are made by their suits. But, on the other hand, last year the local womanizers in Sukhumi beat up my friend Volodya Averbah when he tried to protect his wife and teenage daughter from insolent attacks.

"It turns out that there is nowhere to go in the Soviet Union now. Unless you want to go around with a machine gun," I continued. "Although it's possible to get a good rest abroad. Last year my wife and I managed to go to the Mediterranean Sea in Tunisia."

"Oh!" Lara got excited. "The Mediterranean Sea must be a real treat! Did you get some *putyovki* for your cruise?"

"Well, no, we were presenting a play at the Carthage theater festival, thus combining the pleasant with the useful," I said. "Tunisia is a stunningly beautiful country, and a very hospitable people."

"Do you work in the Ministry of Culture, or what?" Lara asked languidly. "And what bad luck brought you here?"

"Lara, Lara, how many times do I have to tell you that it's not polite to ask people several questions at once? Let him answer your first question and then ask another one." Kolya, who had just materialized on the threshold, reprimanded his partner in a loud voice. He held a kettle in one hand, and a big tray with finger sandwiches in the other. The sausage was Finnish, the cheese fell just barely short of being a French brie, and there was some red caviar, too. Could it be that they brought all this from Moscow? I asked myself. Here one can get such things only through the special distributions for the highest party elite. In Moscow people with connections can get not only red caviar but even the devil himself, horns and all.

"Hello," I said, standing up to greet my host. "It's nice to meet a resident of the 'exemplary Communist city,' here at the end of the world."

"Oh, are you from Moscow, too?" Kolya rejoiced restrainedly, placing the kettle and sandwiches on the table. Then he introduced himself: "Nikolai Petrovich."

I introduced myself and we shook hands. His handshake was firm and self-confident.

"What a coincidence, indeed. I mean that we came to the same landlady," Kolya commented. "Larochka, let's sit down at the table."

"It would be better if we all got into one Sovmin [Council of Ministers] health center!" Lara said angrily. "I bet not only members go there!"

Kolya and I laughed and casually examined each other. He was my senior by ten years, although he seemed to be older despite his well-built physique. His face was wrinkled, the remains of his hair had become salt-and-pepper, and there were heavy bags under his eyes. It was clear that this person smoked a lot, loved to have a drink, and to sit at least once a week the whole night long playing cards with his friends.

"Wait a minute, I have some really good tea with me," I said, and went to my room to bring my Twining's Irish Tea in tea bags.

Lara and Kolya approved of my tea and I gave them what was left in the package as a present.

19

Eclipse in Osh Province

Our peaceful tea party, which had started as breakfast but imperceptibly turned into lunch, was interrupted by the sudden intrusion of a worried landlady. "Oh, those Muscovites, darling little Muscovites! They have pleased people so much, making everyone so happy!" she lamented, waving her arms. "And all this is because of your damned glasnost and perestroika! Whether it was good or bad—we were living as people do, friendly and peacefully, until Gorby came along and screwed it all up."

"Stop talking nonsense, Spiridonovna!" Kolya shouted at the landlady. "Tell us what happened. You're cackling so much I'm getting dizzy."

"Kolya says just the right words. Good work," I thought to myself in passing. "He's such a familiar type—a Moscow boss playing the role of a good guy. He knows exactly how to talk to people."

One characteristic of Soviet culture is that Soviet people are used to distrusting any kind of polite behavior, and they react to it with some suspicion. Politeness, as one of the main qualities of the intelligentsia, was declared to be regressive and ridiculous. This phenomenon derives from the ideology of the Soviet regime which, from the first days of its existence, declared the old intelligentsia simply superfluous for the two main classes of Soviet society—the proletariat and the peasantry—unless their knowledge could be used by the system. The deep suspicion of the authorities toward people who earn their living by brainwork has a quite pedestrian explanation: intellectuals are more resistant to mass brainwashing than other strata of the population. Historians of the movies, for instance, long ago noticed that in all the old Soviet films, soft-spoken representatives of the intelligentsia are always comical figures, who often turn out to be agents of several foreign intelligence services at once. Let us not forget also the subconscious inferiority complex of several generations of semi-educated Soviet leaders, and that Gorbachev was the first head of the Soviet government who completed his education before joining the party apparatus. Lenin was expelled from Kazan University during his first semester, and he finally got a degree by mail. Stalin entered a theological college but soon gave it up and joined the criminal world. All other Soviet leaders, even if they studied somewhere, mainly graduated from the ideological party colleges where nobody studied anything but lies.

I was letting myself be carried away by my thoughts, but I came to quickly when I heard Spiridonovna cry in full voice, "But they're killing each other, they are!" She started wiping with the end of a handkerchief at the tears rolling down her face.

"Who's killing? Who's being killed?" Kolya laughed, looking back at frightened Lara.

"Don't you know, the Kirghizes and Uzbeks are burning each other!" the landlady told us, sobbing and crying. "Our neighbor's sister came last night from Myrza-Ake. She just managed to escape from there. She says what's going on there is awful: they're destroying everything and they have no pity for anyone, neither old people nor children! And what they do with women—it's beyond description, some real tortures!"

"Sit down and calm yourself," I said, trying to hide my anxiety. "Do you want a cup of tea? Pour her some tea, Lara."

"What kind of tea is it, tea on a string or what?" the landlady asked through her tears, seating herself bulkily on a big wooden stool.

According to her, the neighbor's sister, who was Russian herself, had fled with her children, in a state close to insanity, two nights before from her home settlement of Myrza-Ake in neighboring Osh Province. In that settlement, where the majority of the population is

Kirghiz, an anti-Uzbek commotion had flared up. People who had been peacefully living together, in an equal state of poverty, had suddenly grown crazy with hatred toward their ethnic neighbors.

As if by some invisible command, in the morning all Kirghizes tied red bands over their heads, armed themselves with sticks and shovels, and started loading themselves onto buses. Where did they get so many red bands and who allowed them to use state buses? Of all means of transport only cars are allowed to be privately owned. So far, there was no answer to any of these questions. The Kirghiz neighbors said that they were driving to the neighboring town of Uzgen, the district's center, to smash the houses of local Uzbeks. Many of them returned to Myrza-Ake in the afternoon, and then such terrible things happened as could have been seen only in a nightmare. Mobs of Kirghiz youths and teenagers led by adults, armed with guns, went through the settlement checking all houses and yards searching for Uzbek families. Uzbek houses were set on fire by Molotov cocktails thrown in through the windows. Women and children were raped, men were killed after being tortured. Some of them were burned alive. The authorities did nothing to help the victims, and there were suspicions that they in fact had helped the marauders.

"Did they make attempts on the Russians?" Lara asked, growing pale with horror.

"It seems they didn't," the landlady answered, crying. "They just broke into the Russians' houses and demanded they give up hidden Uzbeks."

Not only Russians but even some Kirghizes were trying to hide Uzbeks. Old Kirghiz men tried to stop the pogrom, or at least stop the killers at the threshold of their houses, but the crowd, growing wild, threw them out of the way and beat to death any victims they found.

Even without describing in full detail these bloody events (for instance, the killers were putting out eyes and cutting off noses from live people; wounded Uzbeks were driven to a local hospital where they were finished off with shovels by the crazy crowd), it was clear that rumors of similar actions on the part of Uzbeks had triggered all these atrocities. This mechanism of exciting mobs has always worked without fail in our country. It was behind the 1988 anti-Armenian raid in Sumgait, when rumors spread of Azerbaijanis allegedly killed by Armenians in Nagorno-Karabakh. It was also behind the 1989 attack against Meskhetin Turks in Fergana, where Uzbeks had ascribed to Turks every conceivable and inconceivable sin. And it was also behind the pogroms eighty years ago, when the mob was inspired by absolutely nonsensical lies about ritual killings of Christian babies by Jews.

But the events in Kirghizia differed considerably from the usual wars between ethnic groups in the Transcaucasus because in Kirghizia both sides belong to the same religious denomination. Kirghizes and Uzbeks are both Moslems; moreover, both are members of the Sunni sect. And like other world religions, Islam considers the murder of coreligionists not only the worst possible crime but a terrible sin as well. So in this case it would hardly be possible for the authorities to attribute the clashes to religious discords.

So what was happening? According to the official explanation, which I learned later in Tashkent, the reason for the bloody conflict between Kirghizes and Uzbeks was a disagreement over a large piece of land belonging to a *kolkhoz* named after Lenin and populated mainly by Uzbeks. While the majority of the people in Osh Province are Uzbeks, it is part of Kirghizia, and consequently ruled by the Kirghiz rather than the Uzbek party mafia.

The press reported that the local Kirghiz authorities had transferred this ill-fated allotment of land to the Kirghizes for their exclusive development. But in fact the sequence of events was the opposite. First, Kirghiz squatters seized this land illegally, and then the authorities passed a law ensuring the ownership of this allotment by the squatters. But Soviet people know all too well how cruelly the authorities punish any manifestations of anarchy. If only this anarchy was not sanctioned by authorities themselves, even though secretly. That is why the Uzbek community's rage was pitted not against the squatters alone but against the authorities, who had openly connived with the dangerous course of events and, perhaps, provoked it in the first place. It is not clear why the local and republic authorities did not undertake any steps to prevent the tragedy, particularly since the local police and the KGB, it was later reported, had repeatedly informed the province and republic party leadership about the growing tension. Consequently, one can conclude that either the republic leadership had completely lost its ability to get a clear understanding of the situation, or it was overtly scheming to create this conflict. Another possible conclusion was that such a desire had been imposed upon them from above. For the slogan "divide and conquer" has been successfully put into practice by all the empires that have ever existed on earth, the "Evil Empire" included.

The housing problem in our country has been permanently aggravated since the first days of the Soviet regime. For instance, in the town of Osh, with a population of about two hundred thousand, twelve thousand families have been on a hopelessly long waiting list for decades to get a place to live. And what does that really mean, twelve thousand families? It is more than a third of the inhabitants of the city. Unlike contemporary Russia, in Central Asia families with many children are very common, as there is traditionally no birth control in this region. Three, five, or seven children is not the limit for a woman in Central Asia. The majority of the women who are awarded the decoration "Mother Heroine," which is given to women for having ten or more children, live in the Turkestan republics.

There is one more peculiarity that distinguishes the Central Asian housing problem from that of its Russian prototype. In Russia the ruling class has succeeded in making the urban resident's ultimate dream a separate iron-and-concrete cage, lost in the belly of a many-storied barrack. I mentioned earlier that several generations of the inhabitants of big cities have lived all their lives in communal apartments. To get an idea of what that is all about, try to imagine this: There are several bedrooms in your house, in each of which the city council has settled a family of strangers, with whom you have to share a single bathroom and kitchen. Among them there might be alcoholics, rowdies, disturbed people, people with whom you might be absolutely incompatible, but who cares? It is not difficult to imagine how children grow up in such hellish places. They grow up to replace their unlucky parents in our endless wine lines, which stretch beyond the horizon.

It is different in Central Asia, where first of all people are still attached to the land, and second, where they have by some miracle defended the inviolability of the family. At any rate it has turned out to be impossible to herd them into the communal apartments. Uzbeks and Tadzhiks are traditionally farmers who, like their ancestors, are prepared to live even in jerry-built clay shacks in order not to leave their fields, orchards, or melon plantation. Even in the towns, the most dilapidated house is considered to be preferable to a two- or three-bedroom apartment in a many-storied building. But to build a house, even the most primitive, one needs land.

"Well, at least in the U.S.S.R. there's no problem with *that!*" you might say. "Whatever you may say, the country occupies one-sixth of the earth's dry land." Yet the truth is very different. Land in our country cannot be sold or bought, for it is considered to be the property of the people. Which means, to translate the Soviet Newspeak, that all land belongs to the party *nomenklatura*. The officials distribute it to their heart's content, because distribution is the main function of their exercise of power. Representatives of the *nomenklatura* are prepared to distribute just about anything: funds, apartments, means of production and the labor force, land, goods, foodstuffs, human rights, places at graveyards—the important thing is to maintain a deficit of everything.

In the overpopulated Fergana valley, for instance, a deficit of land was successfully created with the help of the deliberate idiocy of the *kolkhoz* system and the dominance of cotton, forced by "the center" to be the agricultural monoculture. That is, first peasants were coercively driven to *kolkhozes* where they were turned into state slaves, and then they were obliged to grow only cotton.

Naturally, once they found out about the decision of the authorities to allow the Kirghizes to keep the land allotments that they had seized, the Uzbek community fiercely protested, the more so as its members had been cheated many times in the process of the distribution of land. There was a noisy meeting at the seized field, and everyone got excited. Groups of Kirghizes and Uzbeks started fighting, but the two mobs facing each other did not have enough time for a real battle. The Kirghiz police, according to the official information, started shooting in the air, but some bullets went into the crowd. Six Uzbeks were killed on the spot, and there were dozens wounded. The Uzbeks fled, and right there at the theater of military operation the Kirghiz gunmen in red bands made their first appearance. They pursued the escaping Uzbeks. Were they sitting in ambush before that? Did they receive a signal from someone to begin an attack? There were no answers to these questions, although everyone with whom I spoke about these terrible events agreed that all this was planned long in advance. Pogroms and arson spread to other towns and villages, and a real civil war started during the ensuing weeks. Thousands of people dashed away to hide in the mountains, but even this did not help many of them to escape. According to the official media, the number of victims ranged from two to three hundred. And it would certainly have been much higher were it not for the troops that were hastily sent there by Moscow.

Consider it some more: could it have been a precursor of the bloody scenario in Vilnius and Riga in the winter of 1991? Moscow brought in its troops, the same black berets that organized the bloodshed in the Baltics. But if the people there experienced the intervention as trouble, in Central Asia it was an unconditional boon. It is better to have tanks at all crossroads and military patrols, soldiers in helmets and bulletproof vests, in order that the bellies of pregnant women not be pierced with pitchforks right before their husbands' eyes, and the men's throats slowly cut letting their blood out as if they were animals, in front of their wives and children. Yes, after what happened here the sending of troops became inevitable, for only the force of arms could separate, at this juncture, the Kirghizes and Uzbeks who were clinging to each other in a fratricidal fight. Which illustrated for the umpteenth time the old imperial claim that without their "elder brother," the senseless Asiatics are only capable of gathering cotton and eating pilaf on holidays. What kind of democracy do they need, much less self-determination?

Now, were the local party bosses punished for this tragedy? Was it not the party, possessing all local power, which made the decision to distribute the allotment that became the pretext for the bloody conflict? Under Genghis Khan they would have been beheaded instantly for such a lack of foresight. And if they had been found guilty of evil intentions, the execution would have been much more tormenting. But what happened under Gorbachev? Were the guilty persons punished at least to the extent of receiving a party reprimand? No. At the routine Party Congress of Kirghizia which took place literally days after the events in Osh Province, Sadykov, first secretary of the Osh Province Committee, another Sadykov, first secretary of the Osh town committee, and Asanov, first secretary of the district committee in Uzgen, were all elected to the Central Committee of Kirghizia's Communist Party. Later, they would resign under the pressure of public opinion, but they remained members of the Central Committee, which guaranteed that after a short while they would be given new positions as party leaders. An excellent example of the *nomenklatura*'s undrownability! Especially impressive is the later career of Sadykov, ex-party boss of the Osh Province. He was "elected" a member of the bureau of the Central Committee of the Communist Party of Kirghizia and a delegate to the twenty-eighth Congress of the CPSU—"elected" as one of the most worthy Communists of the republic, to solve the problems of the country and the whole world, along with other worthy Communists.

Yet we did not know any of that in the first week of June.

The landlady returned to her house, and we were still sitting at the table, cold tea in our cups, frightened and depressed. Like the majority of Soviet people, we had long since grown accustomed to announcements about catastrophes and social cataclysms in our long-suffering country. And like the majority of Soviet people, we long ago worked out special defense mechanisms to protect our psyches, mechanisms which make it possible for us to keep on living in the face of constant stress. It is one thing when you read something in a newspaper or even watch it on television, but when you can smell in the air people being burned alive somewhere nearby, it is a completely different story.

"We ought to return to Moscow," Kolya said resolutely.

"I have to go to Tashkent," I responded, trying to control my indignation. The details of the slaughter, described by the landlady, reminded me in many ways of last year's attacks against the Meskhetin Turks in Fergana, which I watched on an amateur video. But this collision surpassed in its horror everything I had heard or read about before.

Poor Lara remained in a state of shock. For the third time she tried to draw on her almost extinct cigarette.

"It is probably better not to delay our departure," I said. "We have to decide how to get out of here—via Frunze or via Alma-Ata? And shall we take a bus or go by car?"

"Via Frunze!" Kolya answered. "And we'd rather fly."

"You have some strings you can pull at the airport, haven't you?" Lara inquired after Kolya lit her cigarette with a click of his lighter.

"Who knows?" Kolya shrugged his shoulders, evasively.

Which meant that everyone should take care of his own transportation. I thanked them for brunch and we said good-bye to each other. I did not have a television, and the Moscow radio show "Beacon" gave sparse information about the events in Kirghizia, so I did not know how my family was reacting to the news. I did not succeed in getting through on the telephone to my wife in Moscow, which made me feel uneasy. What did they think in Moscow about this massacre in Osh? Were they even paying attention to this new bloodshed, in the endless struggle for their own survival? Well, they could express their horror, stretch their hands in bewilderment: last summer Uzbekistan, last winter Azerbaijan, and now Kirghizia. It is always somewhere far away and perhaps not so frightening.

And what about Tashkent? There were quite a few Kirghiz students in Tashkent's many institutes, and the classes had not yet ended. What if, in response to the anti-Uzbek mob in Osh, anti-Kirghiz uprisings were to start in Tashkent? God save us! I did not even want to think about the blast of violence in Frunze that would follow such attacks in Tashkent.

It was interesting to ponder what was happening on the other side of the lake, where the more respectable public was taking its vacation. Also, what was going on in the Uzbek boardinghouses around here? What if Kirghizes began to war against Uzbeks not only in Osh Province but in Issyk Kul as well? These and dozens of other questions were swarming in my worried consciousness as I tried to determine the course of my future actions.

Having seen the roaring crowds at the bus station and at the airport, I understood that it would not be possible for me to get out of here over the course of the next few days by public transport. In other words, I would do better trying to get to Frunze by hitchhiking. I spent the whole day looking for a ride, and only in the evening, when I understood the futility of it all, did I return to my shack.

To my surprise, my neighbors had not left either. At any rate, lights were burning in their window, and I could hear some activity in their room.

"Is that you?" Lara asked across the partition in an almost singsong voice, hearing me enter.

"Yes," I said. "Haven't you flown away yet?"

"Kolya flew to Frunze today," Lara informed me calmly.

"That's interesting." I was astonished. "And what about you?"

"I will go tomorrow morning," Lara replied. "He couldn't get tickets for one flight. And we'll go together from Frunze to Moscow. In the event that he can get the tickets, of course."

"He'll get the tickets!" I reassured her. "The main thing is to get out of here."

"Oh, yeah," said Lara. "Would you like to have a drink?"

"A good idea!" I responded. "Do you have any tea left?"

"Why tea?" Lara was surprised. "I have something better than tea. Come on over!"

When I entered the room I saw that Lara was drunk. A half-empty bottle of an expensive Daghestan cognac was on the table. I am not fit to be a moralist, but drunken people exasperate me. Perhaps all this was written on my face, because Lara said defiantly, "So what?"

"Can you hiccup as well?" I said angrily.

"Wait, don't leave!" Lara asked. "I simply felt very frightened. The landlady told me a lot of new horror stories. It seems that at night some scary horsemen are riding around, doing all kinds of terrible things to people. Especially to women. She went to spend the night with her Kirghiz neighbors. I went with her, but it was so dirty and cooped up that I decided to return here. It's good that you didn't leave yet. Sit, come in and sit. Why are you standing in the doorway?"

I shrugged my shoulders and sat down. The situation threatened to become onerous.

"Do you know who I am?" Lara asked, pouring more brandy in her glass.

"I know!" I snorted, getting unexpectedly embarrassed.

"How did you guess?" Lara laughed.

"You have a too inaccessible air! In our country only professional courtesans can afford to have such a regal expression on their faces."

"Look at him, he's so clever!" Lara stood up from the place where she sat, arms akimbo, a drunk Barbie doll in shorts and a pink sleeveless T-shirt. "So, do you like me?"

"No," I replied angrily. "Your kneecaps are too sharp."

"Don't get angry!" Lara suddenly changed her manner and sat back down at the table. "I've seen so many of you guys in my life that I can see what you are right away. There's no sense in acting like a saint in my presence."

"You're afraid of some horsemen, and because of that you get drunk and try to cheat your fears by arguing with Kolya and me? If you are really a professional priestess of love, you must realize that I don't have any claims on you, territorial or otherwise."

"That's exactly what drives me crazy!" Lara laughed. "You don't look impotent or gay. Is it true that I look so lousy? Or are you afraid of AIDS?"

"Life is more complex than it may seem to you from your bed-sheet," I replied, getting seriously annoyed. "Change your clientele for variety."

"But how?" Lara sighed. "I don't work with foreigners, because I don't want to be an informer and a free lay for the KGB. And among our people, only young racketeers and aged underground millionaires have any decent money."

"Which is better?"

"Of course, the old men are better!" Lara said with great conviction. "They are kinder. The young ones can beat you up and take your money and even bet you in a card game, as though you were a thing and not a person."

"Did someone lose you like that in a card game?" I asked, remembering my surreal encounter with the nocturnal drunkard in Samara.

"I haven't been lost that way, but my girlfriend Tan'ka was."

"How did it happen?"

"Well, she was married to a real bastard, a chauffeur who drove a boss in the trade administration. A handsome guy but crazy, especially when he got drunk. And she was a real beauty: tall as a model and black-eyed as a witch. First he bet and lost all of his belongings: furniture, stereo sets, a car. And then his wife."

"How could it be?" I pretended that I could not believe it. "Can it really happen nowadays?"

"Don't give me that crap," Lara replied. "Haven't you ever heard about sharks?"

"Yes, I have," I admitted. "That's something from the criminal world. Sharks are, I believe, professional card players, who play illegally for big bucks. And if someone can't pay, they kill him. Something like that, isn't it?"

"That's right." Lara shook her blond locks. "But if one has no money to pay his debt, they play for murder, too. For instance, the loser has to go in the street and kill the first stranger he meets.

Otherwise, they will kill him. The rules are quite simple, indeed."

"Who won your friend Tan'ka?"

"Oh, this awful man! A real big shot. In a camp he did surgery on himself without any anesthesia. Can you imagine that?"

"No, I can't. Maybe it's not really true?"

"That was no story, you can bet your booties!" Lara was indignant. "Tan'ka told me all about it herself. She wouldn't lie. When he was released from prison camp, he got a two-bedroom apartment, a car, and a gun, all on the same day. But then they separated."

"And then what happened?"

"Then she became a call girl."

"Where is this Tan'ka now, in Moscow?"

"No, she's in the camp. She's a convict."

"Why is she a convict?" I was surprised. "They don't arrest people in our country for practicing this most ancient profession, do they?"

"They sure as hell do!" Lara replied. "Especially if you refuse to collaborate with the KGB."

"Then did she refuse?"

"No, she was sentenced for something else."

"What did she do?"

"She did absolutely nothing!" Lara sighed. "The cops simply came to arrest one lot and by chance she was among them. The cops found a syringe and some drugs in her purse. So they stuck her with a case of narcomania and something else on top of that, and she got five years."

"That's a sad story," I said softly.

"And are you interested in such stories?" Lara asked. "I can tell you one hundred such stories. It's interesting to talk to you," she continued. "You don't try to take the underpants off your conversation partner. At least not immediately. That's pleasant."

"Good night," I replied. "I apologize if my snoring annoys you even through this thick wall."

It was drizzling in the street. Somewhere far away, dogs were barking. Somewhere even farther away people were killing each other, trying to torture their victims as cruelly as they could.

"It's foolish that you left," Lara remarked across the partition. "And what if they kill us tonight? At least there would be something to remember before we died."

"Remember Kolya!" I said. "I also have someone to remember. But nothing bad will occur tonight."

"How do you know?" Lara laughed with frustration. "Are you a clairvoyant, or what?"

"When some danger is imminent I always feel it."

"With what part of your body?" Lara asked wearily. "With my stomach," I answered and closed my eyes.

20

"Many-Storied Buildings—Dwellings for Egoists"

The ethnic upheaval in Uzbekistan did not frighten only the Kirghiz partocracy: the Kremlin was bewildered, too. Over the course of the last two decades, the population of Uzbekistan has almost tripled, to approximately twenty million. That moved the republic to third place in terms of population in the Soviet empire, immediately after Russia and the Ukraine. (To compare, the population of Lithuania is 3.7 million, that of Moldavia 4.3 million, and that of Georgia 5.4 million.) It is quite possible that Uzbekistan can catch up with the Russian Federation (147 million population) and the Ukraine (51.7 million population) in the middle of the next century, considering the present rate of growth of its population. But for Moscow, which was quite determined to keep at least its colonies in Central Asia and the Transcaucasus, Uzbekistan's annual increase in population is already a serious problem. The crux of the matter is that the number of Turkic peoples in the U.S.S.R. is increasing steadily, while the Russian population is steadily decreasing. Incidentally, the majority of Turkic peoples are Moslems.

Being Moslem means something quite different in the Central Asian and Caucasian republics of the U.S.S.R. than in the Middle East and North Africa. Moscow exaggerates the significance of the Moslem religious factor in its former colonies, in keeping with the proverb "Fear hath a hundred eyes," in order to play on the conflicts between the Christian West and the Moslem East. In actual fact, during the seven decades of Communist dictatorship, Islam in the Soviet Union was long ago transformed from a religious doctrine to a mode of ethnic self-expression for oppressed national minorities. Islam today is a fact of national identity and psychology, as well as a body of customs and traditions, rather than a denomination in the usual sense of the term.

More than fifty million Soviet citizens, mainly Turkic peoples, regard themselves as Moslems. Although they follow the popular customs in their everyday life, few of them observe the religious rites. Most of them cannot even name the five main rules of Islam, the execution of which makes a person a Moslem. I often witnessed the bewilderment and disappointment of Arabs visiting Central Asia and the Transcaucasus when they saw how foggy were the notions of the local residents about their religion. The visitors were at a loss: how can one sincerely consider oneself a Moslem and not practice the main rites of Islam?

Yet, people in these places have thought and still think of themselves as Moslems, and that fact most of all exasperates and scares Moscow. Even in the terrible years of the Communist terror and ideological bigotry, the stubborn Caucasians and cunning Central Asians tried to retain their everyday style of life. Certainly, they attended the meetings, pretended that they were taking on some idiotic socialist obligations, carried the portraits of their snout-faced leaders to the holiday demonstrations. In short, they were not squeamish about observing the conventional forms, but no one was deceived. Even the highest local partocracy, which condemned with official fury what it called the "feudal-religious prejudices" of its various peoples, continued to circumcise its sons and bury their colleagues according to pre-revolutionary rites, with hired mourners and the reading of prayers.

Moscow was perfectly aware of the insincerity and unreliability of its colonies in terms of sharing the official ideological values of the Soviet regime. Political hypocrisy as a fact of Soviet life was especially glaring in the ethnic republics, which is why the intense growth of the local population has induced well-grounded fears in the Kremlin.

Even under Gorbachev, the non-Russian peoples of the U.S.S.R. used to form a little more than half of the empire's population, and the possible consequences of this new ratio are obvious—assuming, of course, that the Moslem republics remain a part of the Commonwealth of Independent States, in one way or another. It is possible, of course, that in the foreseeable future Russia may cease to be an imperial center and become itself the colony of its former colonies. Just a few years ago, such an event seemed improbable, but history is keen on surprises, sometimes even the most incredible ones.

In any case a rebelling Central Asia will not be anything like a small, defenseless Lithuania. But Central Asia was in no hurry to rebel, for several reasons. One of them was a lack of deep-seated anti-Communism, which considerably influenced the course of events in other parts of the empire. That can be explained by the fact that unlike the peoples of Russia, the population of the Central Asian republics were quite aware from the first that the party clans that rule them have nothing to do with Communism. Party demagoguery could befuddle party officials themselves but not the simple people. The root population, seeing that they are governed by Moscow's puppets, was satisfied to know that at least it was a local and not a Russian *nomenklatura*. And the specific kinds of ideological garnish the center has used for the management of its colonies have really become irrelevant, especially in the last two decades. Corruption, pervading all the social and state structures, and an unhidden political cynicism of the powers that be have contributed to the establishment of an overall lack of faith and political nihilism.

But the rules of the game were still in force, and the ruling clans had to make believe that they followed them. False slogans painted on building façades, hundred-foot-tall portraits of General Secretaries on every corner, ridiculous editorials on the pages of local newspapers, the phony enthusiasm of reports about the fulfillment of state plans for cotton (the actual figures were usually inflated by millions of tons)—all this deafening hullabaloo never stopped even for a minute, always in keeping with the "latest governing instructions" from Moscow. Each time the Kremlin bosses changed their classical party suits for ideological miniskirts and then went back to Stalin's military jacket, riding breeches, and boots, the Central Asian partocracy, putting on its phony smiles, had to follow the changing trends of political vogue themselves. The main thing for the apparatus is to stay in power; the ideological vestments it has to wear really do not matter. Political principles in the Soviet East and in the Soviet West are really the same because there are in fact no principles. And only the Soviet Communist system is to blame for that.

But times have changed and the relationship between the former center and the ruling partocracy of Moslem republics is now much more complex. In some republics, as for instance in Azerbaijan, the dependency of the local apparatus on Moscow by 1990 has grown to an incredible extent because of the overtly anti-Communist moods of the population. Without direct military support from the center, such local Communist regimes would perish in a matter of hours. In other regions, more stable in a political respect, for example in Turkestan, the leaders of the local Communist parties suddenly started talking about greater economic and political independence for the republics, sometimes borrowing the nationalistic verbiage of their political adversaries from nascent opposition parties, popular movements, and fronts. If you take into account that Central Asia has always been a source of raw materials for the Soviet empire, the anxiety of the Kremlin, faced with the prospect of losing these valuable appendages, is quite understandable. It is also clear that any strain in the relations between the various Central Asian republics and especially between their respective party-mafia ruling clans answered the vital interests of the pre-breakup center in this part of the world.

Now let us look at the situation from the viewpoint of the ruling partocracy of the Central Asian republics. On the one hand, in summer 1990 they still demonstrated their loyalty to the center, as they have always done, since they realized that the Central Asian republics still had a long way to go to reach the relative independence of the Baltics, Armenia, or Georgia. The leadership in these places belonged to a new political generation that came to power independently and often contrary to the center's directives. Meanwhile, the Central Asian rulers until the failure of the hard-line coup d'état in August 1991 were still nominated and replaced by Moscow. The post of the republic's highest party leader was then automatically combined with the post of the president of the republic (following the model set by Gorbachev, who, even after the attempted hard-line coup, announced to his astonished savers in ludicrous zombie-like manner about his unshakable faith in his dear Communist Party. Furious, Yelstin however ordered him to shut up and immediately dismantle the rotting party machine). Yet in 1990 all the general secretaries of the Communist Parties of the republics had to share their power with the KGB bosses of their republic and the military district commanders. They were never nominated from among the local *nomenklatura*; they were always subjugated directly to Moscow. (This situation continued until the recent total disintegration of the center.) On the other hand, even prior to the breakup of the Soviet Union the leaders of the Central Asian republics were no longer just the center's puppets, puppets who just several years before that could not possibly have imagined themselves operating beyond the existing political system.

By the middle of 1990 they realized completely that even in the case of the republic's secession from the U.S.S.R., their chances of keeping power in their republics were quite good. This aspiration proved to be true by the end of 1991 when the evil empire had finally fallen apart, yet none of the Communist leaders of the post-Soviet Moslem republics had gone. The totalitarian structures of the Soviet empire, exactly reproduced in the Central Asian republics, together with the clannish, mafialike character of the party-state power, provided a firm foundation for such endurance.

Any opposition, yearning to become a political Hercules, was just twitching its legs in the cradle, and still lacked the strength to clean the post-Bolshevik Augean stables. The local Communist parties rushed to replace the word *Communist* on their signboards with *socialist* or *national democratic*. This apparently pleased some innocent Western sovietologists, but the rest of the world discovered quite soon that the substance of the political system in post-breakup Central Asia remained exactly the same. "Well, who cares?" you may ask. The White House, though, pretended it did, as its concern about the evident lack of democracy in hard-line-dominated Uzbekistan, Tadzhikistan, and Turkmenistan was publicly declared. "First they have to prove their sincere commitment to democracy and a free market; then we may consider our diplomatic recognition of those republics," was repeatedly said by American officials. Alas, this glorious statement failed to find full-scale implementation in reality. A good old double standard was here used again as Washington postponed recognition of

Uzbeks and others, but promptly established diplomatic relations with neighboring Kazakhstan, which was uncompromisingly ruled by an authoritarian regime backed up by the unsinkable apparatus of the newly repainted and renamed local Communist Party. Why such preferences? There is no mystery at all. By a twist of fortune, simply because part of the Soviet strategic arsenal happened to be stationed in its territory, Kazakhstan managed to wake up one morning and surprisingly find itself among the arrogant members of the International Nuclear Club. Kazakh hard-liners had enough common sense to decline any demands by Moscow to return intercontinental missiles to Russia. As soon as they did so, they received immediate worldwide diplomatic recognition. "Therefore," concluded the rest of the post-Soviet Moslem republics, "if you want to be treated respectfully, you just ought to possess some nukes."

But even without them, all Central Asian leaders feel themselves cozy enough upon their thrones. It is also necessary to make allowances for the peculiarity of the political culture in the Central Asian region, which is linked with a certain national-cultural mentality. For instance, reverence for elders is highly developed there. That tradition is often transferred to the realm of politics, even if on a merely formal level, and it influences the political ethics and the rules of the political game as well.

For party bosses of Kirghizia or Kirgizstan (with 4.3 million people), Turkmenistan (3.5 million), and Tadzhikistan (5.1 million), the Uzbekistan of tomorrow, with its swiftly growing population of 20 million people, portends a rather ominous future. In neighboring Kazakhstan, with its 17 million inhabitants, a significant growth in population was achieved in the last decades mainly because of a flow of Russian and Ukrainian settlers, who finally outnumbered the root population. What makes the powerful party clans in the republics bordering on Uzbekistan uneasy? Certainly, a fear of losing power. Political independence, achieved by the secession of each republic from the U.S.S.R., may probably lead to new alliances of former Soviet republics, this time on a regional level. But who knows what kind of relations there would be with the new center, especially since the past and present of local relationships have been anything but cloudless. Is it not better to preserve the status?

However, the ethnic intelligentsia is deeply opposed to that idea, and it has proposed from its ranks new pretenders to power. At first, as a rule, they have supported the political slogans of Moslem and Turkic unity. Then as they enter the political reality of today's Turkestan, many of them come to understand rather quickly how far the most beautiful abstract ideas are from being realized in this life.

On June 8, 1990, after more than twenty-four hours on the road, I finally reached Tashkent. First I hitched a ride on a truck and went from Cholpon-Ata to the town of Issyk Kul, which had earlier been called Rybachii ("Fisherman's Town"). Then I managed to become the third passenger in an intercity cab going to Frunze. My fellow passengers were an aged couple, depressed and scared by the threatening turn of recent events. Their son had been arrested for participation in an antigovernment meeting on the square in front of the local Central Committee, and they were heading for Frunze to get him out of trouble. The driver, a Soviet Korean, on the other hand, was very excited and was trying to convince us that the unrest was provoked by local criminals using the mass disturbances as a cover in order to plunder banks, jewelry shops, and rich inhabitants, such targets having been marked long before.

The Kirghiz capital, which was formerly shady and green, now looked like an active volcano at the moment of eruption. At the bus station where I came to try to leave for Tashkent, crowds of enraged Kirghiz youths were storming buses to go to Osh Province to destroy Uzbeks. The overall hysteria was inflamed by rumors that Kirghiz babies had been thrown into fires by Uzbek crowds in Uzgen. The usually rude cashiers and arrogant drivers were scared to death by the raging crowd, against which ordinary patrols could do nothing. Special troops were defending the building of the Central Committee of the local Communist Party, and the administration was apparently too frightened to send them to other parts of town that had been turned upside down. From odds and ends of conversations that I overhead it was clear that new and terrible anti-Uzbek violence had occurred at two city markets, with casualties on both sides. Student disturbances had grown into criminal excesses, which had continued for several days. There were shootings at night, and demonstrations in the daytime, with crowds breaking windows and overturning buses. Some people were demanding that the government resign; some were simply expressing to the whole world the rage and hatred that they had accumulated during years and years of unrelieved poverty.

The party bosses barricaded themselves in the building of the Central Committee, and to all appearances were imploring the capital to declare martial law. That was later done, in fact, after the raging violence had subsided.

I succeeded in exchanging a couple of words in the center of the city with several young men, evidently hurrying from one melee to another. They said they were students at the local polytechnic institute. I asked them to explain what was going on in the city, and one of them, half-smiling, answered that they were "sick of living in the most Soviet among all the Soviet republics, which looked more like a political Disneyland than a normal state."

"And what do Uzbeks have to do with it?" I asked, rashly.

"They are too fertile, and they need new living spaces," one of them answered studiedly.

"Wait a minute—who is he?" the third one cried out, growing pale.

They could beat me up, I thought nervously, but I did not feel the usual coldness in my stomach.

"I'm a journalist from Moscow," I said as calmly as possible and put my bag on the ground, ready to ward off an offensive. Four excited lads against one wandering geopolitician—not an encouraging ratio. Once I had been in a situation where two big guys were holding my arms, and a third one was pounding me with his fists, after which all three of them had fun for five more minutes kicking me with their feet. In such circumstances the most important thing is not to fall down—but in case you do, try to cover your head with your arms, pull your legs together, assume the fetal position, and tighten all your muscles.

Fortunately this time I did not have to make use of my knowledge of self-defense, because my clothes, which had caused such animosity in padded-jacket Cheboksary, were, on the contrary, coming to my aid in Central Asia. Long live the Central Asian taste for casual clothes and walking shoes! After they had taken my measure, the students read, moving their lips, the inscription "Bugle Boy" on the pocket of my summer shirt. Its foreignness was evidently approved of. Judging by my appearance, I was hardly a Tashkent agent.

"It means 'signal-man,'" I explained with a sigh of relief, referring to the inscription, and leaned over to take the handle of my bag. At this moment a shattering blow threw me to the ground. Yet apparently Muscovites were treated better here than Tashkent dwellers, because the attack did not continue and damage was confined to my Sakar camera. Squatting on all fours I looked at my compatriots, who were quickly leaving the scene. Then I tried to stand up so that a patrol would not take me to a "medical sobering-up station."

In the evening I managed to make a deal with a driver of a bus leaving for Tashkent. In the beginning he had no intention of talking to me, for there was no place on the bus. People were sitting even in the aisle, right on the floor. The driver was just pulling onto the road when I came up to him. When I examined his face for a second, I understood that I had to pretend that I was a criminal.

"I have to get out of here," I informed the driver in a singsong voice, trying to mimic Soviet criminal jargon. He leaned down toward me, trying to make out what kind of person was addressing him from the pitch darkness of the evening. If I had asked him in normal language, he would have cursed, slammed the door, and left right away. But what if I really was a representative of the criminal world? Having seen the hundred-ruble note in my hand, he coughed a bit and then asked cautiously:

"Will you go without a seat?"

That meant that I had to stand for the nine hours of the overnight journey.

After the first hour in the bus I had a terrible headache. My feet were dead tired, my back was in pain and, besides all that I was dying to sleep. Passengers with regular seats made believe that they did not notice those who were sitting on the floor in the passage, and the latter grumbled with a disturbed air when those who were standing touched them as they shifted from one foot to the other in order to disperse the pins and needles in their limbs. Everyone felt threatened by the others and hated them, a characteristic of our whole society. The only difference was that the driver, unlike Mr. President, at least knew where he was taking us.

However, I was lucky as usual, since a few passengers, sitting on the floor in the aisle, got off in the village of Merke, after an hour and a half. Judging by their conversation they were going to stand in line at the local co-op store, which, rumor had it, would tomorrow be selling some imported footwear.

The driver gave me a piece of plywood and I established myself on it with a maximum of comfort, leaning on my travel bag with its old US Air sticker. It was a far cry from those lucky ones snoozing in their seats, but those passengers who were still standing gave me an unmistakable look of hatred.

The strain of the previous day was gradually subsiding. Seething Frunze was left behind, and there were still 370 miles of night driving to Tashkent. My fellow passengers were quiet, seemingly in the grip of fear even when they were asleep. The bus stopped once, in the middle of the night in a big empty field.

"Men to the left, women to the right!" the driver announced with a businesslike air, and all the passengers drew to the exit, grumbling and groaning. There were not even any of the usual jokes that people make in such situations. After answering the call of nature under the stars of the steppe, people reluctantly returned to the stuffy environment of the bus.

Near morning, before we reached Tashkent, in the village of Leninskoye, two more people got off the bus, and I sat in a seat, as broad as one on an airplane. There was no use in trying to fall asleep at this point, and my new neighbor, to all appearances, had already had a good night's sleep. By and by we started a conversation. He turned out to be an Uzbek from Tashkent, returning from a trip to see his son in military service. Quite unexpectedly for me he started to talk not about the events in Osh Province, nor about the cruelty of the *dedovshchina*—the initiatory "pecking order" in the army—but about the harmful impact of many-storied buildings on the Uzbek national character.

"The more they build many-storied buildings in our republic, the more problems we have," his monologue began.

I looked at him in astonishment, then turned my gaze out the window at the steppe landscape. It was already dawn, but it was still a long way to the Tashkent valley. There were no many-storied buildings in the vicinity, only one lonely Kazakh yurt looming on a hill, among bright morning tulips. A woman was sitting in front of a clay hearth, kindling fire. It was difficult to discern from afar whether she was old or young.

"Problems? What problems?" I asked absentmindedly, absorbed in my own thoughts.

"Many-storied buildings are dwellings for egoists," answered my fellow-traveler with conviction. "They are good only for those who aspire to comfort and goods."

"What's wrong with that?" I was surprised.

"It depends on the cost!" my neighbor said. "Formerly we had no cockroaches, no rats. Only cats and dogs. And what *aryks* we had!"

"What *aryks* did you have?" I asked. *Aryks* are little channels that separate sidewalks from roads in Central Asian towns.

"There were splendid *aryks* in the past," this strange man said with an air of inspiration. "There was an ideal cleanliness here in the past. And now—an entirely antisanitary condition. I'm forty years old, and all our cleanliness has died before my eyes. Everything has drastically changed, especially in the past twenty-five years. We haven't been protecting nature, and that's the result. We cannot even get rid of rats. Huge rats dash back and forth along the *aryks* from which we used to drink water, because now there is dirt and refuse there. And it's impossible to fight it."

I remembered how when I was a kid I went floating in an *aryk* with my brother in a big zinc-covered laundry tub. Its sides rubbed against the banks growing with thick grass, but the flow was so strong that it did not get stuck anywhere, and, though it banged its bottom on underwater rocks, it also carried us into the future. My brother wanted to become a sailor, but he became a diplomat. Then he was exiled from the country where he was working because he had a romance with a local girl, and then he became a philosopher. Strangely, the same KGB officer who exiled him from Budapest in 1974 also exiled me in 1981 from Baghdad because of a romance I had with a young girl who later became my wife.

"In the past every family had a ram," my interlocutor went on, as he had not received a reasonable answer from me. "We tilled our lands ourselves. In front of every house there was at least a little patch of land. The elders grew roses, and then gathered in teahouses, with flowers behind their ears. They joked and laughed. Nowadays no one's laughing."

"What's to be done?" I asked. "Where's the way out of the mess we're in?"

"The bigger the city, the more it takes from nature," my environmentalist companion answered, sighing.

"Well, and what do you think about the possible independence of Uzbekistan?" I asked him point-blank. I was going to meet an old acquaintance of mine in Tashkent, the poet Mohammed Solikh, who like many other intellectuals preferred active involvement in politics to literary activities in the years of perestroika. But unlike many others who do not go beyond idle talk, he had founded a democratic party, called Erk (Freedom).

"For as long as we have lived, we have always thought that we were happy. But it turned out that there is trouble everywhere," he answered without a shade of surprise at such a question. "I believe that we have to secede from the Soviet Union. Each republic should be separate, because every people has its own culture, language, and customs. Any representative of a certain people is always attracted to his own nationality, isn't that so?"

I shrugged my shoulders noncommittally.

"But this is an instinct," he insisted. "It's not nationalism. It's simply that human beings are made that way."

It is pertinent to remember at this point that the word "nationalism" is regarded almost as a swear word in the Soviet political lexicon. In Arabic, on the contrary, it is almost always meant as praise. In English it is a rather neutral working term, the emotional tinge depending on the adjoining adjective and how the talker himself feels at the moment. In view of such discrepancies it is really no wonder that the leaders of different states who impute different meanings to the same notions cannot reach an agreement.

"But what about people of other nationalities?" I asked him. "I have in mind those who were born and grew up on this soil. For instance, Russians. There are almost two million of them in Uzbekistan. What do you think—do they have a right to stay here when the republic secedes from the U.S.S.R.?"

"Oh, yeah!" he answered without any hesitation. "But people of other nationalities have to respect the local customs. The interests of the root nationality have to be regarded in the first place."

Oh these interests of nationality! We Soviets are all so bewitched by them! Why is no one in our country talking about the interests of personality?

The next day I called the Writers' Union of Uzbekistan and arranged a meeting with Mohammed Solikh. He is young, tall, and slim. But the expression of his intelligent eyes is always sullen, and his face is stern. It has nothing to do with the fact of his being a very important person, since he was the same before, about nine years ago, when my close friend Yura Lassky, who was also a friend of Mohammed Solikh's, introduced us to each other. Yes, Mohammed Solikh had gone far in these years—both as a person and as a political figure. As I remember, in one of his early poems an ant threatens the sky amid the sky-splitting torments of a thunderstorm. Now he writes: "...so that nature, peering at me, knew its own grandeur."

In the first years of perestroika there was a coup in the Writers' Union of Uzbekistan. Brezhnev's old guard faltered and retreated, leaving the battlefield to the generation of thirty- and forty-year-olds. Then Solikh became one of the secretaries of the Writers' Union of Uzbekistan, making use of his position in the *nomenklatura* for the formation of the first legal political opposition in the Soviet period of Uzbekistan's history. On the base of the popular-front movement Birlik (Unity), and with the help of political comrades-in-arms and allies, Solikh managed to organize the group Erk, which became the foundation of a new democratic party of Uzbekistan.

After the first minutes of our meeting, which are normally dedicated to inquiries about business, family, health, and common acquaintances, I told him that I wanted to ask him a few questions about his role as cochairman of the democratic party and a member of the Uzbekistan parliament.

"The aim of our party is, naturally enough, complete independence," said Mohammed Solikh. "Uzbekistan might become a member of the confederation or secede from the U.S.S.R. Time will indicate which way to go. We need to undertake a popular referendum, and only it will decide. But the law about secession from the U.S.S.R., which was promulgated in Moscow, doesn't suit us. It's suitable for other republics as well, because according to this law those republics that contain, alongside the root nationality, other national and ethnic groups cannot secede from the U.S.S.R. But even according to this law, if our people vote for secession from the U.S.S.R., we'll be able to do it. But it won't be simple. Because Central Asia is the main material source of the Soviet Union, the conditions for secession that we'll get will be considerably different from those that are offered to the Baltic republics. Russians might let go of the Baltics, on definite conditions, to be sure, but they'll try to hold us back with all their might."

"And are you sure," I asked, "that someone else would vote for secession besides the intelligentsia?"

"Now other social forces are awakening, too," Mohammed Solikh said with conviction. "The bulk of our population lives in little villages, but nevertheless their consciousness is not as enfeebled by cotton-gathering as we used to think. Despite the fact that people's ability to think about something other than bread has been crushed by the yoke of poverty and false ideology, the population of the republic hasn't forgotten how to think. We're heading to the point when the question of secession from the U.S.S.R. will be pronounced in full voice. If we do not raise it now, if it is not discussed in the sessions of the Supreme Soviet, it doesn't mean that the republic doesn't think about it at all. Soon there will be a new session and we'll try as hard as we can to pass a declaration of independence."

"What you are talking about expresses the viewpoint of your party. But are people thinking in the same vein well represented in the local organs of power? In local Soviets, in province Soviets, in the Supreme Soviet of the republic?"

"Yes, certainly. Our adherents are not as numerous as we would like them to be, but compared with previous years, there are many people who think in a new way and want to change the existing order. Of course, there are many fewer of them in comparison with the other republics, with the Supreme Soviets of the non–Central Asian republics."

"By the way, have the local authorities acknowledged your party? As far as I know, the popular movement Birlik is still refused official registration."

"Officially we're not acknowledged yet. But we already have about four thousand members, and there are even more people supporting our platform. Birlik is a popular movement, and we're a political party, which arose on the base of Birlik."

"I heard that you have your own newspaper. Can it be freely bought?"

"Oh, yes, of course, but from our public distributors only. Our party, Erk, sets as its main task the political independence of the republic reached in a peaceful way."

"But what about mutual collaboration with Turkic peoples of other regions? For instance, of the Caucasus, Transcaucasus, the Volga region, and Siberia?"

"By all means. In our program there is even a point about the restoration of a single cultural community. In a moral sense, this is one of the major points. We have planned a number of meetings and already held one of them. We met with delegations of Tartars—both Crimean and Kazan. But, unfortunately, it's not easy to gather all Turkic peoples at once. But we'll do it of necessity in the future. Cultural unity of the Turks is part of our strategy. In the twenties and thirties we were speaking almost the same language. So we'll also work on this task, the task of restoring the cultural unity of Turks."

"And what about Turks who are not Moslems?"

"Religious belonging doesn't matter. We're interested in ethnic ties. With Iakuts or Altais, for instance."

There was one more topic, which we, perhaps, had subconsciously pushed to the end of our conversation: the tragic events in Kirghizia.

"We sent our representatives there as soon as we found out about the catastrophe," Mohammed Solikh said, visibly growing more preoccupied. "They call us every day. Unfortunately, the situation is not under control, or rather it's not under our control. Passions flare up and who suffers from that? The peaceful population as usual, defenseless people. I can't tell you anything else, as there is no complete information about the events in Osh Province yet."

"We'll never get complete information about those events," I said, and shook his hand as we parted.

21

The Hero's Gold Star

I moved away from Tashkent many years ago, yet I still loved it at a distance, and the longer it had been since I lived there, the more uniquely precious everything associated with this huge, friendly city seemed to me. Fortunately, I had so many opportunities to go to Tashkent that very soon I was cured of my nostalgia, for I discovered that when it began to flow over me from time to time amidst the gloomy and endless Moscow winter, I was associating it not so much with the city but with the irretrievable times of childhood, youth, and young adulthood.

Tashkent itself managed beautifully without me, continuing its unhurried two-thousand-year-old way through time, gradually changing its appearance and growing upward and outward. The circle of my close friends dissolved; they all had new things to do and worry about, and many of them now saw each other only during my short annual visits. During one of these reunions I realized with unexpected pain that it probably was not worth gathering all my former friends together, for people should be brought together not only by recollections of the past but by concerns of the present, and perhaps also by common hopes for the future.

* * *

Not long after the death of General Secretary Brezhnev, Sharaf Rashidov, the first secretary of the Uzbek Communist Party, who had ruled Uzbekistan for more than twenty years running, also died. Death overtook him on his personal train when he was crossing his domain, tormented by the usual fear of the next change of power in Moscow. Remember the problems Vova Liberman's mother, Mira Mordukhovna, had in connection with defending her dissertation, because competitors for scholarly degrees were obliged to cite only living party leaders in their work? Problems somewhat similar in nature, although more complicated, had arisen among the party leaders of whole republics. It was not so simple for a member of the "old team" to form a good relationship with a new party imperial leader, especially when the imperial leaders began to replace each other every year, regularly changing their cabinet in the building on Staraya Square at the miserably misused Kremlin wall. I say "misused" because through the years the Soviets filled it so full of deceased upper-level party members that it became a vertical cemetery.

Replacing the henchmen of deceased general secretaries was often accompanied by scandals and even by arrests in the highest echelon. That was especially characteristic of the period when the terminally ill former KGB chief Andropov came briefly to power. He had at his disposal sufficient incriminating materials to ruin any powerful *apparatchik* who was annoying to him.

Rashidov was lucky to die a natural death. They buried him no less pompously than the first Egyptian president, Gamal Abdel Nasser, whose funeral I saw in 1970 when I worked in Egypt. Yet the cautious people of Tashkent, unlike the residents of Cairo, did not throw themselves from balconies and roofs as a sign of despair. And they turned out to be right. At first the ashes of the Uzbek leader were placed in a tomb at the center of the city. Then, without any explanation, as it has always been done in the Soviet Union, Rashidov's ashes were secretly moved to his native land in Jizak, and at the spot of his former tomb they planted a flower bed overnight. However, the Soviet people long ago became accustomed to the unpredictability of the past in their country. Therefore, no one was especially surprised when after a time it was explained that the years of rule of this true Leninist and Hero of Socialist Labor, Sharaf Rashidov, were by no means as cloudless as the court historians and party chroniclers had described them.

Meanwhile, within the Uzbek party mafia, a life-or-death struggle was raging among several clans. Several cases of suicide by higher bureaucrats were staged, and other top bureaucrats were arrested. Palace revolutions followed one after another, and Kremlin interference was required to stabilize the situation. Moscow did not want to lose its Central Asian properties because of internecine war at the higher levels of the local party apparatus. Having become entangled in the intrigues of the local *apparatchiks*, the hard-line Kremlin finally became furious. The "little brothers" had obviously lost their sense of moderation, and it was time for them to come to their senses. Especially since the people, having heard endless talk about the self-purging of the party from Gorbachev, then the new leader, expected some concrete action. It was declared that Moscow was sending a special brigade of the U.S.S.R. procurator's office, with inspectors Gdlyan and Ivanov in charge of investigating the mass crimes of the Uzbek party elite. However, they undertook the job too zealously; in the best Soviet tradition, they did not trouble themselves overmuch with procedural formalities. Disclosures were not only sensational but simply monstrous. Information leaked to the press that for many long years, the deceased member of the Politburo, Rashidov, had not governed the republic; rather Adylov, the most powerful Soviet mafioso, actually governed behind his back. Of course, compared with the epochal crimes of the Communist regime, the excesses of Adylov were not so impressive. The man had his own small army; he tortured and murdered defenseless peasants or put the "guilty" into his own prison. How much better was the "lawful" power of the Bolsheviks, maintained and continuously strengthened by unprecedented violence and terror? Let us remember the 60 million Soviet citizens, including Uzbeks, whom the Bolsheviks destroyed during more than seventy years of rule. They also tortured them and held them in prisons and camps, reducing them to the level of silent slaves without any rights. What of it? And did the party, after subjecting the country and its citizens to so much misery, repent of anything? Did it not refuse to acknowledge its own crimes? Only the names of the local Communist party changed, but the people who made up the system remained the same.

Nonetheless, the cynicism of the so-called Uzbek affair surprised even the worldly-wise Soviet people. The Uzbek Don Corleone

Adylov did not go underground, but was a completely official figure. He headed one of the largest Uzbek collective farms, was elected a deputy of the Supreme Soviet, and even received the title Hero of Socialist Labor. Think on this fact: a criminal offender receives the highest government award of the Soviet Union. And those who decided knew about his criminal career. The official press, including the national newspapers, wrote a multitude of laudatory articles about his "progressive experience in farm leadership." Documentary films were made about him; they dedicated enthusiastic television shows to him. He participated in sessions of the Supreme Soviet and even, it seems, was a delegate to the regular congresses of the Communist Party of the Soviet Union. At that time in his personal prison, located on the grounds of his collective farm, people were fastened to the walls with chains and subjected to medieval tortures.

The only ones who dared to protest were simple Uzbek peasant women. It was widely publicized that during the last decade in Uzbekistan 240 women, after dousing themselves with gasoline, burned themselves alive. They were mostly young women and girls. Even in the years of the rise of glasnost, the Soviet press could not explain the reason for this horrible phenomenon. The suicides departed without farewell notes, without previously making any political accusations. They simply poured gasoline on themselves and turned into living torches.

Tashkent continued in those years to be called a "beacon of socialism in the East."

After the first sensational disclosures of the Uzbek party mafia, which turned out to be under the control of a criminal, it became clear to many that this kind of thing could not happen in a totalitarian state without the center's knowledge of it. The underlying reason is that the Moscow party bosses could close their eyes to a great deal, all the more easily since they had plenty of their own worries along these lines. The clues led to the very top, to Moscow. In particular, the name Egor Ligachev is mentioned, he who was then considered second after Gorbachev as a figure in the Soviet imperial hierarchy. Indications were cited in the press of what was found under investigation of the Uzbek party leaders and even sums of bribes he had supposedly taken. I say "supposedly," because unlike the condemned members of the Brezhnev gang, Ligachev was not brought to trial and consequently his guilt was never proven.

Nevertheless, the situation took an extremely undesirable turn. With the scandal the investigators, Gdlyan and Ivanov, were pushed aside from handling the matter, and when they began to appeal to public opinion, they were simply removed from the job. However, fortunately for them, they managed to become deputies of the U.S.S.R. Supreme Soviet, which protected them from immediate further reprisals. Almost all of those under investigation were given their freedom after a while, and the Uzbek partocracy (naturally, with the blessings of the Moscow partocracy, and with the aid of the mass media which was subject to it) was able to make it appear that the purpose of the investigation was not to uncover the crimes of the Uzbek party mafia, but rather that it was a malicious crusade by two investigators to compromise the entire Uzbek people.

Yet let us not forget one peculiarity of the Uzbek mentality: however bad Rashidov or his successors were, they were still Uzbeks. The Moscow bosses, representing the same unfair and cruel system, are the same kind of villains but still they are also foreigners!

Local patriotism is a factor of no little importance. It is to be found in Uzbeks of every cultural and social level to about the same degree. Turkestan has a rural culture, whose physical and literary monuments have been preserved to this day. The peoples of Central Asia are justly proud of them and certainly consider them a part of their own history. The Uzbek partocracy, especially its well-educated elite, recruited from the local cultural and scientific intelligentsia, is not an exception in this regard. For example, Rashidov himself began as the editor of a regional newspaper and served as president of the Writers' Union of Uzbekistan during the later years of Stalinism.

His literary legacy consists, practically speaking, of one work. His subject is simple and unpretentious. The party charges the hero, the chief of a collective farm, with beginning to develop the Golodnaya Steppe. But he is not sufficiently heroic and does not immediately realize why he should toss millions of rubles uselessly into the wind when it is possible to invest them with greater benefit in half-ruined old farms. A still more heroic female party organizer appears, who explains to the poor chief that the concerns of the party are directed exclusively toward the welfare of the people. Joyful paisanos come out of the bushes and ask the female party organizer to lead them to the bright future. All abandon their homes and native village, and, singing joyfully, ride to the Golodnaya Steppe to grow new millions of tons of cotton for Moscow.

At the very beginning of his career, when Rashidov was still only a humble *nomenklatura* worker at the regional level, the future party emir of Uzbekistan fabricated this story. Later, already in the post of president of the Writers' Union of Uzbekistan, he transformed it into a large novel. Having become first secretary of the Central Committee of the Communist Party of Uzbekistan, he charged his assistants with remaking this novel into a trilogy. I was well acquainted with Lilia Shcherbakova, who asserted that she wrote the Russian text of the trilogy for Rashidov, which was then translated into Uzbek, and then under the name of the Moscow *nomenklatura* writer, again into Russian. When Rashidov became a candidate member of the Politburo, his multivolume masterwork was translated at the major Moscow publishing house Progress, which issued it in huge editions in all the main languages of the peoples of the world and then happily turned the entire edition into pulp.

It is funny that in the last decade of Rashidov's rule, membership in the Writers' Union of Uzbekistan was fashionable among the highest echelons of power. Even Yakhyaev, the formidable minister of internal affairs of the republic, was a member and held the title of people's poet of Uzbekistan; the obligatory performance of songs to his words was the curse of Uzbek radio and television.

The majority of party-state bosses at the time of Rashidov were writers, i.e., at least they were people who knew how to read and write. Which, of course, enabled the preservation and continuation of the tradition of Oriental "enlightened" despots, robbing and plundering their people, but not begrudging part of the plundered gains going to the erection of public buildings, road construction, and patronage of the arts and sciences.

Compared to the ruined roads of central Russia and Kazakhstan, some of the automobile routes of Uzbekistan can seem like real highways. After the famous earthquake of 1966, which occurred on the morning of April 26, Tashkent was almost completely rebuilt. The imperial sweep of Tashkent's downtown includes a monstrously huge square named for Lenin. By the way, that granite statue of him is one of the largest in the Soviet Union. By its dimensions it reminds one of the legendary King Kong in scale. Only it is not naked but in stone dress with the inevitable three-ton cap in his giant fist, pointing the way to the bright Communist future.

With the death of Rashidov an entire epoch in the life of Uzbekistan ended. But would it be better for the people in the new epoch?

22

A Wake at Dawn

I spent three weeks in Tashkent, but I never managed to relax completely. The melancholy pictures I had seen during the previous leg of my journey hovered relentlessly before my eyes. While I was wandering the boundless plains of Russia and Kazakhstan, I had dreamed of Tashkent as a Promised Land, but once there I came to understand that my rosy anticipation was just a dream. The feeling of total uncertainty about the future, and the portent of an overall catastrophe, characteristic of the country's outlook at large, were exacerbated by the events in the region, which had utterly demoralized the inhabitants of Uzbekistan's capital city. Fear of the upsurge of crime and terror ruthlessly distorted human souls. Women stopped wearing jewelry like earrings, since they could be torn out of their ears. People were robbed and mugged in broad daylight, on public transport. The corpses of raped and mutilated women were constantly being found in the city canals and in deserted places. People who owned new cars were threatened by the possibility that racketeers might torch their homes and torture their kith and kin. Lines of armored vehicles stood on the shoulders of suburban roads, and although the official word was that military exercises were taking place in the region, no one believed it. Many people were terrified, expecting that armies of killers from Syrdarya or the Fergana valley would surge into Tashkent in a matter of days.

Hundreds of thousands of people of dozens of different nationalities inhabit Uzbekistan's cities, especially Tashkent. As in the other Central Asian republics, these long since "unrooted" minorities tend to prefer the urban way of life, while the overwhelming majority of the indigenous local nationality is connected in one way or another to agriculture. In Uzbekistan agriculture means cotton monoculture, which under the *kolkhoz* system dooms peasants to total poverty and lack of rights. Soviet propaganda used to call the Uzbek peasant *khlop-korob,* which means "cotton producer," but the new word *khlopkorab,* or "cotton slave," pops up quite often in the press nowadays. During the years of perestroika the predicament of the "cotton slave" has become worse than it was before. The unemployment level in agriculture has reached a million and a half in Uzbekistan. Finding no jobs in the village, peasant youths strive to settle in the cities, but because of the residence-permit regulations, they almost always find that impossible. They direct their resulting rage against ethnic minorities. "How is it that we, people with our ethnic roots here, have no right to live in our own capital, provincial center, or regional center, while they— Russians, Tartars, Koreans, Jews, Armenians—may live there?"

The cruelty of 1990 attacks against Meskhetin Turks in the Fergana valley, the outbreaks of brutal violence in Syrdarya province, and recent pogroms against Armenians and Jews in Andizhan demolished all trust among the different national groups. People of the "unrooted" nationalities, Russians among them, have suddenly realized how defenseless they are against demonstrations of force on the part of the local population. Suddenly great numbers of people have been seized with ambition to emigrate. Jews, Armenians, and Germans have rushed abroad by the tens of thousands. Slavs and people of other nationalities who are not allowed to emigrate leave for Russia, where no one wants them since there are enough problems without them. But it is impossible to stop this flow of population.

Larisa and Volodya Averbah, my old friends in Tashkent, told me the story of something that happened right before my arrival. The daughter of some friends of theirs, a young woman who had just married a student from Ecuador, within three days went from happy newlywed to young widow. She nearly lost her mind the night her husband came home after encountering some hooligans, holding his own eye in his hand. Besides other numerous traumas, he had a fractured skull, as a result of which he died in agony three days later. He was treated in an ordinary hospital, which is of course in no way like the hospitals for the *nomenklatura*. Because of the shortage of orderlies the dying patient had to go on foot for his X-rays and blood tests. The surgery on his skull was performed with the help of a hand-held brace and the drainage tube was made from the finger of a surgical glove. But even this operation was delayed for a day because there was no razor to shave the hair on his head. Razors are a deficit item in the Soviet Union and the patient's relatives had to find one themselves. Another patient, lying in the same room, took pity on the young woman and lent her an old rusty razor, which the young woman herself used, sobbing all the while, to shave the familiar curls from the head of her dying husband. By a cruel irony of fate he was a Marxist and believed in Communist ideals.

Ecuador, one hopes, will reevaluate its policy and temporarily refrain from sending its students to the regions of heightened risk. But what can the local residents do? As a result of the wild outburst of crime, the representatives of many nationalities perish, Uzbeks among them. No wonder quite a few people look for salvation in the return to the customs of the old, pre-Bolshevik life in Central Asia, when there were no locks on the doors and the city thieves were as well-known as, say, the city madmen.

My mother's neighborhood is considered to be one of the most conservative in Tashkent. It was always characterized by traditionalism, a nonacceptance of the "new way of life" that had been imposed by the authorities during the previous decades. There are no concrete apartment boxes here with their motley multinational populations; there is no hustle and bustle in streets crammed with people and transport. People here live in their own houses, closed off from the world by high fences; the shady streets are well-tended and uncrowded, and people know each other by name.

My late father bought our house back in the middle of the fifties, and it cost him one-tenth of what it would cost now. There was not even public transportation in that region at the time, and for some years my father drove my brother and me around in an old Willys, which the United States had supplied the U.S.S.R. under the provisions of the Lend-Lease program. To install the telephone in our house, my father had to buy wooden poles and hire workers to post them along the road, because our house stood almost a kilometer away from the main telephone line. In those far-distant times a telephone was considered a great rarity in our neighborhood, as was a television for that matter, and so our neighbors used to come to our house with their whole families to call somebody or to watch television. Both appliances stood on the glassed veranda, always ready to serve anyone who wanted to use them. I remember that at the end of the fifties we also bought a tape recorder, huge and heavy as a safe laid on its side, which seemed to people at that time like a miracle.

Those times have long since passed, and this *makhallya,* as this sort of community is called in Uzbek, long ago became one of the most respectable and well-off in Tashkent. For the most part it is populated by upper-middle-class people, which in Uzbekistan means tradesmen, the senior staff of colleges, hospital directors, in short, people of means and a certain position in society. All of them have their own houses with big orchards, full of fruit trees and hothouses, and several cars usually stand in a garage. Color televisions and telephones long ago became objects of everyday life, and videos are now popular among the young generation. Computers and fax machines are not yet in vogue, but when necessary they will quickly become common elements of daily existence.

It is surprising, but neither the seventy years of Communist dictatorship, with all of its freezes and thaws, nor the latter-day perestroika with its economic chaos and outbreaks of ethnic violence, have noticeably changed the code of behavior and the interaction among neighbors here. Sometimes it seems to me this code has not changed for centuries. Many of the same rules operate in any Uzbek *makhallya,* for they derive from traditional patterns of behavior in Uzbek culture. For instance, everyone, even the toddlers playing all summer long without trousers, address each other using the formal second person plural instead of the informal singular "you." The elders here get the kind of respect that old men in Moscow only dream of. Adults do not dare smoke in the presence of their parents. The first cup (*piala*) of tea is always offered to an elder or to a guest. Daughters-in-law, no matter what authority they might hold in their jobs, try not to contradict their mothers-in-law in anything and pretend to obey them unquestioningly. If someone wants to pass a message to a neighbor, he sends his son. The boy rings the gate bell and asks not for the head of the family himself but for his own peer, requesting him to pass the information to the addressee. A stranger never maintains eye contact with a young woman even if he starts talking to her.

Yet despite this scrupulous attention to convention in the *makhallya*, the local people pay scant attention to the laws of the state, following them only because they have to and only as far as necessary. No one believes in the formal institution of law as such.

In the land of arbitrary rule it is not laws that govern people but people who govern people, with all their string-pulling and bribes. This is the reality that everyone learns with his mother's milk. In Tashkent, money is treated with great respect, no matter whether it was made legally or illegally. How can laws be held in high esteem if the authorities themselves have for decades behaved according to the code of the criminal world?

Unlike Russian authorities, in neither Central Asia nor the Transcaucasus have the authorities succeeded in inculcating the habit of feeling envy toward a well-to-do neighbor, at least if he is of the same nationality. Here it is not shameful to be rich. Even families with small incomes show great hospitality and hold big celebrations on important occasions. People might be living from hand to mouth, but when the time comes to marry their son, for instance, the wedding as a rule turns into a grandiose feast where many years of the parents' savings are spent.

The main family events of this kind—weddings, funerals, circumcisions—take place with the active participation of the *makhallya*. Communal spirit is still very strong and not infrequently the residents of a *makhallya* collect big sums of money as charity for those who do not have enough money to organize these basic rites. A celebrating or grieving family has to receive, over the course of a couple of days, anywhere from a few hundred to fifteen hundred guests. The meals are offered in the orchard, or if it is not big enough, in the street in front of the house. In this case huge canvases are stretched over the street, between the houses, and the street is closed to cars. The *makhallya* owns many folding tables and benches, and countless quantities of cheap dishes as well as gigantic caldrons for pilaf. And, of course, all this is absolutely free. The pilaf which we discussed in a previous chapter is the basic ritual entertainment but not the only one.

Personal invitations are sent to official guests only, neighbors

(*Left*) Mary, me, and my wife, Alexandra, in the last moments before our Red Odyssey got under way. Alexandra looks distressed about the potential dangers of my journey. Mary is trying diplomatically to ease the tension of the farewell scene.

(*Bottom*) The great auto mechanic, Vova Liberman, with his children, Motya and Ksusha, and his wife, Sveta, next to him. His in-laws, the unforgettable Shlupkin and his wife, are on the flanks, the Chuvash granny in front of them, while the *The Knight in the Tiger Skin* serves as a backround for the happy family in Novocheboksarsk, Chuvashia (chapter 3).

Soviet roads between cities usually have no divider lines to separate traffic and can be especially dangerous at nighttime. The lack of road and exit signs is another feature of highways in the Soviet provinces.

(*Above*) The Russian technocrat, Sergei Dobrynin, from the city of Samara on the Volga River, with his cheerful wife, Alla. Following an old Soviet custom, they presented me with a ceremonious tea accompanied by traditional attempts to unravel the mystery of the Russian soul (chapter 7).

(*Left*) The Russian beauty Liubava and the brave Vova Liberman by the Volga River in Samara.

(*Above*) Liberman, the Mozart of auto service, struggles with the rear axle in the middle of nowhere.

(*Right*) The children of workers at the Aktyubinsk iron alloy plant in the lobby of Damolis dormitory, Kazakhstan (chapter 11).

Railroad conductor Ergash: "Why are you taking my picture? Are you from the police or what?" (chapter 11).

(*Left*) Akyn Esenbai, the beloved of the gods, improvising one of his love songs for his admirer, Rosa (chapter 13).

(*Below*) The market in Dzhusaly, where seeds are the main merchandise—as if people were birds (chapter 13).

Nina Karavai, now eighty-seven, a retired teacher, fought for justice after the local authorities tried to throw her out on the street (chapter 14).

Bakyt, an archaeological worker, with a local Kazakh peasant woman selling *kuzhe-ochitpa*, the Kazakh national dish (chapter 15).

Polat, a private cabby in Chimkent, Kazakhstan, who once received two bullets for his fare, his car taken for change. Yet he survived miraculously and didn't give up his otherwise cozy profession (chapter 15).

(*Left and above*) A famous poet Iranbek Orazbayev and his wife Fatyma. Their teenage son was shot to death under obscure circumstances in Alma-Ata (chapter 16).

The Kazakh expert on national problems, Rustem Dzhangushin, firmly believes in the post-Communist unity of the Turkic peoples of the former Soviet empire (chapter 16).

(*Above*) These Kirghiz refugees didn't want their names revealed because of fears about the bloody interethnic clashes in Osh province, Kirghizstan (chapter 19).

(*Below*) Armored vehicles and tanks on the roads of Central Asia became a usual part of the local landscape.

(*Below*) Valera Gusev, a living legend of Tashkent, in his mountain hideaway, avoiding the passion of two sultry sisters (chapter 23).

(*Above*) A leader of the Uzbek democratic party and an outstanding poet, Mohammed Solikh (chapter 20).

(*Right*) Pop star "Oscar," the Stevie Wonder of the former U.S.S.R. (chapter 29).

(*Below*) A Tadzhik knight, Safar Abdullo, who is always telling the cruel truth and takes to heart everything occurring in Tadzhik literature as if it is taking place in his own family (chapters 25, 26).

(*Above*) A gargantuan sculptural composition in front of the Union of Tadzhik writers: two Soviet classicists, Maxim Gorky and Sadreddin Aini, discuss the leading role of comrade Stalin in Soviet literature (chapter 25).

Parviz Tursun-zade, a musician and son of the writer after whom a town in Tadzhikstan was named (chapter 27).

(*Above*) Loik Sherali, a genius of Tadzhik poetry, framed by party bureaucrats, who decided to take advantage of his popularity (chapter 25).

(*Above*) Everyday life in Dushanbe (chapter 25).

(*Right*) A scene from the Central Asian bazaar: "Behave yourself, stranger. I told you, no pictures!"

The bright girl, Firuza, can explain everything about silkworms. The eggs are put in special bags, held under the armpit, and hatched by the natural warmth of the human body. Only married women with children are entitled to this job (chapter 27).

Malame Maksumov, a retired prison guard and an ardent Stalinist, whose only possessions are portraits of Lenin and Stalin, and his abused but rebellious wife. I'm hiding behind them (chapter 28).

Gel'dy Bairamov, a grandson of the legendary president of Turkmenia, who doesn't care about the Muscovites' idle chatter of civil freedoms because he believes that democracy, Soviet-style, means violence and bloodshed (chapter 29).

Leila, the disgraced president's granddaughter, with her daughter Sel'bi, and her cousin Nargiz, a Turkmenian Cinderella (chapter 29).

Bairam Bairamov, a Central Asian wise man and son of the legendary president of Turkmenia, an amateur cook who cooks for thousands (chapter 30).

(*Above and below*) Preparations for a wedding party in a Turkmenian village: calories and cholesterol are not concerns (chapter 30).

Newlyweds, Turkmenian-style (chapter 30).

Dancing at a wedding party in a Turkmenian village (chapter 30).

(*Right*) A Baku intellectual, Rauf, my Azerbaijanian Virgil, who escorted me through the circles of local political hell (chapters 32, 33).

(*Below*) Newlywed victims of Moscow's January 1990 military crackdown in Baku (chapters 32, 33).

The children in Baku smile like children everywhere; God forbid them to experience what their parents endured during the horrible years of "triumphant Soviet Communism."

(*Left*) Ghamid Kharizchi, a Khomeini follower, opposes the complete disintegration of the Soviet Union as an ideological state because, according to him, Russia is a Turko-Slavic organism in need of a unifying idea (chapter 32).

(*Below*) Azer Mustafa-zade, a wise politician and prominent member of the top-ruling bureaucracy in Azerbaijan (chapter 33).

The leaders of the People's Front of Azerbaijan on a hunger strike. On the *right*, Issa Gambarov; on the *left*, Panakh Guseinov (chapter 33).

The archpriest of the Russian Orthodox Church in Azerbaijan, Reverend
Georgii [Yury Novakovsky] (chapter 33).

come without invitation, and no one expects them to bring real presents. Any stranger can become a guest, too.

One evening, about five days after my arrival in Tashkent, my mother informed me that I had to go to the wake of a neighbor, a person who lived in the next street who had died the other day.

"Who's that?" I asked her, trying to remember who she was talking about.

"Don't you remember? He was a judge and your father's acquaintance. He lived next to Santalyat, where they sell hotcakes, and his elder son became a department chairman in the Institute of Marxism-Leninism. His third daughter married Tashmat, who studied in the Institute of People's Economy but later became an opera singer."

"Oh, yeah?" I said, astonished, because I could not remember any of these wonderful people. I had left this community almost a quarter of a century before, when I was just nineteen. "And what if I don't go?" I asked cautiously, for I had no particular desire to do so.

"You'd better go," my mother said. "All the *makhallya* knows that you have come from Moscow, and if you don't go people might think that you have become quite conceited."

Our Tartar family was the only Russian-speaking family in the whole district, and even though my parents were absolutely fluent in Uzbek and maintained good relations with their neighbors, neither I nor my two younger brothers ever became part of the local ethnic scene. The middle son became a diplomat, then a philosopher, and the youngest a pop singer and movie actor. My personal rating among our neighbors was even higher because I knew Arabic and worked for several years in Arab countries. From a local viewpoint, this was a great virtue, for Arabic is the language of the Koran (even though no one is able to read or understand it now). Besides, many *makhallya* elders do not see any difference between Egypt, where I worked twice, and Saudi Arabia, where I have never been in my life. For them all the Arab countries are "Arabstan," and anyone who has been there is considered to be a pilgrim who has returned from the Holy Land.

In the past, different cultural and ethnic backgrounds not only peacefully coexisted in Tashkent but were on very good terms, so it was not particularly strange that while I was not accepted in the *makhallya* as "one of the guys" I was nonetheless not regarded as a stranger either. In other words, I did not argue with my mother, because I knew that she valued good relations with the *makhallya* very much.

Hundreds of people usually come to the wakes, which are held on the day after the funeral, on the fortieth day after death, and on the first anniversary of the death. Those in attendance are not only relatives, friends, and acquaintances of the deceased, but his professional colleagues as well, who enjoy such occasions because they take place during working hours. No one would be surprised in Central Asia or in the Transcaucasus if, calling on some person at his job, he was told "He left for the funeral" or "Today everyone went to the wake of our accountant's relative. Please call again tomorrow."

The wake starts at dawn and can go on until late at night. Guests come and go in an endless flow, but each party has a special time. I was invited among the earliest guests, which might be interpreted as a sign of respect.

My mother woke me up very early in the morning and attempted to feed me some breakfast. After I escaped from a fried mutton leg and a full pot of *pelmeni* dumplings I went out to the street, still cool in the morning, the street that was familiar to me from my childhood. The cherry and apricot trees standing along the road had already lost their blooms.

In front of almost every house young women, looking quite sleepy, in light baggy dresses and long flowery wide trousers, were sweeping and watering the sidewalk. They wore sharp-nosed rubber galoshes, which in keeping with a local custom are worn on bare feet. The sweepers were junior daughters-in-law, who are responsible for cleaning the street in front of the house. It is believed that the state of the sidewalk in front of a house characterizes the family at large, so young women regard this responsibility very seriously. I was walking in the middle of the street, which was completely empty in that early morning. The women looked at me cursorily, and politely greeted me in Uzbek, evidently trying to figure out where a person of such an outlandish appearance could come from so early in the morning.

At the gates of the home of the deceased, his sons and several local elders in snow-white turbans were sitting on chairs brought from inside. On the occasion of the wake everyone wore greenish-blue quilted gowns wrapped by red and white waist bands. Unlike the elders the other men had *tyubeteykas* on their heads—small black folding hats with a peculiar ornamental design of white embroidery symbolizing a box of cotton.

I slowed down in order not to be the very first guest. Anyway, I was not ready for a prolonged conversation with the relatives, as I did not remember either their names or occupations. At that moment a cavalcade of cars, consisting mainly of white and black Volgas, appeared at the end of the street. That brand of car, and especially in those two colors, is considered the most prestigious in Uzbekistan, for only the *nomenklatura* uses it. The cars stopped, the doors slammed, and the first party of guests moved into the yard.

The sons stood up, and the elders in white turbans started nodding their gray beards approvingly, evidently referring to the long line of cars, which evidenced the respect that some serious people had for the relatives of the deceased. I hurried up and joined the tail of the line of guests that went past the relatives, shaking hands in turn with each of them.

"Ah, Marat-aka, come in," one of the sons said affably, and I recognized him at once as the barefooted boy who many years ago poured water from the *aryk* on me while I proudly rode past him on my first two-wheeler, on this very street. But what was his name?

Across the yard were wooden tables and long benches, covered with carpets and blankets. The guests had silently passed to the yard and were sitting at the tables. At this moment another party of people arrived, and places were quickly found for them as well.

"Who will say the prayers?" an aged Uzbek sitting in front of me asked sternly and everyone responded:

"You say them."

He agreed and started to tune himself, but something seemed to disturb him, because suddenly he addressed me: "Why don't you wear a *tyubeteyka*?"

"Because I'm not Uzbek," I said. "I'm a neighbor."

"But I thought that this was an Uzbek *makhallya*," he said, addressing no one in particular and knitting his thick eyebrows even more than before. But there was no time to procrastinate, for at a wake everything is done quickly and without much talking. Holding his hands in the shape of a little boat and closing his eyes he quickly whispered the first sura from the Koran, turning the long *a* sounds into no less long *o* sounds, in keeping with the Central Asian fashion.

The first sura, the so-called al-Fatiha ("Opening") is rather short and many elders know it by heart, although they do not know how to translate it. The man started saying the prayers fluently, but then he got confused and became silent, trying to remember the next line.

"*Iyaka nasta'in*," I prompted him quietly, and he opened his eyes, looked at me with hostile surprise, and finished the prayer.

All of us moved our open palms along our faces and said, "Amen." After this, obeying a sign of the senior person, boys dashed to the table with large round dishes of pilaf in their hands. These were volunteers, youths from the neighborhood. Their job is not paid and is called *khizmat*, which is quite adequately translated as service.

People had started cooking the pilaf late the night before and it had just become ready, spreading round its delicious smell. The cook was not to be seen, but firewood covered with white ashes was still smoldering under the *makhallya*'s huge caldron. Each dish, called a *laghan*, was for two persons. People are supposed to eat using their hands and mainly keeping silent, only inviting the fellow-eater to partake by an urging gesture and saying "*Oling-oling*," which means something like "Come on, help yourself."

When I took out a spoon that I had brought from my mother's house, my fellow-eater could not help smiling, and I was immediately punished for doing that by a disapproving glance from the gentleman who had said the prayers. Despite the fact that the plate was large, the portion of pilaf was barely enough for the two of us. No matter how big the caldron, it is impossible to feed everyone. That is why another meal would be made ready by the afternoon, a mutton soup or something simpler.

The boys took the empty dishes as adroitly and nimbly as they had brought them, and then they served dozens of little kettles with black or green tea that had been poured from a gigantic public samovar. The tea was the signal that the wake had concluded for the first group of guests. We had only to listen to the same prayer and leave our places for the next party of guests. But before that we had to drink our tea.

In Central Asia people do not drink tea from cups; in their place small round *pialas* are used. A small amount of tea signifies the respect of the host or the person who pours the tea from the kettle, and his readiness to treat a guest many times.

A friend of mine, Professor Larry Penrose from Hope College in Holland, Michigan, once got into a funny situation because of this custom. At the Uzbek Academy of Sciences, he was received by the local bosses, who were very anxious, since it was the beginning of the seventies when Americans in the Soviet Union were a great rarity. Larry had greatly impressed them with his knowledge of the Old Uzbek language. When the tea was brought in, the stern faces of the academicians cheered up a bit. The youngest of them, having caught the motion of eyebrows from the eldest, poured Larry's *piala* with extreme respect; that is, he splashed only a small amount on the bottom. Larry thought that according to the ritual one was supposed to rinse the cup out before drinking. He took the *piala* from him and, finding an appropriate vessel, an ashtray, poured its contents out without hesitation. The academicians exchanged glances in utter surprise but did not say anything, having concluded that Larry was following some American custom they did not know about. The junior academician put his left palm to his heart and took Larry's *piala* and poured in it the same amount of tea. Larry, somewhat at a loss, again poured its contents into an ashtray and went on talking about plans for his trip through Uzbekistan. One of the academicians, who turned out to be a plainclothes colonel of the KGB, quickly left for another room and made an urgent call to Moscow to get instructions on how they should act in this strange situation. The possibility could not be excluded that it was some kind of imperialist provocation, which was being discussed daily in Soviet newspapers. Then the junior academician, sweating from extreme tension, poured Larry a third *piala*. Suspecting that something was wrong, Larry got nervous and decided to take his time before pouring the contents into the ashtray, particularly as the ashtray was already full of tea to the very edge. Pretending that he was driving away a fly, Larry put his *piala* on the table and waited to see what would follow. Sighing with relief the server poured tea to the other participants of the meeting, even faster than it was necessary. Then Larry finally saw that he had to drink the tea instead of rinsing his *piala* with it.

23

Surgery Without Anesthesia

In the sultry Tashkent night she was standing under the bright fluorescent light of a street lamp at a deserted streetcar stop; her big black eyes glowed like those of a cat. They could be seen about a mile away, sparkling in her pale, ivory face. But how killingly beautiful she was we saw only when we drove up. She raised her hand, and I pulled over.

"Where do you need to go?" my friend Valera Gusev asked her in Uzbek.

"There!" the girl answered vaguely in Russian, and pointed with her hand away from the old part of the city. I sensed a strange aloofness in her voice; it was as if a robot-android were talking to us, one that had already accomplished the tasks set by its master and was now indifferent, since whatever it did it was destined for the recycling center.

I cautiously pushed Valera aside, as he was radiating the energy of his flaring emotions onto the midnight wanderer without being aware of it. The girl presented a really strange picture. An explanation of how she was dressed probably makes no sense. She was wearing something light, short, and no doubt very expensive. In cities like Tashkent, people know how to dress, and there are even special styles here that do not rely for their inspiration on Moscow or Paris. But the problem was that this enigmatic creature was not dressed in Tashkent style, nor was she attired in Soviet youth fashion. Her clothes were more exquisite. In our country her mode would be called, ironically, the "expensive woman" style. All that was missing were the gloves and the hat; the blue-and-white plastic bag with a Rothman's ad printed on it seemed in sharp dissonance with the rest of her outfit. A Dior purse would have been more in place. But the expression on the beautiful face of this woman was as deadpan as a mask.

"Where is your 'there'?" I asked, rather foolishly, because we had to go in exactly the opposite direction, toward the Old City, where my mother's house was.

Valera turned around and looked at me meaningfully. His look signified, If you are my friend, we will drive her wherever she wants to go.

Suddenly the midnight lady clattered her heels over to our car and slipped into the backseat. I snorted, feeling the incongruity of her air and our jalopy. She was too chic for the old Moskvich that I had borrowed from one of my friends for a few days.

"Come on, boys, enough of this foot-dragging," she said, destroying her romantic image. I was somewhat at a loss. By all appearances, she was a hard-currency prostitute who had somehow blown away from the Moscow International Trade Center to Tashkent's Lenin Boulevard. Despite their complex relations with the KGB on the one hand, and with criminals on the other, hard-currency prostitutes make good money and can afford outfits that cost as much as the annual income of an average Soviet person. But this girl did not speak as though she was from Moscow, and she did not look Russian either.

"Well, where shall I drive, then?" I asked without turning my head, for some reason aping the boorish manner of a Moscow private cabbie who makes quick money by picking up drunken foreigners.

"Let's go to my place," Valera exclaimed joyously, immediately reacting to the sudden turn in the plot.

"I won't sleep with you," the woman answered. "But let's go."

Of course she spent the night with him. Moreover, they developed a crazy romance, which with its tense passion and rapid-fire denouement could have competed with some of the heartbreaking Indian melodramas that are so popular in Uzbekistan.

It was strange that all this happened to Valera Gusev, my old friend from Tashkent, who had seemed to grow exhausted in recent years from the constant discrepancy between the desired and the real. He had achieved much of what he had aspired to in this life. For instance, he was a graduate of two institutes—the Institute of Physical Culture and the university's department of journalism. He had been married to the daughter of a high-positioned party bureaucrat (*appa-ratchik*), but the marriage did not work out, because both partners were completely unfit, psychologically, for family life. After he joined the Union of Cinematographers of Uzbekistan he was able to stop going to his state job every day. He was well known in Tashkent as a script writer and an author of detective stories. He also created texts for songs and operas. He was quite independent financially and had a certain status in society. His friends, both male and female, loved him. But somehow everything that had earlier brought him joy suddenly stopped exciting him. He bought an old military van and set it in the Tashkent mountains, right on the border between Uzbekistan and southern Kazakhstan. When he could not be found in the city, his friends would know that he was again in one of his sulky moods, and had left to be far away from the onerous Soviet reality.

Nature could heal Valera's fits of black melancholy but not for long; each time his stays in the city grew shorter and his spells in the mountains grew longer. However, I was fortunate enough to find him in Tashkent. As always, we communicated as if we had never parted, although more than a year had passed since our last meeting. Valera is one of my oldest friends, and my family receives him as a relative. That evening we were just returning from being with Borya Shelepov and Larisa Tsoi. I had been looking for a car and a fellow-traveler to accompany me on my journey at least half of the way to Dushanbe. The road, however dull it might seem, was really dangerous, and an old friend would make a dependable and comforting companion.

But that woman on the street overturned all our plans.

A week later, Valera appeared at my place for the first time. He looked exhausted and depressed. In our circle, discussing one's personal life even with friends is not acceptable, and therefore I started talking about quite prosaic matters, something about Uzbekistan's new trade regulations, which had just been introduced as in other places: now only people with local residence permits in their passports could buy things in stores. But Valera limply waved this off.

"All the same, they are stealing and they will continue to steal," he said, talking about Soviet tradesmen.

"What about our friend Novogrudsky? Did he finally find himself a fiancée?"

In the late seventies Boris Novogrudsky had emigrated to Canada with his wife and daughter, but his wife left him soon after and married a more prosperous person. In the last three years he had come to the Soviet Union twice in order to get married, but because of the great numbers of young Soviet women desiring to leave the U.S.S.R., he could not make any choice. Having slept with dozens of candidates he arrived at the sad conclusion that their readiness to share his bed was explained not by the fact that he was himself so irresistible but rather by their horror of the impending civil war and desire to escape. However, in Canada polygamy is not allowed, so he could save only one woman. But where was the guarantee, he wanted to know, that she would not leave him as soon as she got her permanent residency?

"I wish I had his trouble," Valera said with a sigh, and then I understood that I was witnessing a classic case of the tragedy of middle-aged love. That state was depicted with great pathos in pre-Islamic Arab poems about men who completely lose their ability to talk about anything but the subject of their passion. But semiliterate sons of the desert are one thing, while my enlightened and sophisticated friend is another.

After I had driven them to Valera's home that evening, the woman agreed to stay at his place. But almost immediately after I left she complained that her liver was aching and added that she had recently had hepatitis. It was not surprising at all, Valera thought with compassion, because he knew that many Soviet people get infected in clinics and hospitals due to the lack of disposable syringes. Another reason is that the vegetables and fruit are contaminated with pesticides and the drinking water in many southern regions of the country is dangerous, too. He turned off the music, pushed away the glasses of brandy, and offered to call an ambulance.

"I don't need any ambulance," she said. Her name was Gulya; "Gul'" in Uzbek (or, to be more precise, in Tadzhik) means "flower."

"Why not? Let them come, give you a shot and some medicine," Valera objected in surprise.

"Don't you know our doctors?" Gulya said, answering a question with a question. "I'm used to doing everything myself. I always carry a syringe and medicine. Are you afraid of intravenous shots? Some men, you know, faint at the sight of a needle piercing someone else's vein."

"I won't faint," Valera promised, but started having serious doubts over that story about hepatitis.

After she gave herself a shot Gulya became a new person. From the sullen, silent, pale beauty she was transformed into a merry, tender, and naughty child who ultimately fascinated Valera. He always used to think that his best woman was yet to come, but suddenly Valera thought that he had never met anyone better than Gulya. He tried not to think about what she was and who had taught her the art of love. It is difficult to deceive yourself when you're over forty. In the morning he took an empty ampule out of the garbage and tried to read what was written on it.

"Fentanyl," Gulya prompted, suddenly emerging from behind him. "It's a painkiller, but not a very strong one."

"That's a narcotic," Valera echoed angrily and looked her in the eye.

Gulya put on an innocent air and smiled gently at him, saying, "That's right."

"So you're a drug addict?"

"Of course not," Gulya said self-assuredly. "It's just that I was raped in eighth grade. After that I could never be with a man without giving myself a shot."

"How did it happen?" Valera asked, turning pale with rage.

"It's none of your frigging business, mister." Gulya laughed, cautiously freeing the empty ampule from his clenched fist and throwing it in the garbage. "Look, you cut yourself. Where do you keep your iodine?"

Over the course of the next five days they were together constantly. Once or twice a day Gulya would go home to change clothes and to find out from her grandmother who had called. Her father was a rather important Uzbek official, but because a new "team" had just come to power in the republic he was going through difficult times. It seems that he was even being prosecuted for something or other, but like the majority of party bureaucrats from the old guard, he got off with only a scare—because of a lack of evidence, Gulya would say, laughing. Her mother, Russian by national origin, had died long ago and Gulya maintained no contacts with her father and his new family, because they had lost all hope that she would ever play according to the rules. When he was still in power her father had secured a two-bedroom apartment for her in a decent district of Tashkent, close to the Alai bazaar, where she lived with her maternal grandmother. The old woman was very fond of her granddaughter and never asked her why she did not come home for so long. Probably she had no idea what her little Gulya had become, her Gulya that she had nursed from the cradle. Long ago, when she was young herself, like the majority of Soviet people of her generation, the grandmother had been poisoned by Stalinist propaganda about the bright future that had to be built at the cost of their lives for the sake of their children and grandchildren. She had even worked in the Komsomol—the Young Communist League—and perhaps could have made a modest party career, since she had been quite beautiful when she was young. Many women in the party apparatus show some traces of former beauty. But misfortune had befallen Gulya's grandmother, and in her heyday she underwent unsuccessful surgery on her face that left an awful scar on her cheek, accompanied by a tic from a damaged facial nerve. She almost stopped going out because she was ashamed of her mutilated face.

"The first impression is really awful," Valera said while I waited with him for a taxi on the street. I was listening to him almost without interrupting because I understood that he needed to let it all out. I was almost ideally suited for hearing such a confession for two reasons. First, we had been friends for almost a quarter of a century. Second, I was leaving soon.

Gulya had introduced her new friend to her grandmother, something that apparently had almost never happened before. That same evening, Valera met Gulya's elder sister, who had by chance come to visit the grandmother. That, too, happened quite rarely, because Gulya's elder sister, Yulduz, had been married for a few years and had a four-year-old son. She worked as an engineer in a huge state research institute whose projects had resulted not only in the calamitous rerouting of the waters of local rivers and streams but even the destruction of the Aral Sea.

Despite the fact that they looked very much alike, the sisters were absolutely different women. The older one, according to Valera, was meeker and more feminine than Gulya, even in the way she looked. She was as tall as Gulya but her legs were plumper and her shoulders more sloping. Her clothes and her hairdo were much more modest than her sister's, and unlike Gulya she had a healthy complexion and businesslike, restrained manner. She had probably guessed what her sister's life was like but preferred not to interfere. They were never especially close and only saw each other on rare occasions, because Gulya did not like Yulduz's husband.

To put it bluntly, she hated him. Some time before she had even wanted to kill him. But then she decided that it was not worth depriving her infant nephew of his father and her sister of her rich and influential husband. The reason for this hatred was both simple and awful: he was the man who had raped her in such a rough and cruel manner. What was even more awful for her was that he was constantly reasserting his claims and had recently achieved what he wanted by force. He had been a featherweight boxer in his past and maintained the ways of a ferret—a brisk predator with movements nearly imperceptible and therefore especially terrifying to his victims.

"Do you know how he did it?" asked Valera in a breaking voice. "First, he hit her in the solar plexus, so that she almost fainted. And then he cut his own initial with a razor blade on her ass. So that she would not resist the next time."

"But where did he get a blade?" I mumbled. "It's a deficit item, you know."

Valera looked at me wildly.

"Excuse me," I said, confused. "It's just that I know that you can't get them, even in hospitals."

"But not in the Fourth Central Directorate," Valera replied in anger. The Fourth Central Directorate is the name of a network of medical institutes that take care of party *nomenklatura* only.

"Why isn't he afraid of her going to the precinct? Or complaining to her sister?"

"First of all, he's a respectable person in the republic, while she is most probably registered with the police as a prostitute. Besides that, she's a drug addict. And he brought her some morphine that time. Otherwise how would he lure her to his friend's apartment? The most awful thing is that she has run out of drugs again and went back to him. Only the day before yesterday she was boasting that she would give it up but yesterday she began feeling withdrawal symptoms, so she sent me to the devil and crawled back to him."

"Well, what are you going to do now? If you don't have any definite plans I would like to suggest that we go right now and buy a pistol and kill this bastard. Second, you will marry Gulya tomorrow, and she'll give birth to three children. She'll throw her needles down the drain and enter a pedagogical institute to teach future eighth-graders how to behave."

"Stop it!" Valera cried out. "You weren't so cruel before."

"Sorry," I said wearily. "I was just trying to make you understand how foolish what you're planning to do is. Don't be a donkey—remember your first marriage! How long will it all last—a week? Or a month? You are giving her hope, and nothing will come of it all the same. Are you able to dedicate the rest of your life to the moral resurrection of another person? Don't you overestimate your own strength? And why did you decide that a fallen woman could be made happy living with such a capricious, unstable, and jealous person as you? Why, you'll be mad with jealousy toward her past."

"But I have to do something," Valera moaned, "or I'll go nuts."

"Seduce her sister," I said suddenly, but immediately took it back: "No, don't do that."

As if to spite me, the first cab to appear in the half hour that we had been waiting came right at that moment. It was a licensed private cabman. In Tashkent, unlike Moscow, private taxi owners prosper.

Valera threw me an insane glance and climbed into the green Zhiguli, which took him roaring into the night. Certainly wisdom consists of knowing the limits of what is possible for you and rejecting attempts to achieve the impossible. But as the old bullshitter Gorky wrote, we "sing a song to the insanity of the brave." I sympathized with the emotional cataclysm that had overcome my friend Valera Gusev, for it reminded me of the half-forgotten time when our friendship was just beginning.

About ten days later, Alisher Turgunov called me. During the last few years, he had completely matured and become a big administrator. He was too decent a person and too independent to try to climb up the ladder of the party apparatus. But like any other extrovert with managerial inclinations, he was bored without some turbulent administrative-organizational activity to keep him busy, and therefore felt completely at home in the troubled waters of economic chaos. He was always thrown into some emergency or other, called upon to save collapsing structures by changing them into something new, something that corresponds to the current state of affairs. In the summer of 1990 he headed the Uzbek Association for Business Collaboration with Foreign Countries, which he had recently created himself. Like many similarly monstrous new arrangements, the association was engaged in God-knows-what kinds of activities. Yet it was not Alisher's fault; such was the Soviet economic reality that everyone mimicked feverish activity but accomplished absolutely nothing, or close to it. Under the conditions of economic uncertainty, which contributed to the continuing party control over economic contacts with foreign countries, talk about enterprises having independent relations with foreign partners was a complete deception, or a self-deception. Like any other sensible practitioner, Alisher was far from entertaining any partocratic fantasies about the state of affairs. But he believed in the possibility of a reasonable course of events, and thought that sooner or later the moment would come when his association would be able to do what it was created to do—that is, to be an intermediary between the local industrial enterprises and foreign partners. And he tried not to think about how far he was from his aim.

"Do you know where Valera Gusev is?" I asked him just in case.

"He went to the mountains," Alisher answered. "Why, do you want to see him? If you want I can arrange a car to drive you there."

"Can you arrange a car to drive me to Dushanbe?" I asked excitedly.

"No, I can't," Alisher said regretfully. "Dushanbe is another republic, and the traffic cops check business documents and driver's licenses on the way there. You know yourself what times are like now."

"Yes, I know," I said, sighing. "Okay, then let's go to the mountains to see Gusev, at least."

"Are you going to Gusev's again?" my mother asked quietly. She had been present during my phone conversation with Alisher. She was still afraid that my bachelor friend would show me a bad example in his relations with women.

"Yes, but I'm going with Alisher," I answered with a smile for I knew that she thought of Alisher as a serious person. He had not been an angel himself in the past, but ten years ago he had settled down and made a nice family, consisting of a young wife, a charming daughter, Kamola, and a funny, chubby son, Sanjar. Besides, my mother had worked for many years with his mother, and they were friends, too. Valera's parents had been killed during World War II, and so he was brought as a baby from Byelorussia to Uzbekistan, where he grew up in a Samarkand foster home. He used to tell me that the main event of his childhood was a trip to Moscow, in the early fifties, to the Exhibition of Economic Achievements of the People's Economy. Valera had bred a gigantic rabbit that weighed about forty pounds. His trip to Moscow had been his reward for success in animal husbandry.

Alisher picked me up on Saturday, in his own car. His wife, Umida, sat with the children in the backseat, and I sat in the front. Alisher had a surprise for me, which was that he and his wife had recently bought a house in the mountains in the same village where Gusev's caravan stood. Unlike Gusev's unfaithful girlfriend and her elder sister, Yulduz, who were strongly Russified and had lost their national identity, Alisher's wife was an incarnation of typical Uzbek matriarchal virtues. Of course, she was dressed in European fashion and spoke Russian without any accent, but her manners, the way she maintained a conversation and listened to her interlocutor, were like a translation from Uzbek. At one time she taught Uzbek folk dances to children, but after her second child, Sanjar, was born, she left her job. There was no financial necessity for her to work with such a husband as Alisher.

"The former owners were anxious to leave for Russia and they didn't haggle very much," Alisher answered when I asked if he had to pay a lot for such a house.

The highway into the Chimghan mountains was familiar to me from childhood. We used to go there a long time ago for skiing and sledding, and later as students we worked there in children's summer camps as teachers and team leaders. On a clear day, the snowy peaks of Chimghan, just fifty miles distant, are distinctly visible in Tashkent.

In the past it was possible to go to the mountains not only by special buses but by city cab as well. Now everything looked quite different: a patrol car stopped us at the exit from Tashkent, and a dusty armored troop carrier was standing nearby with its machine gun pointing toward the highway.

"There were disturbances in the Parkent region this spring," Alisher said. "There was some shooting; people were killed and wounded. It wasn't only the soldiers who were shooting—the people from the crowd were armed as well. The police station was burned, and the building of the party district committee was damaged. But don't worry, it wasn't near here. It was about fifty kilometers away."

"But why is an armored troop carrier standing here?" I asked.

"They say they're trying to catch some armed gang," Alisher responded.

Then he told me yet another Tashkent story about the chief of the province traffic police unit, who was sprayed with bullets by some unknown attackers from a neighboring car.

"And no one was caught," Umida added from the backseat in a calm voice.

The road was beautiful and maintained in good condition. Local inhabitants call it a "government highway," for it runs by the compound of the official recreational residence of the Communist Party leadership, with its special medical institutions and the state and private dachas of the Uzbek party functionaries.

Approximately twenty miles from Tashkent is a small town called Chirchik, built right after World War II. Numerous chemical industries are located there, and have contaminated the environment for almost five decades. As you approach Chirchik, you begin to see an impressive array of poisonous smoke of every color of the rainbow spewing from tall chimneys rising from the factories.

"A man was arrested here recently when they found that he was keeping a two-barreled, rapid-firing cannon in his backyard," Alisher boasted, not without a glimmer of patriotic pride.

"Against whom was he going to wage war?" I asked.

"It's not known yet," my friend responded, "and in any event, there were no cinders on the inside of the barrels, which meant that he hadn't fired it yet."

Illegal arms sales long ago stopped being a sensation in our country. Recently our newspapers informed their readers that the authorities intervened in the sale of a combat tank somewhere in the Transcaucasus. It does not surprise anyone that Armenian fighters even use air power in their war against neighboring Azerbaijan. Of course they do not have any jets, only prop agricultural planes and helicopters.

Somehow we began talking about birth control. Strictly speaking, there is no such thing in Central Asia. Sporadic attempts on the part of the center to control the growth of the Central Asian population were reduced to naught by the complete inability of industry to provide people with the necessary appliances and pharmaceuticals. The only mechanical means that one can get is the so-called Soviet spiral, but using it causes uterine erosion, which leads to even more awful consequences. But even if some alternative appliances were to appear in the pharmacies, only city dwellers would show interest in them. Residents of rural areas, who constitute more than half of the Central Asian population, still rely primarily on nature and on God to prevent too-frequent pregnancy.

The Soviet women who have legal abortions in ordinary hospitals go through the most terrible experience. Because of the constant deficit of drugs, abortions, widely available, are done in the majority of cases without general anesthesia. Instead they give women shots of aspirin. Because of the wild screaming of the patients, doctors often work too quickly and do not empty the womb as thoroughly as necessary. As a result, about half of the patients have to return for a second procedure. In Russian it is called "a purge." Recent announcements on the boards of maternity homes read "Only people with passports showing a residence permit for this district can get on the list for a purge."

The vilest thing about our system of "free" medicine is that although any kind of anesthesia you might need, imported drugs included, is always available in the hospitals, you have to bribe the doctors to get a shot; moreover, bribes will not be taken from just anyone. Women usually have to pull strings to pay for their treatment. Otherwise, there would not be a deficit. On the other hand, not everyone is rich enough to afford bribery, such as a high school girl who gets an abortion without telling her parents. Now imagine the women sitting in line waiting for surgery: they can hear all the screams behind the half-closed door. And they look with hatred at those who did not scream.

Having left Umida with the children at their house, we went to see Valera Gusev. On the way Alisher politely expressed his displeasure at the conversation in the car.

"Have you forgotten that in Uzbekistan it's not courteous to talk to women about such things?" he reproached me. "But why?" I was confused. "Your children don't understand Russian, and your wife is an adult person. And then we were speaking not about some concrete case from someone's life but about the problem for millions of our women compatriots, on the whole. Many of them have to have several abortions each year."

"But I'm against abortion in general," Alisher said.

"That's another topic." I shrugged. "Is it still a long walk to Valera's caravan?"

"About twenty minutes," Alisher replied and started talking about his plans to build a resort for hard-currency tourists in Chimghan.

Valera met us joyously at first, but then he became sullen again. Alisher, it seemed, knew nothing about Gulya and therefore I did not want to ask Valera about the further course of those events in his presence.

"Let's go to my house," Alisher said to Valera. "We have brought lots of food with us. Marat's mother made a whole pot of *manty*. Umida made a salad. Come on, you look too sour!"

"*Manty?*" Valera's face became bright for a moment and he started to salivate. "Let's go."

Manty are something like big ravioli with a mutton-and-onion filling. They are not boiled in water but cooked over steam in a special pot, called a *kaskan*. This dish is held in great esteem not only in Uzbekistan but in other republics of Central Asia as well.

After dinner Valera and I walked to the river in silence and sat on boulders, warm from the sunshine. Valera tore an unripe apple from a tree and cautiously bit into it. I wrinkled my face, imagining how sour it was.

"So, it's completely kaput," Valera informed me sullenly, having spit out the bite of apple onto the ground.

"It's completely kaput only when someone is dead," I objected. "I hope everyone is alive and in good health?"

"Alive but not in good health," he responded. "She came all covered with bruises the next day. You yourself can imagine where these bruises were."

I nodded silently. I did not want to know more about this awful story. But Valera was so much swallowed up by it that I started worrying for his mental state.

He had driven Gulya away and immediately felt sorry for doing that. But she left and disappeared completely. The grandmother knew nothing of her whereabouts and was quite anxious, sensing that there was some trouble. Valera visited their apartment several times, and once ran into Gulya's elder sister at the entrance. They started talking, and Valera invited her to his place, out of despair perhaps.

Despite all her outward appearance of well-being, her marriage was unsuccessful—how could she be happy with such a husband? Yulduz came right up to Valera and, closing her eyes, asked him to kiss her.

"Oh, God!" I said. "Did you really do that?"

"But you yourself advised me to do it." Valera looked at me reproachfully.

But the new affair did not bring him any joy. After the narcotic intoxication of Gulya's passion, the restrained caresses of the elder sister irritated him with their lack of skill. But the genie was already out of the bottle: after five years in her joyless marriage, Yulduz had fallen in love with Valera with the enthusiasm of a neophyte, grabbing onto him as onto the last straw.

"She's going to divorce her husband and move into my apartment with her child," he informed me gloomily.

"And what if Gulya returns?"

He started groaning as if from an unbearable pain.

"Is that why you came here?" I asked.

"Yes, I ran away in the most disgraceful way. But it was a stalemate situation. I don't want to see anyone at all. And I don't want to see you, either. Leave me alone, all of you! I want to be alone."

He started trudging uphill toward his caravan, absolutely indifferent to what party was in power in the U.S.S.R., or anything else having to do with this world.

24

The Unapproved Route

Meanwhile, as the Soviet bureaucrats say, the "question" of the car hung in the air. Of the dozens of my friends and acquaintances in Tashkent who have cars, not one was willing to rent his car, or to join my expedition as a Liberman the Second. It did not help either to persuade or plead with them to "share the glory." Nor was anyone swayed by the great sums of money that I offered in increasing amounts, as at an auction. The common motive for refusal was sadly identical: "Old man, you have not chosen a fortunate time for your journey. We don't need money or glory. Life, as you know, is more valuable. Who will feed our children if something happens?"

Among the latest horrifying rumors, a story was circulating about policemen stopping cars on the road. "Your documents," people in military uniform reportedly would demand, and while you were getting your papers, they would put a pistol to your temple and pull the trigger. Then the dead bodies would be thrown by the side of the road, and the car would be stolen and stripped for parts. As I said earlier, the price of a car sold for parts on the black market often exceeds the price for whole cars. But the main thing, of course, is that it is so much easier for the thief to cover his tracks. It is strange that not one of the storytellers tried to determine whether it was bandits dressed in police uniforms or policemen earning their living by robbery. Of course, the former is more likely than the latter.

Recently the all-knowing *Literaturnaya Gazeta* published a scathing feature story about a regional procurator who upheld the law somewhere in Voronezh oblast, and who killed his lover with an ax, but not out of jealousy. The motive for the murder was robbery, for the victim worked as the chief accountant of a business, and that day she had received at the bank the wages of several hundred employees. In the former U.S.S.R. people's wages are paid in cash. This murderer-in-uniform, by the way, was married and had engineered his lover's disappearance as an escape for the purpose of stealing the money she received at the bank. And everything would have worked out for the young rising representative of the *nomenklatura*, but as it always happens, by chance the dismembered bodies of the accountant and the cashier he had also murdered were discovered.

The day before, a local resident had tried to sell his new Moskvich, and members of a local gang had surrounded him. With blackmail and scare tactics, they forced the owner to sell his car at a ridiculously low price. When he refused and tried to drive away, they grabbed crowbars and methodically smashed the car into smithereens. Seeing what his property had turned into, he grabbed a sawed-off shotgun from behind the seat and killed two of the attackers. The remaining ones opened fire with pistols and riddled the poor wretch with holes.

Another unfortunate made a deal with bandits while his wife remained sitting in the car. "You sold the car to us as is, i.e., with your wife," the gangsters said, laughing and not letting the terrified woman out of the car. In order to "redeem" her, her husband had to return the money he had just received for the car. As a result, he got his wife back, but the bandits got the car for nothing. The deal was made, and he could not do anything to change it.

Very often, victims do not go to the police, not only because they know just how real the racketeers' threats are. At the moment a deal is made in any commission store in the whole territory of the pre-breakup Soviet Union, the buyer and the seller inevitably break the law since a fictitiously low price for the car in question is always listed in state documents. That is explained by the usual restrictions of the state, that what is on paper is always more important than reality. For example, a store appraiser (naturally, a mafia member) establishes the selling price of an automobile of three or four thousand rubles, when its market price is ten times higher. Fictitious buyers promise the owner thirty thousand rubles, but the documents are drawn up to say three thousand. After that, when all the documents are already drawn up and it is time to pay, the owner of the car, now already its former owner, suddenly realizes that they are paying him only as much as is stated in the document. In the language of those who make a detailed study of trade, this is called "conning the mark." If the victim tries to raise a fuss, the perpetrators give the deceived person some fists in his teeth and advise him to appeal to the police.

That is only small-time swindling in comparison with how the Communist state suddenly acted toward all its citizens in January 1991. The Soviet right-wing elite made tens of billions of rubles by "conning" almost three hundred million "marks." This was accomplished by the removal from circulation of all fifty- and hundred-ruble banknotes, the currency in which the majority of the population was paid during the past year. Most of them, and pensioners as well, had stored their pitiful savings in these two ill-fated denominations. The government permitted only monthly wages to be exchanged for legal tender, and only three days were set aside for the exchange. On the first declared day, no exchanges occurred because there were no instructions. On the second day, they changed money for workers, and on the third day, for retirees. Thousands of people waited in endlessly long lines; a few died of heart attacks. The mafiosi just laughed, since only they and the *nomenklatura* knew about the caper ahead of time and had long ago exchanged their green and brown paper bearing Lenin's profile for the new money or for dollars at black market prices. According to Victor Gerasimov, then president of the U.S.S.R. Gosbank, about forty-six billion rubles were withdrawn from circulation: that is, about one third of all Soviet money. According to the authorities' estimates, anywhere from seven to fifteen billion rubles were in the hands of speculators and the nouveau riche of perestroika, against whom this action was apparently directed. The rest constituted the savings of ordinary citizens.

Help, as always, came from an unexpected source. It was Galya Otemisova, she whose trolley pass was not punched because she asked about it in Russian rather than Uzbek, even though the Uzbek words for "trolley," "punch," and "pass" *are* Russian. At one time she was a classmate of my brother Tahir, and all her life she had been unrequitedly in love with him. Therefore she was a friend of my family, and she always tried to help me during my visits to Tashkent. After many long years of working in the cultural department of the city council, she had developed numerous connections and acquaintances, without which it is virtually impossible for a Soviet person to live a decent life under the existing system.

"Lucky man," she said when she called once early in the morning. "My friend Gal'ka Sakevich is driving her car from Tashkent to the Crimea. They are planning to go through Samarkand, Ashkhabad, Krasnovodsk, Baku, Tbilisi, and so forth, all the way to the Crimea."

"That can't be!" I almost fell out of bed with joy. "And who is going with her?"

"Her husband and their adult son," Galya said. "If this arrangement suits you, I will settle things with her, and then I will call you back."

"Wait, when are they planning to leave? And why are they going somewhere at a time when all respectable people are sitting at home?"

"I think they want to move to the Crimea. You know how many people have left here now."

"But you aren't planning to leave Uzbekistan?" I asked.

"Who needs me, with two children?" Galya giggled. She had recently divorced her husband, who, like his former boss, Yakhyaev, the minister of internal affairs, combined service in law-enforcement organs with membership in the Writers' Union.

"What kind of car are they driving?" I asked.

"A Zhiguli, Model 9. Do you have any other questions?" she asked with mild sarcasm. The Model 9 Zhiguli is considered the top car automobile in the U.S.S.R. People call this car *utyug* (iron) because it resembles an old-fashioned iron in shape.

After that, everything got progressively worse. The next day she called again and said that the republic VDOAM had not approved their route and had not signed the road list.

"What kind of agency is VDOAM?" I said in a disappointed voice. "Why must the route be approved? It's not a rally or an auto race."

"VDOAM is the All-Union Society of Auto Fanciers," Galya angrily explained. "If they have a road list from VDOAM, they would be considered as a team, and would have a chance of getting a room in hotels, as well as obtaining the guaranteed amount of gas for the whole approved route. Without the road list, this is like a private trip, and no one will be interested in their problems."

"Why didn't they sign the route—because of Turkmenia or Azerbaijan?"

"Horseradish is not sweeter than a radish," answered Galya, quoting the old Russian proverb, meaning that neither alternative is better. "In Turkmenia there are armed bandits on the roads, especially between Ashkhabad and Krasnovodsk, and in Azerbaijan there is virtually a civil war. Don't you read the newspapers?"

"In my opinion you yourself don't read the local papers," I snapped. "You have papers that are like those in Brezhnev's time. They don't write anything about this. All they can write about is the continuing leadership role of the Central Committee of the Communist Party of Uzbekistan and the indestructible friendship of the peoples."

"How do you like that! There's a Muscovite for you." Galya was offended on behalf of the local press. "All non-Uzbeks support Karimov's policies," she said, referring to the first secretary of the Central Committee of the Uzbek Communist Party and thus, automatically, the president of Uzbekistan. "Who the hell needs such democracy when they slash and burn the people? For us here, democracy is understood not as demonstrations with placards but as pogroms with blood-letting. This is not Moscow—"

"Fine," I interrupted, "but what are they going to do now, your friend Sakevich and her family?"

"They got a route approved through northern Kazakhstan, Chelyabinsk, Ufa. In short, through Russia, a huge detour. Still, it is not so awful. If they die, it will not be from bullets but from hunger. They say there is no food in Ufa."

"Where is there any?" I answered sadly, thinking of the Urals and the European part of Russia.

There remained one last tried and true way: an intercity taxi. From Tashkent to Dushanbe on the Road of State Importance M-34 was only 285 miles and could be managed in about seven hours of good driving. Of course, to stop a taxi on the road and tell the driver that I planned to go to Dushanbe was out of the question. In the first place, hardly any driver would take the first passenger he met for such a distance, and in the second place, I could not myself trust the first driver I met.

In spite of strong protests from my mother, who was horrified at my traveling, in her opinion, in such a strange way, I finally found a sensible and dependable man in one of Tashkent's taxi stands who agreed to take me to Dushanbe for one thousand rubles. I understood that I was overpaying him about one and a half times, but the people who recommended him were my friends, and therefore I decided that I would not likely find a better alternative.

Kissing my weeping mother, I promised her that in August I would absolutely come to see her again, and that then, like all normal people, I would fly on an airplane. I leaped into the front seat of the old, beat-up Volga with checks on the side, and commanded the driver: "Forward!"

He looked askance at me, started the engine, and floored the accelerator.

The early summer morning, it seemed to me, was beautifully appropriate for the beginning of the next stage of my journey. What of the fact that the motor rattled too loudly, and the interior of the car smelled strongly of gasoline? The country winds pleasantly ruffled my hair, the midday heat was still far off, and the not-too-lively M-34 cheered my eyes with a typical Central Asian landscape: green acres of planted fields, tall shapes of pyramidal poplars along the road, distant lines of low mountains on the horizon.

The car was old but quick, and we reached Yangiyul without any adventures. Even the state auto inspection stations, to my surprise, did not stop us.

"State taxi," proudly explained my driver, whose name was Sergei. He was somewhat gloomy for his twenty-two years. He had a Soviet-made portable stereo tape player in his car, which was attached with a cord to the cigarette lighter on the dashboard. When Sergei put in a cassette by a rock group called Depeche Mode, I asked if he had earphones.

"It is illegal to drive a car while wearing earphones," he said, looking at me with indifferent, light-colored eyes.

"Then turn it off," I requested.

"We usually don't ask passengers if we can turn music on or not," Sergei said with pride. "But since this is a 'charter flight,' then all right, that's the way it is."

Then, when he got bored with being arrogant, we chatted, and I found out from him much that was interesting. After finishing school, he wanted to become an officer and even enrolled in a military academy, but he was disappointed in the army system, and after the first year he turned in his resignation. Since, according to the law on universal military obligation, he was required to serve in the army two years, or three in the navy, after leaving the academy he was sent to serve a term as a soldier in the construction battalion that extended the railroad line through the thick, impassable forests of Siberia.

In the Soviet army first-year soldiers are subjected to highly refined physical and spiritual terror from the older soldiers. The tradition of "nonregulation" dependence of the young before the old had its beginning in the cadet barracks in czarist times. But it has reappeared in recent decades in the open criminal coercion of the young by the older men. This infection penetrated the army from the corrective labor colonies, as well as from colonies for juvenile delinquents, which tens of millions of Soviet young people experienced. The liberal press organs regularly feature mothers' letters about their sons, young soldiers who became invalids or died as a result of vicious nighttime massacres in the barracks. However, any attempts to initiate conversation about reforms in the military in the official military press, as before, are considered a "criminal attempt to undermine the defense capability of our great homeland."

As a former military student, Sergei was not really considered a greenhorn. Nonetheless, in his new position he had his share of rather cruel experiences. In the end, after coming out of the hospital, where he had been taken with broken ribs and a crushed hand, he managed to adapt and even to be assigned to one of the most desirable military posts, the local stokehold. To maintain a round-the-clock fire in the furnace, loading coal with a shovel, was not considered burdensome work, since the others had to lay railroad ties, even in minus 16° Farenheit weather. After the slave labor of prisoners, the construction battalions were considered the most convenient and cheapest—they were virtually unpaid—source of unskilled labor.

The Uzbek contingent in the military unit in which Sergei served was badly represented, and Azerbaijani soldiers were the "top dogs." Conflicts between contingents of soldiers of different ethnic groups in recent years have become a serious problem for the Soviet military, from which it is possible to draw the obvious conclusion that the armed forces have the same problems as society as a whole.

Seeing he had an interested audience, Sergei told me about the Uzbeks' recent spontaneous demonstrations in the Tashkent region known as Chor-Su. The latest violent death of an Uzbek soldier was the cause. He had been killed in the barracks at the hands of soldiers of another nationality. His parents obtained the body of their son, and when they opened the coffin, they saw that his head had been cut off, then sewed back on. A huge crowd gathered at the funeral, and they bore the litter with the youth's body not in the direction of the cemetery but rather to Lenin Square, in order to have a protest meeting. Special forces and police blocked the demonstrators' way; however, they managed to avoid mass confrontations since representatives of the authorities promised to investigate what happened.

"Now in many Union republics, people demand that draftees spend their service on the territory of their own republic," I said.

"Well, then they will pressure the people of nonnative nationalities," answered Sergei. "You see, there are no republics of pure national composition."

For him the issue of interethnic confrontations had a purely practical significance. His father was Tartar, his mother Russian. Recently he had married a girl whose father was Jewish and mother Armenian. Like many Russian-speaking residents of Tashkent, he did not know the Uzbek language and thought that he could easily live in the lap of this culture, which he considered Russian.

"Like an Englishman in India," he explained unexpectedly. "They can live there and not know the local languages. And no one drives them out of there because of that. Why should I go away? I was born in Tashkent; my parents were born in Tashkent, my parents' parents were born in Tashkent. Why should we consider ourselves nonnative? My wife and I are expecting a child," he continued, looking ahead at the road, leading off into the mountains. "What will his nationality be? Previously he would be considered Soviet. But now? What if Uzbekistan leaves the U.S.S.R.?"

"But do you want it to leave?" I asked, guessing at his answer. Behind Sergei invisibly stood tens of millions of Russians who had been born and lived their whole lives in Union republics beyond the borders of Russia.

Sergei thought, then shrugged his shoulders: "Not really. I do not want to leave. Politics doesn't interest me. I have a home, a family. I want to live and work peacefully. It is too bad that this will not be so, for the higher-ups"—he spat out the open window—"can't share power among themselves."

"And you are not afraid to remain in Uzbekistan?" I asked Sergei. "What if, God forbid, after uprisings against Meskhetin Turks, Armenians, and Jews, conflicts with other nationalities begin? For example, Uzbeks with Russians?"

"No, I am not afraid," Sergei answered phlegmatically. And he explained why. His answer astonished me. I never thought that there existed such a view of the problems of inter-ethnic relations. Sergei believed that any possible direct violence against Russians in Central Asia would immediately affect the Uzbek mafiosi, both those being freed and those being sent for terms in prison camps on Russian territory. The criminal world separated the Soviet Union into spheres of influence in its own way, and the interests of local nationalism were not taken into consideration. The criminal world in the U.S.S.R. is virtually nonnational and lives by its own precise laws, obligatory for all members of this gigantic community, independent of their national origin. Of course, bands of street hooligans and even individual professional bands can be grouped by purely national characteristics. For example, the members of one group, who earn their living by rackets in Moscow, are Chechens, but their boss may be subject to Russians, Koreans, or Jews.

Since violent uprisings in the national republics—it is unimportant who has ordered them—take place with the participation and often under the leadership of criminal elements, there is no random chance involved in the choice of targets of the violence. That is why, so far, Russians have never been the victims.

Carrying on such a jolly conversation, we rather quickly approached the border between the Uzbek and Tadzhik republics, about one-third of the way. The Syr-Darya region of Uzbekistan through which we traveled was well known to me. The Golodnaya steppe located there was where I had gone every year when I was a student to pick cotton. Chinaz, Syr-Darya, Gulistan, and Yangier were the towns that flew by the window, alternating with endless fields of still unopened cotton. The scene evoked elegiac recollections of events of that faraway time when each love seemed the last, each fight decisive, and great hopes for the future were so stupid that it is even strange that many of them nevertheless came true.

However, even today students of Uzbekistan leave their studies for six to eight weeks every year for compulsory agricultural labor. If for urban students picking cotton might conceivably be considered as a kind of adventure, for schoolchildren of the rural regions of Uzbekistan cotton and everything connected with it are a real damnation. It was in reference to rural children that the word "cotton slave" was first used in the Soviet press, and for all the talk over the past five years about the conditions of their lives, almost nothing has changed. Evidently, it will not change, since the Communist Party of Uzbekistan declared at its last congress that the *kolkhoz* structure as before remains the firm basis of the agricultural republic.

After we refueled in Uzbek Yangier at a gas station for state automobiles and passed the neighboring town of Khavast, we soon crossed the border into Tadzhikistan.

Tadzhikistan is the most mountainous of all the current Soviet republics. Mountains make up nine-tenths of its territory. It is the smallest republic in Central Asia in territory, but not at all in population. The population of the republic is 5.1 million people. Of them pure Tadzhiks number three million, Uzbeks 1.1 million, and Russians five hundred thousand. The remainder represent other nationalities and ethnic groups of the Soviet Union, the total number of which exceeds 130.

"Do you know that Tadzhikistan is in first place in the country in the rate of population growth, outstripping even Uzbekistan?" I asked Sergei.

"Really?" He was politely surprised. "Do you know the actual figures?"

"Yes," I answered, digging into my papers. Here they are for the 1980s:

Tadzhikistan:	+33.7%
Uzbekistan:	+23.7%
Turkmenia:	+27.0%
Kirghizia:	+20.9%
Azerbaijan:	+16.5%

"And Russians?" Sergei asked.

"I don't have separate data for Russians," I said, leafing through my travel notebook, "but as a whole I can say about Russia itself: 5.6 percent."

"Not very much." He took a deep breath. "But by total number they are still far ahead of us."

"No, not so far," I retorted. "If Central Asia maintains these rates, by the beginning of the next century the U.S.S.R., even in its current borders, will be primarily a Moslem country."

"How about that." Sergei whistled. "The first child, God willing, is born, and immediately I will be busy with the second. We need to be fruitful and multiply."

The next population center on our route was the city of Ura-Tyube. The road gradually rose, and after Ura-Tyube we had to negotiate two mountain passes, both at an altitude of about eleven thousand feet.

"Haven't you heard what happened among the Tadzhiks in February?" I asked Sergei.

"I don't know," he answered. "There was some kind of turmoil. In comparison with what was going on in Uzbekistan or is now going on in Kirghizia, nothing special. They say that about twenty people died."

"What nationality were the people who died?"

"I don't know," Sergei said. "They have written very little about it here. Or I haven't come across it."

Indeed, the February events were the first of several actions of the local population against the authorities of the all-powerful party apparatus. The actions failed each time.

Central television, TASS, and the influential party press, just as they did after the January events in Baku, knew how to convince public opinion in the country that an eruption of nationalist extremists was taking place in Dushanbe under the banner of religious intolerance. The liberal Soviet press honestly tried to understand the situation, but the facts were so contradictory, and the actions of the enraged crowd so far from the tradition of European parliamentarianism, that nothing else remained but to drop all attempts to understand events in Dushanbe until a better time.

Before the journey to Tadzhikistan, I developed for myself a rather precise plan of action. From among my many acquaintances and friends I chose two key figures. In Dushanbe there were two people: Loik Sherali, a leading Tadzhik poet and public figure, and Safar Abdullo, the well-known literary critic, politician, and brilliant polemicist. Loik Sherali was a U.S.S.R. people's deputy, while Safar Abdullo was a member of the Presidium of the people's movement for perestroika, Rastokhez (Renaissance), and a member of the board of directors of the Assembly of Democratic Movements of the Peoples of Central Asia and Kazakhstan. We were on friendly terms with Safar, since in recent years he had temporarily lived in Moscow and taught at the Literary Institute. Through him I got to know Loik and translated one of his books into Russian. In the mid-1980s it was published in Moscow, and then republished in Dushanbe. In the Tadzhik capital lived another person whom I very much wanted to see, the talented pop singer, composer, and guitarist Parviz Tursun-zade. At one point we had worked together as translators in Iraq and were close friends, but I had not seen him in about ten years. Arriving late in the day in Dushanbe, I said my final farewell to Sergei, who, in spite of all my persuasions, decided to start on the return trip immediately, since he had to put the car in the garage before nightfall. With a heavy bag across my shoulder, I entered the familiar house of the Writers' Union of Tadzhikistan on Putovsky Street, full of decisiveness to put my plan into action. However, like many other wonderful plans, this one collapsed almost immediately. Since the time I had called my friends from Moscow, many days had passed and not one of them was there.

Loik Sherali had fallen ill and was in the *nomenklatura* hospital. Safar Abdullo, having arrived from Moscow, immediately left for his native village somewhere near Pyandzhikent, almost two hundred miles away by mountain roads. I received the bad news from the second secretary of the Writers' Union of Tadzhikistan, a man by the name of Pshenichnyi, who, it seemed, was the only person who was in his office that day. Like all *nomenklatura* members, he acted very self-important, but his attitude toward me was very welcoming and friendly. My credentials had just been confirmed by a call from the central apparatus of the Writers' Union of the U.S.S.R. from Shavkat, a consultant on Tadzhik literature whom I had called several days earlier from Tashkent, requesting help in reserving a room at the Dushanbe hotel.

Pshenichnyi offered me green tea to drink and said that a semi-luxurious room was reserved for me in the Central Committee hotel.

"Central Committee? Semi-luxurious?" I asked in surprise.

"Yes, the Central Committee." He smiled in response. "For good people, everything here is just like before."

I hummed an aimless tune. Perhaps it was necessary to explain to Pshenichnyi why I had come here.

"I want to write about the February events," I told him. "Will you give an interview?"

"I will," he said and called his secretary to make some more tea.

25

The Fallen Angel

What happened on February 12, 13, and 14, 1990, in Dushanbe was a complete surprise, according to Pshenichnyi and the other party bureaucrats. Pshenichnyi said they knew that something was going to happen but no one supposed that it would result in such events. Around the ninth or tenth of February, rumors started to spread that a large group of Armenian refugees from Baku had arrived, and that the local authorities had promised to distribute apartments to them immediately. Simultaneously, some emissaries from Azerbaijan arrived, too, and, as it became known afterwards, they started to organize counteractions. So there were some rallies, especially in those districts where there is a lot of building and development. Neither the Soviet nor the party organs managed to neutralize these rumors. When a comparatively small group gathered on February 11 in front of the building of the Central Committee, their single demand was "Get rid of the Armenian refugees." It seems that there were some attempts to break into houses where the Armenians were staying, to make them leave the republic. The city authorities promised to evacuate all the refugees and asked for twenty-four hours to do so. On the next day, February 12, the crowd gathered again in front of the building of the Central Committee, but this time the question of Armenian refugees didn't come up. There were other

requirements, mainly that the leadership of the republic—the first secretary of the Central committee, the chairman of the Supreme Soviet,
and the chairman of the Council of Ministers—resign.

But the officials of the Central Committee refused to go out to
speak to the crowd, which then started throwing stones at the building and later tried to set it on fire. The police were trying to defend
the building but they didn't have enough officers. Then the riots
started.

"I was passing by the square at the time," said Pshenichnyi. "The
police started shooting into the crowd. They said that there was an
order to fire, but now the authorities are insisting that there was never
such an order. Several people were killed, twenty-two in all, over the
course of those days. Finally the crowd rushed into Lenin Street, started
breaking into stores, kiosks, jewelry shops. But it didn't look right.
The rowdies appeared to be very selective."

When I asked him if there were any attempts to spread the trouble
to other parts of the republic, he said they tried to bring in the southern districts, Kantibe, for instance, but it didn't work. Some buses
were stopped, the idea being to send students by bus to organize
raids. But somehow it didn't work. The authorities so far haven't been
able to find out who organized these actions. Three forces were mentioned as possibly being behind it all: extremist nationalists, criminals,
and power-hungry bureaucrats from the rival clan, in that order. Now
some trials are under way. A few people are on trial, a few people have
been released, but they can't tell who the main organizers were. Even
the party press gives different interpretations of this tragic event. For
instance, Rastokhez, the people's movement for perestroika, which
has published, illegally, two issues of its newsletter, is being blamed.

"And what's your personal opinion?" I asked him. "Who was the
main moving force of the February events?"

"My personal opinion is that these February events were not anti-
Russian," he said. "Most probably, it was a struggle for power,
because a working committee *was* established, a new government, in
fact."

"What if we look at these events from the standpoint of those who
are called the extremists: what was their ultimate goal?"

"The development of national culture, freedom for the development of the Tadzhik language. More independence for the republic…"

"Independence or secession?"

"Such slogans—about seceding from the U.S.S.R.—weren't voiced, although there were some calls to establish a Moslem republic. But they didn't find support."

"And what was the reaction of the Russian population?"

"After the February events twenty-three thousand Russians left Tadzhikistan as refugees. And people continue to leave. We don't know how things are going to turn out."

"Especially for the present leadership," I said. As it turned out, one year later Mahkamov, the first secretary of the local Communist Party and the self-appointed president, was ousted.

We then discussed the relations between the Tadzhiks and Uzbeks, which is a very sensitive subject. Pshenichyi said that the Tadzhik intelligentsia believes that the demarcation between Tadzhikistan and Uzbekistan, made in the 1920s, is wrong. They have in mind the cities of Bukhara and Samarkand, of course, with traditionally Tadzhik populations, which belong to Uzbekistan. The Tadzhik intelligentsia is afraid that a politics of assimilation is being undertaken toward the Tadzhiks living in these areas. At first their demand was actually to create some cultural autonomy for Tadzhiks in Uzbekistan. Now, according to Pshenichnyi, they have calmed down. The example of Nagorno-Karabakh has shown that making those kinds of demands leads only to a dead end, as was demonstrated by the bloody conflict between neighboring Armenia and Azerbaijan. (This conflict will be discussed in more detail in Chapter 32.)

"In almost all of the Soviet republics, there are now rations for industrial goods and foodstuffs, while the stores serve only people showing passports with the local residence permit," I said. "What limitations are there in Tadzhikistan?"

"We have only one limitation so far, and that is on exports. Goods bought in the republic may not be taken beyond its confines. And even this is *so conventional*. We are talking about big shipments, of course. When this limitation was introduced, people made a lot of noise, but in fact it's insignificant."

"So one can live here? Everything's in good order?"

"Oh, yeah, on the whole everything is all right."

"Was martial law lifted?"

"Well, we have a curfew now. It's in effect from one o'clock in the morning till five o'clock in the morning, so [laughing] I don't recommend you go out at that time."

I left my bag at the guide's old desk and went out into the wide, hot street. It was getting close to evening, but the sun sets late in summer, and the cool was still far away. In a little park in front of the Writers' Union building, among some shady weeping willows, a gargantuan sculptural composition had been erected: Maxim Gorky and Sadreddin Aini, his Tadzhik colleague (and, incidentally, a good writer) are sitting in gigantic chairs at a Gulliver-sized table, leisurely discussing the leading role of the party in Soviet literature. Old Aini is leaning on a stick, which is the size of a mast on a small yacht, while Gorky has crossed his elephantine legs in a rakish way, hooking his Herculean wrists under his knee.

A noisy Eastern bazaar was in session across the road from these favorites of the Soviet state, forever frozen in bronze. I thought that the bazaar must seem to the statues, from their height, something like a disturbed anthill. I passed through the underground passage occupied by Gypsies and beggars to the other side of the street, and entered another world. Sharp music, a dissonant mix of dozens of different Indian and Iranian melodies, blared out at the crowd from loudspeakers. Calls of the vendors, the honking of cars, the bleating and bellowing of animals, the incessant babble of many languages—all this fused into an endless cacophony. Herbs, vegetables, and fruit, heaped up in bright multicolored hills, were a joy to behold, if not for their prices then at least for their shapes and colors.

I noticed long ago that at the Central Asian bazaars, the youths mainly sell meat, women sell berries, the grown men vegetables, and only old men sell sweet fruit and the white grapes that were Alexander the Great's favorite treat. Oh, these magnificent gray-bearded traders in the turbans of Koranic patriarchs! Their very solemn appearance prohibits any rebellious idea of arguing or bargaining with them. But people haggle, making noises and waving their hands, while the old men look at them silently. Certainly in comparison with the prices of traders at Moscow markets, the local prices seemed quite moderate, although for people with a below-average income, they were still "biting," to use the Russian idiom. I have seen old Russian women buying just one apple, and bugging the vendor to give them withered apricots or crushed tomatoes. Here, the trade was oriented toward other buyers and, judging by appearances, it was flourishing. The co-ops were selling homemade flat cakes whose recipes have not changed for centuries. Bewitching aromas were rising from the small piles of spices exhibited as if in showcases. Shashlik makers were organizing pageants, fanning meat that crackled on the red-hot ashes. The smoke from the shashlik hung over the line of waiting people, who could not take their watering eyes off the metal sticks piercing the meat they craved. The most hungry among them were drooling and looking jealously at those ahead of them, measuring whether they would get their dish this time or have to wait for the next portion to be cooked. All this luxury brought to my mind half-starving Aktyubinsk and the empty shelves of the stores in Cheboksary. In the crowd of local residents dressed mainly in the European manner were a few women in white head kerchiefs and frocks made from silk khan-satin, iridescent in the sunlight. Peasants in faded green *tyubeteykas,* short gowns made from coarse calico, and white trousers tucked into boots with soft soles were pacing about like lords.

I remember how I was surprised in Iraq by my friend Dovlat Gaziyev, an interpreter from Tadzhikistan. Before he came to Iraq, Dovlat had taught in his native village, Nul'vand, situated high in the mountains; for six months a year it is separated from the whole world by snowdrifts and landslides. He came to Iraq with his wife, who had never left her native *kolkhoz* before. Within exactly three days he asked to send her home because it turned out that it was time for her to give birth to a child. The bosses were shocked, for according to Soviet rules pregnant wives were not allowed to go abroad with their husbands. "How did they overlook it in Moscow?" the officers from the personnel department grieved. "He certainly greased some palms," they thought. But there was nothing to do; the pregnant woman was sent back to the U.S.S.R., for it would never do to spend the state's hard currency for a local maternity house.

"Was it worth it to travel so far for three days?" I asked Dovlat. "You had to go from your village to Dushanbe, from there to Moscow, then to Baghdad, and from there to Basra. And now your wife has to go all that way back alone, at the end of her ninth month.

Perhaps she could stay and give birth to a child here? After all, we have free medicine, and our party bosses would have to pay her hospital bill all the same, according to the law."

"No, it's just impossible," Dovlat said with a laugh. "We have three more children at home. We left them with our neighbors."

"How's that?"

"She wanted to see the world, and I decided, All right, let her go! Maybe she won't ever have another chance to leave her native village in her whole life."

I returned to the Writers' Union, where Pshenichnyi was "organizing" a car to take me to the hotel by handing out big gift-wrapped packets, which contained generous gifts of a Tadzhik nature. Having thanked him for the car and hotel, I said good-bye and headed toward the entrance. The three-story building of the local Writers' Union is a big square with an inner courtyard-orchard. Besides offices for Writers' Union officials, the building also includes offices of the local literary journals and a Tadzhik writers' newspaper. I wanted to find some of my acquaintances, and so I went along the corridor, looking into every office in turn. Quite unexpectedly I saw Safar Abdullo, sitting calmly in one of the rooms, peacefully reading some proofs.

"What a sight for sore eyes!" I yelled joyously. "And I was told that you were not in Dushanbe."

"Well, then, who are you talking to, huh?" he replied with a smile and we embraced. It turned out that his regular column had been prepared for publication, and he had come to Dushanbe to read and approve the proofs.

It was almost evening, and I was dead tired, so we decided to wait until the next morning to get everything done. I arranged with Safar to meet the next evening and went to settle in at the hotel of the local Central Committee. Simple mortals have no access to such hotels, for they are mainly for the provincial and regional *nomenklatura* when they come to the capital of the republic for party conferences, seminars, and congresses, or for private reasons. Important nongovernmental visitors from Moscow are also put up in this place—famous scientists, for instance, or directors of big military factories and plants, illustrious cinematographers, journalists from the central newspapers.

The highest Moscow party *nomenklatura* stay in special mansions and state-party dachas.

The hotel entrance was barred by a stern-looking cop with a pistol on his belt. Obviously he loved his job, because he read attentively all the passes of people trying to enter the hotel, and he even held some of the passes up to the light. But no one argued with him because everyone understood that this person was put in his place to defend the hotel from strangers—that is, from all those whom the party forbids to be here.

An affable, aged administrator checked my reservation in her journal, looked at the Moscow residence permit in my passport, and then asked which view I would prefer: the inner courtyard or the fountain at the entrance.

"The sound of splashing water is very calming," she said. "Some people don't like to sleep with the air-conditioning on, and such a cool and fresh air rises from the fountain."

"Air-conditioning?" I asked, unable to believe what I had heard with my own ears. "Better with air-conditioning, if it doesn't rattle."

"Oh, no!" she objected softly, giving me a key. "You won't even hear it. The air comes directly out of the wall."

In broad terms, all hotels in the world are the same. This one struck me by the fact that everything here was working: the television, the radio, the air-conditioning, the light bulbs in their lamps, and the faucets in the bathroom. Even the foreign toilet, which looked like the armchair the pilot of a spaceship would sit upon, worked normally, imparting a real pride in the achievements of technical progress. The sheets were white, the floors were polished, there were even brushes for clothes and separate ones for footwear. The hot water was hot and the cold water was cold, and the pressure in the shower was so strong that it could make you fall down.

When the maid brought me a kettle of tea and left, cautiously closing the door behind her, I started crying, quite unexpectedly, for the first time in fifteen years. I was sitting on the bed, naked and silly, crying. I was crying over my miserable country and her humiliated citizens, I was crying over that girl with a broken face from Cheboksary and Iranbek's son killed in Alma-Ata, over both the Uzbek women voluntarily burning themselves alive because they did not want such a

286 / MARAT AKCHURIN

life and the Meskhetin Turks who on the contrary wanted to live and did not want to be burned, for that old lady from Moscow who sold me an orange radio set and the Aral Sea that had perished because of cotton; I was crying over Vova Liberman who lived in two little rooms with his five relatives. I was crying over the perestroika that had transformed itself into a civil war, over the young soldiers whose ribs were being broken this same moment in the barracks, over the blond Barbie with her three old husbands and her friend Tan'ka who was now being raped by jail guards, and over the Moscow poet Balashov who believed that Jews are aliens who came from outer space to destroy our planet, and...Why, where did Balashov come from anyway? I wondered, sniffing, and then recalled that he was from Dushanbe. At that point I decided to stop, although I had not really cried over so very many people.

Suddenly I smiled at something, I do not know what. And then I fell asleep. My untouched tea got cool, fanned by the air-conditioning.

I dreamed I was standing in my mother's yard and looking at the blue morning sky, and a smiling Jesus Christ, walking on air, was floating slowly toward me with his purple cloak flapping around him.

The hospital of the Fourth Main Directorate, serving the republic party bosses, unlike the hospitals for the rank and file, left an impression of spacious cleanliness. There were no wards holding dozens of patients, no cots in the corridors. There were enough nurses and janitors, and even the hospital yard was spacious and beautiful, reminiscent of the Garden of Eden.

Naturally, it was also under police protection, and it was not clear that I would have gotten in there were it not for Pshenichnyi, who in the morning sent a *nomenklatura*'s Volga to pick me up at the hotel. As everywhere, the affability of the guards depends on the license plates of the car, and on how familiar the faces of the passengers are. We were allowed to enter without any questions but without a salutation either.

I was going to see Loik Sherali, who is incredibly popular in Tadzhikistan. His popularity might be compared with that of a movie or television star in the United States. I have noticed many times what great power famous writers and poets enjoy in the Soviet Union. In Tadzhikistan, where there is a tradition at least two thousand years old of written literature, this phenomenon is even more pronounced than in other places. I remember how struck I was when during one of his public recitations Loik Sherali stumbled while reading his poem and the whole theater full of people, in one voice, prompted the poet on his next line. It was six or seven years ago that I translated his verses, but even now I remember certain lines:

There are no orators—we are looking for a stutterer.
The ax is lost—we are looking for a needle.
We have blown our harvest away in the wind.
And we are looking for a single grain.

And

All our life is—the hope for love.
And all that was on earth is—love.
You think the sun is bringing light to us.
But it is love that is bringing light to us.

Loik never wanted to publish his verses in Russian, for he believed that even the best translation does not render the music of the original.

"Why should I present myself as some wretched beggar?" he used to tell me. "Our Tadzhik-Persian poetry has amassed such a rich tradition during the last one thousand years that any word in my poem evokes dozens of associations in the mind of a cultured Tadzhik. And what will result in Russian?"

"You underestimate the traditions of Russian culture," I would reply, irritated. "We have a two-hundred-year tradition of translations from Eastern poetry into Russian, so any successful word in my translation will evoke approximately the same associations and allusions to a cultured Russian as the original does to a cultured Tadzhik."

"That's the whole point, that 'approximately,'" he said, laughing. "And why do I need this 'approximately'? Everything in poetry should be precise."

The medical department where Loik was treated was on the first floor of a two-story building, spacious in an ancient fashion. There were no guards at the entrance to the building, and I went inside without being stopped. He was not in the ward, and a pretty nurse who seemed not to be surprised by my intrusion told me that he was undergoing a medical treatment. He was getting a mudpack, she corrected herself after looking in her journal.

In order not to miss Loik I went to the building where balneological treatments and physiotherapy were given. I looked into a couple of rooms and saw that the *nomenklatura* also suffers from physical imperfections. I decided not to take chances and waited for the great poet in the lounge. A black-and-white television was on, and I sat there for half an hour, enjoying a show in Tadzhik about a *kolkhoz* chairman who headed his business for fifty years and now, having received one more Lenin order, was thanking our dear Communist Party for its fatherly concern for the Tadzhik people.

Loik appeared unexpectedly. When he saw me he smiled affably. We shook hands, and I asked him about his health. He looked pale and tired, and the striped hospital pajamas added even more to this impression. Like many extraordinary personalities, Loik radiates around himself an invisible energy field. When people of this type enter a room, one can feel their presence immediately. We went out to the yard to walk. It was pleasant for me to see how the young nurses froze when they saw him, followed him for a long time with their eyes, pensively biting their young lips.

"I would never have thought that you would come from Moscow to ask me about my health," he said, looking at me with the cunning eyes of an ancient Persian Dev, a magical being in Oriental folklore.

Who do those Aryan wrinkles in his cheeks remind me of? I thought in passing, and suddenly remembered Shlupkin, Liberman's father-in-law. "I had no idea that you were in the hospital," I said.

"Did Pshenichnyi tell you that I want to talk to you about what's happening in the republic?" I asked directly, putting aside all Eastern obliquenesses.

"And do you know that all materials concerning the February events have to be cleared through the Central Committee?" Loik smiled cunningly. We came up to a latticed wooden pavilion, entered, and sat down on its railings opposite each other. Loik made up his mind at last and said, "All right."

"What's the reason for the February outburst?" I asked. "Why did it happen?"

"I believe," Loik replied, "that the outburst of violence was a response to social injustice. A universal social injustice reigns here, in all walks of life. Wherever you look—from the procedures for getting an apartment to those for placing and promoting the bosses—everywhere you find corruption, regionalism, string-pulling. And even more, as you probably know, Tadzhikistan holds the last place among the fifteen Soviet republics in terms of economic production and the living standards of its population. Although we have Communism Peak and Lenin Peak in our mountains, the level of life below them is just awful. The death rates of children and women are almost the highest in the U.S.S.R. Do you know that children here can't drink their mother's milk?"

"Why?"

"Because it's toxic. The women work at cotton plantations, where poisonous chemicals like defoliants and pesticides are used in great quantities. And in the village stores there's absolutely nothing, just empty shelves, no milk even. So mother's milk is poisoned and there's almost nothing in stores. So what can come of it but babies dying in the first months of their lives from emaciation? And that is only one example. The state of our people is simply miserable. Perhaps that's why the discontent of the people took the form of such an outburst of anger. The Armenians were just a pretext. I don't know who was the main object of the crowd's rage—Mahkamov, the first secretary of the Central Committee of Tadzhikistan, or the whole government in general. Look what happens with our resources. Cotton is the staple of our agriculture but we have no cotton industry in this republic. The entire harvest goes to Russia and what are we left with? We have businesses named Tadzhik Gold, Tadzhik Cotton, Tadzhik Furniture, but the republic has neither gold, nor cotton, nor even furniture. I think that the people's discontent with such a state of affairs will only increase with time. The republic should own its own natural resources, and the people should see the results of their toil."

"But do you think you can achieve that without a transformation of the economic system itself?"

"Now we are working out a concept of economic independence for Tadzhikistan, but we have a very long way to go before it's realized. The cotton example shows that first we have to build our own industry and then say that we want to process our own cotton."

"But people in any country will be happy to buy raw cotton."

"They will, to be sure, but the price is different. When you yourself produce fabrics and clothes, the market offers you other prices. And then these plants and factories will ensure employment for the people, which is no less important for us. Our own working class will come into being. We never had a working class before. Not a really conscious, fighting, thinking working class—nothing like that."

"But isn't it late to set one up? The world has gone pretty far from Marxist idealization of the proletariat."

"Our republic hasn't gone through the stage of capitalism, and therefore the level of our public consciousness is rather low."

"But don't you think," I asked, smiling wryly, "that the very terms 'capitalism' and 'socialism' in our country are too ideological? Isn't it simpler to distinguish between the advanced and backward countries? According to this classification, we are unfortunately a backward country."

"I think that there are people here, too, who understand that what matters is not the terms but something else."

"What's that?"

Loik didn't answer and only shrugged his shoulders.

"All right," I went on, "and what do people think here about the fact that in both Moscow and Leningrad Communists have lost their former majority in the city councils? Does anything like that happen here?"

"Nothing of the kind." Loik mechanically rubbed his dimpled chin. "There are no such strivings in Tadzhikistan, I have heard no discussions of it whatsoever."

"And what about the democratic party? Or Rastokhez? Do they have any chance to play a real role in the republic's political life?"

"The Communists succeeded in completely compromising and blackening the Rastokhez by blaming them for the February events. Although Rastokhez, on the contrary, was trying to pacify the raging people, to prevent trouble. There are many good guys from the intelligentsia in Rastokhez—scientists, writers, poets. But they were driven underground after the February events. They published two issues of their newspaper. No one knows where they do it. There's nothing especially seditious there; they write ordinary, normal things. But we are not used to them yet. Throughout the whole Soviet Union, these are all quite ordinary themes, open for discussion. Here they are banned. Even the popular movement Rastokhez is still not registered as a public organization. Drafts of its charter are still lying on a lot of tables—in the Central Committee, in the Council of Ministers, but they are now refusing to register it, using the February events as a pretext."

"And what about the democratic party?"

"It seems that it will be allowed, although I haven't familiarized myself with their statutes yet. I think that any party is a dictatorship, although if the democratic party won't aspire to a dictatorship, I'll welcome it. But no party can feed the people. The Communists made noises about the bright future for so many years, and it resulted in—phooey! And if such a mighty party as the Communist Party can do nothing, these little parties that are mushrooming now won't be able to do anything either, because they don't have any strength. They won't be in a position to compete with the CPSU because they lack the economic base that Communists have created for themselves at the state's expense. I'm not even sure that they will be able to win any influence in the parliament, but time will tell."

"It seems to me that the events in Tadzhikistan depend to a great extent on how the situation is developing in the center."

"Yes, of course, but the RSFR is quite different too. People feel less enthusiastic about Yeltsin here than in Russia."

"And let's imagine that Yeltsin wins over Gorbachev, and the Communist regime in the center collapses?"

"Then the Communists will arrive here to ask for political asylum." (Which really happened in August 1991!)

We looked at each other and laughed.

"Can it be that everything is so stable here?"

"Yes, so far," Loik answered, "but we'd better not comfort ourselves with illusions."

"So, what's the matter? Do people here feel respect toward a strong central power?"

"They feel respect and are afraid of it. They are more scared than respectful. For instance, after the February events, people started to berate Mahkamov just as they berate Gorbachev; even worse, they started calling him an executioner because he ordered the troops to shoot into the unarmed crowd. But it's all just backbiting. Only recently we traveled with him around the Lenin region. Everyone we encountered said the same thing: 'Everything is good, everything is beautiful!' We went to one *kolkhoz,* where all the people gathered, and then one of the elders got up, prayed, and almost kissed Mahkamov. So he asked the elder: 'Is everything all right?' And the elder replied: 'Everything is good, Comrade Mahkamov, everything is excellent.'

"Then I could not stand it anymore and said: 'You write letters complaining to the Central Committee and Political Bureau almost daily. So why when the *padishah* [Oriental monarch] himself has come do you keep mum?' And only then did they begin to tell the truth. One of them got up and said that there's no sugar in the stores, another said that they can't get land for allotments, still another that there are no doctors. So much pain, so many problems are there. This is the East. They bow to you when they see you and put their hands to their hearts, but stab you in the back as soon as you depart.

"So what about Mahkamov?"

"What about Mahkamov? His power is only based on the bayonets of soldiers. They say that as soon as the curfew is lifted, a sequel to the bloody events of February will start."

"He's not popular among Tadzhiks?"

"Certainly not!"

"And what about among Russians?"

"The Russian-speaking population supports Mahkamov because he has a firm hand."

"And what was the public reaction to your trip with Mahkamov?"

"I received a lot of insults on the phone because of that trip. Because they broadcast it on television. Because they say I was traveling with an executioner."

"And were the callers anonymous or not?"

"The whole point is that they were anonymous. I would ask them: 'Who are you?' But I never received an answer. They were saying that I revealed my true self by traveling with an executioner. And everything that I've written before, all my thoughts and feelings—it turns out that all that was lies. It was lies because I'm not on the people's side."

I kept silent, for I did not know what to say. At least I understood why he turned up in a hospital. I had nothing to console him with. These were his own relations with his people. The only thing that I knew for sure was that time would pass and that Tadzhiks would call this the era of Loik Sherali. And there will be just one line in fine type dedicated to Mahkamov—at the most.

"Why is Dushanbe called 'Monday'?" I asked.

"Before the beginning of the twentieth century there were three big *kishlaks* [villages] here, and the total population was almost seven hundred thousand. Bazaar day was on Mondays here, and for several centuries in a row, people came here on Mondays from all the neighboring villages."

I took a picture of Loik Sherali, using my last film. He has the eyes of a fallen angel. The mob loves to throw its former idols from their pedestals.

26

Hats with Corners Turned Down

So, how is he?" Safar Abdullo asked when he found out that I had met with Loik Sherali in the morning.

"Depressed," I said. "When I asked him, as I was leaving, what he was working on now, he grew even gloomier and answered that his writing hasn't gone well for a long time. In the Soviet Union, a lot of people's writing isn't going well nowadays."

Safar's expression changed. He took to heart everything occurring in Tadzhik literature, as if all these events were taking place in his own family. Many *nomenklatura* writers hated Safar with all their hearts for his straightforward responses to their works, which were dedicated to serving the ruling ideology. Even before perestroika he never restrained himself as a literary critic, and he was always telling the cruel truth right in the faces of the literary bosses—be it in a review, a public talk, or an informal conversation. Maybe that is why he had nothing in Tadzhikistan—neither a state job, nor an apartment, nor even a permanent residence permit. But he never lost heart, and he served his beloved Tadzhik literature selflessly. I was always impressed by his ability to come up with very long fragments from medieval and contemporary Persian and Arabic poetry, appropriate to the subject of conversation at hand. When I first knew him, I confess that I assumed he was inventing all those quotations on the spot, because his inexhaustible fund of poetry was too astonishing and endlessly variegated. I went so far as to check some of his quotations against Russian translations, to make sure that they were authentic; then I felt ashamed of my incredulity.

"Mahkamov decided to take advantage of Loik's popularity with the people," Safar said, rolling his glaring eyes. "He wanted to improve his image at Loik's expense. You know, don't you, that in every Tadzhik house there is one of Loik's books resting right next to Hafiz's *divan?*" (Hafiz was a medieval Tadzhik poet, and *divan* is the Tadzhik word for a collection of poetry.)

"But it turned out the other way around," I said. "Loik became almost a traitor in the eyes of the people. Why did he go with Mahkamov?"

"Well, what would you do in his place?" Safar asked. "Imagine that you are a living classic, and some party *padishah* invites you to his office, asks you about this and that, and then says, 'Let's go see how the people are living.' Naturally, Loik didn't refuse. And then they make a big deal about this trip in the media—there was a whole propaganda show about it on television, a report in every newspaper: Mahkamov with Loik standing next to him. I called Loik myself the next day and asked, 'What's all this about?' Of course when the people see their favorite poet beside such an odious figure as Mahkamov... After the kinds of things that happened in this republic, the political leader of any civilized country would have resigned of his own accord. And Mahkamov not only remained in his place but grew some deeper roots. Thanks to Mr. Gorbachev, who introduced the rule that the highest party job goes automatically with the highest state position. That was unheard of, even under Stalin."

"And what really did happen in February?" I asked my friend. "Who was operating behind the scenes? Criminals? Nationalists? Some alternate party leaders fighting for power? Is it possible that no one really knows what it was? Or perhaps everyone knows but is afraid to say out loud?"

Safar looked at me with his fiery eyes and it seemed that even the hairs on his head were standing on end from indignation. If the hair on a person's head is the halo of his soul, Safar's soul, judging by his hair, was raging with emotions. "Afraid? Who's afraid of them? It's they who ought to be afraid!" He told me the radical Tadzhik intelligentsia's interpretation of the February events.

For many years the party elite or, more accurately, the political mafia, which is united by close family connections among several powerful clans, ruled Tadzhikistan. Only by belonging to one of these clans was it possible to make one's way to the main party, state, and managerial positions of the republic. Working in this self-reproducing way, the Tadzhik party mafia was quite satisfied with the status quo. Naturally, it considered any proposals that threatened to interfere with the existing structure of power as extremely dangerous and objectionable.

The main source of possible jeopardy for the ruling party elite became the people's movement for perestroika, Rastokhez. Like the majority of other Central Asian opposition movements, it was headed and directed by the national (mainly humanitarian) intelligentsia, which put forth calls for more cultural, economic, and political independence. Rastokhez had elaborated, among other proposals, an alternative conception of economic independence for the republic.

Elections to the Supreme Soviet of Tadzhikistan, to name the deputies who would have the right to solve many questions concerning the republic's future, and elect its president, were coming up. If strong groups of deputies from Rastokhez and other new public organizations managed to operate in the local parliament, the ruling mafia's monopoly would be seriously endangered. And so it started an offensive.

"The main initiators of the February events can't be found," Safar said, poking his finger right in front of my eyes, "because those who are looking for them are in fact the initiators."

"What are you driving at?" I asked, surprised, politely dodging his gesticulations. "Are you saying that the party bosses organized an uprising against themselves?"

"They didn't organize it, but they did provoke it." Safar pounded his fist on the table. "And they achieved the best possible results. The main thing was to blame Rastokhez for the bloodshed, exposing it before the whole country as a bloodthirsty terrorist organization. Naturally, in our new parliament the majority is now made up of hard-line Communists, just like before—people who would vote for Mahkamov.

You wouldn't believe how many times Abdulzhabbarov (one of the leaders of Rastokhez) attempted to get a hearing of the conclusions of the commission on the February events on the agenda of the first session of the Tadzhikistan Supreme Soviet. But the Communist deputies don't want to know what the commission found out."

"And what other public organizations are represented in the parliament?" I asked. "I heard something about the Vahdat People's Front in the city of Ura-Tube, Oshkoro in the city of Kulyab, Ekheyi Khudzhand in Leninabad..."

"Formally, none," Safar replied. "You know, don't you, that the directive of the presidium of the Supreme Soviet of Tadzhikistan regarding the registration of public organizations has been suspended?"

"Perhaps they registered too many organizations?" I guessed.

"That's the whole point: none of them were registered." Like an opera hero Safar burst forth with furious laughter. "Just fancy, first the mafia announced its directive concerning the registration of public organizations and then it suspends it, having registered none of them."

"Oh, I like that logic. Why, for God's sake, would they create another headache for themselves?"

"The February events have other consequences, too. For instance, if local Russians before were backing glasnost and democratization even more than the Tadzhiks, now every last one of them is calling for stability and order. Which, of course, only the victorious Communist Party of Tadzhikistan can ensure with an iron hand. Although there is one unexpected side effect to these events."

"The mass emigration of Russians?" I asked. It was not difficult at all to guess what it was. The same tendency was under way in neighboring Uzbekistan, to say nothing of Kirghizia or Azerbaijan.

We were sitting at the counter of a half-empty café of the Writers' Union. An aged white-coated counterman, who was also the cashier, was shuffling his feet, having nothing to do. He listened to our loud conversation for a long time, moved his bushy eyebrows in sympathy, nodded and sighed noisily at the most dramatic moments.

"Yes!" He couldn't restrain himself at last, and interrupted our conversation. "If they were born in Tadzhikistan, if they love it and consider it to be their motherland, why do they leave it in these difficult times? Most of them are qualified specialists, as you know. They go away leaving a vacuum behind them. There's no one to replace them! And why were no local specialists trained during all these years? Earlier, in the 1920s and 1930s, when the Russians were coming here, they tried to learn Tadzhik before anything else so that it would be easier for them to teach their students. And so far people retain a positive memory of them. All of them live here, many are already retired. And people feel respect for them. But this tradition was soon forgotten. In our time it's not necessary to know Tadzhik to live in Dushanbe."

"Why," I objected, "one hears people speaking Tadzhik in the streets."

"He means something else," Safar explained, not surprised at all by this man's intrusion into our conversation. "The Russians had to learn Tadzhik. The linguistic milieu itself made them do that. And now one can't say that Dushanbe is a Tadzhik city. It's not a capital for Tadzhiks. If Russians make up just 10 percent of the population of the republic in general, more than 60 percent of them reside in Dushanbe. Although many are going to leave now."

"But maybe they have reasons to be afraid?" I asked slyly.

"What is it they are afraid of?" Safar got indignant, while the man behind the counter started shaking his head violently as if denying any threat to the lives of Russians. "Twenty out of twenty-five killed in the February events were Tadzhiks. A fool would understand that the uprising was against the party and not against Russians. And that Tadzhik was proclaimed the state language, so what? Is that a reason for leaving? I think that the Russian-speaking population is leaving the republic not because it has conflicts with Tadzhiks but because the living standards here are twice as low as in the Soviet Union in general."

"Don't you exaggerate? I didn't get the impression that people here live worse than they do in Russia or Kazakhstan."

"Go to the countryside and you'll see," said Safar. "Even new galoshes are a big event for a family there. And do you know how they eat?"

"I know," I answered, "flat cakes and tea. It's the same in Uzbekistan."

We tried to pay the counterman for the green tea that we had drunk, but he refused to take money, saying that he considered us to be his guests.

"If you had an opportunity to address Americans, what would you tell them?" I asked him.

"Americans?" he asked again in surprise. "Let them learn Tadzhik. It's a very simple and beautiful language. Maybe they will make use of it one day!"

Safar and I went out and decided to go to the bookstore and then walk to my hotel.

"Is Tadzhik very different from Farsi?" I asked Safar. "Are they just dialects of one language?"

"Tadzhik is Persian-Farsi transliterated with Russian letters," Safar replied. "But nothing good ever came of it. They took away the old alphabet and thus cut the Tadzhik people off from their ancient history and culture. This monstrously sly Bolshevik act did terrible damage to the national culture of the Tadzhik people. Why? Because letters are culture-producing for a Tadzhik. Can you imagine Pushkin writing in Russian but with Arabic ligatures? That would be crazy, wouldn't it? But this nightmarish experiment was conducted in the U.S.S.R. on many peoples, Tadzhiks among them. I believe that it was a cunning policy."

"What's so cunning about this policy, tell me!" I snorted. Many Soviet and Western intellectuals are keen on ascribing refined cunning and slyness to the Bolsheviks, although they most often were led by nothing more than ordinary cruelty that resulted from their own lack of culture and purely proletarian hatred for the cultures of other peoples that are incomprehensible to them.

"Why? The formal reason they gave was that the Arabic alphabet is difficult to learn. But as a former teacher of Persian-Farsi in the Moscow Literary Institute, I am entitled to say that my students— Russians, Latvians, Georgians—learned the alphabet in just two weeks. And this language wasn't native for any of them. Why then is it more difficult for Tadzhiks, whose ancestors were using this alphabet for ten generations? No, all this talk about the Arabic alphabet being too difficult for Tadzhiks is a blatant lie. So it turned out that in just seventy years Tadzhiks have lost their letters, their cultural legacy, and their cities."

"What about Dushanbe? Or Leninabad? Are you going to give it back its ancient name of Khodzhend?"

"In Dushanbe Russians make up the majority of the population.

In Leninabad Uzbeks are the most numerous ethnic group. As far as the restoration of its historical name is concerned, it's true that the people are demanding the return of the former name. When it was renamed into yet another 'Lenin's city,' for that's what Leninabad means in Tadzhik, it was done on the pretext that it was 'by request of the working people.' In fact, as you know, no working people requested it. The Bolsheviks just impertinently renamed Khodzhend Leninabad and Dushanbe Stalinabad. Well, Stalin was dumped, but so far we can't do anything with Lenin. The party functionaries stand firm on this point."

While he was saying this, Safar's facial expression suddenly changed. The Eastern way of describing this transformation might be to say that "the invisible hand of Providence pushed a button, and the projector of his soul showed a new slide on the screen of his face." I traced the direction of his admiring gaze and saw on the other side of the street a spectacular young woman in summer sandals, a short white skirt, a lilac T-shirt with the monogram V on it, and a little purse hanging from her shoulder. She was walking with the quick stride of a professional ballerina, not looking around, shaking her short hair the color of hay.

"Lena!" I shouted, trying to be heard over the noise of street traffic, "Lena Kisel!"

By strange coincidence, the woman Safar had admired was my friend Lena Kisel, a brilliant dancer in the ensemble Brothers and Sisters, which my wife and I had brought to Tunisia the previous winter for a tour. I introduced the two of them, and Lena and I proceeded to reminisce about our time in Tunisia.

"Yes, our journey to Tunisia was like a fairy tale," Lena said dreamily. "Do you remember how we swam in an enclosed pool after the discotheque and then had dinner in a late-night restaurant?"

After the bleak Moscow winter and the criminal public in the Moscow restaurants where Moiseyev's group worked, the luxurious four-star hotel on the shore of the warm Mediterranean Sea, with its respectable European clientele, could easily seem like a paradise on earth. This hotel belonged to the biggest company in Tunisia, with whose proprietor I had signed a contract to organize a fortnight of Russian culture and cuisine during Christmas and New Year's.

"And do you remember that official from the Saudi Foreign Ministry who wanted to buy you," I said, smiling, "that one who would come to the pool and look with crazy eyes at how you and your friends were posing as Russian mermaids?"

"Why, in fact he did buy," Lena said. "Only it wasn't me, but...Well, you probably can guess who it was."

Safar was moving his honest eyes from Lena to me and back again without understanding whether we were serious or kidding.

While we were talking we crossed to the other side of the street, where Lena had been walking before she met us.

"But, unfortunately, I have to hurry up," Lena said suddenly. "I work in the circus now, and I have to get to the show early. But come to one of the performances sometime. We'll be working here for a long time."

She walked away in her quick beautiful step, swinging her hips as if she were a model on a podium, knowing that hundreds of curious eyes were staring at her.

"Yes," Safar said. "There are none like her among our women."

"Is that good or bad?" I asked him with curiosity. We proceeded into the bookstore.

During a whole week, I walked around Dushanbe either with Safar or alone, meeting people and asking them about life in the epoch of perestroika and glasnost. Unfortunately I met no one who was happy with his life. The poor people were complaining that prices keep rising, and that it was impossible to make a living on honest labor, while the enterprising ones were talking about the crime rate and the unwillingness of the authorities to think about anything but keeping their privileges. The representatives of the *nomenklatura* were berating the center because, they said, "Moscow has completely let people get out of hand and confused the whole country with its idle talk about democracy."

Russians were afraid because Tadzhiks had begun speaking of Russians as their enemies. It had never been like that before, Russians were saying; it was the nationalists who stood behind it. The nationalists in fact were swearing not only at Russians but at Communists, too, because of the debased Tadzhik language and the building of grandiose power stations in the mountains, where the danger of earthquakes as a result of tectonic fissures exceeded all admissible norms.

The awful talk about taking back the ancient cities of Samarkand

and Bukhara from Uzbekistan had stopped. Perhaps the endless nightmare of the Azerbaijan-Armenian war over Nagorno-Karabakh had sobered up some hotheads. Uzbeks and Tadzhiks had coexisted peacefully for centuries in the confines of the same Central Asian states, and that is why the fact of artificial breeding of two potentially opposed socialist nations from two closely connected ethnic groups provoked an understandable indignation on the part of local politicians.

Safar and I once even had a big argument on the subject of the origin of Tadzhiks and Uzbeks. It happened in a very exotic place—in a *chaikhana* (teahouse) on the bank of Varzob River, many miles from Dushanbe.

"Let's go eat shashlik," Safar said suddenly one night, having driven to my hotel in the early evening. This time he was at the wheel of an incredibly ancient car. "Lamborghini?" I asked just in case.

"Moskvich," Safar answered proudly and laughed. The car belonged to one of his relatives who had two cars.

According to Soviet rules, one family is forbidden to own two cars of the same brand. Thus those people who can afford two automobiles of one brand must employ cunning. The car that Safar drove now was officially his car, since his relatives put it in his name, but in fact it did not belong to him. Safar drove for many years without a license, yet without feeling any guilt or fear, which characterizes the local attitude toward laws and regulations.

"And what about traffic cops?" I asked.

"Five rubles if he's a Tadzhik, ten rubles if he's an Uzbek," Safar answered.

He was driving rather recklessly, and speeded up when he was going downhill to forty miles an hour.

"Why don't we drive to Samarkand in this old heap?" I said, egging Safar on to an escapade.

"To Samarkand?" Safar was apparently interested in the idea. He was from Samarkand himself. "But the roads might be checked by patrols, and I have no license."

"I'll take all road expenses on myself," I answered. "And I can drive a car. I have a license, to be sure, even an international one. In the presence of the proprietor of a car any person with a license can drive."

"But how will I get back?" Safar started thinking. "It's one thing to talk to traffic cops in Dushanbe, and another to drive on the inter-city highway in the epoch of intranational conflicts. These Uzbek cops will make short work of me, a poor Tadzhik."

"All right," I said, knowing that a thorn was in my friend's flesh. "I'll look for something else."

There was a table set next to the river, from which cold air was ris-ing. The river's source was high in the mountains, and the quick-flow-ing water had no time to get warm under the rays of sun. The *chaikhana* was state-owned, but some private enterprises had a con-tract with it for making shashlik, so the prices were altogether astro-nomical.

A boy brought some green tea in a kettle with a tin spout and *pialas*. A boisterous company of local men and Russian women who were obviously not locals were sitting at the next table. The women were probably organized tourists from a neighboring tourist center.

"Are the tourist centers open now?" I asked Safar, who stuck out his chest and stretched his quite impressive shoulders like a character in a movie, under the approving gaze of the women at the neighbor-ing table.

"Don't you see the female tourists? That means that they're open, doesn't it?" Safar answered, squinting with his fiery gaze toward our neighbors. One of the mysterious features of contemporary Soviet life which has struck me many times is that despite the increasing eco-nomic chaos and the complete muddle everywhere, many of the old businesses keep running as if by a miracle. Around the whole country entire trains with goods are waiting for months on sidetracks to be unloaded; huge factories and plants are stopped because of undersup-ply from their partners and a lack of raw materials; thousands of *kolkhozes* only pretend to be carrying out economic activity, doing harm to themselves and to the state, while some provincial tourist bureaus go on working as if nothing is happening. So they load trains with curious and undemanding Russians and bring them to the muti-nous Baltics, seditious Georgia, warring Armenia, or to Central Asia, splashed with the blood of its massacres.

"Safar, will you stop staring at those fellows' women friends," I whispered fiercely. "You know that they'll beat us up if you don't stop."

"A huge guy like you, afraid of some greenhorns?" Safar curved his eyebrow like a good guy from a Western. "We'll lose them in a flash."

"I don't want to lose anyone." I got really angry. "As if there was something worth fighting about here! What shall I do if they break my camera, or dunk it in the river?"

"No harm, you'll go to America and buy a new one," Safar said, and addressed the neighboring table. "Girls, have some melon. This is the real Kanibadam kind."

"Listen, don't bug us with your Bukhara melon," one of the boys said in Russian with a terrible accent, so that the women would understand that they were under his protection.

"Do you know who you are talking with, sucker?" Safar yelled at him in a scary high-pitched voice in Tadzhik, his face growing red.

"Excuse us, *domullo* [professor], we didn't recognize you," the guys said either seriously or taunting Safar, and putting their hands to their hearts they bowed politely.

"That's better," my friend answered contentedly and, pointing with his hand to the melon cut into two parts with its sweet juice pouring out, repeated, "Help yourself."

One of the women got up and walked provocatively to our table. She was reminiscent of the stereotypical image of Soviet woman on American television: she was fat, badly dressed, and dowdy. And tipsy.

One of the guys made an attempt to get up and follow her, but the others stopped him and it seemed to me that I heard in the rapid flow of their urging the familiar word "Rastokhez." I knew that Loik Sherali was a national hero. Could it be that my friend Safar had also entered the Tadzhik Hall of Fame? Or was I hearing things?

Smiling absentmindedly, the woman picked up a piece of melon and took a bite. Chewing pensively she suddenly introduced herself: "Nadya!" Then she moved backwards, saving her energy and painstakingly keeping her equilibrium on the way.

As a diversion from this unpleasant episode I started an idiotic argument with Safar about the ethnogenesis of Tadzhiks and Uzbeks, and as a result he forgot about the neighboring table but almost had a falling out with me for the rest of his life.

I understood, of course, that arguments on such inflammatory subjects could hardly lead to anything good. In our country, where intolerance of other viewpoints has been raised to the status of state policy and one people is subjugated to another, abstract arguments on the nationality question always threaten to metamorphose into actual violence.

"But why don't you speak about the fact that before the eighth century there were neither Uzbek-Turks nor Tadzhik-Persians in Central Asia?" I said, treading on Safar's tender spot. "When Central Asia was conquered by Arabs in the eighth century, its population consisted mainly of Sogdians, but the contemporary inhabitants of Tadzhikistan and Uzbekistan keep hardly a drop of their blood in their veins. The ancestors of contemporary Tadzhiks were Persians from Khorossan who converted to Islam and served in Arab troops as fighters for the new religion."

"So they settled in cities," Safar answered, accepting my challenge. "Don't you know that the word 'Tadzhik' also means 'city dweller' in some medieval dictionaries? Tadzhiks and Persians were living in cities while the Turkic peoples were living in their yurts on the steppes."

"Nothing of the kind," I answered. "Turks were living in cities, including the Central Asian cities, several centuries before the Arabic invasion. Have you forgotten about the Great Turkic Khanates—the Western and the Eastern? And what about the Eftalite kingdoms, whose people were called the 'white Huns' and who had their own lawful state even in the times of the pre-Christian Roman Empire?"

"That's a good lawful state, indeed," Safar said, growing indignant. "You know, don't you, that an Eftalite woman was the wife of all brothers at once. And if her husband had no brothers—"

"Then she had to fold only one corner on her hat and not all of them—depending on how many husbands she had," I interrupted my friend sharply. "I have read academician Gafurov, too. And so what. Polyandry exists in Tibet even now. And what would you say if I mentioned another fact—in Pendzhikent, which was part of Tokharistan at that time, a man had the right to marry any woman, including his sisters and even his mother."

"So what?" Safar teased me. "Polygamy still exists in the Soviet Union. Or perhaps you never heard about it?"

After a pause, I rushed into hand-to-hand combat.

"The Turks and Persians in Central Asia are both imported ethnic groups," I said. "In the thousand years before the Bolsheviks, their ethnic belonging was determined by religion and not by language. In Central Asia with its Turkic-Tadzhik bilingualism what was important was to be a Moslem; your nationality, Uzbek or Tadzhik, didn't matter. Nationality in general is a European notion, and it was never reliable in Central Asia. But the Bolsheviks came and first created Uzbekistan with an autonomous Tadzhikistan in its confines, and then separated Tadzhikistan into another republic. As a result the descendants of Persians from Khorossan, the conquerors of the eighth century, living in Samarkand and Bukhara, consider themselves Uzbeks while the descendants of the Turks, who twice invaded the territory of contemporary Tadzhikistan, once in the eleventh and then again in the sixteenth century, consider themselves to be Tadzhiks."

"*Domullo,* would you like us to cut him into pieces?" said the guys sitting at the next table, jumping forward.

"No, he's a guest," Safar said. ("How you regretted turning them down!" I joked later, parting with him before leaving Dushanbe.)

"Don't argue, boys." The women intervened, feeling high from their drinks. "Don't quarrel. We won't annoy anyone, we're enough for all of you."

27

Firuza Means "Turquoise"

Parviz Tursun-zade was yet another person whom I wished to visit before leaving Tadzhikistan. I had last seen him in September 1980, on the border between Iraq and Syria. It was the first week of the Iran-Iraq War, and Soviet leaders had decided to evacuate the families of Soviet specialists and some of the Soviet personnel in Iraq. Parviz was among them, and I was in the group that accompanied this caravan of refugees up to the border with Syria.

I had become acquainted with Parviz when I started working in Iraq, and we became friends rather quickly. At that time I thought Parviz had one big drawback: he was a pathologically humble, not to say obsequious, person. Of course, by Soviet standards that quality is considered to be an undeniable virtue. The system aspired to see its citizens become just like that: unpretentious, patient, and submissive.

Parviz was a first-class guitar player. He was young at the time of Beatlemania in the sixties. But his infatuation with rock music turned into a real tragedy for his clan. His father, then chairman of the Writers' Union of Tadzhikistan, was regarded as a living treasure and state writer *numero uno* of Tadzhikistan. Back under Stalin he started getting all conceivable and inconceivable state premiums and government awards, including the most prestigious—Hero of Socialist Labor—and by the end of his life he was almost at the top of the *nomenklatura* pyramid of his republic. Later, he even had a city named after him. Without a doubt, this man was an outstanding character, and he had great authority in Tadzhikistan, to say nothing of his firm connections with the upper echelons of Moscow partocracy.

And then suddenly there was an awful disappointment: the eldest son, the favorite Parviz-zhon, for whom such proud parental plans had been hatched, gave up a splendid career—any career would have been possible for him—and discredited his father by strumming on a stupid guitar. It would not have been so bad if he at least played some national musical instrument and sang Tadzhik songs, but he became completely shameless: he grew long hair and sang in a womanly voice in an incomprehensible imperialist language.

Eventually, the parents decided to marry the poor musician off, for there were scores of available brides from families with high status. A daughter of the minister of finance of the republic was chosen at last. Since the wedding was on the highest level, the gifts included keys to a new apartment, an automobile, and sets of furniture produced in other socialist countries (which are much more prestigious than Soviet furniture).

But fate interfered in this luxurious life. When Parviz's father died, his wife's parents decided that Parviz was not such a good match for their daughter. So they came up with a contract for Parviz to go abroad with his wife, who turned out to be sick when it was time to go and stayed at home with her child. During all his stay in Iraq, Parviz tried to get his wife to come to him, but each time, in accordance with her parents' plan, she would delay her arrival.

"Get ready for a divorce," I told Parviz when we parted, as the caravan of buses started moving slowly across the Syrian border to the port of Latakya, where ships were waiting to take the Soviet refugees by sea to Odessa.

"Never in my life," he answered, sitting at the window of the bus, for he loved his beautiful wife and his little son.

Yet he had to get divorced; it was a long, sad story. Later, he married another woman, gave up on his romantic dreams, threw away his guitar, and became a director of the museum dedicated to his great father. Several years passed, and he had two more children by the time his job lost all attraction for him. Parviz then became a professional photographer and turned to his guitar again, playing at weddings and other family gatherings.

"And he could have become a secretary of the party committee of a big city," Safar said pensively when we had a conversation about Parviz. "Or an academician. Or, in the worst case, a minister of foreign affairs of Tadzhikistan. Especially if there were no perestroika."

Several days later I left the hotel of the Central Committee of Tadzhikistan, because, according to my friends, by staying there I could attract the attention of the local mafia, which would not like my meddling in its affairs. I thought that to be quite convincing, and without even making clear what wing of the mafia they were talking about—party or criminal—I said good-bye to Pshenichnyi and to Safar. I went to stay with Parviz, thus going underground.

We met as if we had never separated. This ability of many of my old friends to pick up a friendship after a long separation as if nothing had ever happened sometimes astounds me. I called Parviz many times whenever I came to Dushanbe but I had never caught him in the city. Then he changed his telephone number and completely disappeared from my view. I learned his new number, thanks to Safar, but Parviz was not at home, and so I left a message with his wife.

That same evening a hotel receptionist called me to say that a visitor was waiting for me downstairs. I understood at once that it was Parviz and told the receptionist to let him come up to my room. Ten minutes passed and there was no Parviz, so I decided to go downstairs myself. "He just went upstairs on his own," the receptionist said with a look of dismay. "He didn't have his passport, and so I couldn't write him a pass."

I caught up with him in front of the elevator, and we happily hugged each other. He had hardly changed at all; even his facial expression was the same.

"I just arrived from out of town, and my wife told me that some Marat called. And although we haven't seen each other in exactly ten years I realized at once that it had to be you, I don't know why."

"Telepathy!" I said, patting him affably on the back. "Why didn't you ever call on me in Moscow?"

"I don't like Moscow," Parviz confessed openheartedly, "and besides, I was afraid that you had no time for old friends."

By Soviet standards, Parviz's four-bedroom apartment was strik-
ing. In one of the rooms there was a carpet hanging on the wall, in
which his father's portrait was woven. Weavers made it to express their
gratitude to the writer for his great literary works. We left the hotel
and went to a restaurant, because Parviz wanted to buy a bottle of
vodka.

"Are you still a teetotaler?" he asked when I suggested doing
without the Green Devil.

"I don't smoke, either," I replied, amazed at my own virtue.

"What joys of life are left for you?" Parviz asked, and went in to
see a waiter, an acquaintance of his, while I stayed in the car. Buying
spirits from waiters, overpaying enormously, is another good old tradition, which helps people get around the Soviet ban on buying alcohol
after 7:00 P.M.

Parviz's wife had cooked a first-class pilaf, which testified to the
fact that I was treated with respect in this house. Then she went to
bed, while Parviz and I sat up until morning remembering old times
and old friends. Neither politics nor the current events in Tadzhikistan
were of any interest to him. It was as if time had stopped for this guy
at some point in the late seventies. He played his exquisite twelve-
string guitar for me, sang some old Beatles songs, then his own new
songs. I called my wife in Moscow. Parviz had met her in Baghdad but
had no idea that she would become my wife. Despite the fact that it
was just before dawn, a sleepy Alexandra was happy that I had called,
and Parviz and I talked to her for a whole hour, passing the receiver
from one to another, talking about how we loved her.

"When will you be in Samarkand?" my wife asked at the end of
the conversation.

"In about a week," I told her. "Why?"

"I miss you," she meowed. "And I've never been there. What if I
come for a couple of days?"

"And what about Mary?" I asked about our daughter.

"She'll come, too."

"Okay," I said impulsively. "Let's check our watches."

There was plenty to see in Samarkand. Human settlements have
existed in this place for more than twenty-five hundred years, though
the fourteenth-century ruler Tamerlane and his grandson Ulugbek, a

man of genius, left the most impressive imprint of all on the city. Samarkand seemed to me the most astounding of all the ancient Central Asian cities, although if I had to live there, I would probably have died of ennui. It is another thing to visit every few years; for me it is a great joy, and no doubt a major disruption in the lives of my Samarkand friends. I loved the ancient center of this city, because among other things I knew some of its long history.

It was only 195 miles from Dushanbe to Samarkand, and I succeeded in persuading Parviz to drop me there. He was invited to provide the music for a wedding at a *kolkhoz* in the environs of Pyandzhent, which was very close to Samarkand. Parviz usually performed with a friend and his wife; Parviz and he played musical synthesizers and sang, while the other man's wife, a young, beautiful Tadzhik woman, sang and performed folk dances. She was a redhead with blue eyes. In Central Asia such coloring is found only in Tadzhikistan. In the Pamir region, some ethnic groups bear genetic reflections of the ancient pre-Islamic peoples—sometimes azure-colored eyes, rather rare among Central Asians, sometimes a light-brown beard that, along with peasant attire, makes a person look as though he were masquerading as Lawrence of Arabia.

Parviz's colleagues were rather hostile when I first made my appearance in the front seat of his car. Their reaction was quite understandable, actually, for in their situation they were even more threatened by strangers than I. They received really high fees for their work, and that, no doubt, attracted the attention of the police as well as the criminals. Parviz's partner looked as if he himself belonged to the mafia; probably he was connected with some local godfathers. Like their counterparts in Moscow, they had to pay a rather high percentage from their income for protection. But then they were quite safe except for threats they might get from amateur racketeers or from criminals on tour, coming for some quick booty to the territories of other bands.

The road A-377 along which we were moving westward, toward the border between Tadzhikistan and Uzbekistan, may have been a part of the ancient Silk Way. Of course, there were mountainous paths in those days, not paved roads. Ancient authors inform us that in some places the paths over the mountainous precipices were so narrow that neither camels nor horses nor donkeys could pass them. Then porters from local villages carried the packs with the goods themselves, and after the pass the merchants hired or bought new beasts of burden.

While we were talking, we passed a settlement called Dardar, ten miles after which I knew there would be a turn to go to Rudaki's mausoleum. In Central Asia the name "Rudaki" is known to every high school student. Rudaki was a great Tadzhik poet and philosopher who lived in the middle of the ninth century. As the ancients wrote, "Neither the Arabs nor the Persians had an equal to him in versification." Like Loik Sherali, Rudaki was close to the ruling court but by the end of his life he had fallen out of favor, gone blind, and been exiled. I can tell you only one story about this poet, which I found in an old reader published toward the end of the nineteenth century. This is a legend, to be sure, but it seems to me that it could have happened.

At a Friday bazaar in one village in the mountains, a strange man was trying to sell an object of unknown use. People were bustling around the salesman, noisily arguing and waving hands, each one having his own idea about how to use the object, but the crowd rejected each explanation on the spot. For instance, an executioner thought that it was a tool for torture, a baker believed that it was a rolling pin, a doctor insisted that it was a device for enemas, and so on. At this moment the blind Rudaki came up and asked permission to touch the wonderful object. When his request was fulfilled, Rudaki held the thing in his hands for some time, smiled and then suddenly brought it to his lips. Everyone stood stupefied and frozen to the spot when they heard the beautiful sounds of a flute. Yes, the object turned out to be a sort of flute that no one had ever seen before. But then people snatched it from the poet's hands, and it was broken.

I had fallen out of the mood I was in, and did not ask to turn down the road to Rudaki's mausoleum. It's probably not his real tomb, I thought. Anyway, more than a thousand years had passed since his death. The bones of a blind old man had long since decayed, but he still existed for Safar, Parviz, and the blue-eyed redhead. Can it really be true that the word is more stable than anything else in the world?

We left our companions in one of the huge houses owned by a

kolkhoz boss, and then Parviz and I were ready to go on driving. The wedding was to begin in the evening, and by all appearances could continue for several days. The instruments and speakers arrived before us from the neighboring province. The bridegroom's father sent a car to bring them from the place where Parviz's team had worked the previous weekend. It was two hours of quick driving to Samarkand, and then Parviz had to drive back again, for he had to return before eight o'clock in the evening.

We had a quick lunch, and decided to roam a little to move our limbs before embarking along the road. I noticed a little coppice of short gnarled mulberry trees. People grow them in Central Asia because of their leaves, which are used as silkworm fodder.

"Silk!" I said aloud, and Parviz looked at me in astonishment. For him, as for the majority of Central Asian residents, the local mode of production seemed absolutely ordinary and natural. Recently I read somewhere that an archeological dig in the Sherabad steppe, in the south of Uzbekistan, unearthed a peasant settlement that existed about four thousand years ago. One of the shreds of clothing that was miraculously preserved in the burial mound turned out to be, as further expert inspection proved, a piece of natural silk. This discovery, sensational in itself, shook the former certainty of scholars that ancient China was where sericulture originated. It is a shame, because I very much liked the legend of how the strictest ban on taking silkworms out of the Chinese empire was broken. China jealously protected its monopoly on the production of natural silk, and threatened with capital punishment anyone who violated this law. But one Chinese princess who married a Central Asian prince smuggled it out in her fluffy hair—which entails at least two possible conclusions. First, interethnic marriages were successfully concluded from time immemorial. Second, the grand dames of antiquity washed their hair more rarely than the representatives of the shampoo industry of those times would have wished. The enamored princess had probably brought in her hair the small eggs that the silkworm's butterflies lay—approximately two thousand to a gram.

Meanwhile, Parviz's partner Bahrom asked him to help install the amplifier and speakers for the evening concert, and they left for about half an hour. I decided to spend this time seeing at least part of the silk-producing process with my own eyes.

While I was walking around the village, a flock of curious children, led by a ten- or eleven-year-old girl, started following me. She had an extremely short haircut, which made her look like the boys, her friends. She had such a clever and good-natured gaze that even I felt ill at ease. She stopped and looked me in the eye. "What's your name?" I asked the child in my doubtful Tadzhik. "Firuza!" she answered and her face brightened with a smile. In Arabic Firuza means "turquoise." Her sociable disposition, too, was unusual because village children in Central Asia reluctantly let strange adults into their world.

"Do you know how people breed silkworms?" I asked her.

"Yes, I do," she replied.

There I was talking with Firuza in a muddle of Tadzhik, Uzbek, and Arabic, accompanied by funny mimicry and gesticulation. We laughed a lot, but she saw that I was really interested in the subject of our conversation and tried to be as useful as she could. She even brought me to the building where cocoons are bred on the leaves of mulberry trees, and to the hellish kitchen where they are boiled in caldrons in order to unfold the silk thread.

To systematize the information I received from Firuza, I later learned the following. The microscopic eggs laid down by silkworm butterflies have to be "revived." This is done in the same way as it was thousands of years ago. The eggs are put in special bags held under the armpit and are thus hatched by the natural warmth of human bodies. Further, only married women who have children are entitled to the job. The young unmarried women are forbidden to do it, because there is a strange superstition that they might harm the productivity of the future silkworms. After approximately two weeks of this warming, tiny caterpillars, hardly visible to the unaided eye, come into being. These incredibly voracious creatures plunge onto mulberry leaves like monsters from a horror movie, throwing off their skin every five or six days as it becomes too small for them.

Only women are engaged in this feeding of silkworms. Children help them. Boys climb up the trees and cut off branches with sprouts and leaves. Girls bring all these branches to the house, mince them, and put them in small trusses. As a rule, silkworms are fed in the houses while the people live out of doors during a couple of summer months. Strangers are not let in to see the silkworms, lest they be cursed by the evil eye and spoiled. In one such house, I saw women's long trousers hanging over the door as a talisman. Firuza explained to me that silkworms get used to the smell of the woman who feeds them and other people are not only not allowed to feed them but are not even allowed to look at them.

But as a special person who had been to the Arab world, I was permitted to listen to how the silkworms sound when they are eating their mulberry leaves. There is a ceaseless noise in the room—something like an autumn drizzle. In the room, these astonishing creatures work with their jaws twenty-four hours a day, devouring an incredible amount of leaves. They live in small cardboard boxes, and the silkworms from one box can eat the leaves from twenty mulberry trees. The boxes stand on special low tables, whose legs sit in saucers full of water.

"So that other insects won't crawl into their boxes," Firuza explained to me.

In about a month or so, the caterpillars become almost three inches long and weigh several thousand times more than when they were born under a woman's armpit. Now people put mulberry twigs without leaves in their boxes, and the caterpillars weave their cocoons around them, excreting a viscous fiber from their glands. A certain portion of these cocoons are put aside for breeding. A caterpillar falls asleep in a cocoon and turns into a pupa, which transforms into a butterfly. A butterfly mates, lays down new eggs, and dies. The eggs wait for a new Chinese princess, or a Central Asian peasant woman who will put them into a bag under her arm.

"How are cocoons unfolded?" I asked Firuza. Parviz came to ask me whether I was going to get on with our driving.

"Let's go right now!" I said impatiently, "but first let's just look at how they boil cocoons in a caldron."

And Firuza took us to a special room in which big cast-iron caldrons, full of a monstrous brew, were boiling on clay stoves. Steaming half-naked women, looking like medieval witches in clouds of steam, were prying cocoons from tempestuously boiling caldrons with sticks, trying to hook them by the thread. When they succeeded, they hooked the end to a primitive wooden wheel that they slowly revolved with their hands, winding a thread of natural silk.

It occurred to me that those who speak against wearing fur could quite seriously think about natural silk as well. Anyway, there is something barbarous about a species of insect gluttons, completely dependent on human beings, bred only to be fed to monstrous sizes—all for the purpose of boiling them alive in order that people be able to dress in their excrement.

"So, what are your impressions?" Parviz asked when the telegraph poles with sparrows and swallows sitting on the wires started flickering again outside the car windows.

"Unforgettable!" I responded, referring to everything I'd seen in Tadzhikistan.

"And do you know how people found out that they should unfold the cocoons?" he smiled, thinking that I was talking about that hellish kitchen.

"Well, perhaps some poor weaver sold his soul to a devil so that the devil would teach him how to get rich—to marry a *padishah*'s daughter. Is that it?"

"No, it's not that at all!" he said. "Quite the contrary. The Chinese emperor's wife was drinking tea under a mulberry tree, and a cocoon fell into her cup from the tree. A silk thread was poking from it, so she pulled it. And what came of it you can judge for yourself— you've just seen it!"

28

Samarkand, the Oldest City
in the World

At the close of the fourteenth century Timur the Great, otherwise known as Tamerlane, defeated the Golden Horde, as we have noted. By the end of the fourteenth century the mighty Volga state had already grown old and lost part of its former power. If we can speak of states as of people, then the Golden Horde had gone from being a tireless, sinewy soldier, over the course of some one and a half centuries, to becoming a fat and crabby old man. It was challenged by Timur's young state, which, if we continue the comparison, was like a young, energetic giant.

As we already know, the result of Timur's extremely successful clash with his distant kinsmen, represented by the Golden Horde, turned out to be useful not so much for him as for the sleeping princess known as Rus', which had been a captive of the Golden Horde for almost two centuries. Only in 1380, at the battle of Kulikovo, did the Russian princes inflict the first defeat upon the Tartars. The anniversary of this event was celebrated with great pomp in our country a few years ago. No one remembered that in that same year of 1380, in response to its defeat, the Golden Horde carried out a successful campaign against Moscow and, capturing it, restored its power over the Russian colonies.

If we follow the logic of these anniversaries, then soon Uzbekistan must also celebrate six hundred years since the victory of Tamerlane over the state that once occupied the territories of the current Tartar, Chuvash, Bashkir, Samara, Ulyanovsk, and Astrakhan areas, as well as Kalmyk and parts of Kazakhstan. Anniversaries of this type may number in the dozens, but it has never occurred to anyone in the national republics of the Soviet Union to celebrate the past victories of its peoples over their neighbors. Only Moscow officially celebrates the past victories of the Russian state over the peoples of other republics that have become part of the U.S.S.R., calling them victories of Lenin's national policies.

But let us return to Tamerlane, whom fate soon led a second time to the role of victor, yet who could not know all the consequences of yet another of his victories. I am speaking about the serious threat that at the beginning of the fifteenth century hung over Western Europe's Christian civilization from the direction of Turkey. Arising out of the ruins of the Eastern Roman Empire, the Turkish state strove to gain power. And contributing to this effort in no small degree was the clever and fortunate Sultan Bayazet, leader of the future Sublime Porte, who for his valor as a general was called Yildyrym, that is, Bayazet the Lightning Bearer. However, he did not manage to turn the military might of Turkey against Europe. In 1402, at the battle of Ankara, the Turkish sultan's troops were utterly defeated, and Bayazet the Lightning Bearer was taken captive. And not by the Crusaders, but by the Samarkand governor Tamerlane. The European monarchs and the Christian church breathed a sigh of relief, having received a respite that would continue for another century and a half.

Tamerlane, who did not generally tend toward jokes and gaiety, unexpectedly began to laugh when he saw the captive sultan. The sultan, who as a youth had already lost an eye in battle, was frankly ashamed.

"You can kill me," he said to Timur, "but you dare not laugh at me."

"Not at you," answered Timur. "I laugh at the strange whim of fate. You are blind in one eye; I am lame and have a withered arm. To normal people we are freaks. Why then is half the world subject to us?"

Each of my visits to Samarkand showed me new, previously

unknown aspects of the city. But I had always been more drawn to what was unchanged in it—its genuine antiquity. In a strange way it pacified the soul, reminding one of the transitoriness of tyrants and ideologies, including the current ones that spread across these ancient walls their stupid red slogans and self-aggrandizing lies about the unity of the ruling elite with the people.

I had been in Samarkand no fewer than ten times, and always for some kind of official business. For the first time, it was for an international meeting of the Moslems of Asia and Africa, to which I was assigned as a correspondent on a Soviet radio broadcast to foreign countries. On my most recent trip, only a few years earlier, I had come as a member of a large and noisy group of writers from Moscow and the Baltics, when the local Writers' Union invited us to a practical conference on the translation of Uzbek literature into Russian. Uzbekistan is a traditionally hospitable land, and therefore every Muscovite, regardless of the level on which he was received, enjoyed being an official guest of the state organization of the republic.

On this trip, however, I had become used to the private nature of my journey, and therefore I was not disturbed either by the lack of hotel rooms reserved in advance or by the problems I faced with transportation. No one expected me here, and this undoubtedly gave my arrival in Samarkand an element of novelty. Parviz left me in front of the Samarkand Intourist hotel and hurried back, only after receiving solemn assurances from me that there was a place in this wonderful city for me to stay.

My wife, Alexandra, and my daughter, Mary, were flying here the following afternoon, only to return the next morning to Moscow. With the aid of our friends my wife had managed to get round-trip airplane tickets, a feat that by Soviet standards was genuinely heroic. My task was to find a night's lodging for all of us. Of course, I could play the role of a homeless hippie, but in fact I had three respectable trump cards up my sleeve. First, a good friend of my mother's worked as administrator in one of the largest hotels in Samarkand. If she had not retired, a roof over my head would be assured. The second alternative was to spend the night at any of several of my friends' houses, including that of Shukhrat Aminov, who had been my study group mate at the institute.

The most interesting possibility was the third. Almost a year earlier,

I had met an interesting and outstanding young man in Moscow named Ben Benyaminov. At that time I was still actively occupied with a private publishing business, and our acquaintance came out of this work. Ben was one of the leaders of the ancient community of Samarkand Jews, an Asiatic strain called Bukharian in the Soviet Union.

This extremely colorful and distinctive community was at one time large and flourishing. Ethnically quite closed, it did not approve of mixed marriages, which is why long centuries, perhaps even thousands of years, did not wash the classic biblical features from the faces of the Bukharian Jews. They were especially clearly manifested in the solemn appearance of dark-skinned, white-bearded old men and the timid appearance of dark-haired young girls with huge sad eyes.

The sharply increasing threat of interethnic conflicts and some overtly anti-Semitic incidents have led to a sharp increase in Bukharian Jewish emigration to Israel. For example, on the night of February 24, 1990, about a hundred tombstones were overturned or broken in a Jewish cemetery in the area of Rustaveli Street in Tashkent, the work of "unknown perpetrators." As far as I know, this event did not receive any publicity in the Soviet mass media. Moreover, in 1990 there were a number of raids in Andizhan and Bukhara mainly against Armenians and Jews.

Sometimes it seems to me that people who have lived on this land no less than ten centuries leave here not only because they consider Israel their historic home. There is probably another reason: many feel with horror that to remain where they were born is not simply difficult but even dangerous. I will never forget the scene that I once witnessed at Moscow's Sheremetyevo airport. A noisy clan of Bukharian Jews, made up of adults and children of all ages, moved en masse toward customs. On one of the baggage carts they were pushing sat a one-hundred-year-old woman on a pile of suitcases. The sudden change of the great migration did not bother her; she appeared to be absolutely indifferent to everything that was going on around her. Her children were themselves already old, and it was apparent that they were worried. You see, none of them had ever left their native Samarkand during their entire lives. Only the adult grandchildren and young great-grandchildren joked and laughed. Before them were their whole lives and freedom. And they carefully bore their grandmother on a baggage cart, as if she was an old fig tree in a large earthenware pot. God willing, it will take root in the land of its ancestors.

"But where is there to go for people whose historical homeland is not beyond the borders of the U.S.S.R.?" inquire the Slavs, Turks, Ugro-Finnics, and representatives of other languages and peoples of the U.S.S.R. I have also met many such people on my way.

"Where would you like to go?" I asked them, as if I could somehow help. I never thought that so many people wished to leave this country.

"Not for myself; for me it is already too late," they answered. "We want to go for the sake of our children."

One of the most widely distributed illusions among those who dream of leaving is the assurance that other countries are prepared to receive them. They think that free emigration from the U.S.S.R. is prevented only by the absence of the right to leave. The majority have a very fuzzy idea of the fact that it is necessary to receive permission for entry.

I spoke with Ben about all of this after we had discussed the conditions under which he ordered a batch of calendars from me, showing the Jewish religious holidays. Then he invited me to lunch in the Moscow restaurant Uzbekistan, not far from my office. This restaurant has begun in the last couple of years to have a worse and worse reputation, but I considered it impolite to refuse or to suggest another place. In Moscow people invite you to a place where they have some *blat*, not just to any place they wish.

Fortunately, Ben went around Moscow with two bodyguards, for moments after we sat down at our table, a noisy fight began at a large table near the entrance. Obscenities quickly escalated to hand-to-hand fighting with cold steel. The fight continued about ten minutes. Since the participants were racketeers of some sort, the administration, fearing to disrupt their own fragile relationship with them, did not call the police. In order to leave the hall, we would have had to fight our way through the crowd of brawlers. It was simpler to remain in our places and eat our rapidly cooling kebabs, which the waiter had brought a few seconds before the beginning of the fight. Ben's bodyguards shielded us from random punches, and, smiling tensely, we continued our discussion. After the crowd of fighters had substantially thinned out, their ranks reduced by those wounded and possibly dead, Ben, at a sign from the bodyguards, stood up. I stood up after him, and, stepping around the injured bodies, we silently proceeded to the exit.

After that, Ben and I met in Moscow many times, but we went for lunch exclusively to the Malyi Teatr club. First of all, it was closer to my office on Petrovsky Boulevard. Second, the criminals who frequented that restaurant were of a higher class, and did not themselves participate in brawls. Realizing that I had come to Samarkand without an address or telephone number for Ben, I decided to track him down by the deductive method. Leaving my heavy bag with the doorman at the Intourist restaurant (ten rubles), I went to the bazaar, which since the time of Tamerlane was considered to be the heart of this old city. Of course, there were no streets with glass roofs, which my medieval colleagues described in their travelogues; they had disappeared from here long ago. I found a photographic portrait studio, where my experiment in the methods of Sherlock Holmes was to begin. Photo studios here, just like hairdressing salons and shoe repair shops, belong as a rule to a representative of the local Bukharian Jewish community. In Uzbekistan only these three types of private business by some miracle avoided nationalization under the Bolsheviks, and the only people who dared, even during the cruel Stalinist era, to work in the private sector were the Bukharian Jews.

"Do you want to be photographed?" asked a friendly man lazing by the open door of the studio.

"Do you take photographs for a foreign passport?" I demonstrated with a question the seriousness of my intentions.

"Is it needed immediately?" The photographer brought the conversation to a concrete plane, inviting me to stand in place against a background, a white screen made of an old sheet. He was young and most assuredly knew Ben.

"How much does it cost?" I began to determine the price, squinting from the bright light of the lamp he had turned on.

"Do you expect me to do it by the price list?" The man pretended to be horrified. "Then the border guards will never let you out of here."

"Yes, they would," I answered arrogantly, putting a sorrowful expression on my face, since it is categorically forbidden to smile in Soviet documents in black-and-white photographs.

"But you're not Jewish?" he asked from under the black cover, aiming his antediluvian camera at me.

"Chinese Jew," I said, nodding inopportunely, because at that precise moment he took off and put back on the lens cover. That is, he photographed me.

"Six rubles," he said, turning off the lamp. "It will be ready tomorrow. I never heard that there were Chinese Jews."

"They exist. Keep it," I said, giving him money. And as if I was incidentally interested, I asked him, "Where is the store of Ben Benyaminov's father?"

For some reason it seemed to me that Ben's father must have a small commission store.

"Diagonally across from the entrance to the bazaar," answered the surprised photographer. "So you know Ben Benyaminov?"

"Who doesn't know him?" I answered with a satisfied smile, sincerely hoping that we were not simply speaking about someone with the same surname as my friend.

Going into the store diagonally across from the entrance to the bazaar, I asked the sales clerk to call the manager.

"What for?" she asked rather aggressively. Just like all sales clerks in the U.S.S.R., she thought that if someone calls the manager, then it is only because they want to complain about her. "What's the matter?"

"It's confidential," I answered mysteriously. "Call the boss."

The store was indeed very small. There were no other shoppers besides me. Behind a thick curtain separating the selling area from the back room, I could hear a rustling sound. The store manager apparently was standing behind the curtain, listening to our whole conversation. If he thought that I was a racketeer, then he was perfectly capable of holding a double-barreled shotgun in his hands. Or a Kalashnikov machine gun. Or, at worst, a tank of gas, which he could use to defend his money.

"Mr. Benyaminov," I said to him, "can you spare a minute? I'm a friend of your son's."

"Then why did you come to me?" he asked, coming out from behind the curtain. There was no Kalashnikov machine gun in his hands, but mistrust was written on his worldly-wise and wary face.

"I am passing through Samarkand," I said and introduced myself.

"I left my notebook with the telephone number of your son at home in Moscow."

But this man throughout his long life had been deceived so many times that he was not about to believe what I was saying.

"And why did you leave it in Moscow?"

"I forgot it," I answered. "You seem to be somewhat doubtful."

"I doubt nothing," Ben's father answered, annoyed. "I simply see you for the first time in my life. You are a solid man, but you yourself know what kind of times we are living in. God knows why you want to see my son."

"Couldn't you call him and tell him that I'm here?" I asked. "He will tell you himself what to do with me then."

"Well, all right," the old man answered, displeased, and pulled an old black telephone with a bent dial from behind the counter. Hiding it from me with his hand, he dialed five numbers and said in Tadzhik:

"Ben, there is a man here who says he is from Moscow, and that he is your friend. What should I do with him—call Rafik, or do you want to talk to him yourself?"

Then he handed me the heavy telephone receiver.

"Ben, *shumo narzed-me*," I greeted my friend, in the local dialect of Tadzhik that our countrymen have spoken among themselves for many centuries.

"Who is it—Marat? It can't be!" Ben started to laugh. "What brings you here?"

In the morning I met my wife and daughter, and we went to see the sights. After a month-and-a-half separation, it seemed to me that Alexandra had grown even more beautiful, and eight-year-old Mary had become tall and grown up. Both were in Samarkand for the first time in their lives, and I enjoyed playing the role of tour guide. Although in Timur's era Samarkand was reputed to be one of the greatest cities in the world, its remaining historical monuments, by current Moscow standards, were practically next door to each other. Therefore, it only took a few hours to become superficially acquainted with them.

Those who have been to Samarkand on the Intourist tour probably remember the old square, Registan, with its three huge restored *medreses* (Moslem religious schools, which are no longer being used as such), their portals and domes inlaid with blue tiles, and the mosque of Bibi-Khanum, named for Tamerlane's favorite wife. Remember the fascinating story about when she decided to build a new mosque for the return of her husband from his last campaign? The young architect, infatuated with her, dared to promise to build it in time only if Bibi-Khanum would let him kiss her. And the tomb of the same Tamerlane, Gur-Emir, next to whom was buried his favorite grandson and heir, the Emir Ulugbek. It is indeed strange: in a sarcophagus under a huge nephrite epitaph the great soldier and the great scholar found their last refuge, grandfather Timur and his grandson Ulugbek, decapitated by his own son, a fanatic and envious person. Who thought to bury them together? And the Ulugbek observatory. This enlightened monarch left behind astronomy tables that scientists could use even in the twentieth century. There's a legend that if Timur's tomb is opened, horrible disasters will befall the country. Anthropologists opened it just the day before that Sunday in June 1941 when Hitler invaded the Soviet Union.

Unfortunately, our excursion had to be interrupted because of the surfeit of colors, impressions, and information, and perhaps also because of the unaccustomed intense summer heat after a long flight from rainy Moscow. My beautiful Muscovites' eyes began to droop like flowers in a drought. We bought all sorts of things in the market and returned to our one-room apartment provided for me by my friends for those few days that I planned to spend in Samarkand.

After a siesta, when the heat was beginning to abate, but still long before nightfall, I invited my wife and daughter to the next tour, which is not in any Intourist itinerary.

"Now we are going to the Bukharian Jews' *makhallya*," I announced to my wife and daughter, not without some ceremony.

"They will let us come there?" my daughter wondered. She still knew little about different nationalities, but she well understood that in our country there are many interesting places where people are usually not allowed to go.

"Better than that, they are expecting us," I said proudly, and looked at my wife. For ten years of our life together she and I had visited practically every republic of the former U.S.S.R. In Christian Georgia, in Moslem Azerbaijan, in pagan Abkhazia, in Catholic Lithuania, in Russian Orthodox parts of the Ukraine, and in Buddhist

Buryatia we had friends and acquaintances who were prepared to welcome and help us.

As we penetrated the narrow streets of the Bukharian Jewish *makhallya,* the noisy city was quickly replaced by quiet Central Asian alleyways. The blank, windowless walls of the one-story houses and dusty clay fences, extending in dense rows along both sides of the street, closely protected the crowded little yards from the dangers of the outside world. The uniformity was only disrupted by the metallic gates and massive wooden doors, from which the noses of curious children poked.

Convinced that we had finally gotten lost, I knocked on the first gates we reached and asked how to get to the house of Jewish culture. A young lad, opening the door, offered to lead us. In about five minutes he took us to a house which, as he explained, had previously been a hospital. "Previously" meant before Bolshevik rule. People met us guardedly at the inner courtyard, but upon hearing Ben's name, they smiled.

"He's busy right now," they said. "They have a Hebrew lesson. Come in and wait."

"Of course," I answered, "only tell him that I'm here."

Ben came out right away, and we exchanged a joyful handshake. Ben, at just twenty-five, looked too young to be the leader of the community. He tries to look older than his years, but it does not work. Neither his thick black beard nor his sedate bearing help, nor does his strict custom of dressing only in black and white.

He had already been in Israel, and planned in the near future to settle there forever. He does not go there now, because he believes his main task to be the evacuation of the whole Bukharian Jewish community.

Right next to him shines with earnest energy his deputy and friend, Raphael. Raphael is a brilliant conversationalist, and to listen to him is a pleasure. Ben is always silent and serious, but behind his restrained manners you feel a hidden fire. Raphael scatters sparks, like fireworks, but his eyes remain sad.

I introduced them to Mary and introduced Raphael to Alexandra. She had met Ben in Moscow.

Raphael started to tell Alexandra about his *makhallya.*

"The Bukharian Jewish community of Samarkand," Raphael began in the voice of a tour guide, "is one of the most ancient in Central Asia. As early as the twelfth century, Istudella wrote that the Jewish community of Samarkand numbered almost fifty thousand people."

"Perhaps he exaggerated that figure somewhat," noted Ben. "At any rate, I wouldn't rule it out."

"Well, whatever," answered Raphael. "The Jews lived here a very long time, and there were a great number of them. But by the end of the sixteenth century there had been so many attacks on Samarkand that the city almost ceased to exist. Then a great proportion of the Jews moved to Bukhara. They began to come back here only in the seventeenth century."

"When was this *makhallya* formed?" Alexandra asked.

"The land and the buildings of the *makhallya* where we are now were acquired in 1843 by Kalantarov, a merchant of the first guild," Raphael said.

"For how much?" asked Mary.

Raphael looked at her with interest and said, "What a bright little girl! How old are you?"

"Eight," Mary answered with great dignity.

"Don't digress," corrected his friend Ben. "She asked how much, and you asked her how old she is."

"For thirty thousand Bukharian tanga," replied Raphael. "Unlike all other parts of the world, it was bought all at once and as a whole."

"Religious communities often acquire large parcels of land with all their buildings as private property," I noted thoughtfully. "I don't remember exactly, but it seems that the Mormons own whole cities, where even police access is prohibited. No trespassing."

"This doesn't apply to us." Raphael again laughed. "Although the deed of purchase was kept, which states that this very land belongs to these very Jews. Then trade began to develop actively; textile shops appeared, spinning shops, and so forth. All signs were written in Hebrew."

"That is, in Hebrew letters, but in our language," Ben added.

"In the Tadzhik dialect," I explained to Alexandra and Mary.

"In general, life here seethed and bubbled with vitality," Raphael said. "Here in this house, for example, there was a large synagogue. After the revolution they located a clinic here. There were thirty synagogues in this *makhallya*. You see this house? This was the museum of

Lur'e, the first Hebrew museum associated with the museums of London and Paris."

"Why is everything in the past tense?" I asked. "Where did all of this go?"

"They destroyed it," Raphael answered unconstrainedly. "In 1937 everything that didn't have a direct relation to the building of socialism was destroyed. The particular feature of this area was that a memorial plaque could be erected in almost every house here." As we walked along the street, he pointed out different old buildings. "For example, in this house was born Khalilov, one of our best choreographers. In that house was born Nar'yanmarov, one of our best film directors and the author of the large series of films on the era of Firdous. In this area were born and grew up the artists Elizarov and Kalantarov. Here lived Mulakandov, the well-known singer. Another Mulakandov, the best tamboura player in Central Asia. The singer, Talmasov. All here, on this little scrap of land. Here lived the best merchants. They traded in Paris, in London, in Kazan, in Moscow. People lived very intense lives. New people continuously came here. The community was constantly replenished with arrivals of Jews from Bukhara, Shakhrizyabs, and Karshi. The revolution and the establishment of the new rule strongly influenced the Jews. These were people of the air. They made money in real estate, they sold, they bought. And here was the end of economic freedom. No one knew what to do, what to work on next. People began to be ruined. The Bolsheviks wanted to drive everyone into factories and plants. They began to organize Jewish collective farms. It was all horribly preposterous. The result was that by the end of the 1930s, everything was closed or forbidden."

"We have now restored the Hebrew inscriptions," Ben said. "Jewish life has generally become very intensive. But people fear pogroms. In Andizhan, for example, there was a horrible pogrom; they burned twenty-two houses."

"What is a pogrom?" asked Mary.

We looked at each other and were silent.

"I was there and saw this cruelty; it was horrible," Raphael said in a quiet voice. "You see, there never were any pogroms here in Central Asia. It always seemed to us that it was somewhere far away, in the small towns of Russia, that this kind of thing was possible, and only long ago. And suddenly it turns out that it is here, right behind your door."

"The motives?" asked Alexandra. "Why do they do it?"

"Motives?" Raphael repeated. "The most absurd. They threatened the homes of the Armenians, and then they knocked down the neighboring homes of the Bukharian Jews. After that, as Gdlyan discovered here during the Uzbek affair, the attitude toward Armenians here became terrible."

And he told what I had already heard in Tashkent, about the war between the Uzbek and the Armenian mafia in Tashkent, about the horrible death of the head of the mafia of the Tashkent Armenians, and many other stories that make your blood run cold.

I took Mary by the hand and we went out front. She talked to me about her life, about the fact that she learned to jump rope twenty new ways, that older girls mistreated her on the playground, that this year no one was going to vacation at the sea, and that Grandma Farida had such a bad telephone that when she called she could barely hear anything.

"And now we will go and visit a very interesting man," said Raphael, once more his jolly self. "The fact is that he is an ardent Communist. As a real Communist, he has no property at all. Only portraits of Lenin, Stalin, Brezhnev, Chernenko, Andropov, and Gorbachev. All the gorgeous images are displayed. He especially loves Lenin. He says that he, like Lenin, also has no children. He is a miserably poor man. But he built over the gate something like a shrine to Lenin. Inside is a portrait of Lenin and, by Jewish tradition, a single candle burns, but above it is a red banner."

We walked to a narrow dead-end street that ended with an aged gate. An old portrait of Lenin hung over the door, in front of which a single candle burned in a menorah. The spectacle was more than surrealistic.

But when the host himself came out to meet us, the effect became even more majestic. This man looked like a twin of Stalin's.

Ben kept discreetly silent. Raphael was like a stage director who, after a successful premiere, came out to the front of the stage to take a bow and to receive bouquets of flowers. Alexandra and Mary examined with undisguised interest the Stalinist cap and mustache. What surprised me more than anything was the hand-rolled cigarette made from a page of *Pravda*.

"Hello, Iosif Vissarionovich," I said, clearing my throat. "May I take your picture?"

"Let's go into the yard," "Stalin" said in a trembling Georgian accent. "Why stand on the street?"

We went into a dark little yard and were even more surprised. Directly over our heads were nailed large portraits of all the general secretaries in order of their appearance on the Russian throne, with the solitary exception of Khrushchev. Stalin, Brezhnev, Andropov, Chernenko, and Gorbachev stared at us, looking like brothers. Apparently, the creative daring of the court artists was limited by some sort of secret instruction, preordaining the drawing of leaders precisely in that form, eternally young but with a wise fatherly squint. The portrait of Stalin was the largest, and that of Gorbachev was the smallest.

"Why Gorbachev?" I asked. "Do you like glasnost and perestroika?"

"No," he answered. "It is a mistake of the party. But he is General Secretary, and we are obliged to love and respect him. He is the father, and we are his children."

"And where is Khrushchev?" I politely inquired.

"Bad man," the host snapped shortly. "Why, he slandered Stalin."

"A pathological case," I said quietly to my wife. "Don't get into an argument. There is no point. The life of a man is lived, and you cannot change anything."

We were introduced. The host's name was Malame Maksumov. He was seventy years old. I asked him to tell about himself.

"My father was the first Soviet policeman among the Bukharian Jews," he said. His voice was low and slightly hoarse. The hand-rolled cigarette in his dangling hand had already gone out, but the smell of the burned paper and the rotten tobacco made me want to sneeze.

"And you?" I asked. "You went to war?"

"Yes, in the Stalinist-Uzbek division, under Kursk."

"And after the war where did you work?"

"I worked in a prison."

"As a guard?"

"Yes. But I had a tender heart. And when they let me, I left there."

"To where?"

"To be a fireman. In recent years, before I retired, I was a fireman."

His wife came out of the house. She was scrawny, lively, and a little slant-eyed.

"Are you from a newspaper?" she asked, seeing my camera and Dictaphone.

"Something like that," I said. "But basically we are friends of Ben and Raphael's."

"Then you better not take his picture, but tell him so he won't beat me!"

"Only don't start a new fight in front of our guests," Raphael said to the old woman in Tadzhik. "Or you won't be allowed into Israel."

"We won't go anywhere from here," said Malame, not looking at anyone in particular. Again he lit his hand-rolled cigarette.

We went into the house, which consisted of two tiny low-ceilinged rooms practically without furniture. In one an old metal bed barely fit, with piles of rags instead of sheets. Several nails were stuck in the wall. On one of them hung a half-rotted military greatcoat. In the other room the only furniture was a table moved up against the wall, covered with an old oilcloth and two wooden chairs. On the wall hung several faded black-and-white photographs. Some of them were rolled up in a tube. Others were still stuck on. In one, Malame was in the uniform of an NKVD soldier; another photograph showed him with a saber at his side.

"What is their floor made of?" Mary asked me in a whisper.

"Of clay," I said. "Here everything is made of clay: the walls, the floor, and the roof."

The poverty of this home was scandalous. The next level lower could only be a cardboard box like those the New York homeless sleep in. But these people ended up in such a poor situation because for various reasons they did not fit into the system of their society. Malame had been an indispensable component part, one of the millions of "reliable cogs of the system," a system that only robbed him for all his loyal service. The sole reward he received from Communism was an old cap and mustache.

"Give me something to drink, please," I asked Malame's wife, and she ladled out some water with a cup from an old bucket standing in the yard.

There were no water pipes in the house, just as there never was a refrigerator, or a washing machine, or a television. They had to carry water from a water tap on the street.

"I want to go to the toilet," said Mary.

"Can you wait till we get home?" I asked.

"It's harmful to wait," Mary answered in Alexandra's voice, and set out herself to search for lost horizons. Or a toilet.

29

The Disgraced President's Granddaughter

We overslept the next morning, and then the cab that we ordered did not come, and as a result Alexandra and Mary missed their plane. We decided not to waste our time trying to find out why the cab had failed to come. Even if we succeeded in getting through to the taxi booking office, it would not have changed anything; no one is responsible for a failed order. Therefore we preferred to dedicate ourselves to another problem: how to get new air tickets.

We did not want to ask Ben for help, as we had formally parted with our Jewish friends the day before. We had also visited Raphael and his merry mother and bid farewell. The same evening, after a walk around the fairy-tale burial sites of the local medieval rulers, called Shakhi-Zinda, or immortal monarchs, Ben brought us to the cooperative kosher restaurant for dinner. It was situated in the big yard of some private house and looked like a rather pleasant, clean place. There were electric lights in the trees, and in the middle of the yard there was even a kind of fountain. Following the local tradition we ordered a kebab of fresh sheep's liver with tomatoes and onions. We talked mainly about the publishing business and the possibilities of selling our firm's editions in Samarkand. But neither Ben nor I was as enthusiastic as the previous year. Perestroika had come to a dead end, and it would have been naïve at this juncture to count on a big future for a private business. Also, Ben was planning to leave for Israel at some point in the next two years. My future was much more uncertain. We were parting in a rather sad mood, for we understood that we would not see each other again soon.

My friend with whom we had been staying had departed for several days for Bukhara. To call our other friends, only to plunge them into the pandemonium of getting air tickets to Moscow, would have been both inhumane and discourteous. If you stay in a person's house, you may ask him for help since you are his or her guest. But it is impossible, according to local etiquette, to request a favor, even from a close friend while visiting his city, without first spending some time with him. In this case, there was no time for such niceties. So only one choice was left: to deal with the problem of negotiating with the local Aeroflot ticket offices all by ourselves.

After several hours of Machiavellian efforts we went through a chain of acquaintances from a Tartar barmaid to a Russian cop, then to a Tadzhik porter, then to an Uzbek ticket cashier, and finally to a commuter plane leaving directly for Tashkent. It would be much simpler to get tickets to Moscow from Tashkent, and in any case my mother would be happy to see her favorite daughter-in-law and granddaughter.

My next destination was the city of Ashkhabad, which is the capital of yet another Central Asian republic that materialized on the map of the Soviet Union in 1924 by Bolshevik decree: Turkmenistan, also known as Turkmenia. It is the fourth largest republic of the pre-breakup Soviet Union, and twelfth in terms of population. A little more than 3.5 million people live there; about 2.4 million of them, or 68 percent, are Turkmens. The second ethnic group comprises Russians. There are fewer than half a million of them, and their numbers are not growing. Unlike its policy in the majority of the Union republics, Moscow has not created artificial conditions to encourage Russian immigration here. The center's indifference to one of its southernmost colonies is no doubt due to the fact that the vast majority of Turkmenia's territory is desert.

Russian and West European authors of the nineteenth century

usually depicted Turkmenia as a rather gloomy place. "This territory," says one Russian document from the middle of the nineteenth century, "looks like a fruitless, wild desert which provides no conveniences for settled life. The often stony, and sandy, and even more frequently shale steppe grows with feather grass only along the Atrek River, close to the Persian border, where the Turkmens grow grain. The nomads have only small pastures in this territory of over half a million square miles, and they use water from wells, salt water for the most part."

Let me note that alongside the deserts there are ancient oases with a lot of water and quite arable soil. But Turkmenia holds next-to-last place in the U.S.S.R. in terms of population density; Kazakhstan ranks last. Turkmenia is one of the most conservative among all the former Union republics; the population was utterly indifferent to the slogans of democracy that Gorbachev put forth when he was still a reformer.

By a fluke, I happened to get acquainted in Tashkent with the son of the person I was going to stay with in Ashkhabad. These two were the son and grandson of Nurberdy Bairamov, the former president (or, to be more precise, chairman of the Supreme Soviet) of Turkmenia, who was replaced in Khrushchev's time for an attempt he made to pad the republic's top party *nomenklatura* with members of local party cadres—in other words, by Turkmens rather than Russians.

The grandson, Gel'dy, could not tell me much about his legendary grandfather. The name "Gel'dy" is rather widespread among Turkmens. It is translated as "Arrived" or "Appeared," which is a confirmation that grateful parents send to the Almighty on the occasion of the birth of their long-awaited child. Sometimes sons are called "Holiday Arrived" (Kurbangel'dy) or "Well-being Arrived" (Omangel'dy). Another widespread version of such names ends with "-berdy," which means "The Giver." For instance, the name of the outstanding grandfather of my new acquaintance was Nurberdy, which means "The Giver of Light." For comparison we might recall that the Turkmen's neighbors, the Uzbeks, often give their children the name "Tukhta" (another version is Tukhtasyn), which means "Let's stop with this one!" or "That's enough!" In other words, by giving a newborn this name, its parents are informing Providence that they already have enough children, and that they will not be able to feed any more. At present this is probably the most reliable means of birth control in this part of the Soviet Union.

But to understand what Turkmenia is today one has to look into its past. Let us begin with the extensive empire founded by the tribe of Turk-Seldzhuks, which from the eleventh century dominated not only Central Asia but also the Middle East for a whole century. Even Baghdad was part of Seldzhuk's empire at that time, while the Khalif of Baghdad was deprived of political power by the Seldzhuk Sultan Togrul-bek. It was exactly at that time that the disparate tribes of Turks-Oguzes and part of the Karluks and Kipchaks received the common name "Turkmen."

That does not mean, of course, that the process of their ethnic consolidation had really begun at that time. Even in the twentieth century, Turkmens are still divided into tribes that differentiate themselves culturally in everyday life. Each Turkmen tribe has its own dialect and traditional carpet designs. Each tribe also has its particularities in clothes, customs, music, and folklore.

Fleeing Genghis Khan's invading troops, some Turkmen peoples and tribes left for the Near and Middle East. Other tribes ended up in the territory of contemporary Pakistan and India. Tamerlane took away the majority of the territory of modern Turkmenia from Khoresm-Shah after which Timur's ancestors tried for half a century, not without success, to revive the agriculture and crafts that had been decaying since Genghis Khan's invasion.

During the next centuries Turkmens never had their own state. Some tribes were engaged in nomadic and pastoral animal husbandry; others combined agriculture with domestic crafts and fishing on the Caspian Sea. Beginning with the sixteenth century Turkmenia became an arena of long wars between Iran, the Uzbek Khoresm khanate, and the Bukhara emirate that is considered with good reason as their own by both Uzbeks and Tadzhiks. The Turkmen tribes gradually got involved in this struggle not only passively but as active participants, siding with one side or another.

But the wheel of history screechingly turned one more time and a new force appeared in the local political arena in the middle of the nineteenth century: the Russian empire. It had many reasons for becoming interested in its increasingly decrepit neighbor, Central Asia, which had found itself completely left behind by the emerging industrial revolution. Serfdom had just been abolished in Russia, and some of the liberated peasants appeared to be ideal settlers for the recently conquered Central Asian territories. The Civil War in the United States had resulted in the sharp curtailment of cotton imports to Russia, which was now trying to find new sources of raw materials for its textile industry. The Russian empire was aspiring to retrieve, as quickly as possible, some of the international prestige that had been undermined by its defeat in the Crimean War of 1853–56. But the most important factor was probably rivalry with England, which was itself casting lustful glances toward Central Asia and the Transcaucasus. It is not clear what the fate of this huge region would have been if the British Isles had been closer to it, and Her Majesty's emissaries prompter and luckier.

The next stage in Turkmenia's history is called in official Soviet histories "the voluntary joining of Turkmenia with Russia." In fact this "voluntary joining" was carried out as a result of a long military campaign, which Russia undertook with the general aim of conquering Central Asia. The colonial war to get the Turkmen tribes to submit to Russian rule lasted for sixteen years, from 1869 to 1885. After the forcible subjugation of the Bukhara emirate and the Khiva khanate, more than half of the Turkmen tribes that had been under Bukhara's and Khiva's control automatically came under the rule of the Russian crown. The rest doggedly resisted the "voluntary joining," but in 1881, as a result of the storming of the Geok-Tepe fortress, not far from contemporary Ashkhabad, the Russian troops gained their ultimate victory. With a powerful artillery cannonade, about ten thousand of the intractable defenders and residents of the fortress were killed, including, of course, the civilian population.

Strangely enough, Gel'dy knew almost nothing about that. During the hour of our flight from Tashkent to Ashkhabad we talked about everything except the motley past of his once-freedom-loving people. It appeared that the history of the Turkmens did not excite him very much. The boring lies of his high school and college teachers certainly contributed to that. The forthcoming competition of singers and performers called "The Voice of Asia," scheduled to take place that summer in Alma-Ata, was of much greater interest to him. A musical group in which he was a vocalist and drummer was going to take part in that competition.

My brother Oscar, who also was invited to participate in that festival, told me later that the event which most impressed the participants and spectators was not the singers' performances but rather a funny event involving Kazakhstan's Communist Party secretary of ideology. At the ceremony for the opening of the festival, after the mullah read his prayer (which was a sensation in and of itself), the main Communist ideologue of the republic sat down on the floor in the central aisle and asked for some *kumyss*—fermented mare's milk. This action was intended, of course, to demonstrate to the many thousands of young people in the audience the allegiance of the party leadership to folk customs.

Ashkhabad met us with its usual sultriness. After landing we were kept in the plane for a long time. The plane quickly started to heat up, and soon all the passengers were sweating. "You can immediately tell that deodorants are a deficit item here, as well as soap," I commented diplomatically.

"Anywhere but in Turkmenia," Gel'dy responded. "We don't even have rations for food."

"That's great," I said, wondering if perhaps that was the reverse side of the local political system's conservatism.

Someone was having heart pains. Children were crying and gasping for lack of air. A young Russian mother was inculcating the Soviet psychological attitude into her five-year-old son's brain: "Don't you see that everyone else is putting up with it? You must do the same. Why do you think that you are better than others?"

At last someone, apparently from the crew, jumped out the window and brought a ladder, which looked like a metal scaffold for painting walls. The door opened and we tumbled out of the plane.

Outside, however, thanks to the dry climate, it was easier to endure 107 degrees Fahrenheit than 90 degrees in Moscow after a summer rain. Except for our bags, which we had taken with us inside the plane, we had no luggage and did not have to wait for the plane to unload. We came out to the square, and suddenly I felt something strange, as if my memory had just pulled me back twenty years. Around us there were no people, and it was quiet. Kiosks were selling the usual trifles. The antediluvian sparkling-water machines were working as if they were brand new. Even the drinking glasses had not been stolen. Right in front of the roadway leading from the square, there was a gigantic portrait of Lenin with a Turkmenian face, under which was stenciled in huge letters "What vouchsafes our victories is our allegiance to the party!"

I looked around incredulously and stared at Gel'dy. He seemed contented and was obviously happy to come back home.

"Look what's written there!" I laughed, pointing to a red transparency with an idiotic inscription: "To win over through labor—is to strengthen the peace!"

"What's so funny?" Gel'dy got offended. "Are you against the strengthening of peace?"

"No," I answered peacefully, "I am not against it. But who are those one ought to 'win over through labor'?"

"The devil knows!" Gel'dy smiled, seeing that I was not going to demonstrate my Moscow snobbery toward attempts by the local party apparatus to embellish its hometown with visual propaganda.

"Look, empty cabs!" I was amazed by the half-forgotten sight of a line of taxis with checkers on their sides.

"Those are intercity cabs," Gel'dy said, putting a damper on my delight. "They need passengers to the suburbs. And here they are, the private owners. They are waiting to take passengers around the city."

In our cab, the radio was playing loud Azerbaijani music. I was just about to ask the driver to turn it down when he turned it off.

"What's going on?" I asked Gel'dy. "Are cab drivers in your town so considerate of their passengers?"

"Oh, no." Gel'dy laughed. "It's just that we were driving by a cemetery. And when one drives by a cemetery one has to turn off the music."

"Aha," I said. "I haven't seen anything like that, even in the Arab countries. Are people so religious here?"

"Religious? No, it's just a folk custom. Do they treat the deceased without respect in Moscow?"

"Why, no. But people mainly cremate their corpses there."

"What's that?"

"Well, burn them."

"Fascists!" the driver suddenly interrupted. "How can you burn the dead?"

I looked at him, trying to figure out his nationality. From behind and in three-quarter profile he looked like a Persian Azerbaijani; there are many of them on Turkmenia's territory. I decided to take a risk.

"And do you know that your ancestors were fire-worshipers?" I told him. "And that they didn't recognize any other way but burning their dead?"

"What?" The driver blew his top. "We were always Moslems! How dare you insult our faith!"

"That's right, but before Islam," I said in a conciliatory voice. "There was no Islam until the seventh century, and people lived also in the sixth century and in the fifth century and even earlier, you know. They also believed in God. They are not to blame that the Prophet Muhammad (peace be with him) was born centuries later."

"In the Koran nothing is said about what was before it," the driver said with conviction.

"How can you say that nothing is said there?" I objected cautiously. "Just the opposite. Adam and Moses, Noah and Solomon, John the Baptist, and Jesus himself (may peace and the blessings of God be on them all), to say nothing of many others, are messengers of God mentioned in the Holy Book." Here I strained myself trying to recall an appropriate quotation from the Koran. At the university they made us learn by heart a dozen quotations from this book as a requisite for passing. To be sure, my knowledge was not sufficient for a serious religious debate but it should have been enough for a dispute with a cab driver.

"Moreover, as it is said in the Koran"—I coughed and quoted in Arabic and then translated—"For we assuredly send amongst every people a messenger, serve Allah, and avoid evil."

At this moment we drove up to the place to which Gel'dy had asked to be taken when we first got in the cab, and the driver braked sharply.

"Here we are," Gel'dy said joyously, as we simultaneously took out five-ruble bills.

"So you can read the Koran," the driver said with respect, politely pushing away my hand and taking five rubles from Gel'dy. "That could be a good occupation here. You know, at weddings, funerals and so on."

"I'm thinking about it," I answered, and we got out of the car.

Gel'dy's parents were not at home. His mother was on duty for her twenty-four-hour shift at the hospital, where she worked as a doctor, and his father had been invited to a wedding. We learned all that from Gel'dy's elder sister Leila, which means "Night." She was holding her six-month-old daughter, Sel'bi, in her hands. The baby was constantly moving because of an oversupply of energy: clenching and unclenching her tiny fingers, jerking her hands and legs, rolling her head in order to reach some objects that attracted her attention, and making funny grimaces at the same time.

In contrast to the heat of the street it was rather cool in the semi-darkness of the house. In the hot regions of Central Asia, the custom is to hang heavy curtains over the windows, opening them only after sunset to let in the night coolness. During the last ten years air-conditioning units made in Baku, the capital of Azerbaijan, under a Japanese patent have been installed in some houses. But like any other home appliances, they have always been a deficit item, and since the beginning of the war between Azerbaijan and Armenia, they have completely disappeared from stores. The Bairamovs had air-conditioning but they had no telephone. However, they didn't turn on the air-conditioning because they were afraid that little Sel'bi would catch a cold.

Gel'dy's parents lived in a large old apartment building. Once upon a time, in the beginning of the sixties, it was probably considered a prestigious home. It was a five-story building, without an elevator, made of iron and concrete paneling, which in the Soviet Union is the staple material for constructing many-storied buildings. Brick is only for the top *nomenklatura* families.

Gel'dy's family's apartment consisted of three smallish rooms, an antechamber, a small kitchen, the bathroom, and a large glassed-in balcony. "That's where I'd better ask to stay," I decided, for all the main rooms were obviously overpopulated. One of them served as the master bedroom; in the second bedroom, Leila and her husband and daughter were living temporarily; in the third room, which also served as a living room, Gel'dy himself slept. Besides that, a relative from Khoresm province also lived in their apartment. She was a fourteen-year-old girl who did not know a word of Russian. She had just recently arrived from a far-off village and was very shy with me. As far as I understood she was here playing Cinderella's role, for the Bairamovs had evidently brought her here to help Leila nurse little Sel'bi. But she did not seem to consider it an onerous task, for in Central Asia such work is quite normal for teenagers, and it was clear that she preferred to live in the city rather than in her village. Her name was Nargiz, which means "Lotus." Like many girls from the country-side she had no idea of her own beauty and therefore behaved quite naturally, that is, with the awkward grace of a colt. She washed her niece's diapers and was quite satisfied with her existence.

Unlike taciturn Nargiz, Leila not only spoke perfect Russian but she also judged everything firmly and rather sharply. She looked as though she was just twenty years old, and in fact she was even younger, but one could feel that she had an exceptional personality and had had some extraordinary experiences for a young Turkmen woman. Turkmenia is the only republic of the Soviet Union where the absolute majority of women still wear long traditional dresses that have been invariably in fashion for the last thousand years. When they come to Moscow Turkmen women look rather exotic, but in Turkmenia itself people stare at those who are dressed otherwise. Like every-where in Central Asia and the Transcaucasus, married women must appear in public with covered heads. The last custom, however, is ubiquitously ignored, especially in the towns. Still, the village women and town women from traditionalist families continue to wear ker-chiefs or tuck their hair under light scarfs.

"Go find father and tell him that our guest has already arrived," she ordered Gel'dy in the self-assured voice of an elder sister.

"Where will I find him?" Gel'dy replied. "And what if the wed-ding is out of town?"

"He left the phone number of people who know where the wed-ding is," Leila said. "Go, call from a pay phone."

"Wait," I said. "There's no rush. It's only four o'clock, and the wedding is sure to begin in the evening. Perhaps Gel'dy wants to take a shower and have something to eat."

"What shower?" Leila laughed. "In this time of day we never have enough water pressure in the pipes. But we do store water in cisterns, so he can rinse himself."

"Then don't use up all the water," I said. "I'll go next."

After we drank some tea and ate some grapes I had bought from private vendors on our way to the house, Leila succeeded in motivat-ing her brother to look for their father and began to interrogate me about everyday life in Moscow. At the same time she went on skillfully interacting with little Sel'bi—putting something in her hands, taking away some toy that Sel'bi was trying to put into her mouth, changing her diapers, giving her some boiled water to drink. Nargiz was sitting silently in an armchair in front of us and did not participate in the conversation.

At first, I did not intend to get involved in long conversations, for I was tired after the road and all that heat. Looking from time to time in the direction of the cool balcony with its air-conditioning, I was ready to attempt a polite escape from protocol and go have a good nap for several hours.

But in the course of our conversation I soon sensed that my interlocutor's mentality differed very much from a typical Central Asian woman's way of thinking. There was the unmistakable influence of some other, nonlocal culture in her behavior, her intonations and gestures—to be more precise, of an urban youth subculture, but not Moscow's or St. Petersburg's, and yet particularly not that of Kiev but most probably of some Russian provincial place. She was, after all, the granddaughter of an outstanding person, of the president of the republic who had dared once in his life not to obey Moscow's order. And so I decided not to hurry and to get involved in the conversation in earnest. Unlike the conceited *nomenklatura* children, the children and grandchildren of the former president of Turkmenia did not make a big deal of their background. The moment he fell out of favor with Moscow he lost all his *nomenklatura* privileges, and so did his offspring.

It is noteworthy that the mutinous gene that the KGB discovered in the DNA molecule of the disgraced statesman for some reason was inherited only by his granddaughter. In any case, unlike Leila, her brother Gel'dy and his parents, to whom I was soon introduced, impressed me as rather complaisant and unpretentious people. It is difficult to say what Leila's ambitions were, but she evidently felt restricted by the circumstances of her life. Hers was a character with a surplus of passion and revolutionary stirrings, as a result of which instead of peacefully getting her college degree in her hometown of Ashkhabad, she found herself for some reason in the small town of Redkino ("Radishville") in the Moscow area.

"And what were you doing there?" I asked, surprised.

"I was studying," Leila answered.

"What were you studying, if it's not a secret?"

"Personal computer operating. There was a professional-technical school there that offered a degree in personal-computer operation."

"What computer systems were you taught?" I asked.

"IBM and Macintosh," Leila answered.

"Which one do you prefer?"

"I don't know," she said. "They didn't really give us any idea of what it was all about. The only thing we mastered were computer games."

"Well, that's something," I said, "if one remembers that the majority of your republic's inhabitants have never seen a computer in their lives."

"Have they seen a computer in Russia?" Leila asked defiantly. "Perhaps, only in Moscow."

"You didn't like to study there?" I asked.

"No!" Leila responded resolutely. "They don't like ethnic minorities there. Petrov, the director of the vocational school, was a rascal. Once he said to me and my friend Sanya, a Kazakh girl from Alma-Ata, 'Why did you come here? It would be better if you stayed at home to graze your sheep; there would be more sense in that.'"

At that moment Gel'dy appeared on the threshold and announced, "I found Father! Let's go, he's waiting for us."

30

Bukhara Carpets with Anchors

Leila and Gel'dy's father, Bairam Bairamov, son of the ex-president of Turkmenia, had an unusual hobby. He was an amateur cook.

"Big deal!" you will exclaim. "What's so strange about that? Everybody considers himself an amateur cook. You yourself told us something about pilaf on the bank of a river."

"But wait a minute," I reply. "Bairam Bairamov doesn't cook just for his family or for a party of half a dozen friends; he cooks for one thousand or fifteen hundred people at once. He cooks for weddings, and people consider themselves really lucky if they succeed in getting him for such an occasion. All his summers and autumns are booked three months ahead of time. After the secretary of the local Committee of the CPSU, the bride's and bridegroom's parents, and of course the newlyweds themselves, he's the most respected person at a wedding."

Oh, yes, a wedding in a village is a great event, which for the local residents overshadows absolutely everything not connected with it, including the news of the world. People talk about a wedding long before the appointed day and often recall it long after it has ended. In some exceptional cases, grandiose and outstanding wedding celebrations rise to the status of historical events for the inhabitants of a village, becoming a reference point in the local calendar. "Don't you remember, it was the summer when the foreman Amandurdy married his son who almost ran over our camel with his tractor?" a wife might remember in the middle of winter. And a husband, dreamily closing his eyes, would immediately echo, "Of course I remember! You are talking about that wedding when a guest from Moscow with a camera that flashes with lightning came to see the cook from Ashkhabad? Oh, the meat was really good that day. And the musicians were playing so fast that stupid Annapes fell while dancing and broke his ankle."

Bairam Bairamov has a melancholic personality, the temperament of an Eastern mage. Certainly he works at a scientific research institute, where he is an engineer and earns a modest salary. But in truth an historian is imprisoned inside this man, just as an artist is imprisoned in Vova Liberman's father-in-law from Chuvashia.

Bairam stood in a white apron before bubbling caldrons, stirring their contents with a long-handled spoon. We had become acquainted just half an hour before. I was interested in his views about what was going on in Turkmenia, but he was more absorbed by global problems.

"There's another tempo of life here," he remarked philosophically. "No one is in a hurry. In Moscow you are always hurrying because you are afraid to be late, knowing how big and accessible is the world. And we live as if in another dimension, practically behind a little iron curtain. No one has a good idea here about how people live in other parts of the country. To say nothing about other parts of the world. Or perhaps they don't want to know, so as not to get upset. Just look what the local newspapers and television are saying. Do you know that we have an almost official censorship on the most popular shows on Central television?"

He told me that national broadcasting stops after the evening news show "Vremya" ("Time"), which presents the official point of view of the Soviet government about what is happening in the country and abroad, so that the local viewers will not see and hear how far the quasi-independent showmen could go if unrestricted. (The best shows from Moscow, in terms of real information, are broadcast late at night.)

In front of a clay hearth, under the caldrons, a bundle of old newspapers for kindling was piled on the floor. I bent down and pulled out one of them at random. It was a copy of the *Evening*

Ashkhabad from March 12, 1990, just four months old. "TO BE A COMMUNIST IS MY CHERISHED DREAM!" one of the headlines informed us. I looked through the text and read, "The perestroika generation enters the CPSU. Perestroika gives birth to a new party vanguard..."

"Even *Pravda* gave up this style about three years ago," I said. "What kind of readers are they thinking of? Aren't they ashamed of themselves for publishing such nonsensical stories?"

"They are thinking of us," Bairam said with a melancholy air, "as of the residents of Socialist Turkestan. The most stable republic among the brotherly republics of the Soviet Union."

"But what's the secret of that stability?" I asked. "According to the Moscow press, 40 percent of the workers and 50 percent of the peasant families here live under the official poverty level. In your republic there is the highest death rate among children in the country: fifty out of every thousand die. For comparison, in Japan just five out of a thousand die."

"What does it have to do with Japan?" Bairam was surprised. "They suffered from nuclear blasts in Hiroshima and Nagasaki but they didn't have such a political system as we have. Our system fits ideally for the purpose of monopolization of all spheres of governing and human life by the ruling elite. Or rather, it's the other way around: they created that system, having accommodated it to their needs."

"I believe that they have invented nothing new," I said, smiling doubtfully. "It's just that Central Asia still is in the stage of feudalism in the realm of politics."

Bairam nodded, continuing to fiddle with his spoon. "That's exactly the case. The relations between all political bosses and their subordinates on any level are built on a medieval pattern: the power of a superior is absolute and it's sacred for the junior. The mechanism of interaction works in one direction only: from above downward. Those who are below can't affect those who are above them, not because they don't want to but because it's impossible in principle. And as far as Communist cant is concerned—does it really confuse you? What's important is that a real mechanism of power stands behind it and quite real people operate it. And they would never give up their positions. When was it ever the case in the East that people voluntarily abrogated their power?"

Well, in the West, too," I said, "people are reluctant to give up power. But the political system there rests on different principles. Rotation of political leadership, relative accountability of the lawmakers, or rather their electability, at least."

"But that's what our party bosses are afraid of above all," Bairam said. "That's why they don't allow any meetings or the creation of popular fronts."

"Can it be that in all of Turkmenia there's no other public political organization except for the local Communist Party?"

Bairam objected. "Well, there's the Komsomol, and the children's pioneer organization named after Lenin."

"No, I'm serious," I said, laughing. "I was told in Moscow that in Ashkhabad there's a historian named Marat Durdyev who is attempting to create here either a popular front or an informal organization like Aghzy-Birlik."

"Oh, I know," Bairam replied. "They meet in the building of the Knowledge Society." The Knowledge Society is a government organization devoted to the advancement of science. "Once they even tried to organize a rally in front of a monument to Makhtumkuli [the Walt Whitman of Turkmenia], but the local police and the KGB broke it up. You are well informed. How do you know about that, if I may ask?"

"It's not a secret," I said. "I heard about this person from my Azerbaijani friends in Moscow. And my friends in Alma-Ata and Tashkent told me about Aghzy-Birlik."

"They are Pan-Turkists, aren't they?" Bairam said, showing interest. "Are you a Pan-Turkist, too?"

"No," I answered, "I'm a Westernizer. Incidentally, they are not Pan-Turkists either, at least not in the political sense. Now only political romantics allow themselves to talk about a unified Turkic state. One may only discuss this idea theoretically. It's as difficult to realize it in practice as any other beautiful utopia. Those who have in their hands any real power in this region are not interested in the creation of such a state in the first place. The most ambitious goal that might be achieved in the near future is that the republics of Central Asia would sign contracts about the direct supply of each other with certain kinds of agricultural production, bypassing Moscow's intervention."

"Moscow wasn't built in a day," Bairam said. "While the Baltics are fighting for their political independence and the Caucasians are waging fratricidal wars, the cunning Asiatic rulers are winning step-by-step more and more economic independence."

He wiped sweat from his forehead and beckoned a Turkmen woman standing nearby.

"Go tell the hosts to bring another portion of sliced meat," he asked her in Turkmen.

It was more difficult for me to understand spoken Turkmen than Uzbek, Kirghiz, or even Azerbaijan. I was not used to either its sound or its grammar, although some words common in all the Turkic languages were absolutely familiar.

"And do you know that his elder brother is the Soviet Union's ambassador to Bolivia?" Bairam asked unexpectedly.

"Whose brother?" I didn't get at first who he was talking about.

"Well, you have asked me about the historian named Marat Durdyev," Bairam explained impatiently. "His elder brother, Tahir Durdyev, is the Soviet Union's ambassador to Bolivia."

"A funny coincidence," I said. "They have the same name as my brother and I. But these are not Turkmen names."

"Their mother is Tartar," Bairam said.

Meanwhile, the guests were arriving. I left Bairam and went for a walk around the scene of the approaching feast. It was a large vacant plot of land on which stood several rows of tables with long benches on either side. At the end was a truck trailer that had been transformed into a brightly lit stage for the musicians. They had already turned on their equipment, which included "light-music"—a special appliance consisting of hundreds of electric bulbs that were shining with all the colors of the rainbow, turning on and off in time to the rhythm of the music. The band played very loudly, with equipment suitable for big concerts like those that the Moscow rockers loved to give a few years ago at overcrowded stadiums.

The bride and the bridegroom had not arrived yet, but I saw Gel'dy's face flash in the crowd. He hustled through the crowd toward me.

"So, how's it going?" he asked.

"I have been to Uzbek, Tadzhik, Russian, Tartar, Kazakh, Armenian, Korean, and even Greek weddings, but I have never been to a Turkmen wedding before."

"Well, there won't be anything special," Gel'dy said. "First they'll sit at the tables and stuff themselves, then they'll start dancing."

"But it's that way everywhere," I told him. And then I asked, "But will they fight? At Russian weddings sometimes they also fight after the dances."

"No, we're strict about that," Gel'dy promised. "You can't even approach young women here. But of course we communicate all the same." And he laughed.

"So how do people dance, then?"

"We dance side by side but without touching each other," Gel'dy explained. "You'll see for yourself soon."

The guests rather quickly sat themselves at the tables, or rather the men did; strangely, the women were still standing. They crowded around the tables and watched the men eat. All of them were wearing long closed velvet dresses of dark blue, cherry, or green, all cut from absolutely the same pattern: a rounded closed collar, some embroidery on the chest, a little bit more near the waist, and then—straight down to the floor. Turkmen women are considered to be the most beautiful in Central Asia, and there were quite a few beautiful, almost doll-like women's faces in the crowd.

One Western traveler who spent fourteen months in captivity in a Turkmen tribe in the 1860s wrote that Turkmen respected their women more than other Moslems, but all the same the women had a lot of work to do. Every day they had to grind grain for the family's meals. Besides cooking, Turkmen women wove silk and wool, sewed, knitted, made felt, carried water, washed and painted silk and wool, and, most important, made carpets. Many of these responsibilities are still obligatory for village women today.

As is well known, marriages in Turkmen tribes were formerly made as purchases. A father, or, if he was not alive, a brother or a nearer relation on the father's side of the family, sold a woman, often before she came of age. Now, in accordance with the Turkmen republic's laws on marriage and the family, marriage is defined as "a voluntary union of two parties, based on mutual love, with the goal of establishing a family," and eighteen is considered the legal age for marriage.

Naturally, this law is violated like all other Soviet laws. During the time of stagnation, Brezhnev's era, that was one of the few sensational news items allowed in the central press. About once every two or three years there would be an item in one of the major Soviet newspapers about the "feudal elements" in the life-style of some petty Central Asian boss who started a second family or married a woman who was not of age.

Despite Gel'dy's prediction, everything was remarkable at this wedding. The newlyweds were very young and timid and touchingly ashamed to so much as look at each other. Or they pretended to be ashamed. Probably in three and a half years they will have at least four children. A secretary from the district party committee took the microphone away from the singers, extracted a bundle of paper from the inner pocket of his jacket, and began a long, confused speech. After the first forty minutes, no one listened to him.

"What is he talking about?" I asked Gel'dy, with whom I sat at the far end of the table.

"About the district's achievements in socialist competitions," Gel'dy replied, adding, "He looks exactly like Fidel Castro, only he has no beard."

It was clear from this reference that Gel'dy, like most Soviet people, believed that Cubans sincerely enjoy listening to the hours-long speeches of their leader.

Then people started bringing the food that Gel'dy's father had cooked. The main course consisted of deep-fried pieces of meat, with a lot of fat, followed by chicken cooked the same way.

The next day was Sunday, and so Bairam did not have to go to his state job. As I supposed, I got the glassed-in balcony as my bedroom for the night. The bed was made right on the floor, but I was quite comfortable, especially since I was allowed to turn on the air-conditioning, which worked almost noiselessly.

In the morning my bedroom was transformed into the dining room; all that needed to be done was to fold the bed and put it in the corner. When I returned from the bathroom, a clean tablecloth was laid on the floor, and our plain breakfast was awaiting us. Unlike yesterday's exotic fare, it was a standard Soviet affair: hard-boiled eggs, bread, butter, and sausage.

"Can one really buy all that in your stores?" I tactlessly asked. In the East such questions are considered to be impolite.

"One can get anything," Bairam said dryly. After yesterday's work at the caldrons, he looked tired and sleepy. Despite the fact that it was early in the morning, it was rather hot in the street and by mutual agreement we lay at the table with naked torsos. Not being in the habit I found it rather difficult to eat while lying down, and so I sat in a Turkish manner with my legs crossed under me. But even so I was not comfortable, and I started to get pins and needles. Bairam, on the contrary, easily managed without table and chair and even delivered a little speech about the advantages of eating on the floor.

"Why aren't the others eating with us?" I asked.

"Gel'dy's still sleeping," Bairam replied, "and the women have already eaten."

Bairam's wife returned from her duties early in the morning, and was terribly surprised to find an unknown person sleeping on her balcony. But then, having made sure that all the members of her household were safe and sound and peacefully asleep in other rooms, she reasonably decided not to make a ruckus and to let events unfold on their own. Bairam had forgotten to tell her about my visit—or perhaps he did it on purpose, since his wife did not approve of some of her husband's acquaintances. Dubious characters they were, from her point of view. After we introduced ourselves, she excused herself and went to bed, for her night in the hospital had been rather tiresome.

At teatime I praised the carpets; the apartment was full of them. In Turkmenia, unlike Russia, they are not considered as objects of luxury, because quite often they take the place of all other furniture. Bairam, a walking Turkmenian encyclopedia, overwhelmed me with information about Turkmenian carpet weaving, its history and the present-day state of the industry.

The manual techniques used to produce carpets here have not changed very much. As Bairam told me, in the old days the carpets were woven outside. For that purpose a special appliance made of poles was dug in the ground. Women wove with the help of two big crossbeams on which a woof was fixed. Carpets were woven with an iron tool consisting of five or six plates arranged like a comb. Each family had its own design, which was passed from one generation to another, from mother to daughter. Bairam told me that some Turkmen clans living near the Caspian Sea included images of anchors in the designs of their carpets.

I told him, "Most people believe that Turkmens are inhabitants of the deserts, whose only occupation is the breeding of horses and camels."

"Nothing of the sort," he replied. "Turkmens, especially those who lived on the shores of the Caspian Sea, were always fishermen. They went out in the sea on board their small fishing boats and using primitive tackle caught sturgeon. Then they sold it to Persian merchants or to Russian merchants from Astrakhan, and also ate it themselves in large quantities. They even stored it for the winter."

"Did they store fresh or salted fish?" I asked.

"Neither, they stored fried fish, fried in caldrons of fish oil until the fish became red. And then it was stuffed into fish bladders and dug into the ground for storage. So, not all the Turkmen tribes were engaged in carpet weaving. Some members of the agricultural and urban populations never did it. They simply bought their carpets."

"And what's the difference between Turkmen and Bukhara carpets?" I asked.

"There is no difference," Bairam informed me. "The so-called Bukhara carpets are basically Turkmen carpets. They were named so in the times when some of the Turkmen tribes were subjects of the Bukhara emirate. Bukhara merchants simply bought them and then sold them in Russia and Europe, putting their own name on them."

Then I asked, "Is it true that the Turkmens found oil even before Turkmenia became a Russian colony?"

"Yes," he replied, "and quite extensively, too. By the beginning of the nineteenth century, about sixteen hundred tons of oil a year were being exported, mainly to Persia, in exchange for wheat and fabrics."

"How did they get it? There were no derricks at that time, were there?"

"Very easy," he answered. "They got it from wells. There were more than three thousand of them. The technique was quite simple indeed: the wells were dug in a primitive way, not very deep. The edges of these wells often crumbled, and the holes got very dirty. Turkmens delivered their oil themselves, too. They brought it in barges to the Persian coast. Wood for building their ships they obtained from Iran, and after they established relations with Russia, from Astrakhan."

I also found out from Bairam that during the first years after the

Bolsheviks came to power Ashkhabad was renamed Poltoratsk, after one of the Communist leaders who had been in charge of the bolshevization of Central Asia, along with a commander named Frunze. By a caprice of Stalin, the capital of Kirghizia remained Frunze, while Ashkhabad received its ancient name again (with the addition of one letter: formerly it was Askhabad; now it is Ashkhabad).

In the afternoon we went to see the historian Durdyev, but he was not at home. We met his mother, an affable person. Unlike Bairam, who lived in a state apartment, the Durdyevs had a big house that stood among shady trees deep in the yard behind a high stone fence. The hostess's name was Mariam. She offered us tea and started a light and clever conversation. I asked her when her son would get home, and she replied that it would not be soon.

"In the evening?" I asked.

"No," she responded. Then she looked straight into my eyes and added, "Maybe in a month. Maybe later." She must have seen the question forming in my mind, for she calmly said, "They put him in a madhouse."

On our way back we had to wait for a taxi for a long time. Perhaps because of the terrible heat the streets looked absolutely desolate.

"What do you think?" I asked Bairam. "Is he really sick, or is it a preventive action against an active supporter of perestroika?"

"From the point of view of the local authorities, they are the same thing," Bairam answered imperturbably.

"But then why is his mother so calm?"

"Don't forget that she has four sons," Bairam answered, placing a stress on the word "four." " And one of them is an ambassador of the Soviet Union. Do you understand how important it is for Turkmens that one of them represents the empire on the world arena? Besides Russians, only Ukrainians, Christianized Jews, Tartars, and Armenians have been Soviet ambassadors so far."

"No," I objected. "Uzbeks, for instance, have served as Soviet ambassadors as well, to Syria and to Sri Lanka. But what does this have to do with Durdyev's mother?"

Bairam was surprised at my dullness. "She's a statesman's mother. That is her dominant identity. It means that anything that the state does is right. And with all her mind and all her heart she's on the alert to defend the interests of her 'main' son."

"With her mind—yes," I said, ruminating, "but with her heart—no! You don't know Tartar women well."

A day later I saw Grisha Rybin at the entrance to Ashkhabad's store for military personnel. We were both so stunned by our encounter that for several moments we were poised like two giant lizards, ready to duel over territory. But instead we smiled from ear to ear and started patting each other on the back and shoulders and saying a lot of cheerful nonsense. We had last seen each other exactly twelve years ago. Grisha was at that time serving as a military doctor in a small garrison situated in the middle of a white-hot desert about fifty miles from the Caspian port of Krasnovodsk.

By some twist of fate I fell into this military unit twice in my life, and each time for half a year. And all this because in my military card under the heading "Military-educational profession" it said "Arabic interpreter." In accordance with the law of compulsory military service the district military committees could conscript any Soviet citizen as a reservist regardless of whether he had already put in a full term of military service or not.

The first time I got into this mess was while I was still studying at the university. At that time our whole student group got caught, and the district military command cruelly cheated us. They told us that they were just calling us up for a two-week military training program which we were going to have to go through anyway the following summer. "So you might as well do it in the winter so as not to spoil your summer vacation," a gray-haired colonel told us, smiling in a fatherly way. "Don't take anything with you but a toothbrush."

And we, six twenty-year-old fools, went to the military unit with nothing but our light briefcases, which were just becoming fashionable at that time thanks to Sean Connery, and we got stuck there for six long months. Once we had slipped into the tenacious embrace of the Soviet Army it was not easy for us to break loose. When the Egyptians finished their studies, we were sent to war with them, for what was called "a probationary period."

In a year we came back, but we had hardly enough time to finish our university studies before we were called up again, this time for two years; and once more they sent us as military interpreters to Egypt. The second time, though, I was luckier—I did not go to the front. Because I was at the 2+ level, I was appointed as nothing less than an interpreter for the military adviser at the commanding headquarters of military aviation. The commander there in those years was Hosni Mubarak, now the president of Egypt. Because of my young age I did not understand that I was observing an outstanding statesman and the future ally of the United States in Operation Desert Storm. At that time what I liked most about him was that he taught me how to play squash and even gave me as a present a squash outfit and an excellent racket.

But it was not Hosni Mubarak I met at the entrance of the military shop but Dr. Grisha Rybin, so let us return from far-off Egypt to visit no less far-off Krasnovodsk.

I was happy to see my old acquaintance. "How did you come to be here?" he asked me, as for the twenty-fifth time he pounded my back with his enormous fist.

"Gorbachev is to blame!" I exclaimed, hitting Grisha's shoulder with the same camaraderie. "Who are you for—Gorbachev or Yeltsin?"

"I'm for Yeltsin," Grisha answered without pondering. An angry young man came up to us and said, "Comrades, don't block the way."

"Aren't you hot in your jacket?" I asked him affably, after which Grisha and I walked away and stood in the shadow of a tall plane tree.

"They have guns under their jackets," Grisha informed me.

"Do you carry a weapon?" I asked.

"What for? I'm a doctor," Grisha replied. "Although there is one in the storeroom at the sergeant's."

"He surely sold it a long time ago to Armenians or Azerbaijanis," I joked. "So, are you still serving in Krasnovodsk?"

"Where else? That is, not in our military unit outside the city, but in a military hospital in Krasnovodsk itself. As you see I'm already a captain; soon I may become a major, and then I can retire."

"Who will let you go?" I laughed. "Everyone loves you, you know."

"My wife loves me, too," Grisha announced proudly.

So at last he had married! He was always dreaming about someone like the Decembrists' wives, who followed their husbands to Siberia, someone who would share with him all the vicissitudes of fate.

"Only she lives with her parents, in Astrakhan," he said as if he had intuited my thoughts. "She says that she can't spend more than three days in Krasnovodsk. So we fly to see each other: she flies to me, I fly to her."

"Well, this guarantees a permanent honeymoon until your retirement," I said encouragingly. "What are you doing in Ashkhabad?" I asked, suddenly recalling that we were 350 miles from Krasnovodsk.

"Now we take our patients to Ashkhabad and not to Baku," Grisha responded.

"Are you telling me that you brought someone in a Red Army ambulance to Ashkhabad, and now you are going back to Krasnovodsk?"

31

The Iron Smile of Krasnovodsk

When I was in school, I always thought that the name of the city of Krasnovodsk (that is, Red Water City) was a rousing revolutionary metaphor. However, when I visited there for the first time, I immediately understood that I had been in error. The water flowing from the water taps there was in fact reddish-brown, apparently caused by rust or some other compound. Because of this water, Krasnovodsk natives and residents all have bad teeth and unhealthy skin. But one had to cherish even such awful water, because it was severely rationed, especially in the summer. In our military unit, for example, the water only operated one hour in the early morning and one hour late in the evening, which at summertime temperatures of more than 113 degrees Fahrenheit drove me crazy. But then I bought a large pot that held almost four gallons, and I cooled my rage by pouring the stored water over myself at any time of day. After that, the fact that sand crunched in my teeth could be considered a minor discomfort.

The main problem in Krasnovodsk was not lack of water, however, but the evil dispositions of the worst segment of the local population. The authorities for some reason selected this city for administrative exile of the "non-working element." Moscow was considered the "model Communist city." But many people lived there who, from the point of view of the authorities, were unworthy of Moscow residence permits: prostitutes, alcoholics, and people who avoided "socially useful labor"—or, for example, those who, after being released from imprisonment in corrective labor camps, had been deprived of the right to live in large cities. Those were the people who were exiled to Krasnovodsk.

The drive from Ashkhabad to Krasnovodsk took about ten hours, but in spite of the vicious heat, I spent those hours feeling completely comfortable. The military license plates and the red cross painted on the dark green sides of the car kept to a minimum the possibility of undesirable delays on the road. I even took a nap on the litter that was set in the car like a narrow hospital cot. But we spent most of the time in conversation. We spoke about our common acquaintances, of whom almost none were still in the garrison; about the horrible times that we were all living through; about the plague infecting our economy, and about the epileptic fits afflicting the political life of Moscow.

In Krasnovodsk itself, in Grisha's words, life was virtually unchanged.

"Because previously it was worse than anywhere else, so we were better prepared for perestroika than anyone,"he joked mirthlessly. But in comparison with civilians, it had previously been a little easier for the military, because in little stores on the unit grounds they sometimes delivered some food and industrial goods that the residents of the surrounding area had never heard of. Now even that no longer happened.

"But how do the people live? Why are they so patient?" I asked, almost rhetorically. "Apparently this is their only life; there will not be another one."

"But who worries about that?" answered Grisha. "When you don't have the basics, no one thinks about lofty matters. The soul is covered with scabs and scars; it hardens, and people become evil and aggressive."

"What does 'aggressive' mean from the point of view of medicine?" I asked. "Does it mean that people are manufacturing additional hormones?"

"Of course," answered Grisha. "Testosterone levels in saliva have become several times higher than the norm. That used to be the reason people drank alcohol, and now drinking has become a problem. Now there is more home brew, or people poison themselves with chemicals."

We recalled a senior lieutenant who died in his sleep. He had drunk until he lost consciousness, then began to vomit and choked to death.

"This was suicide," I said. "His wife didn't want to leave Moscow, so she wouldn't lose her residence permit and her job. He had no prospect of advancement in rank. You see, he was already past thirty, but he had only progressed to senior lieutenant. They did not discharge him from the army because he had not served his allotted time. And he began consciously to destroy himself. Like a Manichaean."

"Well, if everyone is so quick to take offense, who will serve in the army?" Grisha observed philosophically. "Who are these Manichaeans—some sort of national group or what?"

"No, they were followers of a religion in Central Asia," I said. "The people believed that their real life is ahead of them, and that the present life is only an annoying delay on the way to the future. And so they destroyed themselves by all available means in order to get to heaven more quickly."

"Just like us," sighed Grisha. "Seventy years have destroyed our country for the sake of the bright future."

"No," I said. "We are God's chosen people. All the other peoples should see in our example that it is impossible to go this way. An experiment that ends in a negative result is just as valuable as one with a positive result."

Grisha laughed. "I don't remember that I agreed to let someone conduct experiments upon me."

"You're not thinking like an army doctor," I said, making my diagnosis. "It is immediately obvious that you have studied in Leningrad."

"No." Grisha shrugged his shoulders. "I think that everything would have been different if Lenin's teachings had not been distorted. The old man was largely right and foresaw many of today's catastrophes. But he was not listened to, and here is the result. And don't argue with me." He laughed, having seen that I had opened my mouth for further debate. "I am an inflexible Leninist."

"Inflexibility is a sign of paralysis," I said angrily, but I did not try to continue arguing. Everyone has the right to his own point of view. The main thing is not to be shot for it. Everything else can be endured.

Of all the cities in the Soviet Union, Krasnovodsk is the least appealing for tourism. Its main attractions are the oil industry workers' palace of culture, built after World War II by Japanese prisoners; a three-story hotel, the Krasnovodsk, built in the 1970s by Soviet prisoners; a couple of movie theaters in which teenagers are usually fighting; three seedy restaurants where the local criminals and frightened out-of-towners go; and, of course, the seaport, with a ferry crossing to Baku. In the downtown district, made up of two and a half streets, there are large apartment buildings, mainly two- and three-story ones, also of postwar construction, and therefore, as they say in the U.S.S.R., "without amenities." The facilities are outside in the yard.

The population of Krasnovodsk is quite a varied mixture, and Turkmenians here are a clear minority. Russians first settled here in 1715, sent by Peter the Great, who was searching for a way from the Lower Volga to Central Asia and India. A detachment led by Prince Bekovitch-Cherkassky built a fortress here and moved on. However, the khan of Khiva, by the name of Shirghazi, immediately grasped the threat posed to him by his great white neighbor. He defeated the Russian detachment and sold the survivors into slavery, except for Prince Bekovitch-Cherkassky, whose head he ordered to be cut off. Thanks to this uncivilized behavior, the Russian occupation of the Transcaspia was put off for another one and a half centuries. In the first half of the nineteenth century the Russian empire revived its so-called scientific expeditions to the eastern shore of the Caspian Sea, which, as Soviet sources now acknowledge, really had a military and political purpose.

Stepping onto the square in front of the Krasnovodsk oil industry workers' palace of culture where I used to walk, and breathing the familiar smells of rotted fish that the hot gusts of wind brought from nearby canning factories, I almost thought, "Home, sweet home." But I happened to remember, and with a great sense of relief, that this time I was only a visitor here.

I spent the night at Grisha's in his bachelor's furnished apartment, and the following morning, before first light, the screeching whine of small motors woke me up. In my half-awake state, it seemed to me that a team of Lilliputian prisoners was felling the forest with toy chainsaws. But then I remembered that although in the Krasnovodsk Province there were a great number of corrective labor institutions, there was no forest and none expected in the near future. I looked out the window and saw that the motors were mounted on gasoline-powered model airplanes, tethered to strings, which were wailing about in circles. Several adults and about two dozen children were flying them, most likely a club of young airplane-model makers. The government always encouraged technical creativity in children, since in any such crowd could be standing the inventors and engineers of the future, whose talents could come in handy for the military-industrial complex. In the Soviet Union many leading figures of science and technology were born far from Moscow or Leningrad, in just such joyless population centers as Krasnovodsk.

Newcomers have always ruled Moscow and, consequently, the whole country. That rule applies not only to the party and political elite but to every area of human activity—military affairs, science, technology, the arts. Maybe that is why so many of our leading public figures combine in themselves natural talent, assertiveness, and vital energy with a low level of inner culture, and with cruelty and indifference to the destinies of their fellow citizens as individuals.

From the point of view of biology that is easy to understand: if these self-made, or party-made, men had reflected upon and sighed over each broken flower (that is, every extinct species, polluted river, ruined forest, every Chernobyl, every ethnic group of the U.S.S.R. plunged into catastrophe), they would not have fought their way to the top of the imperial pyramid, but humbly stood in lines for vodka with their fellows in their native Krasnovodsks and other Soviet Peorias. But on the other hand, we now see to what a deplorable condition "the children of the scullery maids" and their posterity have brought the country, after governing it for many decades. Russia continues to live in hopes of an "enlightened monarch," but where to find him? Can he grow up in the provincial cities, where all hope for an enlightened life has been extinguished?

I said good-bye to Grisha, who had to go to work, and I left for the port in order to buy a ticket on the ferry to go by sea to Baku. As strange as it seems, I managed to do this almost without any problem. Perhaps it can be explained by the fact that the ferry still goes six or seven times a day, as it did formerly, although the number of passengers has declined. Just a few years ago many automobile drivers used this passage as the shortest and most convenient route from Central Asia to the Transcaucasus and the Caucasus. Today, of all the cars waiting for the ferry, I did not see a single Central Asian license number, or even one from Moscow or Tashkent.

The ferry was a large, clumsy ship, which could carry slightly more than two hundred passengers. I counted about fifty passenger cars. There were no tickets for either two- or four-seater cabins, but I was not particularly annoyed by that. First of all, you never know what kind of group you will end up in. Second, to go by sea took only thirteen hours, so it was possible to manage without sleep, since my third-class ticket provided me only with a chair. We were supposed to arrive in Baku around eleven o'clock at night. The main thing was not to be late, since my friends in Baku told me that their curfew was very strictly observed.

Poorly dressed, surly men, women old before their time and worn out from a joyless life, children with the eyes of downtrodden old men—these were the companions on this voyage. Everyone was going somewhere, hoping for something, wanting something, which meant that they were all unique and interesting people. But there was something like an invisible barrier between me and them, alienating me from everything that constituted the essence of their lives. Strolling on the deck and exchanging random glances with them, I saw enmity and mistrust in their eyes. Was I an alien to them? Sometimes it is easier for people of one cultural level to find common ground with each other, even if they are from different countries, than with their own countrymen from different social classes. As never before, I suddenly felt my foreignness, the complete irrelevance of my life experience with regard to the attitudes and values of the passengers on this ship. In order to soothe the painful feeling of loneliness arising in my soul, I began to remember everything I could about the next destination of my journey: Azerbaijan.

I did not know its ancient and medieval history as well as I knew the history of Russia or Central Asia or the Middle East. But I have some very close friends in Azerbaijan from whom I learned in conversation much that was interesting about the past and present of that place. I want to tell about two of them, because I counted on their help and advice during this visit to Azerbaijan, my fifth or sixth over the past several years.

I met Azer Mustafa-zade in Iraq when he came as part of a delegation from the U.S.S.R. Writers' Union just before the Iran-Iraq War began. Later, when we were both in Moscow, Azer and I maintained a rather close friendship, and our families were friends, too. His wife, Wafa, was a music teacher by profession, by birth the daughter of a member of the highest Azerbaijani *nomenklatura,* but the most important thing was that she was a fascinating, brilliant woman. I was sincerely sorry when Azer left Moscow, where he had prospered, to return to his native Baku with his wife and young daughters. But I completely understood the reasons that impelled him to that critical turning point in his life.

Azer was an extraordinary man who possessed a sharp and penetrating mind, and was obviously drawn toward a political career. He was a notable figure among the people who worked on the Writers' Union governing board, but nonetheless, at a certain point, the influential but humble post of consultant on Azerbaijani literature stopped being a fulfilling task for him. Like any successful bureaucrat in his early forties, he had every reason to think that the peak of his career was still far off. Just then a prestigious post as deputy of the foreign commission of the U.S.S.R. Writers' Union opened, for which, because of his experience, education, and ability, he could easily expect to be chosen. However, he was summarily rejected because he was not Russian. In this country a person's movement up the career ladder beyond a certain level always depends directly upon that person's nationality. In Azerbaijan it was better to be Azerbaijani—and in Moscow a Russian.

Then he decided to leave for Baku. In Azerbaijan the possibility of a serious party-government career opened up for him. Apparently Azer's situation was favorable, because they asked him to become deputy chairman of the state committee of Azerbaijan for press, printing, and book production. This appointment was a clear slap in the face for his former Moscow bosses, since their subordinate was now joining the highest *nomenklatura* of the republic, which meant that he was gaining access to perquisites of the distribution system at a level higher than their own. With the beginning of Gorbachev's perestroika,

Azer took an even greater step forward and obtained appointment to the position of head of the ideological department of the Central Committee of the Communist Party of Azerbaijan. Someone who occupies this position becomes one of the dozen highest leaders of the republic and possesses almost unlimited power over millions of his fellow citizens.

Contemporary Azerbaijan had nothing in common with those still quite recent times when the whole republic was hung with gigantic portraits of Brezhnev and placards with his idiotic saying: "Taking great strides is socialist Azerbaijan." This slogan was very successfully parodied by my second Azerbaijani friend, Rauf Gasanov, who once said with his biting wit: "Taking a great dive is socialist Azerbaijan."

I also met Rauf in Iraq. At that time he was quite a young interpreter, working abroad for the first time. We amused ourselves when we could. But Rauf was also a serious conversationalist, and I sometimes found out rather strange things from him. For example, I learned that Azerbaijan, more than seventy years ago, managed to maintain a democratic republic for two years. The official history course, which we studied in high school and at the university, ignored this period in the history of the Transcaucasus, limiting itself mainly to curses and insults against the independent national governments of Georgia, Armenia, and Azerbaijan of that period.

"Do you know," Rauf asked me once, "when and where the first democratic republic in the Moslem world was formed?"

"If you throw out the word 'democratic,' perhaps in Turkey?" I proposed hesitantly.

"No." Rauf laughed triumphantly. "it was the Azerbaijani Democratic Republic, formed in 1918."

He told me that in the republic full civil and political rights were guaranteed to all citizens, regardless of their nationality, religion, class, profession, or sex. Officials of different ranks were accredited by England, France, the United States, Italy, Greece, Denmark, Switzerland, Poland, Finland, and Belgium, and full diplomatic relations were established with Iran, Turkey, Armenia, and Georgia. The Supreme Council of the Paris World Conference acknowledged the sovereignty of Azerbaijan, and on that occasion a ceremonial session of parliament took place in Baku.

"Ninety-five parliamentarians of all nationalities, including Russians and Armenians, attended," said Rauf. "There were nine political factions, and a coalition government was formed among them."

"Fantastic," I said, ashamed of my ignorance. "But what about the English? Wasn't there an occupying force, led by General What's-his-name in Baku?"

"Thompson," said Rauf. "Well, in August 1919 they left Azerbaijan, the Communists brought in their forces from Russia, and they stayed there forever. You know how that ended."

"How that ended" referred to the incredibly cruel repressions that befell Azerbaijan over the next thirty years, when hundreds of thousands of human lives were destroyed. It was not difficult to count them because they did not hide, and they were always in sight. Nails were driven into composers' ears and into writers' eyes. Musicians' hands and teachers' tongues were cut off. That is what happened, and today neither the executioners nor the victims are still alive. But it was easier to bring those who survived into the bright future. In succeeding generations the fear of totalitarianism gradually turned into cynicism and unbelief. Azerbaijan itself was turned into a thoroughly corrupted satrapy of the Kremlin, yielding complete control to strong personalities like KGB General Gheydar Aliyev, who for long years was first secretary of the Azerbaijani Communist Party—i.e., a complete dictator like Ceauçescu. However, at that time the first secretary of neighboring Georgia, Eduard Shevardnadze, was also a police general, which did not keep him from subsequently becoming U.S.S.R. Minister of Foreign affairs and then later a leader in the pro-democracy movement.

Just like his Georgian colleague, Aliyev became an influential member of the Politburo and moved to permanent residence in Moscow. At some point he was rumored to be a possible new Stalin. But the rumors were exaggerated, since in our time any possibility for a political career in Moscow for someone who speaks Russian with an accent was much more limited than it was for old bullshitter Joe. Now both generals are in retirement, but it seems to me that either one or the other could return to fully active political life.

One of Brezhnev's last visits to a Union republic was to Azerbaijan—or rather Aliyev dragged him there by force, in order to demonstrate how the people respected the general secretary, and to give him a saber and a samovar made of gold. Along the entire route of Brezhnev's entourage, the police burst into people's homes and demanded that they hang rugs on their balconies in accordance with ancient tradition. In olden times that was how they greeted monarchs returning from victory after winning battles. At each intersection professional and amateur folk groups danced. The crowds of citizens of Baku on both sides of the street raised flags and were ordered to smile. When the aged leader reached the central square and tried to get out of his car, a thousand-voice chorus and a gigantic military orchestra greeted him so loudly that the poor emperor recoiled in surprise, farted, and almost fell to the ground. This scene was directly transmitted to the whole country on television.

"But don't we deserve the leaders that we get?" a youth cried last year, when police with truncheons broke up an unsanctioned meeting on Pushkin Square in Moscow, and he ran away, dropping on the ground a portrait of Gorbachev with a Stalinist mustache drawn on him.

"No, it is that our leaders deserve the people that they get," answered a middle-aged man, recoiling from the policeman's truncheon.

32

À la Guerre comme à la Guerre!

Everything that I saw, heard, and learned in Azerbaijan has lain like a heavy stone in my soul, and I do not believe that I shall ever be relieved of its burden.

Like everyone who watches television and reads the newspapers, I knew that Azerbaijan and Armenia were having a conflict which, long before my arrival in Baku, had grown into a true civil war. In the Commonwealth of Independent States there were three attitudes toward this tragedy. Some people, absorbed in their own misfortunes, simply cannot imagine the true scope of this agonizing situation, and are only dully aware that somewhere down there in the Transcaucasus "those non-Russians are quarreling over something again." Others, depending upon the information they have received, their education, and their own life experience, come out in active support of one or the other warring side. I am part of the third group, perhaps the smallest one, because I think that responsibility for the conflagration of national intolerance lies in large measure with the pre-breakup Kremlin itself. Official Moscow naturally always expressed yet another point of view of the causes for the Armenian-Azerbaijani war, calling the local mafias in both republics the instigators. But that is only partly true. Of course, from the beginning, perestroika put them on the alert. However, the central leadership always had the means and the determination more or less to ignore the dissatisfaction of their henchmen in the provinces. But the point is that in this situation the interests that were being infringed in the Transcaucasus were those of the empire itself. Both in Armenia and in Azerbaijan, in the reform process of the first stage of perestroika, a real threat emerged to the political regime itself, which used to be wholly controlled by Moscow. That in itself threatens to bring about the secession of these republics from their seventy-year subjugation to the center.

Then the decades-long smoldering problem of Nagorno-Karabakh was inflamed. Nagorno-Karabakh is a territory within Azerbaijan that is populated solidly by Armenians. If you think that this explosion of interethnic passions is a random occurrence, look at neighboring Georgia, another republic of the Transcaucasus striving for independence. Its own Karabakh was lying in wait in the form of the autonomous province of South Osetia, which is now at war with Georgia in order to bring about a shift in the jurisdiction of North Osetia, which is part of the Russian Federation. And why not? If you look at a map, you will see that unlike Karabakh, which is separated from Armenia by "pure" Azerbaijani territory, South Osetia and North Osetia directly border each other.

Yet now that it has let interethnic wars out of the bottle, the center is unable to put them back in. Interethnic enmity and bloodletting have not stopped separatist tendencies in the region. Moreover, the situations in Georgia and Armenia are virtually out of Moscow's control. Even in Azerbaijan at the end of 1989, the old party-state structures were almost completely paralyzed by the actions of the People's Front. But a weakening of imperial influence on Georgia and Armenia is partly compensated for, if only by the fact that both of these republics are isolated from the outside world by their traditionally unfriendly neighbors, Iran and Turkey. The loss of Azerbaijan is another matter, for it threatens the empire with a serious disruption of its geopolitical balance.

It would, however, be stupid to consider Armenia and Azerbaijan, and the conflict between them, as Moscow's usual "divide and conquer" strategy. As with any neighbors, both the Armenians and the Azerbaijanis had reasons for displeasure and even claims against each other. But I will not be accused of discovering America if I say that as a whole the Armenians and the Azerbaijanis over the course of centuries have coexisted rather peacefully, and not only in the large cities but also in the countryside. At the same time, Armenians have not only lived on the territory of contemporary Azerbaijan, but Azerbaijanis have also lived on the territory of what is now Armenia. (Let us also note that the northern Azerbaijani khanates before the beginning of the nineteenth century were nominally subject to Iran, which conceded them to Russia in the Gulistan and Turkmanchai treaties, signed in 1813 and 1828 respectively. Armenia was not a sovereign state at this time, and part of the Armenian population also lived on the territory of Turkey.) The real conflicts between the two peoples began only at the end of the nineteenth century with the appearance of nationalistic ideologies.

All the Azerbaijanis I spoke with claimed that the nation was in the midst of an information blockade that deprived it of the possibility of communicating to the world its own point of view on the events occurring there.

I met with dozens of people in Baku who had very different political views and convictions. One of the first things I had asked my friend Rauf to do for me when I arrived in Baku was to set up a meeting with a real Moslem fundamentalist. A few days later, he introduced me to an improbably colorful fellow by the name of Ghamid Kharizchi, the single Khomeini follower I managed to find in Baku. He was young, short in height, and bearded. During the conversation he sometimes said part of a sentence in a falsetto tone, and then returned to a normal register. It was probably an Iranian rhetorical method, but it reminded me more of the yodel that American country singers use in bluegrass music.

In Baku, Ghamid Kharizchi was well known for his scandalous interview in the Lithuanian newspaper *Soglasie* [*Accord*], which was then reprinted somewhere in the West and created quite a stir because of his extremist statements. Western journalists declared him one of the leaders of the Popular Front of Azerbaijan, which, in the opinion of the real leaders of this organization, severely compromised it. He told me that he had recently gone to Iran illegally, and was detained on his return by Soviet border guards who let him go after he had established his identity.

Before I began the interview, I asked Kharizchi whether he represented any organization or would be speaking for himself, to which he decisively responded that he represented only himself.

"The secession of the Baltic republics from the U.S.S.R. would be very advantageous for the Turkic-Moslem world of the Soviet Union," he began, immediately grabbing the bull by the horns. "Let everyone who wants to leave the U.S.S.R.: the Baltics, Moldavia, the Ukraine, Georgia, Armenia. You see, this will only strengthen our influence in the U.S.S.R. However, a complete disintegration of the U.S.S.R. would be disadvantageous for the Turkic republics, because the Soviet Union is basically not only a Slavic but also a Turkic nation. We don't need to stand up for the small nations, who are obsessed with the idea of separatism. They don't have a large, unifying idea, while the Russians, the Turkic peoples do. In general, the Soviet Union is a Turko-Slavic organism. And not only in the future, but also in the past. The Russian-Turkic interconnections began long ago, not only on the political level but also in the economic, cultural, and financial spheres."

"How are the Russians themselves responding to your idea?" I wondered.

"For some reason they don't like it," he answered with some distress. "Russian historical science prides itself on the fact that one of the ancient Russian princes was married to the daughter of the French king. And it is horribly ashamed to admit that they all were related to the nomads of the steppe, and later to the Golden Horde."

"Yes, the Russian prince, Aleksandr Nevsky, canonized as a Russian Orthodox saint, was the adopted son of Batu-khan, the grandson of Genghis Khan," I said. "And thus the brother of his great-grandson Sartak."

Kharizchi looked at me from behind his glasses, not without surprise.

"You prepared well for the interview," he said, praising me. Rauf, sitting next to me, could not stand it and burst out laughing.

"This is not the typical credulous Western journalist for you," he said. "He has a master's degree in the history of Moslem peoples."

"Really?" Kharizchi was surprised, and for about half an hour we delved deeply into historical discussions about the transition from a theocratic state to a secular one, and then again back to a theocratic one. Finally we returned from the depths of history like two scuba divers, holding in our hands the treasures of a sunken ship. For what was our knowledge of the past if not the remains of a vanished splendor?

"Europe always invaded the Orient," Kharizchi said.

"But didn't the Orient invade Europe?" I retorted.

"Well, no farther than the Balkans," he answered. "The main European citadels, Italy, France, Germany, and Britain, were never the object of claims from the East. But Europe always strove for India, China, the Middle East, Southeast Asia, and so forth. As a result all the ideological states of the Orient were destroyed. Take, for example, Japan. During the era of the shogun it was an ideological state, but the Europeans turned it into an economic state. Turkey was a military-ideological state, but it was also turned into an economic state. Even the Soviet Union, which was an ideological state, now tends to see a panacea for all its troubles in prioritizing economics over ideology. The only contemporary state that raises the banner of ideology is Iran."

"Why is it so bad for ordinary citizens to be citizens of an 'economic' state?" I asked. "Doesn't it guarantee people a normal standard of living?"

"All economic states are based upon the egoistic idea of Protestantism: 'I, me, myself, it is mine, I am against Rome.'"

"Do you wish to be a cog, a puppet in someone's ideological games?" I asked.

"No, not a cog, but part of some huge unity," he said, his eyes sparkling. "Don't forget that in the East, morality, everyday ethics, and religious principles have a much more stable base than in your culture, based upon Protestant thinking, which has given the world only mechanization, and which turns people into robots."

"Have you been in the West?" I asked. "Maybe there are not so many robots there as you think."

"No, I have never been there," Kharizchi said. "It is enough for me to see what is happening in Russia. Russians are now turning to Europe; they think that Europe will give them something. Europe will give them nothing. The course of history proves this. Remember Dostoevsky and Tolstoy. What they told their people at the end of the nineteenth and the beginning of the twentieth centuries, have Russians forgotten this?"

"Who has read them besides intellectuals?" I answered. "Why do you think that what happens in Russia can to some degree characterize life in Western states that you call 'economic'? Don't you know that Europe considers Russia an Asiatic country?"

"Everything in the world is interconnected," Kharizchi answered mysteriously. "I think that there are mystical moments in history. Events in one country always have equivalents in other regions. For example, events in Azerbaijan are essentially no different from events in Kashmir, Lebanon, or Kosovo. Azerbaijan is a mirror image of Lebanon. America landed its troops, and in response the Hezbollah Party emerged, which finds support in Iran."

"It seemed to me that a flourishing economic state is a more compatible idea for Azerbaijanis," I said. "Neither Communists nor the Popular Front are in a hurry to raise the green flag of the Islamic revolution."

"Don't forget that Azerbaijan consists of two parts," Kharizchi reminded me. "The northern part, which is part of the U.S.S.R., and the southern part, which is part of Iran. And there, in the south, the Islamic revolution has already taken place. If Moscow continues to carry out this policy toward us, it will also take place here."

"It is impossible to make someone drink who isn't thirsty," said Rauf, and reminded me that it was time to go home.

Before my arrival, about two weeks earlier, Rauf had come back from a vacation in an Arab country where he worked for several years as an interpreter. Iraq had been my last long-term foreign assignment, but for Rauf it had been his first. I knew that he had to be in Baku the second half of July, and so I tried to arrange my route in order to find him at home. I stayed for several weeks at Rauf's house in occupied Azerbaijan, and I probably would not have survived without his help.

The street where Rauf spent his childhood used to be that of Lieutenant Shmidt, hero of the revolution of 1905. Now it's called the street of Rashid Beibutov. He is a popular Azerbaijani singer, a tenor who was a living legend. Now a musical theater is also named for him, the director of which wanted for some reason to meet with me. Even from past visits I knew that in Baku people most often set a meeting in the large teahouse known as Chinara, which was located not far from the seashore, right next to the building where Rashid Beibutov lived. This large apartment building was one of the best in Baku. The apartments there were gigantic, and there were even two bathrooms in some of them, which Soviet people consider an unheard-of luxury.

In Central Asian teahouses people recline or sit Turkish-style on a wooden (or, less often, lacquered) bench, covered with rugs and plush blankets. These benches are called *supa* (compare with the common word "sofa," which comes from the same Indo-European root), and one is supposed to climb onto them after removing one's shoes. People play chess, talk softly, and slowly drink their tea from round cups. Laughter is sometimes heard, but usually a sedate hush is observed here.

I saw nothing of the kind in the Baku teahouse Chinara, where the patrons were noisily talkative. If the Central Asian teahouse is, as they say, a "refuge for meditation," then the teahouse in Baku is undoubtedly a political discussion club. If you spend even just a week here, you will have the opportunity to meet almost all the well-known people in the city of Baku: writers and businessmen, musicians and rogues, KGB officers and homegrown politicians. They drink tea here from small, pear-shaped glasses called *armudi*, i.e., pears. The sugar is broken into small pieces, and they suck on the sugar while drinking the unsweetened tea.

Not far from the teahouse, directly in front of the building where Rashid Beibutov lived, there was a small fountain. Streams of water poured from the jaws of a fairy-tale dragon that a mighty folklore hero seized by the neck. In his right hand he held a sword, poised over the head of the monster, and he was ready to inflict the decisive blow.

"Do you know why he does not cut off the dragon's head?" Rauf asked me seriously. "Pay attention to where the hero is looking. He is expecting that the monument to Kirov will now wave its hand to him and say, 'All right, cut.'"

I looked in the indicated direction, and we both laughed. The hero really seemed to be looking at a gigantic monument to Kirov mounted in the distance on one of the highest points in Baku, extending his hand in the inevitable heroic gesture of all official Soviet sculptures.

"Why haven't they removed this by now?" I was surprised to see the monument to Kirov, who was one of the leaders in establishing Bolshevik power in the Transcaucasus. Later Stalin physically "eliminated" him, as he did the rest of his friends and competitors, and then, shedding crocodile tears, he renamed dozens of cities and thousands of collective farms in his honor.

"They haven't done it yet," said Rauf, "but there has probably been a decision made to demolish it."

One of Rauf's many friends, Oktay Akhmedov, the deputy chief of the local OMON (a special police force detachment), came to the teahouse Chinara in civilian clothes, but looking at him, one could unmistakably see the military in this man—a sturdy, athletic build, an energetic, even stiff manner of carrying himself—and with it an eloquence and the ability to express his thoughts convincingly. However, many Azerbaijanis are born orators, perfecting their skills throughout their lives in endless conversations on political themes with their friends and acquaintances. At this point, Azerbaijanis are among the most politicized nationality of all the peoples of the U.S.S.R. Akhmedov was no exception.

"The only thing that is clear," he said decisively, "is that normal people are now in leadership roles in the republic. The makeup of the Central Committee and the Council of Ministers has been completely recast. If before we could be dissatisfied with our leaders, these people for the time being are doing everything correctly. The situation is gradually stabilizing. Economic reforms are being carried out.

"But on the border with Armenia the situation is abominable. Gorbachev's position is incomprehensible: they have completely disarmed us; they left Armenia armed. Why is the leadership of the country temporizing? Is the influence of the Armenian diaspora on Gorbachev so great? I can give you a simple example: special militia units are created and stationed throughout the country. And here they have barely started. If anything happens, there won't be anyone to protect the border. As for the situation on the border with Armenia, we are sending codes and messages to Moscow almost every day, but the central government is not taking any concrete actions.

"It kills me that the world does not know the whole truth about the January events in Baku. It has been mainly disinformation that has gone out through the mass media. The bigger the lie, it seems, the greater are the chances that people will believe it. When on April 9, 1989, the army killed people in Tbilisi, the whole world knew about it. What happened in Baku on January 20, 1990, surpasses the Tbilisi events in scope and cruelty ten times over. How could they think of carrying out such a massive army operation against the residents of a city? Did you know that more than one hundred people were killed among civilians alone, and about a thousand people received gunshot and bayonet wounds? The victims were of all nationalities: Azerbaijanis, Jews, Russians, Tartars...And all ages, including children. Analyze the obituaries in the newspapers after January 20. How many people died from heart attacks and trauma following in the footsteps of their murdered loved ones! If Sakharov had been alive, he would be here, and then the whole world would know the truth.

"The People's Front had the opportunity to seize power here; the central government was afraid, and this was a punitive operation. Who was Vazirov [former first secretary of the Central Committee of the Communist Party of Azerbaijan] before Gorbachev sent him to rule the republic? He had worked abroad his whole life. His last position was ambassador to Pakistan. What did he know about the republic? What did he know about the life of his people? He didn't know shit. How did he come to power through the back door, just as he left through the back door?

"Why did the mass media cast the Azerbaijani people in the role of the villain? If we are so malicious, why was Baku such a multinational city? You know that in other national republics the *nomenklatura* consists mainly of local nationalities and Russians, right? Here is a list published in the newspaper *Azerbaijan* on July 6, 1990, a list of officials who were members of the *nomenklatura* of the Central Committee of the Communist Party of Azerbaijan on January 1, 1988. Look, you will see: sixty-one people of Armenian nationality. And this isn't even a complete list. Why do they say that we discriminated against Armenians? Are Azerbaijanis members of the *nomenklatura* of the Central Committee in Armenia?"

"I don't know," I said. "Probably not in such great numbers. But the *nomenklatura* isn't the point here. You see, there were horrifying massacres here."

"Yes, there were, but—"

"I know," I said, "I know everything that you are about to say. Since 1988 about 160,000 refugees of Azerbaijani nationality have arrived from Armenia. Under fear of physical destruction and under threat of weapons they were driven out of their villages and, leaving their homes and property, came to Azerbaijan on foot, through winter mountain passes, bearing on their backs their half-dead old folks and carrying in their arms their children dying from the cold. And it was these refugees, who ended up homeless and unemployed, who were the main participants in the anti-Armenian rampages in Sumgait and Baku. I read all this in the local press and heard it from people. But is this a justification? Does violence cure violence?"

"I don't work for the KGB, or as a spy," Oktay said thoughtfully. "I have worked for the police for eighteen years. But what I am only now beginning to guess really scares me. From January 13 through January 16, when a horrifying wave of violence swept throughout Baku, the forces were already here, but for some reason they took no action. They say that there were no orders. But why? And do you know what conclusion I am coming to? Both the Sumgait and the Baku massacres were well-planned actions. Armenians themselves took part in them."

"What?" I exclaimed in disbelief. "Well, fine, suppose that Moscow played the Azerbaijanis and Armenians against each other. But why would Armenians participate in anti-Armenian pogroms? No, that's insane!"

"Insane?" Oktay was angry. "Do you know that in Sumgait a certain Grigoryan behaved more brutally than anyone. He is an Armenian by nationality who appeared before the court for the murder of six Armenians. His guilt was proven, and he acknowledged it! Meanwhile, I can guarantee you 100 percent that even now in the city there are no less than one thousand Armenian spies and saboteurs with Azerbaijani passports and names, who know the Azerbaijani language and all the customs no less well than our own countrymen."

"I understand, intelligence work," I said. "*À la guerre comme à la guerre*. Well, what way out do you see?"

"There is no way out," Oktay snapped. "Moscow is taking no measures, which means that we must rely upon ourselves. You see, this is not us crossing, it is them crossing our border; they are attacking our villages. This means it is necessary to construct a real border system with fortified regions every two hundred, three hundred, or five hundred meters. And to create a military subdivision to guard our state borders. To conscript from here for the army, to spend their service here, and not in construction battalions somewhere in Siberia, where people never hold a machine gun in their hands for their entire period of service.

"The Armenians have a well-trained and equipped army. Helicopters and small aircraft. And we who stand against them? Rural policemen with ancient pistols."

"Where did the Armenians get their weapons?" I asked. "And their helicopters?"

"Well, for example, we hear reports like these on television: 'In Erevan a group of extremists seized a city police department and took all their weapons.' I'll bet you one thousand rubles that you can't bring me even one wastebasket from our city department. Do you think they will give it to you to take away? No way. Tell the truth, the police officials voluntarily gave weapons to the extremists. Or, for example, all the agricultural and medical aviation of Armenia. Where is it all? Scattered and hidden in the mountains, and it is impossible to get it back. Or radio transmitters recently produced by the Erevan radio factory—those little boxes made out of Styrofoam. If you want to land a helicopter at night, you won't even need to light signal fires. Or, according to our information, the weapons from abroad—do you know how they got them? After the Armenian earthquake they were delivered by direct airlifts. At first, the cargo went through Moscow customs, and then they decided to bring them immediately to Erevan in order to more quickly relieve the suffering."

"I don't believe you at all!" I said. "This is your counterpropaganda."

"And empty food cans that went to the guerrillas instead of to the people suffering from the earthquake—that is counterpropaganda?"

"Well, fine," I said, sharply changing the subject. "I know that many Azerbaijanis hid their Armenian neighbors during the slaughter, as well as taking their things and even their furniture into storage. Tell me, honestly, were you one of them?"

"Yes," Oktay said, embarrassed. "I managed to protect my son's teacher. And my wife stores things belonging to her Armenian friend. She recently called and said that she will be coming for them soon."

33

A Girl on the Threshold

Do you know that the first classical opera in the Orient was written and produced in Baku in 1908? It was the opera *Leili and Majnun,* by the Azerbaijani composer Ghajibckov," Rauf informed me.

"Oil again?" I asked. At the beginning of the century Azerbaijan was for Russia about the same as the Arab emirates are for the contemporary Western world at the end of the century. Local oil millionaires generously spent their money promoting fine arts, and opera in the Italian style was then in vogue. The most surprising thing was that among the local intelligentsia, the passion for opera has continued to the present day. However, Moscow has used up most of the oil supply there. During World War II all Soviet tanks and airplanes operated on Baku gasoline. For many decades Azerbaijan was the main oil source in the Soviet Union, while the even richer Siberian fields were not discovered until comparatively recently.

Rauf and I were sitting with a group of young Baku intellectuals, once again in the historic teahouse Chinara. We were having an endless conversation about Azerbaijan, its past, present, and future.

"But why isn't anyone laying claim to the Nakhichevan Autonomous Republic?" I wondered. "That's the one separated from the main territory of Azerbaijan by the strip of Armenian territory called Zangezur."

"Because there is a treaty between the U.S.S.R. and Turkey," said Agabek, boiling with a fiery temperament, "stating that Nakhichevan is part of the Soviet Union only as an autonomous republic within the jurisdiction of Azerbaijan. The treaty stipulates that in case of an attempt to change the status of this region, Turkey has the right to send troops there."

I listened to their version of how Zangezur was purged from the Azerbaijanis by Armenian General Andronik in 1917, and about the deportation from Armenia of one hundred thousand Azerbaijanis at the end of the 1940s, still under Stalin. And again about two hundred thousand Azerbaijanis who were driven out of their villages on Armenia's territory during the last two and a half years.

I asked, "Doesn't it seem to you that in the suffering borne by both Azerbaijanis and Armenians, it is the fault not only of our deformed political system but also of the national intelligentsia itself? It wasn't the peasants who worked out the ideology of national irreconcilability."

But I received no answer to my question, because the conflict had gone so far that each of the warring sides is guided only by the strict logic of his own arguments; anything that does not adhere to his logic is considered nonexistent.

Here is another observation: Before the assault on Baku by Soviet army troops, Azerbaijani society was torn by political contradictions. The appearance of an "external enemy," if it did not reconcile the hostile currents, at least to some degree consolidated the Azerbaijani nation.

Agabek asked me, "Why did the Moscow mass media support the stationing of American troops in Panama? Apparently from the traditionally Soviet point of view, this was typical 'imperialist aggression.'"

"Well, the drug mafia, Noriega's drug trafficking...," I answered, not understanding what he was hinting at.

"Not quite enough for aggression against a sovereign state," Agabek retorted. "Have you noticed that the American troops were deployed after Bush met with Gorbachev on Malta? In Azerbaijan everyone understood that Panama was in exchange for Azerbaijan."

"After that," said Rauf, "Gorbachev met with Bush again, and visited America. Before that visit to America, Zorii Balayan immediately left. Do you know who he is?"

"Of course," I said. "He is *Literaturnaya Gazeta*'s correspondent on Armenia, a well-known writer and athlete."

"He gave an interview to Voice of America. To a question about the goal of his visit, he answered that Gorbachev's visit to the United States was coming up, and he needed to know if the Armenian community was ready for it."

"What of it?" I was amazed. "Why shouldn't they be?"

"How little you understand," said Agabek, getting excited. "He is the president of a country in which one republic is at war with another. This is a very delicate issue: can he be a guest of a community that supports one of the warring sides?"

"Whose fault is it," I said, "that there is no Azerbaijani community in the United States? Maybe he would visit it too? In my opinion, you have a persecution mania."

"No," said a sleepy fellow at the end of the table, "he wouldn't visit it. In the Azerbaijanis' public consciousness there is a firm conviction that Gorbachev had some sort of connection with the Armenian mafia in the past in Stavropol and has laid himself open to possible blackmail. In the northern Caucasus case, investigators Ivanov and Gdlyan have obtained some documents with which they could blackmail Gorbachev from either direction."

"Who is this?" I asked Rauf in a whisper.

"He's KGB," he answered, not lowering his voice.

I looked at him in amazement, then at that fellow. Not changing the sleepy expression on his face, he lazily nodded.

"Why are you so surprised? What do you think, that there aren't normal people among us?"

And as confirmation, he repeated a fantastic Baku rumor about some jewels supposedly received by Raisa Gorbachev as a gift from the Armenian community in the United States.

"But she put them in the state storehouse," I responded, since this rumor was also going around Moscow.

Seeing that this whole scene began to look suspiciously like the usual provocation, shall we not draw a curtain on it?

A fable from Baku: When the Red Army entered Azerbaijan at the beginning of the 1920s and overthrew the democratic republic, a vagabond on the street was heard shouting and jumping for joy.

Alongside walked the millionaire Tagiev, a well-known patron of the arts who had built with his own money more than half of the public and residential buildings in the center of Baku.

"What happened, what are you so happy about?" he asked the vagabond.

"What? Now the people will have their own power!" explained the poor fellow. "Now everything will be different."

"Do you think that you will become as rich as me?" said Tagiev, smiling sadly. "No, it is that now I will be as poor as you."

Of the Bolsheviks who came to power then, there were many who had studied abroad before the October coup on stipends that old Tagiev had granted them. They showed a documentary film in Baku about his daughter, who died of hunger in abject poverty. She had dreamed her whole life of writing a book about her father, but the authorities did not permit her any part of the manuscript fund of the Azerbaijani Academy of Science. "Why write a book about Tagiev for the people? Don't you understand that he's an enemy of the people?" they said to her when she asked for permission to have access to her father's confiscated archives.

But it did not disturb the Academy to conduct its ceremonial session and jubilee in the Baku opera theater, which this "enemy of the people" had built with his money.

My other friend in Azerbaijan was Azer Mustafa-zade, a member of the Writers' Union and a prominent party bureaucrat. I knew that some time ago, after one of the recurring palace coups in the republic's Central Committee, he had left Baku for one of the remote regions of Azerbaijan. He was not in exile, for he belonged to the ranks of the tenured *nomenklatura*. He had been put in charge of the regional committee of the Communist Party, which in practice meant that my former friend became sole master of a small feudal state equal in territory and population to, for example, Bahrain. However, his ascension to the regional throne was strongly overshadowed by the troubled reconstructionist times that had rocked and even overthrown far sturdier thrones.

But like any enlightened monarch, Azer believed in his power, and therefore, as they say, he rolled up his sleeves and undertook to carry out his own idealistic reforms in the region. Some of them, such as the repeal of the regulation requiring that men wear neckties in offices, passed without a hitch. However, the rest were very quickly thwarted by the horrible reality of the Soviet political system—the resistance of the local mafia. During the period of stagnation he could have appealed for help to the repressive organs of the republic. But Azerbaijan by that time had already embarked on an era of political chaos, and so he had to rely entirely on his own strength. The alternatives for a latter-day monarch were few. Either he had to accept the existing rules of the game and rule his emirate by ready-made laws, although foreign to him, or he was threatened with an "unfortunate accident" with a long obituary in the republic press and a respectable pension for his family. After soberly thinking things over, Azer decided to take the third way, that is, to give up the throne. And, as always, he turned out to be right.

He left his palatial residence in the capital of the region and returned to his gigantic apartment in the historic Baku building where the great singer Rashid Beibutov lived. When I came to his home, he had just received appointment to the post of general director of Azerneshr, the largest state publishing house in the republic. This post had opened up because the previous director had just died under mysterious circumstances. People in Baku thought that someone took revenge on him for publishing the book *Black January*, which came out with lightning speed after the Soviet crackdown in Baku.

The scene of my meeting with Azer and his family in some imperceptible way recalled my visit with Dobrynin's family in Samara. There were two grown daughters, asking the same questions about life, only in Samara everyone was light-haired, and here they all had jet-black hair.

Of all the refreshments, for some reason what stuck in my mind was a gigantic watermelon with dark green rind and measuring more than two feet around. The hosts washed it down with cold dry wine, and at my request gave me some local lemonade. Azer, as usual, was charming and eloquent; Wafa was caustic and sharp-witted; only the daughters were obviously shy in front of me.

"What events preceded the January crackdown?" I asked Azer. "Could they have gone another, peaceful way?"

"Judge for yourself," said Azer. "At the end of 1989 a session of the Supreme Soviet of Azerbaijan was supposed to be convened, in which new elections for the Supreme Soviet were to be announced. By the authority which the Popular Front had at that time, it had the opportunity to get no less than 40 percent of the votes, mainly city voters. Well, we were going to the building of the Supreme Soviet to make a decision about the new elections, and a crowd of picketers from the Popular Front would not let us into the hall. We said, 'What are you doing? Let us in; we are Popular deputies.' And they said, 'No, no way are you Popular deputies. You must be impostors. The people are for us, not for you.' Well, fine, we finally managed to fight our way into the hall, sat down, and began the session. Then reports began to come in: in the Dzhelalabad region Soviet power had been overthrown. And there followed similar reports from other regions. After several days even the first secretary of the Central Committee of the Communist Party of Azerbaijan could not get to the Central Committee building. All state structures in the republic were paralyzed. Complete chaos and anarchy took hold.

"In the cities the participants in the Popular Front were intellectuals, but in the rural areas many low-class and criminal elements had joined the movement. It was impossible to talk to them. For example, their deputation came to see me in my office. I tried to persuade them for an hour and a half that now was not the time, that it was not necessary to inflame passions to a white-hot state; strikes weren't necessary. It seemed that we came to an understanding, and then they left. After an hour and a half—again a meeting for half a day, again a strike! I called them again. 'What's going on,' I said, 'we just made an agreement!' 'That wasn't us,' they answered, 'that was another faction.'"

"And then the central government decided to use military force?" I asked. "But the leaders of the Popular Front must have understood what they were doing. Why did they have to subject people to danger and force the pickets against tanks? The army was always quartered here—the infantry, the navy, and the air defense. Why did they have to provoke the troops to fire?

"I don't know who opened fire, but someone shot at the soldiers. In general, I think that the leaders of the Popular Front then overestimated their abilities: they thought that that was it, that they could take power into their hands as easily as tearing a ripe apple from a tree. But it turned out differently. Now there won't be such a mad rush after them. They had a chance, but they lost it."

"What is the prognosis for the future?" I asked.

"Prognosis for the future..." Azer thought for a while. "It's hard to say. We have all these other situations for comparison, such as the Baltics, Moldavia, the Ukraine, but the process here is greatly complicated by the Karabakh issue. That impedes all the democratic processes in the republic."

In Baku it is terribly hot, but no one swims in the sea. As they told me, the beaches on the Apsheron peninsula are closed because there is an overflow of some kind of poisonous substances in the waters by the shore. Like many southern cities of the Soviet Union, the seaport of Baku suffers constantly from an insufficiency of fresh water. For example, in Rauf's apartment, there is water in the tap only late in the evening, and even then only for an hour or an hour and a half. But we somehow adapted and used the water economically from a bathtub filled to the brim. The overflow tank also operates only from 11:00 P.M. until midnight; all the rest of the time you have to pour water from a bucket. We wash our hands by pouring from a cup. Any Moscow family would long since have lost their minds from the constant impossibility of either cleaning or washing dishes. But Rauf's wife, Sada, had an angelic nature, and she accepted all unpleasantness connected with the lack of water with an unfailing, kind, patient smile.

The first night I carelessly lay down to sleep on the balcony, and I was almost eaten alive by ferocious mosquitoes. Tossing and turning under the sheet for about an hour and a half, I was completely exhausted, inflicting useless blows at an invisible enemy. Finally, the military patrol called to me from below. There were five soldiers with machine guns in their hands.

"What's the matter?" one of them said in a young stern voice.

"The mosquitoes are eating me alive," I answered, hanging off the balcony eight stories up. Then a door opened behind me, and a worried Rauf beckoned me into the room with gestures.

"What's going on?" I asked.

"Have you lost your mind?" Rauf said angrily. "Do you think you can chat with a patrol in the darkness? If something seemed out of line to them, they could simply open fire. Do you know how many people were killed on balconies in the first days of the assault on Baku? Women came out onto the balcony to hang out clothes and received a burst of machine gun fire in the stomach. My neighbor, who was carrying garbage out in a bucket after midnight, was arrested, and they didn't release him for three days."

The only people I hadn't been able to meet with yet were the leaders of the People's Front. Recently, in the latter part of July, several leaders of the people's democratic movement of Azerbaijan who had imprudently arrived for negotiations in Moscow were arrested by a special forces unit while they were spending the night at the building that houses the republic's permanent representation. Most who had not been arrested had gone underground. It was virtually impossible to make contact with those who remained at large, but I was able to get Issa Gambarov's nighttime telephone number and to arrange a meeting with him. Issa was one of the ideologues of the People's Front of Azerbaijan.

At the appointed time I was driven to one of the headquarters of the People's Front. I was taken to a large room, where two people were sitting on an old leather couch. One of them was Issa. He was pale and grim. His eyes looked searchingly and wisely through his glasses.

"It is doubtful whether any union republic is in the same situation," he said when I asked him to characterize the situation in Azerbaijan. "Perhaps representatives of other republics can argue with this, because each person's problems always seem the most important to himself. But I say this because we are the only republic on which territorial claims are being made, and whose population is under threat by military units."

"Against the background of this danger to the whole republic, and the danger for the people of Azerbaijan, there seems to be no understanding between society and the republic leadership itself. For a long time the People's Front of Azerbaijan was one of the main stabilizing forces in the republic, if you don't count several days in January when the aggregate heat of both the people and of the front itself led to the tragic January events. But as a whole, our main argument was and remains that the path of democratic, nonviolent reforms lies in elections to parliament."

"Is it possible to hold fair elections now?" I asked.

"The most scandalous thing is that the [Communist] leadership of the republic intends to conduct these elections under conditions of a state of emergency. This, in our opinion, is unthinkable. Is this compatible: a state of emergency, a curfew, and democratic elections?"

It seemed that he was right, because later, in the fall, while the state of emergency was still in effect, the Communists won the elections and stayed in power.

"Recently attacks on activists of the people's movement have intensified," he said. "Last week another member of the People's Front was arrested, and another case was fabricated by which this man will be accused of all conceivable and inconceivable sins. And I would also like to add that since July 18 Panakh Guseinov, another member of the governing board of the People's Front, and I have declared a hunger strike. We are demanding that human rights be observed in Azerbaijan and all political prisoners be released."

I knew he was the founder of the democratic party in Azerbaijan, and asked him to tell me more about it.

"In April of this year several of my friends and I announced the creation of the democratic party of northern Azerbaijan," Issa said. "Naturally, we have our own views of the postimperial future of Azerbaijan. The idea of reviving the complete state sovereignty of Azerbaijan unites us with all the other democratic forces of the republic. According to its positions, one can say that our party is a center-right or liberal democratic party. We stand for the priority of human interests over state interests."

"Why can't the Armenians and Azerbaijanis settle their differences in a peaceful way? Are there any outside factors influencing the problem?"

He thought for a while, then said gloomily, "I think the problem is not just between the Armenians and Azerbaijanis. The Soviet hardliners in Moscow exploit the most painful issues in our relationship. The Kremlin has succeeded in manipulating nationalistic tendencies in Armenia based on territorial claims against Azerbaijan. Unfortunately, our neighbors still cannot choose priorities for themselves and understand which is more important for them—freedom of the people and self-determination (about which they talk so much), or territorial seizure. The central government knows very well how to manipulate this conflict, and, unfortunately, the democratic movement of Azerbaijan has not succeeded in finding a way out of this serious situation, in spite of all our attempts to find a peaceful solution."

It was useless to go on talking about the issue—the problem seemed unsolvable—and I decided to change the subject. "And what about the danger of Islamic fundamentalism?" I asked.

Issa smiled sadly. It looked as if he had been over this a thousand times before and was tired of responding to the same old allegation. "As far as Azerbaijan is concerned, talk about this is a provocation by some and disinformation by others. In Baku, a city of two million people, there are only two mosques, as well as two Orthodox churches and two synagogues, and up until the 1990s the Armenian church was still active. Conduct an experiment: ask ten different people on the street how to get to the central mosque in Baku. Let us see how many Azerbaijanis can quickly explain to you how to get there. In Azerbaijan there are six million Azerbaijanis. But before 1989 there were only eighteen mosques. Here there are virtually no trained ministers, no Islamic literature, and only one Islamic school, a *medrese* that opened only last year. So to speak of Islamic fundamentalism in Azerbaijan, in my opinion, is not at all a serious issue. It is possible to speak of something else—about the fact that in Azerbaijan, as in the whole Soviet Union, for seventy years forced state atheism has been propagated, mosques have been destroyed, the feelings of believers have been insulted; in general, there has not been freedom of conscience. Therefore, the people think that among the other freedoms, the freedom of worship must be guaranteed. It is natural that, as in other faiths, some activation of religious institutions has been observed. But to speak of the politicization of Islam in Azerbaijan is to distort reality. Our society was excommunicated from faith in God by too cruel methods and for too long."

I thanked Issa for the interview and went out onto the street. "Where shall we take you?" my stern escorts asked me. "To Freedom Square," I replied. As they told me, it was the biggest in Europe. "On Freedom Square, in Baku you could simultaneously place Red Square in Moscow, the Place de la Concorde in Paris, and Palace Square in Leningrad," the Intourist guide would tell you. Then she might look over her shoulder and add in a whisper, "Before the January events it was literally thronged with millions of people. And they had already put up a mock gallows for the Central Committee officials! Yes, yes, right here on the square. But they didn't hang anyone."

The gallows were gone, but access to the square was blocked by metal partitions, and it was guarded by policemen and soldiers with machine guns. One of them pointed the muzzle of his gun at me, and I obediently wandered along the bank of the Caspian Sea. There I found a bench under the willows, sat on it, and began to look at the sea. I understood that the People's Front had lost this round. After the flood tide comes the ebb tide. The prospect of victory at the upcoming elections to the Supreme Soviet of Azerbaijan under conditions of a state of emergency was next to nothing. Some of the leaders had been arrested, some were in a quasi-illegal situation. Troops were stationed in the city and had introduced a curfew. And the sea continued to live its life, looking like nothing was happening in the city. But it was obvious even to the inexperienced eye of a visitor how this once colorful and welcoming city had changed. For one thing, red crosses used to be painted on ambulances; now, red crescents are. Is that why, during the January assault, the troops opened fire on one of these vehicles and killed a doctor sitting in it? By the way, he was not Azerbaijani but Jewish. His name was Markhevka.

Whether from the nighttime stuffiness or from the surfeit of distressing impressions, that night, for almost the first time in my life, I had a bad case of insomnia.

Malicious atheism, implanted in the souls of Soviet people since childhood, has as one of its teachings that religious ministers do not themselves believe in God, that they became priests, popes, or mullahs only to avoid socially useful labor and in order to live comfortably at the expense of trusting simpletons.

Attaching their own qualities to someone else is a favorite method of the Soviet ruling class. In order to understand how brazenly the state slandered the Orthodox Church, it is enough for an ordinary Soviet man to be in the company of archpriest Georgii for five minutes. I came to see him at the church the next morning when services had concluded and asked if he could spare me a half hour. He agreed and invited me into his office. Something else startled me: with all the ordinariness of his outward appearance and the mundanity of our conversation, a distinct aura of genuine spiritual purity emanated from him, as if for all his fifty years he had lived completely in another dimension, where there are no lies, no violence.

All his life he had served the parishes of the Caucasus and the Transcaucasus until he was promoted to archpriest, but even this high order did not much change his relationship to people and to God. We talked about his life, and about how his Catholic grandfather came from Poland to the Caucasus, and meanwhile in my soul the conviction grew that this person had not once in his life ever deceived or betrayed or degraded anyone. He had not stolen, not killed, and had never even coveted his neighbor's wife. And suddenly I understood that what I considered to be almost saintliness was in fact common decency. "See what the Soviet system has turned us into," I thought sadly. "They have single-mindedly and methodically removed from us what makes a human being human. For decades they have tried to turn us from people into Yahoos. The most awful thing is that the experiment has succeeded. A person who considers the endless chain of humiliations and violations a part of his normal life, a person who spends a great part of his life in endless lines, knowing that he probably won't get anything—that is not the essence created in the image and likeness of God."

It seems I even said this out loud.

"No," the priest answered me, looking at me sympathetically, "it is not so easy to destroy the human essence. Only this morning a little old lady came to me. She was limping; she had fallen, and her leg hurt. I touched her leg and asked how it happened, and she smiled, and said that it was getting better already. She simply wanted attention and interest."

Orthodox priests have the right to marry and have children. Father Georgii had five children and six grandchildren. The priest's wife looked in, smiled with dark blue eyes, and disappeared. I saw that she had a young and open face.

When I returned from my first trip to the United States, friends, of course, asked me about my impressions. And they were often interested to know what had surprised me most of all. I answered that the fleeting smiles that strangers exchanged when their eyes met by chance surprised me more than anything. And for the first time in many years I had met such a person, in this priest.

"When little old ladies tell me that it is necessary to leave here," he said, "that it is dangerous to remain here, I tell them about something that happened during the 1968 earthquake in Makhachkala.

Only one person died from that earthquake. There was a jolt in the evening, and he decided not to stay in his apartment but rather to spend the night on the street. He placed his cot on the ground and went to sleep. In the night a car ran over him. We do not go anywhere away from God—I myself think so, and I preach it from the pulpit. If it is judged to be time to cross over into eternal life, then it happens wherever it happens. To leave people in misfortune is not the Christian way. How can I go away from here if my flock is here?"

"How do the Moslems relate to Orthodox Christianity?" I asked.

"Do not believe when they say to you that some believers have a negative attitude toward others," said the archpriest. "I meet not only with Orthodox believers but also with Moslems. And I see their goodness and warmth of heart to our church. They often come and ask not only priests but also parishioners to pray for peace to return here. Quite a large number of people go to church. On Sundays and holidays three hundred, four hundred, five hundred people come to services. Many young people come and receive baptism. It is nice that the Russian Orthodox Church gives christening to the human soul."

"Christians of other sects—is their presence felt here?"

"Yes, here there are Baptists, Seventh-Day Adventists, and others. Each group has its own meetinghouse and church."

"You said that your grandfather was Catholic."

"Yes, he came to the Caucasus from Poland during World War I. He didn't know a word of Russian. He stayed here and died at the age of 101. I think that this was because of his loving heart. I never heard him raise his voice at anyone or get angry. But my grandmother was Orthodox. She came from Voronezh. They met here in the 1920s. They spent their lives in the Caucasus. And we never sorted out who was of what nationality. That's the way things were. People on our street shared their joys and their sorrows with us. During the war the German headquarters was across from us; soldiers lived in the yard. And in the garden, in our yard, were mud huts where Grandma hid Jews until the Germans left."

"And your parents?"

"Mama died in 1942, and father was missing, so my grandparents raised me."

Then we heard a noise outside, unhappy female voices. We went outside and saw that some angry old women were not allowing several teenage girls into church because they were wearing pants.

"Where are you going without a kerchief on your head, you shameless girls?" one of the old women loudly cried. "You have absolutely no shame. Or hasn't anybody told you how people are supposed to behave in church? Get out of here, do not insult God."

Seeing the archpriest, the women hushed each other and, embarrassed, they fell silent.

"Where is your granddaughter now?" Father Georgii turned with a kind smile to the noisiest woman.

"I don't know, Father," she answered, blushing like a girl.

"But these girls came here," he said. "They are on the threshold. Why don't you let them in?"

Epilogue

They say that they asked the sculptor who made a plaster death mask of Leo Tolstoy:

"Well, how was it?"

And he answered:

"Fine. Only the beard stuck tightly to the plaster."

I also made a death mask of what was formerly the Soviet Union. That country no longer exists and never will again.

I felt this especially painfully by the time I got to Azerbaijan, the sixth and last Moslem republic on my route. I had had enough of the violence and misery the dying Communist system had brought to the people of my country. To witness it in republic after republic, city after city, had drained me. It was time to go back and take care of my own family.

In any case, I was unable to continue my journey by land because the only land routes back from Baku went through regions under curfews and in the midst of territorial war. I flew back to Moscow, to my family.

Flying over the vast expanse of what used to be the Soviet Union, I saw that one-sixth of the world's landmass would not disappear, would not perish, and I envisioned a day when new states would rise in place of the dying empire. And I had hopes that our distant descendants, instead of killing and torturing each other, perhaps at some time would also exchange fleeting smiles if by chance their eyes should meet...

But why can I not, as did that sculptor, calmly say:

"Fine. Only the beard stuck tightly to the plaster."

"But how idiotic was the ideology and inept the leaders," you say, "how cruel was the repressive apparatus and how stupid the economic system? Are you sorry to part with such a past?"

The lace curtain in the wind from my infancy...riding on a tricycle in the park on Sunday with proud parents walking behind...the Prima cigarettes carelessly forgotten by my father on the terrace...the curve of my classmate's knee a whisper away...the first winning competition in fencing...the thousands of books read...the hundreds of friends, and the seas, and strange cities, and the wild strawberries spotted by my three-year-old daughter under a bush in a forest near Moscow... What have Stalin, Khrushchev, or Brezhnev to do with all this? Or the CPSU and the KGB?

They existed not in nature but in people's minds. Including the minds of those hundreds of millions who were murdered by them.

Once, when I was quite young and careless, I wrote a short poem in which, though I did not realize it, I told my whole life.

A baby will cry out of love for his mother.
A young man will cry out of love for a woman.
A grown-up will cry out of love for his country.
An old man will cry out of love for life.

Did I know, setting out on my long road, that this would be a journey from love to loathing, and from loathing to love? And you, my readers, my companions in this strange wandering of the spirit, I part with you, and I will be lonely without you at first. But matters await you in your own country, and I remain on my Red Odyssey forever, awaiting those who are interested in knowing how the last empire on earth has crumbled to the ground.

Index